THE
CORBETT ROUND

THE
CORBETT ROUND

A unique continuous traverse
of 219 Scottish mountains

MANNY GORMAN

Published by Manuel Gorman
Kingussie
PH21 1PA

www.mannygorman.co.uk

ISBN978-0-9927716-0-7

Front cover: Beinn Dearg, Glen Lyon

For the Mums - Betty, Jane and Barbara,
and my Dad, Ricky Gorman, who tied my
running shoes tight.

Ultreia!

I never thought I would write a book in my lifetime and perhaps by the time you finish reading this you will think that I still haven't, but it is not meant to be a literary masterpiece – it's just how it was.

Manny

Contents

Manny

Originally from Kirkintilloch near Glasgow, I moved to Badenoch in 2000, now living in Kingussie with my partner Brenda, our beautiful daughter Maisy and my two handsome sons Manuel and Duncan. Brenda and I both work locally for the Highland Council's Housing and Property Service throughout the fantastic Badenoch & Strathspey area.

I have been running since I attended St. Ninian's High School in Kirkintilloch in the early 80's, introduced to the sport through the obligatory PE cross-country runs that most pupils dreaded, but which I usually won, and perversely enjoyed. After school I graduated into road running and joined Springburn Harriers for a few years. During this time and with encouragement from my Dad, auld Ricky, I got my first taste of hill running - baptised in fire at the Ben Nevis Race in 1987, and have run every year since. After many hard miles from road racing and training I picked up a bad repetitive strain knee injury which, other than the Ben Race, all but stopped me racing for a couple of years. On the comeback I avoided roads entirely, instead trying off-road and hill running full-time and have never looked back.

My interest quickly morphed from simply the running aspect, to the full mountain environment becoming far more important to me. The freedom and exhilaration of moving fast and light across remote hill or mountain-sides, sometimes for hours, sometimes for days or weeks, are not something that can entirely be described by words. It gets in your head, blood and bones; a drug that you crave. I have now run and raced in the hills, on odd occasions successfully, for over twenty-five years, but it is the very long distance journeys that I enjoy most. Continuous weeks of travel in the mountains feel like a lifestyle rather than a challenge - total escapism. Previous escapades include running 450 miles from Ben Hope in the north to Ben Lomond in the south, with 112 Munros along the way, all in 21 days. I have run solo 200 miles coast to coast across Scotland in 8 days from Inverie over Ladhar Bheinn (the most westerly mainland Munro), the nine 4,000 footers, Mount Keen (the most easterly Munro) and finishing at Stonehaven. I have run solo around the incredibly remote and rough boundary of Badenoch & Strathspey- essentially the watershed of the River Spey, 200 miles in 8 days. All good training runs for the Corbetts!

The Scottish hill running community is a relatively small but close-knit family; the competition in racing is fierce and ruthless, but the camaraderie at all other times is second to none. Brenda started running only seven years ago, encouraged after watching my exploits in the hills and enjoying the unique atmosphere at the races. She has since worked her way around many of the popular calendar hill races and enjoys getting out for sociable plods with her pals and peers for a training gab.

We are both members of Westerlands Cross Country Club, a perfectly formed small-to-medium sized running club, based in the west end of Glasgow. A friendly tribe of runners with its 70's roots in Glasgow University as an off-shoot of the

Hares & Hounds, it is stuffed full of brains with Doctors of all possible descriptions, eminent professors, sought after surgeons, high ranking politicians, successful business people, international engineers… and me.

Foreword

In my life I have been so lucky to meet some amazing people and Manny Gorman is one of them.

In 2010 I went along to a lecture in Boat of Garten near Aviemore and met Manny after he talked about his incredible trip, "The Corbett's in 70 days". I had met him before on the hill, and as a hill runner he is one of its celebrities; unassuming men and women with no egos. Today's sports superstars could learn from these people. Manny is of a breed of these unknown athletes. He is a passionate hill runner and one of the finest amongst this unique band of hill folk. They are a very private people, they are a "family" and this book gives an insight into this fantastic sport, their life, the pain and the suffering, but mostly the joy of moving fast through the mountains.

His talk took you on an incredible journey through Scotland's Corbetts and was a magic tale. It was not just a list of mountains but a journey through Scotland's wonderful wild land. He told a great story of the highs and lows of the trip, the pressures, the support of family & friends and some fantastic photographs of the mountains and of the wildlife. I was riveted by the story as were the large audience that night in Boat of Garten. He said after the lecture that he would perhaps try to write a book about it and share his journey with a wider audience. This is now complete.

This book will take you on a journey through Scotland away from the "honey pot hills" with a wonderful insight into this amazing sport and its unique people. This was a special Round and when you read the book you will be taken into the world of marathon mountain days but also a connection with the people involved and the rare wild places which are very special. His friends and family support was incredible; this is a man blessed by great fitness and an incredible drive. I am sure all lovers of the mountains and the wild will love this book as I did; it keeps going right to the end, where there is a sting in the tale.

Enjoy!

David "Heavy" Whalley MBE. BEM
August 2013

An Appreciation

Our journey cannot begin without special mention and thanks to the few and the many.

Chris Upson is a very talented obsessive on just about everything he touches – his hills, his running, his music and his family & friends. He is self-driven well beyond the normal bounds of mere hobbies or past-times, and insists on learning and absorbing every detail of his subjects in order to excel at sharing it out again, which he always does freely and with inspiration. Chris's input to the Corbett Round was from the first whisper to the last gasp and every twitch in-between. From early planning to the blog site, from giving up so much of his own time and holidays to sharing the hills and logistics, to inspiring and stirring up other runners to get involved, and of course at the eleventh hour being there for Brenda, even in the misery of his own illness. Alec Keith summed him up nicely as "A top man to have on your side!"

Another club mate, Johnston Orr, was relatively unknown to me at that time due to us living in the wild north and being detached from Westies (Westerlands Cross Country Club) training and social nights, but quickly became a firm friend along the way. Like Chris he willingly helped out time and again with logistics, blogging, of course running in the hills with me and notably the supplier one of the finest bottles of whisky ever to have passed my lips. His enthusiasm was infectious and I gratefully fed off that.

John Allen MBE and his wife Anne are our near neighbours in Kingussie who took up my challenge of sailing between the Island Corbetts, providing the beautiful yacht Finlandia for ten days of outstanding journey down the west coast. John, himself a mountaineer of some repute, remained patient and faithful to my non-motorised ethic which tested him on few occasions!

Archie Lang and Sandra MacLennan remain both work colleagues and friends; they helped drive on our travelling circus throughout the 70 days. As well as crewing on the first sailing section, every gap in their always busy life schedule was filled with Corbett visits, blogging, mending bikes, cookers, or even delivering newspapers to remote locations! There on the first day and on the last.

Murray Cochrane, and again Sandra, both our Highland Council Housing line-managers at that time; we are indebted for their understanding and support during a family tragedy and still honouring our employer's commitment to our special leave arrangement a year later, and even extending our leave to allow me to complete the round after I overshot my schedule.

All our many team-mates from the fabulous Westerlands Cross Country Club who offered invaluable support; Graham Kelly, Donald Smith, Elizabeth & Neil Adams, Cat Millar, Rt. Hon Al Campbell & Isabel Coombs, John Donnelly, Dave & Mary Rogers, Stevie Bell, Ellie Homewood, Hamilton Semple, Brian Brennan, Dave Calder, Andy & Maria Mott, Dave Riach, Luke Arnott, Don & Elma Reid, Swaz & Jenny Fraser, Steffan Gorgas, Shona Robertson, Pete & Elsie Baxter, Brian Bonnyman, John Bottomley; and in particular Charlie Campbell, along with his sister June, who got out there and shared the hills with us once again, and always being there to support us. A great guy to have in my corner.

Of course there were many, many more to thank...

Allan from Sheffield on the Clisham, Dot with her life-giving doughnuts and her camera, John & Fiona Newman for their sailing & rowing skills, the exceptional Davy Duncan & ever-patient Christine, out of retirement Donald Smith, Ken & Clare Rumgay with late-notice help and accommodation, Colin & Joan Wilson over a tough day indeed, Alan & Tilly Smith with their fine hospitality and great company, Angela Mudge, Peter Porteous, Keith Bootle, Dave & Val Machin, Paul Raistrick, Geoff Simpson & Ali Johnson for their enduring support during and since, Alec Keith, the ubiquitous Squires, Scott & Linda Kennedy, Jim Hall, Peter Bennett for all his biking, Adrian Davis, Richard 'Tricky' Speirs, John Coyle for his bike and hospitality, Mindy Macleod for the Harris logistics and the Beeb interview, Doctor Chris Ellis, Alison Robb and Kirsty Wright for repairing my broken body, Finlay Binnie and Russell Jones for the loan of bikes, and of course the many Bloggers who helped make this story with their contributions and encouragement which always cheered us up and urged us on.

To Mr Kevin Baird, Consultant Orthopaedic Surgeon and Raigmore Hospital, for the outstanding care and repair of Brenda.

Special thanks go to our generous sponsors.

The marvellous Cairngorm Brewery, with Beth Tyler ensuring we did not dehydrate by supplying ample quantities of their isotonic fine ales.

Also to Mike & Jenny Devlin of Mikes Bikes in Aviemore, who kindly donated various gear towards our trip.

Finally, thanks and love to both our families for their support and help, from near or afar, throughout the trip and ever since.

It was all very much appreciated.

Preface

Manny several times makes the comment about the special nature of an extra-long challenge, how it becomes the normal life (a rich life) and the shock is in the stopping. This is the story of one such, a continuous challenge, an unparalleled mountain running feat, of some near disasters and well-merited success: the Corbetts in just 70 days. To add to the pressures Corbetts enjoy a wider distribution (extra islands- beyond swimming!) and they take perhaps more effort than the Munros.

As the first to complete the Munros in a one-off I'm often blamed for introducing this competitive element but it was inevitable. Humans are competitive and competitiveness sharpens senses. Manny saw more eagles on his running than most do in a lifetime of plodding. When I did that Munro round, or linking the country summits of Scotland, England, Wales and Ireland, computers, mobiles, internet or the web hadn't been invented. That's history now. Today's technology gives this account a vividness that sweeps the story along, Manny pacing the reader all the way. Breathless stuff.

To string together this epic set a huge logistical task to service Manny's continuous, yet erratic, progress: running, cycling, sailing and eating and sleeping. It succeeded impressively with that backing of family and the camaraderie of the running and cycling worlds. In this ever more selfish world this is a story of challenge, comradeship, and dedication to lift the heart.

The nicest compliment came from a friend, "Manny, you're an idiot, but a truly inspirational one"

Hamish Brown MBE
September 2013

1. WHY, WHAT & WHERE?

So, why the Corbetts?

First, believe it or not, it was meant to be a holiday and I wanted it to be an experience for Brenda and I to participate in and enjoy together. It had been a few years since my last long-distance soiree, and I wanted something longer than just a few weeks, covering new ground for us in the Scottish countryside. The roles would be simple – I would travel the route entirely non-motorised by run, cycle and sail, whilst Brenda would drive the van, squeeze in as many Corbetts as possible and do absolutely everything else that was required!

Second, they weren't Munros. Not only had that tremendous round of mountains been done several times in different formats over the years, but my good friend and clubmate Charlie Campbell held the record at that time, 48½ days, which was very special to him and to our running club, Westies; I didn't want to touch it while it was his. It was and, although now reduced to 39 days by a slightly different format, remains unique. Charlie is the only person to date to have swum the two sea crossings, from Mull, and to Skye, and also back & forth across Loch Lomond to run Ben Lomond!

Third, it hadn't been done before - as far I as I could research prior to starting. Only well after the event did I hear of an article in the mountain fanzine, The Angry Corrie, of a 1992 round of 133 days by Mike Wilson-Roberts, but sadly no other details of whether it was continuous, or motorised, etc. In any case, the Corbetts ticked a lot of boxes for me; they are big, remote, a lot of them were new to me, the challenge of linking them looked (and proved) considerably harder than Munros, and a lot of sailing was involved. All told, it looked really, really tough - great!

What are Corbetts and where are they?

The original list, defining Scottish mountains between 2500 (763m) to 3000ft (914.4m) in height, with a minimum 500ft drop on all sides, was compiled by John Rooke Corbett of the Scottish Mountaineering Club in the early 1900s. Obviously a character made of the hard stuff, he was only the second person to complete the all Munros, along with the many Munro Tops, along with all of Scotland's 2,000ft hills; a truly remarkable achievement in an age when transport links throughout the Highlands and other parts of Scotland would have been tenuous at best. Public transport, cars or even decent roads in the highlands would have been rare, and it was a similar determination that I was hoping to engage.

There were 219 Corbetts in early 2009, increased to 220 after the scrutinised re-measurement and subsequent demotion of ex-Munro Sgurr nan Ceannaichean, only a few weeks after the completion of my round. Corbett's own travels would have taken him to many areas where Munros do not completely dominate the skyline, including four additional islands, Moray, The Borders, Ardgour and Assynt to name but a few. Also, Corbetts are spread further in every direction of the compass than Munros and feel totally different, being very much individual characters. There is only one true easily attained cluster of five Corbetts near Tyndrum, the rest are spread wildly in threes, twos or singly, inevitably ensuring an awful lot of re-ascent. Linking them together posed a major logistical challenge.

It was summer 2007 when my plot was originally hatched and the massive preparatory machine began to lumber into motion.

2. PLANNING

So I had hatched the idea, but before I could take the first metaphorical or physical steps there was the pivotal question of whether I, we, could get enough time off work from the Highland Council. Brenda and I both work in the same small Housing Services team in Kingussie, covering the beautiful area of Badenoch & Strathspey. Like all local authorities, the Highland Council was under the usual enormous pressures of cost effectiveness and performance, so we were aware it was a big ask, but submitted our request to our Area Manager, Mr Murray Cochrane, with fingers crossed. To our great delight, we received confirmation of permission, under the condition of a combination of paid and unpaid leave, but we had already guessed it was going to be an expensive business! However, we were over the moon and the excitement built as I wired into a mountain of maps and books to draw up a route and schedule; this wasn't an easy process, but highly enjoyable and addictive as anyone who loves the hills will know. The fun of letting the mind run riot whilst pouring over an O.S. map invariably resulted in days that were ridiculous in length and climb, requiring butchering into more realistic days. The 2007 winter weeks and months ticked by into 2008, but day by day the route came together into an approximate 60 day schedule, and I proposed starting in early May.

A huge amount of work had been almost completed. I had arranged with my old skipper and crew from the Scottish Island Peaks Race - Graham Lord sailing Meridian, and with the race organisers blessing, that we could take part in their famous event, having first visited Harris, Skye & Rum, but also to include a few extra diversions on Mull and Arran to catch the other island Corbetts! It was audaciously complicated but everyone was up for it.

One of the last pieces of the jigsaw fell into place with the arrival of our campervan at the beginning of April. We needed a reliable mobile base, and like many people I had simply dreamt of a campervan for years, but now was the perfect time to buy one, a Compass Avantgarde - four-berth, with loo, shower, fridge/freezer, cooker/oven, loads of storage space and a four-bike rack on the back. It was love at first site! We were now frantically trying to tie up a million loose ends before starting in just a few weeks time… but it was not meant to be.

At the time my brother Richard and his wonderful partner Jane were living in Dundee where they had only just moved into their new house, with their nine month old son, Magnus. Jane a drama teacher who loved her role, Richard about to start his new career as a teacher, they were to be married in the coming summer. Jane was a single day older than me and we celebrated our 40th birthdays together at a grand party in their new home just weeks before. Life was just immensely rosy for them and it was a joy to watch. With a shocking bolt from the blue, Jane died on 15th April after a very brief and completely unexpected illness. The world stopped turning. Our hearts had been torn from us, and the only thoughts left for a very long time to come were for Richard and Magnus. I lived in Dundee for the next month to be with my brother and nephew, and cancelled everything we had arranged for the summer. It simply didn't matter anymore; it was as if the Corbett plans had never existed.

As it does with sufficient time, life recovers just enough and moves on. So it was twelve months later, and with exceptional understanding, our managers were still honouring their previous leave commitment to us, for which we are forever grateful.

I had torn up my original route, unhappy with the lack of flow, had re-written it from scratch over the winter months and was now much happier with the final plan and mileage. The all important sailing section had also been totally changed to form the first leg of the journey, still hideously complicated, but giving a much more natural movement to the overall route. Now proposing an earlier start in April, I could no longer utilise Meridian for the sailing, but at least I had a willing crew formed from some good mountain biking/sailing friends, John & Fiona Newman and Archie Lang & Sandra MacLennan, who had a healthy smattering of nautical experience between them. I recall one of the early crew meetings where I was outlining my original plans to them, to try and sail the island sections in a 14ft Wanderer dinghy, in April – everyone went deathly quiet, some even going pale. John slowly turned to me to break the deafening silence with the immortal shark-movie line "I think you're going to need a bigger boat!" There are no super-sized sharks in the Minch, but he was right of course and I was totally naive of what was required. Archie had a Eureka! moment when he remembered that local pharmacist and Cairngorm Mountain Rescue Team stalwart, John Allen MBE, had recently retired and treated himself to a nice new boat, "Finlandia" (a Nauticat 37), so perhaps he was looking for projects to try her out on? It was certainly worth asking at least, and after a flurry of communications proved fruitful, with additional crew available with John's wife and First Mate, Anne. During planning discussions John had warned me that he was still very much learning his sailing trade for enjoyment, and would not be taking any risks in anything over F6/7 if it could be helped, and that Finlandia was never built for speed, but with unadulterated luxury in mind. So a safe skipper with a nice cumfy boat? Oh, ok then!

In an incredibly busy and stressful last few months I had come up with a much improved final printed schedule of 60 days, but knew this would be fluid from the start: two full sets of maps had been marked up with the Corbetts and the route; a ton of provisions and gear had been loaded onto the van; three bikes were loaded and we also now had a better idea of how the van handled and operated - we had reccied a lot of remote and narrow roads for Brenda's piece of mind as driver. I was generally quite fit but certainly not super-fit; I knew the islands and Borders sections over the first ten to fourteen days would make me much stronger and break me into the different level of fitness required to sustain the majority of the journey. I still had plenty of belly-blubber left over from a winter of over-eating and drinking, but knew all such reserves would all be needed in the weeks to come. I had purposely not raced for most of the spring in order to avoid injuries, but even so had been plagued with a niggling knee pain for the last few months. Without much option I had to persevere with light running and cycling, then ceased all running three weeks before the start, crossing my fingers that whatever the problem was would repair itself and disappear before I got to the start line on Harris... fortunately it did.

As if life was not complicated enough, we had decided to refurbish our Kingussie home, requiring us to move out to a rented house in Aviemore for six months, which is where the majority of the new planning took place. As April grew near it was clear that the work would not be finished in time for us to move back before the trip, so we had to pack our life belongings away into storage for the duration and hand back our temporary accommodation – we were homeless and on the road!

Time was up - now we just hoped everything was covered.

3. THE ISLAND CORBETTS
DAYS 1 – 10

The off

On Friday 24th April 2009 we headed to Skye in order for me to catch a ferry the next morning from Uig to Tarbet on Harris. We travelled via Loch Pooltiel, where I was due to land back on Skye on the second day, so that Brenda could see the narrow access road and pier for her to meet the yacht with the van. It was a stunning evening with the Minch almost mirror calm and an orange sunset over the Uists. We had stopped on the remote wee road to take a photo when a taxi drove past and pulled into a nearby house driveway. In a nano-second decision I came up with the idea that we could park-up the van on the pier, take the taxi across to Uig, and Brenda could come over on the ferry to share the first sailing leg back across from Skye – her only opportunity of a sail. I flagged the driver down for a quote for the long drive to the ferry port - £50? Groan, ok, done! We parked up on the pier and quickly threw some stuff into bags and then we were off! We were dropped off at the Uig Hotel at 10pm and only just managed to persuade the extremely miserable wifey to give us a room for the night, which was almost as grim as the non-existent customers or atmosphere in the bar, with just an overpriced bottle of Red MacGregor ale to glumly sook on.

Day 1 Sat 25th April - In the beginning there was Harris
Foot 3 miles & 2,132ft, bike 24 miles (840ft), 1 Corbett

The walk from the Uig Hotel to the Ferry Terminal turned out to be considerably longer than I had anticipated, especially when humfing a gigantic couple of kit bags in each hand and realising that departure time was approaching faster than I wanted. We met our sailing crew Sandra & Archie at the terminal and gratefully took the courtesy vehicle down the pier to the Calmac ferry "Hebrides", boarding with apprehension of the coming adventure.

It was here. All the months of planning and delays were over, it was time, yikes! The weather was dry but cloudy, with distant An Clisham on Harris expecting me, with its head stuck under a blanket of grey cloud. As we sailing across the Minch Archie enquired of how many summits did I think I would get a view from as the journey expanded... mmm? The first two weeks would not provide a great statistic. The craic was good over the sea to Harris with Sandra & Archie, work colleagues & friends, building the excitement for the coming unknown.

By the time we docked in Tarbet I was buzzing. The first job on landing was to seek out Tarbet Stores, where my Westies clubmate and native Harris-man, Murdo

1-3 Harris to Rum

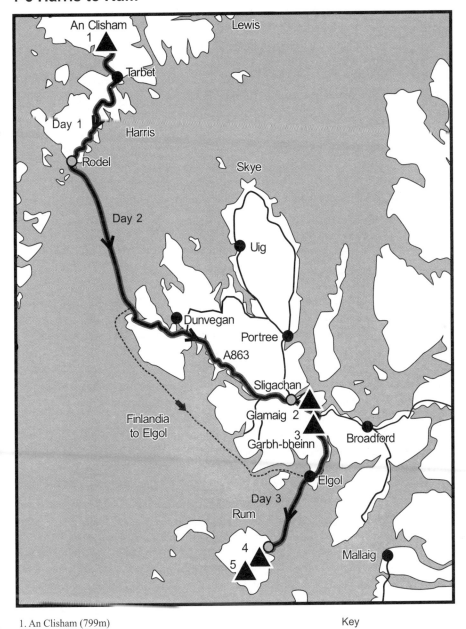

1. An Clisham (799m)
2. Glamaig (775m)
3. Garbh-bheinn (808m)

Key

○ Overnight Stop

Route Taken

▲ Corbetts in Order

MacLeod, had arranged for a borrowed bike to be left for me to pick up. The Tarbet Stores resembled a scene from Steptoe & Son, but a quick enquiry of the Gaelic blethering bodachs from within confirmed that the mountain bike propped at the front door was indeed for me. After a quick photo-call I dived across the road to the bus stop where Murdo had again used his local connections in order to get my bike onto the Stornoway bus (usually not allowed) and driven to the foot of the first hill, the Clisham, thus saving me a 6 mile & 500ft cycle just to get to the start line.

The other three were not coming with me. They were going to have to hang about Tarbet for a few hours to catch a bus south to Rodel on Renish Point, the southernmost tip of Harris, in order to meet the yacht Finlandia and Skipper/1st Mate, John & Anne, and did the only sensible thing under the circumstances – found a pub.

As Brenda kissed me good-luck and I boarded the bus, it caught me by surprise to suddenly be feeling low and in a rut of total anti-climax. I was on my own, no one to share the first Corbett with. The ten minute bus trip was soon over at the top of the hill, and all the other local passengers looked mystified as we stopped in the middle of nowhere whilst I got off, with the driver fishing the bike out from the bowels of the vehicle and shaking my hand good-luck. I would need it.

It was grey, bleak and quiet, but there was a solitary car parked in the adjacent lay-by where someone was getting out. An old fella came ambling over as I sorted out my gear. "Ae up lad, are you going up t' hill?" I replied "Eh, aye...?" This was Allan from Sheffield. His missus, Kay, was still in the car but was adamant that he was not going up the Clisham in the mist, without a map, and on his own at seventy years old, so would I mind if he accompanied me up? He would try to keep up, and I didn't have to wait, really...Well, having no other company and actually really wanting to share the moment with someone, anyone, yes of course!

We left Kay happily reading her paper in the car whilst we set off across the rough ground and started up at a good walking pace. I suggested to Allan that I would walk to the summit with him and then perhaps leave him at the top so I could run back down, and he was happy with this; however as the walk progressed, Allan vented forth with story after story of climbing tales from southern crags and his enthusiasm of hill life was infectious. We yapped incessantly all the way to the top, with a short detour for him to squeeze in some illicit rock scrambling, out of sight of Kay, just before we were immersed in the summit mist. The top, number 1! It was only here I divulged to Allan what I was actually attempting to do with the Corbetts. Without Allan there I wouldn't have got a photo on the first summit nor had such an enjoyable time doing it. I binned any idea of running down out the mist without my new friend and on the descent we agreed to meet back in Tarbet for a beer; me by bike, Allan and Kay in their car. Good craic, several beers and some good grub were scoffed in the The Isle of

Harris Inn before we wished each other well and they headed back to their bunkhouse, me on the bike south to Rodel to meet the yacht and crew.

I chose to ignore Murdo's advice to take the easier west side road and instead rode the much hillier, but much more interesting Golden Road on the east side, via the Bays and through his own home village of Geocrab. Fantastic fun! A road like a roller coaster through tiny, timeless settlements with the wild Minch on one side and rough barren moorland and hills on the other. What a hard place this must have been for families to eke out a living from sea & land, in the days when the crofts were used as such and before a whole generation moved away or died, leaving historic family crofts to be filled as holiday or retirement homes. I was lucky, the weather was improving as the day went on and I was able to see the barren but beautiful surroundings - magic.

A few hours in the saddle, stopping briefly to take photos here and there along the way, I crested a final hill and there was my first sight of Finlandia, at anchor below me. I got a rush of adrenaline up my arms and down my back, all the way to my toes – what a scene! The tight wee sheltered bay was bathed in sunshine with a very attractive yacht that was to be my home for the next ten days waiting for my arrival, and the Rodel Hotel looked inviting on the pier side. A shout out to the boat and a few bodies appeared on deck having been disturbed from their G&T's. I couldn't rush - I just wanted to soak up the moment. After a successful prologue on Clisham the main event was about to start, with a make or break sail down through the western seaboard of Scotland, visiting six islands and finishing in Troon - but very aware that the weather could easily play a joker with the possibility of being storm-bound for days anywhere along the route. Skipper John had been up front in letting me know that he would not be out in any wild weather regardless of my Corbett-clock ticking.

Skipper John Allen MBE is better known in mountaineering circles as *Cairngorm John* - his personal call sign to the many rescue aircraft which assisted him during his eighteen year tenure as leader of the Cairngorm Mountain Rescue Team, extending his MRT career to a remarkable thirty-five years. Since his recent retirement and uncooperative knee joints, sailing had become a new method for him to appreciate the mountains of Scotland, viewed from sea-level.

I had a quick look around the ancient church of St Clement which sits above the bay, and then it was a mad free-wheel down the hill to find Brenda had already booked us into the very comfortable Rodel Hotel for the night. After a good hot bath - the last for a month - the crew assembled for celebratory drinks and a superb meal served up by the hotel owner Donnie MacDonald. The evening outside was absolutely stunning with a bright low sun over a mirror calm bay and Finlandia casting a perfect reflection. Inside, the craic was fantastic and wine was

9

being consumed at a worrying rate... for an athlete at least!

So ended the first day, with Skipper John taxiing the merry crew back out to the yacht, not quite in a straight line, whilst me & Brenny hit the bar with the locals for several nightcaps. I went to bed wondering how good the next two months would be if they were all like this...?

Archie's diary... *I knew it was a daft plan as soon as Manny suggested using our 14ft sailing dinghy to get between the islands. There was part of me (a tiny wee part) which quite liked the thought of giving it a go! I have to admit that when Manny was setting out on this epic I doubted that he would complete it. Not through any lack of effort but purely based on his fairly consistent record of injuring himself every third or fourth outing.*

Day 2 Sunday 26th April - Skye, just add water!
Foot 0.5 mile & 50ft, bike 31 miles (1,319ft), sail 22 miles, no hills

The morning in Rodel broke as beautiful as the previous evening and we bade farewell to our fine host Donnie. We watched Finlandia purr her way out of the bay to our agreed pick-up point off a beach just round the corner. On the collection dinghy with Archie, Brenda was somewhat jittery having never sailed before, whilst I relished the coming journey having experienced the mixed delights of the Scottish Islands Peaks Race several times in the past. This felt just like an extended version of that classic event and indeed would include the three same islands, and a couple of the same hills. The annual SIPR was due to take place in only a couple of weeks time, from Oban to Troon, visiting Mull, Jura & Arran along the way, and attracts some of the top yachts/crews and hill runners from across Britain every year, making it a highly competitive but fantastically sociable weekend. In 2004 I was lucky enough to win the highly prized "King of the Bens" paired with Malcolm Paterson of Shettleston Harriers, sailing on a relatively genteel, but highly competitive, cruising-racer called Meridian, a Sigma-36. (...and to my great delight, again in May 2013, with clubmate Brian Bonnyman, as I pen the finishing touches to this book!)

Our sail across the Minch was relatively uneventful but pleasant, other than poor landlubber Brenda heaving over the side as the wind & sea increased in velocity and resulting motion. The first useful sailing lesson she learned was never to be seasick into the wind...! Another ominous passing form in the water was the massive black shape of a nuclear submarine heading north, like some sort of floating Reaper. By the time we broke into little Loch Pooltiel on the western tip of Skye the wind had picked up considerably and Brenda was ready to hug solid ground like lichen to a rock.

Myself, Brenda & 1st Mate Anne disembarked leaving John, Archie & Sandra to motor-sail south to Elgol to meet me again tomorrow. As it transpired, the rapidly deteriorating weather forced them to change plan the moment they left the shelter of the loch and got blasted by heavy seas and winds, demanding a wise retreat to spend the night at anchor in Pooltiel. With Brenda giving a lift to Anne - due to logistics both were only able to fit in that first sail across the Minch - to pick up Archie's car left back in Uig, I set off on what should have been a straight-forward 30 mile cycle to Sligachan. However, I hadn't even gone a mile when freezing rain started and the wind rose to gale force, to the extent where every turn on the bike meant shouldering a windy side-swipe or hunching over the bars to minimise the resistance. It just got worse & worse. The undulating road was awash and every time a vehicle passed it would give me total drenching in freezing spray. Any respite from the grinding uphill climbs with frozen limbs were not rewarded with a downhill freewheel, as the wind would be in my face forcing me to select a low gear so I could pedal back down again! I hid in a bus shelter briefly, stamping my frozen feet, and sent Archie a text bemoaning my plight, assuming that they were still getting a battering down the west side of the island, but he replied admitting to their hasty retreat back into Loch Pooltiel. Brenda passed me with only a downhill mile to go to Slig, but I was barely moving on the bike, having to fight for every turn of the crank. When I finally got there I was utterly spent and it had taken me three hours for just 30 miles, barely 10mph. The van was heaving about violently in the car park and it had to be moved quickly to shelter behind the hotel building before it blew over! I already knew that doing the days' two hills, Glamaig & Garbh-bheinn, was a non-starter. It was now late afternoon, I was mentally & physically shattered from the all-out battle on the bike, and the clouds screaming over the hills told me all I needed to know about my prospects if I were to attempt continuing. Instead, along with several other unfortunate souls from the flooded campsite across the road, we hid in the bar all night eating & drinking by the fire whilst watching drookit rats coming & going from the storm outside. Mind you, I could think of worse places to be stormbound than Seumas' Bar in Sligachan!

Archie's diary... *As soon we got out of the shelter of the loch the waves were crashing over the bows and John soon decided to return back to Loch Pooltiel for the night. Once anchored we were sheltered from the waves but the wind was absolutely howling. Finlandia swung about pretty impressively on her anchor chain in the swirling gusts as the rain pelted down on the saloon windows. It felt great sitting there in the comfort of the boat having our dinner, drinking beer while the elements raged outside. It felt even better when I got a text from Manny to say he was soaked, knackered and taking brief refuge in a bus shelter (although, I seem to remember his text contained a lot more sweary words than that!)*

Day 3 Monday 27th April - Eilean a' Cheo', The Misty Isle
Foot 9 miles & 5,427ft, bike 9 miles (664ft), sail 11 miles, 2 Corbetts

We struggled to get up after an unsettled night in the windswept wobbly van. It was still pretty miserable but the worst elements of the storm had now passed, leaving me to get on with the two Corbetts in more typical Skye weather – rain and clag. I enjoyed heading off up the loose slopes of Glamaig, the dramatic scene of many a fantastic hill race over the years. In my opinion at least, this is one of my top six "Classic" hill races in Scotland, with a no-nonsense, brutally steep, 2,500ft climb to the summit, and an absolutely hair-raising descent on loose and dangerous rocky scree back to the hotel, to be rewarded by a great night of beer, music & dancing into the small hours! Tonight at Noon, one of the great bands that played for this dance many years ago, announced to the crazed crowd of dancing runners, after having already played their entire set twice over, that "This is by far the most dangerously fit audience we have ever played to!", before continuing once more!

Very early on my way across the moor, and putting it down to yesterdays battering, I felt very lethargic and weary on the first climb and suddenly required an emergency stop for my morning constitutional, only to find to my horror that I appeared to be being eaten inside-out by worms! I enjoy my grub too much to allow any thieving worms to be stealing it, so I sent a quick text to try and get some worming tablets to the boat, but this would not happen before Mull now, and the effects would wear me down far more than I could ever have imagined.

With a little nostalgia the top of Glamaig was reached in a flurry of snow and strong wind, but not being a day to linger I marched straight over the south-east side and started the very steep, slippery and rocky drop, eventually trotting off to the high point of the busy A87 above Loch Ainort. Brenda arrived in the van a few minutes later to allow a change out of sopping gear and have some hot food & drinks, then it was a quick mile of downhill bike to the spectacular roadside waterfall of Eas a'Bhradain, where I set off up the ridge of Druim Eader Da'Choire to reach mist-clad Garbh-bheinn, again in snow. It was a shame the clag was down as I missed out on the spectacular scenery of the Black & Red Cuillins hidden all around me – I will just have to come back on a nicer day. Careful navigation was required on this invisible but very steep terrain and I briefly tried to make sense of a GPS that Archie had lent me to record the whole trip. But after vainly fiddling and freezing for five minutes I surrendered to my technological ignorance and got my trusty map & compass out, finding my way into Choire a'Caise without a hitch. I enjoyed the tricky scree runs off the bealach into the corrie and carefully picked my way down to the footpath leading to the forest car park on the shore of Loch Slapin, where to my dismay Brenda was not to be found! I spotted the van sitting about a mile away by a bridge at the head of the loch, and after some waving, bawling and whistling Brenda finally saw me and drove up to meet me. I was a bit concerned at this, because I knew that Brenda had very limited map-reading skills and finding very exact, but important, meeting points for me coming off the hill in the coming months would be vital, especially in foul weather. I made a mental note, in future to always go over the coming days' route and meeting points in detail together prior to setting off; and it must have worked because this type of hiccup would only happen once more during the remainder of the journey.

Changed again with more food and hot drinks, it was then onto the road bike for a brief but fun fast 8 mile cycle along to Elgol. The recharge of body fuel gave me a buzz, and I flew effortlessly along the road to be met by that world famous view across Loch Scavaig to the Cuillin, unfortunately with its ridge still cloaked in mist. Finlandia, already there, waited for me on a mooring. On the last steep hairpin dropping into Elgol, disaster loomed suddenly. In the split second that it happened, I spotted the multi-coloured sheen off the road surface and knew I was on oil - I also knew I was going to go down! There was a rusty old 4x4 coming up the road too so it was instant decision time – without trying to complete the turn, I headed for the verge which had a steep drop off into broken rocks and jagged concrete, but there was also a very narrow strip of grass. I aimed at it and threw myself off the bike with my eyes shut! I landed heavily, as did the bike, but thankfully both were intact! Worse than the crash - I had to endure the mocking of the decrepit 4x4's ancient driver who had stopped to inform this reckless lowland tourist, in his best Hebridean teuchter twang "Och laddie, you'll have to be careful of the steep roads in these parts, you know!" He was already pulling away and probably missed my best indignant Glaswegian "There's fucking fuel all over the road ya knob!" ...and gushing out from behind his crappy old vehicle!

I dusted myself off, and down at the van in the car park I watched Sandra & Archie walking up the slipway... but all was not well there either! Sandra was being supported by Archie and very slowly hirpled up to meet us. After chuckling at how much they both enjoyed watching me from the boat as I crashed my way down into Elgol, Sandra explained that earlier that morning she was simply stepping down below deck when she felt like someone had whacked her with a club on the back of the leg. Since John & Archie were still both on deck they were in the clear, but it was obvious that something had instead ruptured and I suspected the Achilles tendon, as the foot was almost completely lame. There was no option, she had to go to hospital in the van with Brenda, and I was deeply disappointed for her as all the best island sailing was yet to come. We loaded my gear for the next week or more onto the yacht, bade the two lassies farewell to Raigmore A&E (for the eventual diagnosis of a badly ruptured calf muscle) and in now almost calm conditions, very slowly crept across the sea towards Rum, spotting a couple of porpoises trailing a homeward bound fishing boat. The clouds had at last started to lift and we made no more than a couple of knots for most of the way, but at least the scenery was dramatic enough to stop us getting bored.

Beers were cracked, sails tweaked & coaxed into motion, and Clannad played on the deck speakers with their haunting drones whilst the sun started to creep through chinks in the cloud cover. The Rum Cuillin started to reveal itself above us and we crept into Loch Scresort with Kinloch Castle at its head, where we dropped anchor for the night. Dinner and drams on deck. What a magical finish to the day.

Archie's diary...*On the way to Elgol Sandra somehow tore a calf muscle without seeming to have done anything to cause it and it became clear that the sailing was over for her on this trip. After a while at Elgol the van appeared fairly closely followed by Manny. Even from a distance we knew it was Manny by his riding style, particularly the way he fell off at the first bend on the descent to the pier! Leaving Elgol the clouds were low and dramatic over the Cuillins surrounding Loch Scavaig.*

Day 4 Tuesday 28th April - A Rum Tum
Foot 10 miles & 4,406ft, sail 37 miles, 2 Corbetts

A beautiful sunny morning start to day 4, though I was feeling slightly odd. Archie rowed me ashore and I didn't feel the need to run anywhere, so instead enjoyed a weary stroll around the loch past the castle in sunshine and total silence, other than the birds tweeting at spring. I hauled myself up the Coire Dubh footpath and deciding that I had too much kit with me, planked most of it in the undergrowth to collect on my return. Feeling knackered even at a walk, I traversed around the side of Hallival then up into the mist leading to Askival, which finished in a delightful wee scramble to the summit. Unfortunately once again I was in thick mist, but it cleared very quickly as I started to descend into sunshine. As the cloud burnt off and the view opened up, the rugged beauty of Rum took my breath away – I had never been on the island before but hoped it would not be long before I was back to visit the rest of the hills I would be missing today. I traversed the bottom of Trollaval at a jog then struggled up the final steep climb to the summit of Ainshval. The view was astounding – Askival had now cleared and there were views to Skye, Eigg, Muck and the mainland, all bathed in spring sunshine. I lingered a long while on top soaking up some rare heat, and saw my first sea eagle, with its distinctive white tail, flying below me in rough Glen Dibidil. My spirits soared upwards like the creature beneath me. It was a wrench to descend again but I still enjoyed the traverse around Atlantic Corrie where some stinking wild goats spied me suspiciously as I pretended to copy their surefootedness, stumbling around the narrow trods and climbing up to Bealach Bairc-mheall.

Bloody hell, I was done in - I felt I could have slept for a month. I took another lengthy break overlooking the corrie, scoffing all the remaining food in my pack. My batteries were flat and I was pretty certain it was the gut-worm problem

Days 4-5 Rum to Mull

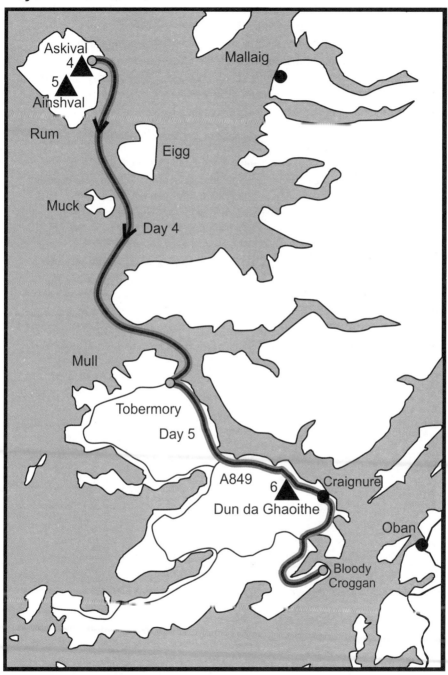

4. Askival (812m)
5. Ainshval (781m)
6. Dun da Ghaoithe (785m)

wreaking havoc with my system. Totally drained, I traipsed back down to the Coire Dubh path and found my hidden gear, then managed to raise my spirits with a good jog back to the shore, cutting a substantial corner heading across some really rough broken ground. I stumbled out the last of the trees and found Archie enjoying a leisurely walk around the shore. I flopped into the dinghy and he taxied me back to Finlandia where a colossal feed was in order to revive the body and soul! My estimated time of three hours ended up a feeble five hours, and felt more like ten, confirming to me that my body was just not working properly. Still, it was a fantastic experience of the island and I was only sorry that I wasn't fit or well enough to make more of it. We set sail for Mull and sitting on deck in the sun, with lots of lovely food, enjoying the splendid scenery made for a very pleasant way to let the body recover. My ongoing worm problem had not affected my appetite – if anything it had increased, after all I had a cast of thousands to feed! I prepared my own substantial feasts and tried to keep hygiene to a maximum to avoid being thrown overboard if I were to infect the crew.

For hours in very light winds we hardly made any progress at no more than a single knot in various currents & tides. The sun shone in a deep blue sky, the island scenery magnificent, wedged somewhere between Canna, Rum, Muck and Eigg. I fell asleep like a dead man and woke to see only a slightly different version of the same scene from hours before. Fortunately I wasn't to know until later of grumblings from the crew on deck about the frustrating pace, and suggestions of starting the engine which were thankfully averted!

Archie's diary... *For hours we drifted along at 1-2 knots, sometimes less, and seemed never to get past Eigg. Despite the magnificent surroundings the atmosphere on board was becoming fairly gloomy. Manny wasn't feeling too great after his run (probably something to do with his wriggly jobbies!) and was a bit pissed off at having lost time off his schedule already. I think John was worried about the weather which although flat calm at that moment was forecast to deteriorate into pretty wild conditions later that evening. He was understandably concerned that we didn't get caught out in foul weather off Ardnamurchan point in the dark. John asked us from time to time what we thought we should do, I got the impression he was hoping one of us would suggest getting the engine going and getting on our way. Manny generally kept pretty quiet at these moments. I usually pointed to a faint ripple in the distance suggesting that there might be some more wind there and we should just give it a wee while longer and would then get busy futilely adjusting sails to try to coax a bit more (or any) speed out of Finlandia. I was aware that a big part of Manny's plan was to cover all of the distance between the Corbetts without using motorised power. I was getting worried that this might be scuppered on day 4 and that this would really put a dampener on the rest of the Round.*

By about 5:00pm we still hadn't passed Eigg and John eventually asked if we really wanted to still be out there at 4:00 in the morning. I had been thinking about those who took part in the Island Peaks Race and sailed throughout the night and was aware of the amount of effort that Manny was putting into this expedition, so I was perfectly happy to put up with a bit of hardship to get the job done. I was however also aware of the possibility of deteriorating weather so told John that if we had to get the engine on due to the weather conditions becoming dangerous then so be it, but I certainly didn't want to give up just because we were fed up.

At that point there was no sign of the bad weather so we plodded on and gradually a breeze filled in as we approached Muck, we picked up speed and spirits on board lifted considerably. By 9:00pm the sun was dipping below the western horizon in a blazing fireball whilst on our port side Ardnamurchan Lighthouse was blinking away indicating that it was just about time for us to turn into the wind and head up the sound of Mull to Tobermory. It was spectacular sailing and I was really sorry that Sandra had missed out on this part of the journey due to her injury.

It soon became dark and as Manny retired below decks John and I tacked our way up the sound into the freshening wind. This was my first experience of sailing at night and I loved it! John was loving it as well, It was a really clear night and I remember him at one point gazing up at the stars and saying "Aah if you could only bottle this you would make a fortune" Having made a fortune from bottling things he should know!

It was during this long slow passage to Mull that I unpacked my new book *Cairngorm John*. This newly released work by my Skipper details his family's migration from Glasgow, then Edinburgh, to the Highlands, highlighting his career as a pharmacist and successful businessman, and by humour, drama and human tragedy explains some of the workings, incidents and ethos of the Cairngorm Mountain Rescue Team. I had bought it many weeks before the trip but thought it more appropriate to keep it to be read onboard Finlandia, with John a captive author available for comments and expansion on his tales. I read *"The Cairngorms in Scotland are a mountain range, a hard reality, a unique and sensitive environment, a playground, a sanctuary, an idea…"* and I hoovered up the first half dozen chapters.

We enjoyed the spectacular marine sunset off Ardnamurchan Point, with its lighthouse winking at us and seabirds cruising around us, I fell into another long deep sleep below deck, and when I roused again it was to the scream of winches and tensioning sails above.

I opened my eyes and felt the strangest of sensations; it was now dark, and lying in my sleeping bag looking up through the hatch, all I could see was a billion stars, wheeling about one way then the other in a perfect black sky. It was similar to being seriously blootered at the end of a great night out, but without feeling sick! The wind had really picked up and was now blowing strong and steady in the Sound of Mull. John and Archie were jabbering away excitedly about navigation lights here & there, vessels on one side or the other, and generally sounding like a pair of schoolboys who were up to no good! In fact they were both revelling in what was their first serious night sail, and made all the more exciting with having to avoid other close traffic and navigate their way safely into Tobermory Bay. I wrapped up warm before hopping up top to enjoy the action and watch us cruise into the brightly lit but quiet bay, to nervously weave between many other parked boats and pick up a mooring for the night. The crew were buzzing from their fun, a highlight of their trip I suspect, but they had had a very long tiring days' sailing, whilst I was able to sleep for long spells. An appreciation of their efforts to help me was starting to sink in. We celebrated a great finish to the day with some quick grub and well deserved drams before bed. It was gone well past midnight.

Day 5 Wednesday 29th April – Mull
Foot 4.5 miles & 2,505ft, bike 34 miles (1,079ft), 1 Corbett

Not surprisingly we were all a bit weary in getting going the next morning, and the first job was to get off the mooring and pull alongside the pontoons for easy logistics in changing crew.

Archie was leaving us and heading home, with John & Fiona Newman – biking & sailing friends from Carrbridge – joining us until we reached Troon, whenever that might be? Both having dinghy and fleet yacht sailing experience, they were looking forward to the challenge, but the first task on hand was to make sure I took my newly delivered worm tablets, thus avoiding plague infecting the ship!

They had also picked up a rather nice looking carbon-fibre road bike for me, borrowed from John Coyle an old running friend, now teaching Technical Studies and bad jokes on Mull. This trusty steed was to wheech me east to Scallastle Bay from where I would climb Dun da Ghaoithe. However there was a hitch – I could not adjust the seat-post, it was seized solid. I could reach the pedals by stretching but I had 20 miles into a head wind to do and I was worried about what this awkward seat position would do. I bade Archie farewell, and arranged to meet the boat again tomorrow in Loch Spelve on the east coast of the island, before setting off on the bike. Within a few miles I could feel the first tell-tale twangs of discomfort in my groin due to over-stretching for the pedals, but there was nothing else that could be done and I just had to get on with it. The undulating road eventually brought me to my staging point, wincing with sharp groin pain, but I hid the bike and took off up the grassy slopes. A steady climb took me into ever increasing winds and by the summit I was struggling to stay on my feet. Far below me in the Sound of Mull a Navy vessel pounded through white horses and I wondered how the crew on Finlandia were perhaps getting bashed about? After being blown over trying to leave the summit and badly staving a finger, I descended very cautiously with my sore groin back to the road before riding into Craignure, finding respite from the wind in the Red Macgregor pub overlooking the ferry terminal. On my second pot of tea I spotted Finlandia thrashing her way up the wild Sound! God it looked horrible, so I texted the crew to tell them so, and how nice it was watching from the pub!

My day wasn't quite finished though. I still had a 15 mile windy cycle to tiny Croggan at the mouth of Loch Spelve to do, which would be the next mornings starting point. After a hasty couple of phone calls, a somewhat exasperated Coyley agreed to pick me up there with the parting words "Croggan!? No-one *ever* goes to bloody Croggan!!" I soon realised why as I dodged monster pot-holes all the way along the loch side to the few houses that exist there, but was rewarded by seeing a Golden Eagle flying at close quarters. I had just arrived in time to find Finlandia motoring her way into the narrow loch inlet and taking what appeared to be a rather odd line, unknown to me actually avoiding charted hidden rocks. John arrived in his car only a few minutes later with Samu his smiley wee boy, and I gave the crew a wave as they dropped anchor off the derelict pier, before being whisked away to spend the night at John's home in Salen. I was spoiled by wine and the beautiful pasta fare freshly prepared by John, whilst his wife Serena nursed their tiny, tiny new baby Adi, and enjoyed a pleasant evening of chilling & chat.

Fi & John blogged... *Excerpt from Crew Log: Wed 29th.*
8am: Finlandia moored in harbour, no sign of life - must have been a late arrival.
12Noon: Crew changeover complete, Archie off/Fi & I on. Also MTB onboard.
Manny departs on John Coyle's road bike - seat too high - ouch - could be uncomfortable, or worse.
Sound of Mull: Motor into strong wind & tide - a bit choppy.
3.28pm: txt msg: "Off hill now"
4.04pm: txt msg: "bloody hell that looks hard work (from the Tea Room at Craignure)" Wind F5-6 on the nose.
5.55pm: Finlandia entering Loch Spelve, strong ingoing tide. Pilot Book says "must aim for submerged rock until a couple of boat lengths then turn to Port" scary or what!!!!!
5.59pm: timely txt msg from M: "get those bloody sails up" He doesn't know what a stressful challenge is

Day 6 Thursday 30th April - A Big Pap
Foot 12 miles & 2,843ft, sail 45 miles, 1 Corbett

It was a very early start next morning, borrowing John's car to get back round to

Days 6-10 Mull to Troon

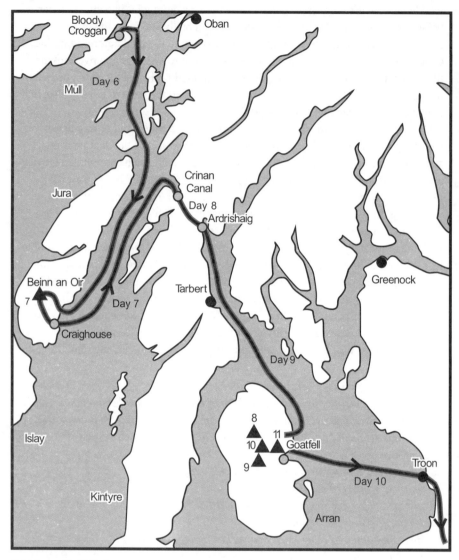

7. Beinn an Oir (785m)
8. Caistoal Abhail (817m)
9. Beinn Tarsuinn (826m)
10. Cir Mhor (799m)

"Croggan!? No-one *ever* goes to bloody Croggan!", certainly never on consecutive days, until now!

With the boat crew already looking lively for 5.30am to catch the right tide, acting-First Mate John picked me up from the shore in the dinghy and we were away, carefully nudging out through the tight opening and escaping into the Firth of Lorn. Wind and heavy rain were the ingredients of the morning as we sailed south and I hid below decks eating, drinking and sleeping. I awoke somewhere in the Sound of Luing and found we had made good time travelling with the tide and were now hosing through the Sound at about 11 knots, with that infamous piece of water, the Corryvreckan, boiling wildly away off to our right. From here heading south the rain started to clear and the sun slowly won the battle to dominate the day, lighting up Jura and her three Paps in a welcoming manner. A magic sail swept us into Loch na Mile, a stunning sandy bay just off Three Arch Bridge and a familiar landmark for the annual Isle of Jura Fell Race competitors; another of my six "Classic" Scottish races. The crew had all perked up after a long morning of cold rain and it was smiles all round as we dropped the hook in the shallow, soft sandy bottom. Having arranged to meet the crew again later in Craighouse, I was rowed ashore once more and followed the west bank of the Corran River up to the bridge, leaving Finlandia looking idyllic in the blue water of the bay. Jura has always been rather kind to me as regards good weather and today was no exception, walking up over the moor in shorts and T-shirt, soaking up the warm spring UV on my skin. However, I was a touch sad that I would only be going over the middle Pap and Corbett, Beinn an Oir, on this trip, as its equally attractive two sisters, Beinn a' Chaolais and Beinn Shiantaidh, only merit the lower "Graham" status of 2,000 – 2,500ft in height. Still, my mind and camera locked in some fabulous images of the whole scene – red deer on the near horizon, like Red Indians ready to attack; the splunging wet yellow and rich green mosses, almost too vibrant in the bright sunlight to be real; the view north to Scarba & Mull and east to Argyll, crystal clear. What a day!

I cruised up to the rocky summit and sat amongst the stone ruins of the old hut there for a good while. The whine of an aircraft approached and I knew what it was before I saw it – a single engine two-seat Tucano T1 fast-jet training machine - which regularly flies over my home in Badenoch with its distinctive high pitched scream, whizzed in from the east and flew very low around the base of Beinn a' Chaolais.

I had to drag myself away from the top before whooping down the rocky south ridge and across the moor towards Craighouse as the light turned to dusk, but stopping every few minutes for just one more look around. The discomfort of my groin strain was thankfully easing, as had any signs of my diabolical worms. The crew were just about to have another pint, wondering where I had got to, when I wandered into the Jura Hotel bar. The yacht sat in mirror calm waters off the pier as I demolished a three course dinner and several pints, along with some good craic to finish the day nicely. Life was good. Then someone spoiled it by telling me the weather forecast...

Fi & John blogged... *Excerpt from Crew Log: Thurs 30th April.*
5.16am: Txt msg: "on my way now, will stop at Spar for a bucket of sunshine" Rain batters off boat roof.
5.34am: M on board, complains of "pulled groin & sore finger"????
Destination Jura via Sound of Luing narrows where Finlandia sweeps through whirlpools & tide rips at 10knots. Skipper John starts engine but doesn't engage gear "just in case we're swept towards rocks"
4.00pm: Arrive Loch na Mile, Craighouse Bay: Paps look stunning. Row M ashore. "Will only be a couple of hours"
8.20pm: Craighouse Hotel: Still no M. All agree to get another pint & some grub before looking for him. Good decision, M arrives soon after, took it easy, sore groin. Forecast. "Strong/Gales S Westerly" Mull of Kintyre out of bounds.
Bugger.

Day 7 Friday 1ˢᵗ May - "We're going to Crinan!"
Sail 26 miles, no hills

The forecast was for SW gales, and with possible tidal delays could mean sailing around the Mull of Kintyre in a maelstrom of violent water & winds. No thanks! Skipper John explained the circumstances in detail to me, possibly expecting me to argue for sticking to the planned course, but I was already in agreement with Crinan the moment I was told of the wind situation. During the Scottish Islands Peaks Race the previous year, running partner Alec Keith and I had vomited our way around the Mull on board Meridian, skippered by Graham Lord, in a wind against tide situation that was only in moderate winds; there was no way I wished to repeat it in gale force conditions. However, things weren't as bad as they might have been. The fickle weather at this early time of year could easily have meant being stuck at anchor for several days, but at least we had an escape route through the Crinan Canal.

After a morning stroll ashore for some shopping and a visit to the new tea room, we re-boarded Finlandia and doubled-back up the Sound of Jura, with growing winds and lumpy seas. As if to make a point, the wind suddenly threw us dangerous googly whilst Skipper John & Fiona were on the foredeck sorting out a sail issue, the result being the Skipper unceremoniously sprawling across the boards and Fi hanging on grimly to one of the main mast shrouds, before both beating a hasty retreat to the cockpit in blasts of sea spray – no further warning was required for me - I hid below, horizontal and in my safe warm sleeping bag!

There is a song which was sung by Dan MacPhail, the engineer on the famous Clyde puffer, the Vital Spark...

The Crinan Canal for me
I don't like the wild raging sea
Them big foamin' breakers
Wad gie ye the shakers
The Crinan Canal for me.

Eventually perfect shelter at Crinan was reached and just as the sun was starting to go down we moored amongst a few dozen other boats in the bay. We had missed getting into the canal system today by several hours, meaning I had dropped another day off the schedule, but what the hell - at least we were still moving. There followed a great evening of food, drink, music and blethers onboard, with Pink Floyd playing live for us, on the flat screen telly at least, before a peaceful nights kip.

Fi & John blogged... *Excerpt from Crew Log: Fri 1ˢᵗ May:*
12.30pm: Depart to catch tide. Canal closes at 5.30pm.
7.00pm: Arrive Crinan & pick up mooring. No hills today.

Day 8 Saturday 2ⁿᵈ May - The Crinan Canal For Me
Mtb 9 miles (243ft), no hills

In the morning I was rowed ashore and walked round the small boatyard to the canal sea lock in time to watch Finlandia nervously edge in; the crew all twitching about deck with plastic fenders at the ready to avoid collisions with the rocky side walls. No worries though, with the boat secured the first lift up to the canal basin began, whilst the crew continually pulled in slackening mooring ropes, fore and aft. We unloaded the mountain bike that had been lashed to the deck since Mull and I reassembled the various parts ready for the trip along the canal tow path. The boat would have to motor through the canal system whilst I, remaining under my own steam, would cycle ahead preparing the manually operated lock gates and sluices.

The 9 mile long Crinan Canal has existed for over 200 years, created in part by engineering luminaries such as James Watt and Thomas Telford, and in that time has survived dramatic collapses of embankments, catastrophic flooding from a burst dam in the hills above, and a total change in the market that plies its waters. Once used for passengers and agricultural freight, it is today recognised more for its shortcut passage of yachts and pleasure craft between the Sound of Jura and Loch Fyne, just like us.

Our day developed into a very pleasurable journey in warm sunshine and good banter with other passing boat crews, whilst soaking up the beautiful scenery of the Moine Mhor mud flats and wildlife reserve, along with the mature woodlands bristling with noisy birds along both banks. It was immense fun stopping and starting at each of the fifteen locks to heave the heavy timber gates and winch open the sluice gates, whilst the skipper tweaked at the throttle and John & Fiona threw ropes and continually adjusted fenders & knots. It was surprisingly steady, tiring work, and I was glad to get the excuse for a breather when hill running pals Katy Boocock & Peter Ferguson with a couple of friends appeared, cycling along the towpath in time to help with the next gate.

At the east end of the canal where there are fewer locks, I shot well ahead on the bike to reccie the pub situation in Ardrishaig, finding the Argyll Inn, and a superb pint of Fyne Ales, Pipers Gold, to quench a thirst... heaven! However, we weren't quite finished for the day and I dashed back out to the canal bank to do the final few locks into the Ardrishaig basin and watched Finlandia cosy up alongside the famous coal fired Clyde Puffer *Vic32*. Tide and wind were against us making any further meaningful progress towards Arran before dark, and we not-too-reluctantly headed for an early pub meal & pints, to reflect upon what had been a fantastic bonus day of nautical fun, rather than just a gloomy delay added to the schedule.

Back on board and everyone having an early night, I sat up in my sleeping bag with a big dram, checking texts to find out that through my slipping schedule I had missed the opportunity of hill company on Arran with friend Damon Rodwell, waiting as long as business and family could allow before having to head back to the mainland again. I managed to write a few scribbles in my diary and absorb a few more chapters of *Cairngorm John*, *"For many of us sport is an essential element in the living of a full and satisfying life. Some will ask: why go to the hill – much as they ask, why kick a large ball around, or hit a smaller one with a stick? For those who need to ask there is no answer. For the rest of us there is no question."*

Fi & John blogged… *Excerpt from Crew Log: Sat 2nd May: Crinan.*
08.00am: Row M ashore then Finlandia motored into canal system. Unload MTB for M to cycle canal path & assist with lock gates. M meets pals from Inverness & forgets lock gate duties.
4.00pm: Ardrishaig Basin: No further progress today, tide & wind direction wrong. Tie Finlandia alongside legendary Puffer VIC32. Fi & I meet Skipper Nick & get guided tour. 2 days now & no hills. All go for early beer.

Day 9 Sunday 3rd May - A Run On Arran
Foot 13 miles & 6,505ft, sail 29 miles, 4 Corbetts
We were first boat out of the sea lock in the morning, and after some quick fiddling with the sails we were off down Loch Fyne with a good breeze and the tide in our favour. The northwest wind veered to westerly and rising in strength, and we were soon heeling over hard on the port side and bouncing in some big waves, making snoozing or reading down below quite difficult, but I managed a

few chapters of *Cairngorm John* before a slumber. However with plenty of good sailing action the morning passed quickly, and it wasn't long before we were belting down the east side of the Isle of Arran and parking the boat at Sannox Bay. This was a change of planned route for the hills, as originally I had expected to come into Brodick Bay from the south and to do the four Corbetts in a clockwise loop; akin to an extended and far preferable route for the Glen Rosa Horseshoe hill race. Instead with the hook dropped at Sannox, John struggled to row me ashore in the teeth of blustering F5/6 swirling wind, all much to the amusement and loud applause of an elderly couple sitting on a bench overlooking the beach. Knackered and red in the face, John managed to pull me ashore far enough to land with dry feet and wished me good luck on the last four island hills before turning to lower the small outboard engine into the water, and cruise effortlessly back to Finlandia. The watching couple now had positively quizzical expressions on their faces... so the guy kills himself rowing ashore directly into the wind, *then* motors back...?! As I approached them I felt the need to explain the "no-engines" scenario and a light of dawning came upon them, but was simultaneously replaced by a look of gawping incomprehension as I told them of my proposed journey.

I left them bemused and trotted off up stunning Glen Sannox into a blasting wind howling straight down from The Saddle - the scene of a famous murder case back in the late 1800s. On my left, high up in Coire nam Fuaran, a Scot John Laurie was convicted - almost entirely on circumstantial evidence - of murdering his walking companion, Londoner Edwin Rose, by shoving him off a crag and smashing his skull to pulp with rocks before hiding him in a rough howf further down the slopes. He was caught apparently on the run, but his initial Death sentence was later reduced to Life in the loony wing of Perth prison, but even so seems quite harsh when some of the evidence actually pointed towards no more than a bad fall from the crag, with Mr Laurie simply making the most of an opportunity and nicking some of the dead man's gear. In those days Life meant Life...

In the wind I fought my way up the newly constructed footpath, saving a journey through purgatory on what clearly must have been a quagmire previously. At the corrie headwall the surrounding crags and jagged skyline confirms just how easy it would be to make a fatal mistake, perhaps like Mr Rose? I picked a direct and steep line up Caisteal Abhail, scrambling over its gnarled rocky top, and took in the stupendous view south across the island in the sun and scudding black clouds. I skirted south of Cir Mhor and headed for Beinn Tarsuinn, taking the opportunity to dump my pack at the col, soon to regret the decision. A smashing rocky climb up the summit, then suddenly day was turning to night as an enormous blackness covered the sky, and the heavens opened in a torrent of hail crashing down on me. It was freezing and painful! I made a crazy race-pace retreat back to the col and almost dived into my waterproofs. God it was wild! I headed up the familiar southwest slope of Cir Mhor with the hail deafening on my hood. By the summit it had changed to driving snow and visibility was down to just 50ft with the wind trying to tear me off the top. I took a quick bearing and dived off the pinnacle into an ever steepening void where I had never trod before, and quickly found myself reverse climbing down some very slippery rocks with agonising cold fingers. Thankfully the slope eased and just 30ft to my right was something more recognisable as the eroded path which I quickly descended onto The Saddle, just as the last of the wintery shower passed over.

A quick bite to eat with cereal bars, and a Complan for good measure, and I took off up the fantastic ridge that leads to North Goatfell and ultimately Goatfell itself, in another snow shower. Approaching the top I was buzzing; despite the weather I had made good time and was flying, adrenaline pumping at the prospect of finishing the 11 island Corbetts and finally hitting the mainland. I texted acting-First Mate John and told him I was on the last top and to get the kettle on, I'd be down in thirty mins. I had pushed on hard over these hills against the afternoon clock, in a little over four hours, hoping there would still be enough light and enthusiasm in the crew to sail to Troon the same evening. Ignoring a growing sore knee, I blasted down off Goatfell at a more reckless speed than was necessary, and trotted onto the beach at Cladach to capture the scene in my mind forever. Low sunshine with fast moving loaded clouds, the colours of the sand & the blue bay and John waiting by the dinghy on the beach with magnificent Finlandia at anchor just off shore, just as the ubiquitous Calmac ferry crossed the water from Ardrossan towards Brodick pier. It was pure magic! I was in a hurry to get off the shore, back to the boat and get the sails up, but John chopped my excitement at the knees. The decision had already been taken to stay at anchor for the night. Phutt...

In an instant I went from being on a massive high to feeling as low as the slimy water in the bottom of the dinghy. I had pushed really hard to meet a self-perceived deadline and had met it, but to no avail. Back on the boat and despite the crew's heartfelt congratulations at finishing the islands (almost) I was in a pathetic sulk, but could not find it in me to come up with a justifiable criticism of the decision. The guys had already pulled off a long sail from Lochgilphead to Brodick, whilst I slobbed about below decks and now they were rightly tired and needed a time-out. I recovered from the blow quickly by my standards, as I am reliably informed that I am a notoriously grumpy bastard when the dark clouds set in. A good beer and things were put right again. The trickiest leg of the journey was *almost* in the bag and well we celebrated, with a salubrious meal along with wine, beers, and drams and a memorable night unfolded as Pink Floyd again played live to us from the flat-screen, whilst our muddled brains tried to grasp the surreal effect of swinging about at anchor with the lights of Brodick flashing past the windows - unforgettable.

From Fi's diary... *The amount of food consumed – after a reasonable breakfast you seemed to just carry on eating and eating... and then go and run it all off up a hill! I think John expended more energy rowing you ashore than you would have done going up the hills that day! Our last night on board, slap up meal, emptying of the drinks cabinet, watching a DVD with music blaring – what a way to spend our last evening together!*

Day 10 Monday 4th May - Troon, The End of the Beginning
Sail 20 miles, bike 34 miles (2,133ft), no hills

Manny's diary... *"woke to blowy conditions, and no breakfast before setting sail for Troon. The forecast F5/6 turned out to be F5/6/7 touching 8! The seas got really wild and sailed on a reefed Genoa only, but still pulled 6-7 knots". With my sea legs well established, and along with big John, I was thoroughly enjoying myself as the enormous rollers put crashing sprays across the bows and our faces. Skipper John and Fi looked slightly more nervous about the situation, and not helped any when a similar sized yacht motoring in the opposite direction, maybe only 3 or 400 metres off our port side, vanished mast and all into a gigantic trough! Yeehaa!!*

Fi & John blogged... *Excerpt from Crew Log: Mon 4th May: Brodick. Forecast: Strong SWesterly.*
Favourable direction. Poor visibility. Fast sail. Stronger wind than forecast. No other sailing vessels. We spot a yacht motoring - hope it's not in distress - couldn't help in these conditions. Pleased I had no breakfast.
11.45am: Troon harbour wall looms ahead. Phew!

As the outer harbour wall approached the crew got busy tweaking things and slowing down the boat, and due to the ridiculous gusts we had already decided that caution was the better part of valour and the engine was switched on, but left in neutral. We sailed into the outer harbour sanctuary with a collective sigh of relief and as we approached the inner marina there was a welcoming committee waiting. Brenda was there along with Archie & Sandra, Anne Allen and also clubmates Chris Upson & Johnston Orr. However, we had relaxed a little too soon, as huge gusts within the marina made parking Finlandia in the allotted pontoon berth extremely tricky and several aborted attempts were made before finally tying up, but not before a very sickening crunch from the port side against a piece of unprotected pontoon metal work – ouch!

Safely ashore for the last time, handshakes and hugs were exchanged on what had been a very memorable journey in its own right. Now, even if the rest of the Corbetts Round was to fail, I knew we had already had the trip of a lifetime and I am forever indebted to Finlandia and her crews for that experience.

11 Corbetts, five views from the top.

Brenda had arrived and parked up in the marina last night, with just fish & chips for company, having completed the long and tough Stuc a'Chroin 5,000ft hill race at Strathyre on Saturday - this year a Scottish Hill Runners Championship counter. After the morning's weather, she was relieved to see us finally sail in.

A celebratory late lunch was devoured in the marina restaurant, Scotts, before some unpacking, washing, showering and re-organising of the campervan, prior to a late and wet cycle to the Bell Memorial in the Galloway Hills, arriving at the obscure wee car park just after dark.

Chris blogged... *Johnston and I headed back to Glasgow leaving Manny to face a 34 mile cycle ride in pishing rain and howling wind into deepest darkest Galloway, to face a fun day out on the Merrick hills tomorrow.*

Manny blogged… *The 34 miles on road bike were tough in the wind and deluge at times, but nothing, nothing, nothing compared to Skye!! Hopefully the weather will improve overnight for a big day over Merrick & Co.*

bob@sandstonepress blogged... *Congratulations to Manny, to the Corbett Round Team, and to the captain and crews of Finlandia, on completing the islands section of this epic journey. With the safe departure of our star author Sandstone's interest technically ends, but I'll be logging in from time to time to keep up to date. Best wishes. Now, I wonder where and when it is to end?*

Skipper John blogged... *Sorry to disappoint you Bob, but your star author is still stormbound in Troon Marina. However as Anne has already commented still having no trouble getting into the pubs!*

Big Dixter fae Tweedsmuir blogged... *Hi Manny, for Monday evening we had the local silver band ready, a cast of thousands of extras, 10's of thousands of well wishers, television cameras. Even Joanna Lumley and half a dozen Ghurkhas. Anyway they couldn't hang about, actually mentioned something about "the swine flew". I said you weren't that fast and I thought calling you a pig was a bit harsh. Anyway we've dismantled the stage, removed all the tents, cleared up the litter and reseeded the trampled grass. They all asked me to say hi when you get down here! Don't worry! We had a whip round and collected £2.80 so we'll be able to buy you a pint! You'll just need to cycle the 14 mile round trip to the pub in Broughton.*

Fi & John blogged... *Impressed at how you can appear outwardly so laid back and casual about the whole event, but underneath obviously took it all very seriously, and put a tremendous amount of effort into achieving your goal (as did Brenda). Thanks to Skipper John MBE & the well victualled yacht Finlandia for a safe passage. Also thanks to Skip John, Manny & Fi for their excellent company throughout. The craic was good & the entertainment outstanding, particularly "Pink Floyd Live at Brodick Bay". Congratulations Manny on completing the Island Corbetts despite your injuries & delays due to the force of nature. (F5-F7 & few F8s). Best of luck and I hope fair weather for the mainland hills.*

4. GALLOWAY AND THE BORDERS
DAYS 11 – 13

Day 11 Tuesday 5th May - God Awful Galloway
Foot 17.5 miles & 5,262ft, bike 11 miles (1,039ft), 3 Corbetts

Manny's diary... *A grim day Indeed! Clouds down to zero!... onto the hills in thick clag, on the compass all the way. Hellish rain, freezing, high winds – horrible.*

I knew when I opened my sleepy eyes what was in store for the day ahead. The rain was lashing off the side of the windswept, rocking van. A hearty breakfast and then full waterproofs were donned ready to do battle with Galloway. I had to carefully navigate my way to the top of my first mainland Corbett, Shalloch on Minnoch, before turning side-on to the howling westerly wind and stair-rod rain to work my way along the completely hidden ridge that led to The Merrick. A fast descent off to the east took me down out the worst of the weather to desolate Loch Enoch, where out the mist I ran past two surprised & bedraggled walkers trying to figure out which way up to hold their map. With a 2006 OMM map and good tip from my clubmate Dave Rogers, I headed straight to a crucial fire break in a thick forest wall, which led me up a gravity defying, near vertical quagmire and out onto a ridge rising to the top of Corserine. As I rose so did the wind, thankfully at my back, and as I ran over the summit it felt as though two hands were obligingly shoving hard from behind, but unfortunately leading me too far down the north-east spur. A tiring flog of a traverse brought me back on route and into the shelter of the forest, but with no sign of Brenda or my mountain bike I set about the 2.5 mile plod down the hard track to Forrest Lodge. Knackered, soaked and hungry, I was less than impressed to find Brenda & clubmate John Donnelly cosily ensconced in the campervan enjoying tea and buns, with my bike still strapped to the bloody bike rack! I had a good break to recover from the hours of battering, a change of clothes into cycling gear, plenty of food & tea, and I was off again to road bike the 11 miles to near Carsphairn, all the time getting buffeted sideways in brutal gusts and lashing rain on flooded roads. Hellish.

By the time I finally drew up on my bike by the van I was totally puggled and the next obliterated hill, Cairnsmore of Carsphairn, would have to wait until tomorrow. Mentally, the day had been very hard going and I just wanted to stop now, but things were about to get worse. I was drenched once more and, with frozen fingers, trying vainly to attach my bike to the rather awkward bike rack when an odd-looking elderly character approached.

This cretin had taken time out of his pathetic life to venture into the pouring rain

Days 10-12 Galloway

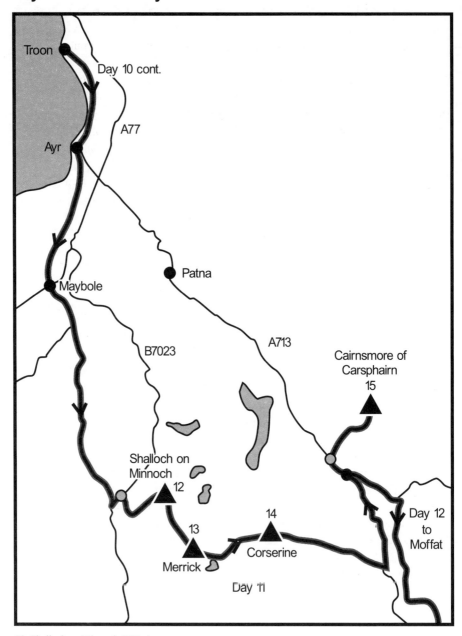

12. Shalloch on Minnoch (775m)
13. The Merrick (843m)
14. Corserine (814m)
15. Cairnsmore of Carsphairn (797m)

and wind to start giving me abuse about parking in the massive lay-by next to the entrance to his house, space enough to park an articulated lorry or two, and causing no obstruction what-so-ever. We had intended being there for only a few minutes, enough for me to load the bike and leave to find somewhere more sheltered for the night, but he couldn't miss an opportunity like this to confirm the pointlessness of his sad existence. He had lit a very short fuse and he could not have chosen a worse moment. He ranted just long enough about his poor sheep on the hill being disturbed or stolen and his house being burgled, for the red mist to come down over my eyes. I laid into him explaining that death couldn't be too slow and painful for him and that the sooner the Colostomy Home for the Moronic realised he was missing, the better for all concerned. He didn't get the message; he persisted and made a near fatal error in raising his walking stick to me. I carefully and diplomatically explained the imminent near-death situation to him, and he lowered his stick, probably not fully understanding how I intended to insert it that far up him if he failed to comply. Brenda had now dashed out into the vile weather to cuff me and drag me into the van just before Farmer Haemorrhoid was sent floating off down the adjacent river. He muttered, farted and splashed off into the misery of the rest of his life.

A horrible end to a quite horrible day, and we found a nearby forest picnic car park to shelter in and ranted about the dreadful old bastard for the rest of the night, with the rain still thrashing off the van.

Graham B blogged... *Sorry Manny, I could have warned you about that guy but had assumed he was probably dead or annoying the inmates of the local nursing home by now. I had a run-in with him 16 years ago.*

Graham K blogged... *It won't be the bike you will be needing, mair like a kayak! Anyone else noticed animals walking around in pairs today ???*

Day 12 Wednesday 6th May - Borderline in the Borders
Foot 18 miles & 5,996ft, bike 54 miles (1,703ft), 3 Corbetts

I think my blog post covered the day nicely...

Day 12 - Moffat, the windy city.
Bloody hell! What a kicking today!
After a gentle start to the day up & down Cairnsmore of Carsphairn (without having to kill the farmer) in 90 minutes and a relaxed breakfast, just as the rain came on once again, we set off for the 50 miler to Moffat. Things went swimmingly, literally. Rain with extra rain took us to Moniaive for lunch for 1 o'clock, and the 15 min break developed into an hour, plus by the time I lost Brenda (following her sat-nag) and found her again, another half hour had vanished, leaving us now pushed for time! Fortunately a reasonable tail wind took us via all the wee tiny

Days 12-13 Borders

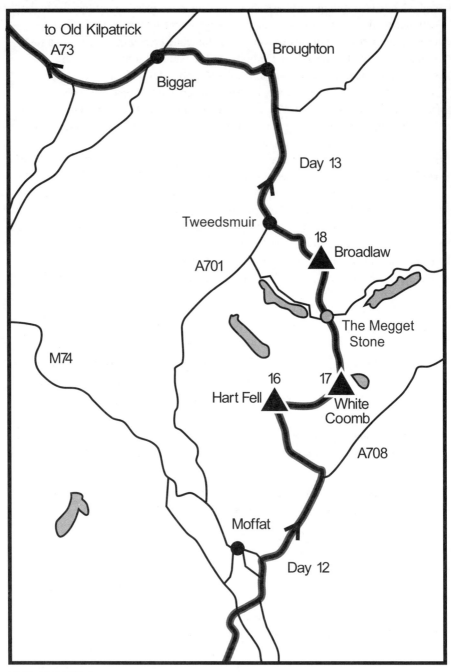

16. Hart Fell (808m)
17. White Coomb (821m)
18. Broad Law (840m)

Day1: Finished - Party! (MG)

Day1: Harris, An Cliseam, with Alan from Sheffield (MG)

Day 3: Skipper John approaching Rum. (MG)

Day 3: Preparing for Rum. (MG)

Day 4: Rum, Askival from Ainshval (MG)

Day4: Archie sails us away from Rum, slowly (MG)

Day 6: Stepping stones to Beinn an Oir, Jura (MG)

Day 7: Fiona & the Skipper go flying, Sound of Jura (MG)

Day 8: Finlandia in Crinan sea lock (MG)

Day 9: Crew John hauls me ashore at Sannox Bay (MG)

Day 12: After a battering on Hart Fell & White Coomb (BP)

Day 15: Focus required on Beinn an Lochain (Archie Lang)

Day 16: Biking off the Cobbler (Chris Upson)

Day 20: Flying down Glen Lyon (BP)

Day 23: With Graham on Beinn nam Fuaran (MG)

Day 23: Beinn Odhar with Johnston, Donald and the boys (Graham Kelly)

Day 23: Manny the Redeemer, Beinn Chaorach (Graham Kelly)

Day 23: Manuel & Duncan were easily bored! (BP)

Day 25: Paul & DHUUUUU!!! on Froachaidh (MG)

Day 28: Leum Ulleim, Loch Ossian (MG)

Day 30: Dave announces No Parking in Dalwhinnie! (MG)

Day 34: Cool bike delivery service in Glen Lee (MG)

Day 35: There was a bit of a head wind...! (BP)

Day 35: Blog it with Brenda! (MG)

Day 35: Sunset, Sgor Mor (MG)

Day 36 Celebrating Corbett 100 at Balcorrach! (MG)

Day 37: Alan and Manny cruising up Ben Rinnes (Chris Upson)

Day 38: Great craic on Meall a Bhuachaille (Alan Smith)

Day 41: Descending Beinn Iaruinn, Glen Roy (Dorothy Carse)

Day 41: Brenda climbs through the Parallel Roads, Glen Roy (MG)

Day 41: Scrambling on Cruach Innse (Archie Lang)

Day 42: Don Reid on Meall na h-Eilde with Ben Tee far behind (MG)

Day 42: Whiteout in June on Meall na h-Eilde (MG)

Day 42: Midged at Fassfern (MG)

Day 43: Leaving Stob Coire a' Chearcaill (Chris Upson)

Day 43: I can see the pub from here! Fuar Bheinn (Chris Upson)

Day 43: Westies do Creach Bheinn (Chris Upson)

Day 43: Sunset over Rum from Ben Resipol (MG)

Day 43: Stunning Loch Sheil & Ardgour (MG)

Day 43: Chris's last Corbett, Beinn Resipol (BP)

Day 44: The campervan make-over! (Archie Lang)

Day 46: Doctors orders! (Charlie Campbell)

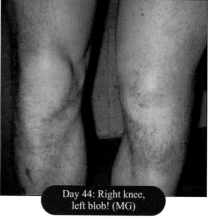
Day 44: Right knee, left blob! (MG)

Day 47: Nervously turning the pedals again with Big Al Campbell (BP)

Day 47: Relief on Garbh Bheinn (Charlie Campbell)

Day 48: Dark Beinn na h-Uamha, Glen Gour (MG)

Day 49: Druim Fiaclach ridge from Beinn Mhic Cedidh (MG)

Day 49: Charlie & Brenda on An Stac (MG)

Day 49: Sound of Arisaig, you had to be there...(MG)

back roads avoiding Dumfries and eventually to Moffat on the horrendously busy A701 in virtually continual rain.

A very brief interlude gave false hope of a dry run in the very low clouds over Hart Fell, White Coomb and possibly Broad Law if light allowed. In fact, the moment I set off from the van up Hang Gill someone pulled out Heaven's bath plug and the whole bloody lot went down my neck! Along the ridge to Hart Fell was reasonable plodding with good trods to follow the obvious route, but in 100ft visibility. However half way across to White Coomb, on a very dodgy compass, things changed dramatically.

The first thing was a temp drop of about 10 degrees, then the heavy rain became cats, dogs, sheep, elephants, woolly mammoths, and the wind gained speed from very difficult to absolutely horrific. All feeling in fingers and face vanished. It was clearly a survival job and I had to get off the hill asap after an epic struggle to touch White Coomb. I got bowled over once in the wind and went deaf in my left ear with rain drops hitting my hood like bullets.

As I dropped below the cloud level my heart sank into my boots when I could see no trace of the road, or van at the Megget Stone! But a bit lower and hurray! the van was just round the corner - Brenda trying to protect it from the dangers of tipping in the wind!

The next hour I would rather forget. When I got to the van I started to shake violently and was slow to remove my sopping garments with frozen hands and the dream of a hot shower was shattered when it turned out the water heater had not operated properly - so got a surprise cold shower! I was so cold Brenda had to help dress me and I climbed into a sleeping bag for about 30 mins with tea to come back to life. Broad Law is now for tomorrow and the 100 mile cycle north may well have to be split.

The last three days of atrocious weather has battered me and I need to step back a bit and hope the weather improves. A very late evening visit to Dick & Jean Wall in Tweedsmuir finished the day on a much brighter note - thank you both for your hospitality.

Archie & Sandra blogged... *God Manny, that was almost poetic. I'm glad you're doing this for fun!!*

Finlandia blogged... *Glad to see that Manny isn't getting it too easy!! Finlandia (aka as The Marie Celeste) is pinned to the pontoon in a Force 8 Gale and that is inside the harbour wall (Force 9-10 outside) At this rate Manny will be finished and safe home before we are! Skipper John and The First Mate are struggling to survive on champagne; rib-eye steak and lobster at the local hostelries. It's a hard life!!*

Alec Keith blogged... *Tremendous effort in the utter pish that is presently passing for May. We all knew you'd done something pretty rank in a former life but there* *must have been more donkeys involved than we'd thought. The weather's due to calm down for Sunday for a few days, so just hang in there for now and keep plodding up those hills. Good luck!*

Day 13 Thursday 7ᵗʰ May - A Central Belter
Foot 6 miles & 1,449ft, bike 70 miles (1,417ft), 1 Corbett

Feeling pretty weary after yesterdays thrashing, we drove back to the Megget Stone from where I toddled gently up Broad Law with the rather surreal surroundings of electronic masts & dishes and other paraphernalia that make it look like the Baddies lair in a scene from a Bond movie. I looked back south to White Coomb, now looking quite attractive with its rolling ridges of grass highlighted by fast moving patches of sunshine - yes, sunshine - it had been a while! I mustered a gentle trot off the summit, on the big ugly scarred access track, down to Crookhaugh where hill running minor-celebrity Dick Wall, of Hunters Bog Trotters infamy, lives with ever-patient wife Jean. I found Brenda coming up the track to meet me, and was glad to just enjoy a walk back to the van together in the sun.

It was another landmark point, the end of the Borders Corbetts, and now a 100 mile cycle through the deadly main roads of the Scottish central belt to get to Arrochar and the start of the huge days in the hills. The high gusting south westerly winds made the riding very hard work, as well as trying to dodge the traffic and the appalling road surfaces. Crouching down on the bars as low as possible, every time I passed a gate opening in a drystane dyke, I would get blasted out into the middle of the road by a side swipe of wind. It was nervy stuff, even in a high vis jacket with front/rear flashing lights, vehicles still tried their utmost to clip my elbow with their wing mirrors on the way past. I had feared the big thundering artic-trucks as the biggest threat; in fact other than the occasional rogue, they were the most obliging in giving me plenty space and I was always careful to give them a good wave of thanks as they heaved past, ensuring any following drivers would usually do the same. It was the 4x4 drivers who nearly ended everything, including my life, numerous times. The way many of these drivers behave smacks of pure arrogance and aggression to all other road users, sitting high up on thrones of power in their big company-owned tin castles, untouchable. Constant blasts of horns, sitting right on the back wheel, cutting me up, no holds barred; 4x4's can and will do anything to get past or over you, on a bike. I fought through Biggar, Lanark and East Kilbride with odd stops at the van for tea and biscuits, but aborted a possible early finish and visit to my parents in Kirkintilloch when I found out my Mum had flu! Sorry Mum x.

I carried on through the dreaded rush hour and actually had some great fun continually overtaking the camper van at traffic lights or in queues of traffic, winding up Brenda a bit more on each passing! Eventually she got clear of me heading into Paisley by running a very dodgy traffic light... she's not competitive at all!? I whizzed down through Inchinnan and across the Erskine Bridge, eventually calling a halt at Old Kilpatrick Library in the nick of time, just as a monstrous black cloud split open and threatened to wash away people, cars and small buildings! It was getting very frustrating dropping bits off the schedule almost every day due to the weather, but I was hopeful that I could make up at least some of it in the coming weeks, with surely some good weather due soon?

The evening was spent meeting up with Munro Maestro, Charlie Campbell, his sister June, and Chris for a few beers and plenty of grub in the Esquire House at Anniesland – the après training venue for Westies over many happy years. Afterwards we parked up for the night at the gasworks at Old Kilpatrick, the start/finish line for the Kilpatricks hill race.

Raining.

5. SOUTH OF THE GREAT GLEN
DAYS 14 – 41

Day 14 Friday 8th May - Rest and be Thankful
Foot 7 miles & 4,233ft, bike 36 miles (7,67ft), 2 Corbetts

Starting off again from Old Kilpatrick Library among puzzled visitors, the rain started almost immediately and I settled into a steady spin, sloshing through constant puddles and taking heavy spray from every passing vehicle. What a start.

Soon after Balloch, on the very busy Loch Lomond-side road, Chris, Charlie and his Dad Ian appeared in a lay-by, and Charlie joined me on his bike for a spin up to Tarbet. Other than An Clisham on Harris, this was the first travelling company I had had in two weeks, but much appreciated on the busy A82. On reaching Tarbet the black skies opened yet again to let stair-rods of rain thrash the ground whilst we dived into a bus shelter to hide from certain drowning. Charlie wisely decided enough was enough and headed back to Glasgow with his dad whilst I paddled on through Arrochar to the Ardgarten visitor centre in Glen Croe, to meet up with Brenny and Chris on the stroke of midday. Horrible heavy hail showers were on a repeat cycle every few minutes and I ate and drank heartily in the van, listening to the pummelling weather, before Chris accompanied me up The Brack and Ben Donich.

It had been years since I had been up these hills and not by this route, so it was a surprise to come across the many fissured cracks in the ground offering weird craggy clefts randomly cut into the side of the hill. There were more sinister giant black splits showing through the long grass into which an unsuspecting leg - or even whole person - could easily drop down, especially if in snow covered conditions! The steady soakings kept us moving to keep warm on the breezy top of The Brack, but on Ben Donich it was a different ball game...

Chris blogged... *20 down. 199 to go!*
Just back from Arrochar where Manny and I got a mighty kicking from the weather on Ben Donich. Conditions on The Brack were fairly tame - just intermittent torrential downpours. But on Donich things got crazy. Sleet, snow and hail blowing in all directions, including vertically upwards pluming out of the corrie below the summit. For several minutes movement was almost impossible as we got battered from side to side. As we staggered down to escape the elements, I could feel my left ear glowing like someone had just punched me on the side of the head.

It was a relief to finally struggle off the top and trot down a final section of track to the van where Brenda had the kettle boiling and hot food ready. A final

Days 14-18 Arrochar to Lochearn

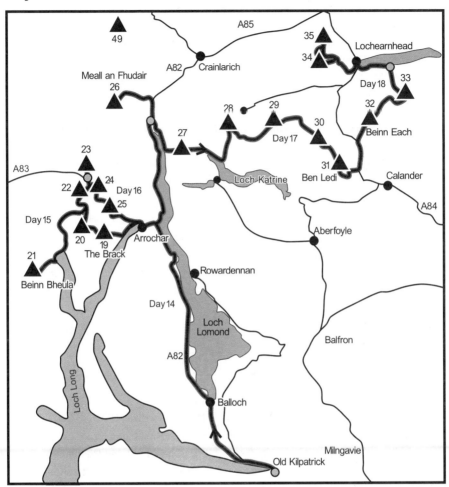

19. The Brack (787m)
20. Ben Donich (847m)
21. Beinn Bheula (779m)
22. Beinn an Lochain (901m)
23. Stob Coire Creagach (817m)
24. Beinn Luibhean (858m)
25. The Cobbler (884m)
26. Meall an Fhudair (764m)

27. Beinn a' Choin (770m)
28. Stob a' Choin (869m)
29. Beinn Stacath (771m)
30. Benvane (821m)
31. Ben Ledi (879m)
32. Beinn Each (813m)
33. Meall na Fearna (809m)
34. Meall an t-Seallaidh (852m)
35. Creag Mac Ranaich (809m)

downhill whizz on the road bike to one of my earliest childhood holiday destinations in Lochgoilhead, where my Gran & Grampa used to have a caravan in the large holiday park. There I called it a day, but in the absence of a decent off-road spot to park-up, we drove back up the hill to spend the night in the van in the rather appropriate Rest and Be Thankful car park.

Still raining.

Graham B blogged... *Sorry I chickened out of a bit of the cycle run this morning. It was chucking it down first thing and I'm not as tough/daft as you guys. Charlie has already proved he is daft!*

Brenda blogged… *I am sitting waiting for them to arrive back at Rest & Be Thankful where at present it is chucking down with hailstones, needless to say I am all cosy in the campervan with a cup of tea.*

Manuel Jnr & Duncan blogged... *Oh-ho, Bren! Why doesn't it surprise me that you're sitting happily in the camper, waiting for them to come back! Wooo! We can't wait to see you tomorrow!!!*

Archie & Sandra blogged... *Good to hear you're taking it easy Brenda, Finlandia is still stormbound in Troon, the first mate reports gusts of 51.5 knots last night on the pontoon!*

Dot's diary… *Approaching the Rest and be Thankful car park, I came upon a drowned rat on a bike – my first sighting of Manny on his round. The drowned rat look became a very familiar one as the weeks went on.*

Day 15 Saturday 9th May - Spring, my arse!
Foot 9 miles & 6,736ft, bike 7 miles (1,030ft), mtb 2 miles (100ft), 3 Corbetts

Yet another dank morning: a quick breakfast and drive back down to Lochgoilhead/Lettermay to start up the first hill of the day, Beinn Bheula. This is a hill I had been up thirty-five years previous as part of a Cub Scout expedition from their outdoor centre located at Lochgoilhead, and just like then it was wet and misty. I set off up the forest track on foot, getting tangled trying to flog through the direct line of an old path among the blocks of plantation trees. Brenny was following behind on the forest track to leave my mountain bike at the foot of a big waterfall for a quick ride out – I'm not sure why I didn't think to ride the bike up in the first place? The ground on the hill was extremely slippy and there was plenty of scope for unwary walkers taking long falls on the steep slopes surrounding the waterfall. The top eventually attained, the descent was exciting on the unpredictable moss and slime, but it was once I was almost back at the bike that I nearly broke my leg, with my foot slipping between a pile of old slimy logs at the side of the track! I hobbled about wincing with pain for a minute or two before riding out the downhill track back to the van in a matter of minutes, passing Brenda jogging back out on the way.

A quick change of gear and a second breakfast were needed before getting ready to jump on the road bike for the long climb back up the glen to the Rest and Be Thankful. Just as I was setting off, my first sailing crew Sandra & Archie drove up, delivering my boys Manuel jnr (12) and Duncan (10), although they ought to have brought their dinghy with them too, as sailing seemed more practical given the conditions! Archie wimped out biking up the hill with me, citing "I would only hold you back" as his excuse, rather than the truth that came out later, "it was bloody pishing down!"

I pedalled back up the hill to the Rest and Be Thankful in quick-time, and had another good feed in the van whilst Archie got ready for a trek up Beinn an Lochan with me, in heavy rain turning to sleet... We set off at a steady plod and the slope got steadily steeper and slippier, until the rain finally fully converted to heavy snow, covering the ground and making it a potential death slide! We continued very nervously using gloved hands trying to grip anything though the freezing wet snow, and a couple of short steeper pulls required complete concentration whilst desperately trying to ignore the consequences of a slip! It seemed to take an eternity, but eventually the angle reduced and we were on safer ground though still in heavy snow. The short ridge on Beinn an Lochain is fantastic – on a nice day, but today was quite different, tip-toeing along half prepared for a slip, with a gaping drop on one side and a very steep slope on the other. It was somewhat amusing having negotiated a short scary knife-edged section, to look back and find Archie on his hands and knees crawling over it - I was cursing not having my camera!

We descended very slowly but at last dropped below the snow level and back into the pouring rain, squelching our way down to the waiting van at the side of the A83 in Glen Kinglas, now with our mountain-biking pal Dorothy Carse in tow. With a glance south-east across the glen I spied the rocky spire of The Cobbler plastered white with snow – I was supposed to be doing that tomorrow – oh God!! Back at the van, a huge feed of pasta was scoffed before a short wheech on the bike down to Butterbridge and get ready for Stob Coire Creagach.

It should be noted here that my running club, the mighty Westerlands Cross Country Club - the best small-to-medium sized running club in the west end of Glasgow - are the organisers of the famous Ben Lomond hill race, just 10 miles east from us, across Loch Lomond. The race was also on today, and I was amazed to learn later that after much deliberation it had gone ahead as normal to the summit, instead of any shortened bad weather course. It proved to be a true test of mountain craft, technical running and stamina with no one left in any doubt as to why race organisers constantly stress the importance of carrying full waterproof body cover at such races. Our race organiser Don Reid made a controversial, but correct decision in letting it go ahead. This event is not aimed at "fun runners" but more for experienced hill runners with some knowledge of what is required in any mountain conditions, and the skills required to remain safe and largely self sufficient, albeit with considerable marshalling and mountain rescue cover also in place. He made his call only after sending a "test runner" to the summit, and also with the advice of other marshals on the hill on the current conditions. Certainly no course records were broken - but neither were any bones, with only one slower runner requiring assistance by marshals after starting to get hypothermic, and walked off the hill under her own steam. Sometimes poor weather can make runners far more cautious than clear weather, where competitors will let loose and go for faster times & personal bests, but of course take more risks in the process, sometimes with resulting falls and injuries, minor or serious depending purely on luck.

Anyway, my biggest humf was that all my clubmates were over at the race on marshalling or organising duties, and not at Butterbridge to shove me up the next hill. The early end of this foul day was in sight, with only one fast solo blast straight up & down Stob Coire Creagach, mercifully with no snow cover unlike its neighbours just across the glen. I ran it in just over an hour and returned to the van to find hill running friend Angela Mudge had joined the entourage ready for tomorrows hills. I quickly showered and changed ready for the drive back over to Tarbet for dinner with everyone in the Ben Lomond Restaurant, a converted church, returning to Butterbridge for the night afterwards.

Yet more rain.

Archie & Sandra blogged... *Manny got another three in the bag on Saturday, we met up with him as he came off Ben Bheula, surprise, surprise it was peeing down again, far too wet for me to get my bike out and join him on the climb up to the top of the Rest and be Thankful (the climb might also have influenced my decision...) I did join him on the next hill, Beinn an Lochain where the rain soon stopped, well not so much stop as change to snow, making the extremely steep and slippy grass even slippier. The narrower parts of the ridge concentrated the mind a wee bit. Back at Butterbridge, Manny devoured another stone and a half of pasta then set off on his own (I would just have slowed him down) to knock off Stob Coire Creagach in an hour and ten minutes.*

Graham K's diary... *I dropped Manny & Brenda a text to see if they needed anything bringing up from Glasgow and a couple of responses came back... Brenda – a rope and harness: Manny – Vaseline and foot powder. My initial concerns & fears about what a "supporting role" actually entailed (and what the Vaseline was for) disappeared when I realised that I had the two mobile phone numbers mixed up in my phone and it was actually Manny who was wanting the rope and harness. This led to more confusion since the planned hills were only Beinn Luibhean (858m) and The Cobbler (aka Ben Arthur 884m). Manny assured*

*me the summit was plastered in snow rather than wanting to take in a classic
climb like Recess Route of Punsters Crack. With that in mind I headed out to the
shops for Vaseline and foot powder… wondering what Brenda had in mind?!*

Day 16 Sunday 10th May - Cobblers to the weather
Foot 11.5 miles & 5,372ft, bike 14 miles (3,75ft), mtb 6 miles (482ft), 3 Corbetts

We woke up this morning with rain thrashing off the van and the initial temptation
to roll over and ignore the world was strong. However after much groaning and a
cup of tea we were off to start from a now SUNNY Butterbridge in good company
with Carnethy Hill Running Club's former world champion Angela Mudge , along
with fellow Westies Cat Miller, Elizabeth Adams, Graham Kelly and of course the
ever dependable Chris, heading for Beinn Luibhean. We made good time uphill,
with the shirt off at long last, drying out my peely-wally wrinkled skin, and the
views from the top were great - only my seventh view in twenty-four hills!

There was a bit of delay on the way off the first top as Angela lost one of her
two pooches, Canna, who was more interested in mountain hares than Corbetts,
much to her mistress's angst! The rest of us gave up looking and headed for The
Cobbler, where I have to admit much knocking of knees and sooking in of bum
cheeks as I scrambled out that infamous rocky wee hole and onto the narrow ledge
to face sickening exposure. I have no problems doing straight rock climbs - whilst
attached to a nice rope, but this was unattached scrambling with no safety net, so
Graham & Chris had at my request put out a nice rope handrail for me to make my
best friend, up and down. Phew, ticked! The others all enjoyed disgustingly
relaxed skips up the same rock!

We soaked up the view of the Arrochar Alps and surrounding hills, all now
steaming in the heat of the sun. It was hard to believe the weather from yesterday,
when where we stood had been under a few inches of snow!

Angela with both dogs now back in tow had caught us up, and all we enjoyed a
superb fast and technical run off the hill as far as the Narnain Boulders, where I
picked up my MTB, kindly humfed up there by clubmate John Bottomley. Any
hope of resting my legs by riding the good downhill path was short-lived with a
rear puncture after only 500 yards, the result of leaping the stone drainage ditches,
and with very bad planning there was no pump or spare tube!! The bike had to be
stripped into separate carry-able parts and humfed back off the hill again by all my
supporting cast – much to the puzzled looks of passing walkers, some of whom
had watched it being shoved up!!

My two handsome boys Manuel & Duncan had managed to walk up the hill a
fair bit with Brenda & Dot and it was great to see them up there, then get a good
run off the hill with Duncan, 10, leading the way! We were soon back at the car

park at the end of Loch Long, with a big bag of sugary sticky heaven – fresh jammy doughnuts! They went down a storm and turned out to be the first of many moral boosting buns to be delivered by newly christened Dot the Doughnut Queen!

Graham took control of my MTB to re-assemble the parts but couldn't replace the tube as the spare I had was the wrong size. Archie then accompanied me for 11 miles of hellish busy and lumpy road biking, north along Loch Lomond to Glen Falloch Farm. Another fuel-stop for food & drinks then it was swiftly off up Meall an Fhudair in glorious evening sun, along with Chris, John and Johnston, taking Brenda's MTB part way up the hill track for me to ride off on the descent, my own bike still out of action. From the rocky summit cairn there were outstanding views down Lochs Lomond and Fyne, and we were surrounded by the snow capped big tops of Crianlarich, Tyndrum and Arrochar. After a short fast descent on foot back to the track, I enjoyed an easy bike ride back to the van to find Brenda out on the hill for a short run too. A magic finish to a great day on the hills - at long last!

While most of my chums headed for home, sadly including Manuel & Duncan back to Newtonmore with Dot, I still had a short ride back south to Inverarnan, tomorrows starting point. Brenny and I were joined by Chris for a splendid dinner in the Ardlui Hotel, enjoying Loch Lomond in the sun. We parked up back at the Loch Long car park on a perfect calm and settled night.

Quiet, no rain tonight.

Random Scotsman blogged... *I never made it up the Cobbler myself, although I had always planned to do so one day. As much as I miss the mountains of Scotland, I can't say reading these posts that I miss the weather much.*

Graham blogged... *Chris and myself headed off to rig the short rocky section from the window, up the ledge and onto the actual summit of the Cobbler. Despite the fact that there was now no snow, Manny still insisted he was a shitebag and rigging the section would save everybody heartache. For every move, he swore and tried to get very intimate with the rock. Maybe that was what the Vaseline was actually for?! At least the harness was not required! On a different note... I would love to have heard some of the conversations from folks heading up the track after we passed running with bike bits.*

Damon & Anna blogged... *Nice one Bigman. Sorry to have missed you on Arran, and again in the Borders. Even sorrier to have missed what looked like a real belter in the Arrochar Alps. Keep it lit!*

Johnston blogged... *By the time I joined Manny mid-afternoon to do Meall an Fhudair, it was glorious sunshine all the way with t-shirts off, expansive views across to the Trossachs.... then a wild, direct descent with no regard for any path until we hit the main track again. Running in heaven today. Just magic.*

Elizabeth Adams reminisced... *I couldn't believe someone as tough and crazy as* *you was nervous about going up the last wee bit of the Cobbler. It was nice to find out that you were in fact human!*

Manny blogged... *Many thanks to Archie for a memorable trip yesterday over Beinn an Lochain in full winter conditions on very exposed gradients. My knocking knees today on The Cobbler were a suitable response to your crawling...*

Day 17 Monday 11ᵗʰ May - Summer at last to Ledi
Foot 28 miles & 10,616ft, 5 Corbetts

With perfect blue skies and a big breakfast I was off from Inverarnan at 9am for the first of the critical "must do" long hill days, with no bike to hide on. Toddling through the campsite next to the West Highland Way with groaning happy campers creaking their way out of tents and wearily stretching, ready for another day of hiking the Way - me too, just a variation on a theme!

A gentle trot for a few miles south down the east side of Loch Lomond past Doune bothy, then I struck off straight up the side of the steep hill choked with old bracken and long grass, with the new shoots of spring just starting to poke through. My puffing and panting disturbed a trio of red deer, but not enough to make them run for cover and stood obligingly to have their photo taken, along with some great shots of mirror calm Loch Lomond. At last the steep ground levelled out after Maol an Fhithich, and I was thankful that it was a clear day as the complex terrain over to Beinn a' Choin would have been challenging in any hill mist. I was two hours to the first of the days five tops, so it was clearly going to be a long day in the heat, and the view far to the east of distant Ben Ledi looked daunting!

I dropped off east to the west tip of Loch Katrine where I decided to accept an extra 2 miles around (instead of +1,600ft over) Stob an Duibhe, which blocked my next Corbett, Stob a' Choin. However the glen holding Alt a' Choin proved to be hard going in the boiling heat of midday, with long tussock grass for nearly 2 miles before higher ground and better footing was reached. The top, at last – five hours for only my second hill! A very fresh and bloody goat's hoof sitting on top of the stone cairn was not the moral boost I was hoping for, but the epic views all around were enough to spur me on again and I headed east once more.

Flogging down, then up and over rough ground once more, to Beinn Stacath - inappropriately translating as "peaky hill" which it is not – more like "rough lumpy hill". Just before the final pull to the top I ran across a fox out in the open. Startled he bolted, but I got a great view of his ruddy coat and bushy tail before he nipped over a knoll and vanished. Then without much warning I found my wheel nuts starting to loosen and energy levels at "shoogly", and I quickly stopped by a wee burn to have a time out. Strawberry Complan to start, then a filled roll for main course and a goody-bar for dessert, with lots of perfect mountain water to drink as I chilled out for fifteen minutes, soaking up the view and letting the batteries recharge for a bit. I had been on the go for six and a half hours in unaccustomed heat without a stop and was feeling weary.

Much revived I took to my heels again and set off, now sensing the beginning of the day's end with only Bens Vane and Ledi to go, but it was still a fair trek to get there first. I had a good soft grassy run down into Gleann Dubh and enjoyed a cooling soak in the cold burn before heading south up a rough path to a small bealach, then climbing south-east for the top of Ben Vane. I climbed fast and pushed far too hard on the tempting short grass carpet. An RAF chopper flew very low overhead, the winch-man sitting with his feet over the side – that's the way to do it! As arranged, Brenda was already waiting at the top for me, enjoying the sun and the views. Sharing our first hills of the trip gave my tired legs a brief boost and I was glad of the company as I started to pay the price for pushing too hard up Vane. My legs were seizing up and twitching with threatening cramps, and it seemed to take eternity to cover the supposedly easy 3 miles to Ledi, which proved to be my Hillary Step of the day. I crawled to the top - I was completely shagged out, and an out-of-condition Brenda was also feeling the effects of her 10 mile excursion. It made me smile to see my old stomping ground, the Campsie Fells, from the top but this was quickly forgotten as we started to descend with knackered legs on the badly eroded rocky path, to the Ben Ledi car park at the east end of Loch Lubnaig, finishing at 7.30pm.

Manny blogged… Now shattered and feet feeling like raw meat we toddled off the path in pain. After emergency rations and a superfast shower, we sprinted to make last kitchen orders, and made it in time for dinner with Swazman and Jenny in the Lade Inn.

My clubmate Swaz and lovely wife Jenny, now living Stateside, had planned to be along for part of the trip, but en-route from South Africa flight circumstances had played against them and could only manage a flying visit to the pub, but for which we were grateful to catch up with them. Unfortunately it wasn't long after dinner before I started to wilt, with rolling head and eyes slamming shut, so much so that I couldn't even finish my beer, much to Brenda's delight!

A fond farewell to our friends and it was a quick drive back to the Ben Ledi car park for the night and a brief blog update...zzzzzzzzz

Day 18 Tuesday 12th May - A Tale of Two Lochs, Lubnaig to Earn
Foot 14.5 miles &7,920ft, bike 10 miles (534ft), mtb 6 miles (772ft), 4 Corbetts

It was a very slow start to the day, sunburnt and aching from yesterday's efforts. 11am saw me creak my way north by bike on the A84 for just a few miles to the south end of Glen Ample, where I was on foot once more. The familiar steep slope of Beinn Each got the legs warmed up and the blood pumping again, but mercifully not at the usual brutal Stuc a'Chroin race pace. It was a cracking day again and thankfully with a good stiff breeze to keep me cool. The high-level ridge trod over to Stuc' was well worn with dozens of hill-shoe stud prints marking the way after the SHR (Scottish Hill Runners) championship counter race had passed only a week before, Brenda included. Due to the island sailing sections of the trip falling behind schedule, Brenda had had time to stop off and do the race before meeting up with me at Troon, thereby later helping secure her a prized Scottish Hill Runners Championship mug at the end of the season!

I had a route decision to make before reaching my next Corbett, Meall na Fearna. The Munros of Stuc a'Chroin and Ben Vorlich stood in my way and the question was whether to contour around or to go over them? I knew the energy preserving option was clearly to go around the south side of the hills, but my feet were still hurting considerably from yesterdays rough terrain, and traversing the steep slopes would only compound that, and I wanted to avoid any blisters at all costs. Also, the very strong southerly wind made the corries on that side of the hills extremely gusty and difficult. No, that wasn't for me and I chose to follow the easy, well worn paths over both hills; easy underfoot, and I was climbing so strongly now it didn't take much too out of me. There was also the bonus of the getting superb clear views from both tops looking far back to Arrochar, and forward to the Comrie hills. The sharp drop off the east side of Ben Vorlich took me to a windless bealach and a crystal clear allt, where I idled to take a good drink.

The short pull up to Meall na Fearna was pleasant in the warm sun and soft ground, with the descent north towards Loch Earn being fast and a fantastic buzz to be moving so fast and effortlessly. Along with the blistering heat of the day, Brenda came up to meet me and it was a great feeling to get back to the van at Ardvorlich and splosh straight into the loch to cool down. The traverse had only taken me a little over four hours, and I could afford a relaxed late lunch before gently biking into Lochearnhead for an evening shift.

Parking in the "Church goers only" car park we nipped off before anyone could catch us; me spinning my mountain bike up the good track into Glen Kendrum, and Brenny trotting gently behind. When I dumped the bike on the track to shoot off up the east side of Meall an t-Seallaidh, Brenda carried on and took my bike up to the road summit between the two Corbetts. It was blowing cold on the top and I didn't linger too long for the clear views before trotting off to meet Brenda at the bealach, from where together we hauled up Creag MacRanaich and hid from the wind behind the small cairn. The view north over Killin to snow patched Ben Lawers in the sun was just magic! Brenda enjoyed her run off on the track, whilst I had a fantastic downhill blast on the mtb for 4 miles, stopping only once to let a herd of about fifty red deer clear the track.

The plan of road biking 25 miles to Comrie was postponed until tomorrow when hopefully the strong easterly headwind would have subsided. Instead we rode/drove back to Ardvorlich by sunny Loch Earn-side for a relaxed dinner and a few fine Cairngorm Brewery ales to end a brilliant day.

This is living!

Day 19 Wednesday 13th May - Loch Earn through Breadalbane
Foot 12.5 miles & 4,708ft, bike 39 miles (2,176ft), mtb 16 miles (595ft), 3 Corbetts

A repeat of yesterday's weather with beautiful skies, but still the stiff easterly wind remained and a head-on 24 mile road bike beckoned. A solid breakfast of the now well tried and tested muesli with Complan, followed by tea and toast, set me up nicely for the first single-track road section along the south side of Loch Earn. This was great fun, whizzing through the twists and turns along the rolling road, and juking in & out the way of passing cars. Loads of camping "fishermen", some with the entire family along for the trip, were creeping out of their gaudy tents all along the loch-side (wherever a car could be half-parked) stretching their early morning limbs with fat guts bursting from under t-shirts or Old Firm uniforms. One crowd of jakeys had already started on breakfast...fags, Buckfast and tins of cheap lager - it was about 9.30am. I suspect from the mess around their camp that they had been trying to hit the fish with the empties!

Once on the main A85 and out of the shelter of the loch-side woods, the strong headwind took effect and I had to hunker down low on the bars. After peching slowly past Comrie by a few miles, a huge agricultural leviathan crept out onto the road 500m ahead of me and turned in the direction of Crieff . I jumped hard on the pedals and only just managed to get on its tail before it accelerated up to a mighty 15mph, but I was grateful just to get out of the headwind. I tucked tight in behind him and drafted a free ride all the way to Crieff – bonus!

I turned direction into the Sma' Glen and the wind was now in my favour for the final few miles to meet the van parked at the side of the bonny River Almond, at Newton Bridge. Brenda met me at the back door with an ice-lolly, magic! After a huge lunch of pasta, pies and doughnuts I headed off on the mtb, now wind assisted, down stunning Glen Almond. This was new ground for me and I was captivated by the steep-sided glen and interesting historical sites with information boards along its length. Half way down the glen the track picks up the Rob Roy Way, a long distance walking route that weaves its way around the surrounding area.

From the top of Auchnafree Hill I was offered good views of Loch Turret and Ben Chonzie. Now there's a weird Munro – Ben Chonzie looks great from various angles, including the top of Auchnafree hill, but when you're actually climbing it,

Days 19-21 Glen Almond and Glen Lyon

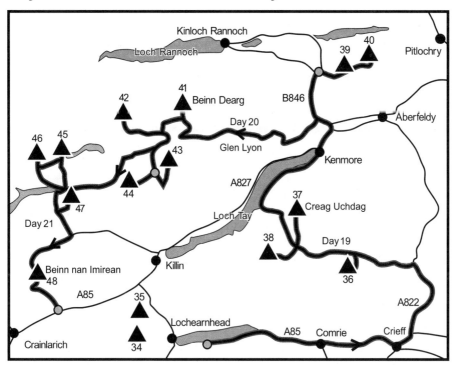

36. Auchnafree Hill (789m)
37. Creag Uchdag (879m)
38. Creagan na Beinne (888m)
39. Meall Tairneachan (787m)
40. Farragon Hill (783m)
41. Beinn Dearg (830m)
42. Cam Chreag (862m)

43. Meall nam Maigheach (779m)
44. Beinn nan Oighreag (909m)
45. Sron a'Choire Chnapanich (837m)
46. Meall Buidhe (910m)
47. Meall nan Subh (806m)
48. Beinn nan Imirean (849m)

it feels nothing more exciting than a dod of lumpy heather - dull. I cracked on further down the glen enjoying the views and the biking, eventually parking up in an old shieling where I launched up Creagan na Beinne. The sunshine was pulling me on and I scooted to the top and back in no time, then a short push with the bike over a few hundred metres of soft track to the other side of the glen, to the unused house of Dunan. Pulling up to the very windy trig point of Creag Uchdag I had that odd feeling of déjà vu. The view south from the top looked strikingly familiar to that from Auchnafree Hill – the lochs, dams and similar hills. The view north to the Ben Lawers group, with their summits still snow patched, was tremendous.

The final blast east on the bike toward Loch Tay was fantastic; wind assisted and downhill, very fast, almost too fast on a few bends! I could smell the burning brakes at the bottom, where I met Brenda sitting cumfy with the sun awning out, in a camping chair with book and drink to hand, but most put out that I was back early. Get back to work! A quick feed and drink, then it was onto the road bike for a final 14 miles along lovely Loch Tay and through Kenmore, to finish with a grinding slow climb on tired legs up the B846 to the old limekilns at the summit. A great day, although only three Corbetts, but we marked the moment with a couple of well earned beers, sitting outside the van watching a splendid sunset across little Loch Kinardochy, with magnificent Schiehallion towering above the forest.

The day was rounded off nicely with a great feed and good company, gratefully staying over at Christine Wilson & Davy Duncan's house in Aberfeldy... and, a real bed!

Day 20 Thursday 14th May - The Lyon Roars
Foot 19 miles & 8,284ft, bike 23 miles (1,240ft), mtb 6 miles (zero ft), 5 Corbetts

Starting off fresh from the lime kilns, I made short work of Meall Tairneachan with its nice wee stone trig point. Sadly the next section was everything I expected it to be - horrible. The route over to Farragon Hill goes through a working opencast baryte mine, and I choked my way through the dusty roads with various giant trucks lumbering around the place. I was half expecting to get chased down by some jobs-worth wearing a hard hat in a jeep, but I nipped through sharpish and out the other side to enjoy the plod up Farragon. The top was getting blasted by a brutal wind from the east and I struggled to stand to touch the top, then unfortunately I had to turn and come back through the industrial dustbowl. I chose a different line of tracks in case anyone was watching or waiting for me to show up again, but escaped out the top unopposed, in time to meet Davy with my mtb which he had kindly lugged up the long uphill access road to the edge of the mine. I couldn't get away quick enough from this place – it was alien and didn't belong, what a bloody mess. I screamed down the long hill but backed off a wee bit when I nearly missed a corner!

Food, drink and onto the road bike to whiz down to Fortingall, past its famous yew tree, and into amazing Glen Lyon. With a big tail wind I was absolutely flying along, in top gear up or down hills. Brenda's mouth was wide open with surprise when I pulled up alongside just after she had stopped the van at our pre-arranged stop. Hee hee!

It was very warm now, and I was glad of the wind to keep me cool, but I was wary of burning, so caked up well with sun cream before heading off up Beinn Dearg through a shield of forestry. A steep climb up the south side took me to the flat top and all around the views were brilliantly clear. I could look back over the last four days of hills and was rather chuffed at the amount of ground I had covered. A couple of quick self-timer photos and then it was a great soft grassy run-off down towards Innerwick, but cutting off east up a good track to Cam Chreag. The plan was to meet Brenda and Davy who had pushed my mtb to the top of the track, but they had already summited and left immediately because of the high winds, somehow missing me on the hill. I had already spotted my bike left by the track so knew that they were not far away, and after topping the cairn soon caught up with them on two wheels. I blasted on down at high speed, enjoying the rock dodging and jumping drainage ditches, to finally screech to a halt at the Innerwick car park with a big grin on my face!

The day got even better; running chums Joan and Colin Wilson of Carnethy Hill Running Club had just arrived and were soon getting ready to do the next hill with me. I had the familiar quick change and feeding frenzy then onto the road bike to pedal across Bridge of Balgie and a few miles up the narrow Ben Lawers road. Grateful for all his help today, Davy was heading home to Aberfeldy promising to see us again later in the trip, whilst Brenda was sorting the van out and getting dinner ready.

So Joan and Colin accompanied me up the short fast climb to the top of Meall nan Maigheach with great views down the glen in the low sun, but ominously gathering clouds. A wee bit of debate about the highest point had us trotting about various minor bumps, before concluding that the first one - with the big cairn as a clue - was in fact the top! Back to the van and another fine evening of food, Cairngorm Brewery ales, and good company once again.

Day 21 Friday 15th May - Glen Lochay was a Breeze
Foot 21 miles & 7,685ft, bike 14 miles (988ft), mtb 7 miles (279ft), 5 Corbetts

Charlie blogged... *Despite the weather deteriorating back to the pish again for our hero & heroine, oor Manuel slam dunks another 5C day, consisting of Beinn Nan Oighreag, Sron a' Choire Chnapanich, Meall Buidhe, Meall nan Subh, and*

Beinn nan Imirean. Has this guy never read the SMC handbook, it's just not the done thing to do multiple Corbett days, 1's and 2's are the norm. Then again, Manny never was normal. By my very simple arithmetic, that means the Gormanator has grabbed a full day back from the dropped ones – brilliant!

I knew the good weather couldn't last, and the early morning brought pouring rain belting off the side of the van, with strong winds shifting to blow hard from the southwest. A quick breakfast, then reluctantly out into the mire with Joan & Colin to fight our way up Beinn nan Oighreag. In clag we found the top but by then I was frozen, my fingers hurting, so it was a relief to turn and have the wind at our backs and get warmed up with the run off back to the road, where we changed into dry gear and huddled in the van guzzling gallons of tea and food.

Ho hum, back on the bike and fight against the wind, west down Glen Lyon to Pubil. From here Colin joined me on a short loop over Sron a'Choire Chnapanich and Meall Buidhe. The clag was really thick on the top and a precautionary compass bearing was taken to avoid any messing about. The wind on the side of Meall Bhuidhe was ferocious and we struggled up, nearly getting bowled over on a few occasions! Any conversation between us was impossible and we were glad to get down again to contour around the top of a small bump and return to Pubil, where the girls had kept the van cosy warm, drinking tea, nice.

No such luxury for me. All change and off again, biking up the very lumpy and twisty Lairig nan Lunn road, which we had reccied several months previous to make sure we could safely get the van over and into Glen Lochay. From the road summit I was able to make a very short excursion to what must be one of the easiest Corbetts to attain, on good day – however this was a minging day! The SMC book will tell you that The Hill of the Soo (or raspberry) is only a mile and 310m of climb, but, on days like this it's not that simple. The clag was seriously thick and the top of the hill is very gnarly with many minor hummocks and knolls to bewilder anyone without map or compass! I was careful to stick to an accurate bearing, and was thankful to walk directly onto the hidden top where I double-checked my position on the gps gadget from my bumbag. A quick ten minute trot back down to the van to find a surprise visitor had hunted us down.

Westies clubmate Brian Brennan had arrived laden with sack loads of delicious choccie biscuits and Walkers individually wrapped fruit slices, perfect hill food! Brian being a globe-trotter for BP over many years had stockpiled a warehouse full of British Airways complimentary goodies from departure lounges around the world, no doubt contributing to the recent near financial collapse of the company! I gratefully stowed away the first of many instalments of bagged calories. After a brief blether over a cup of tea and promise of his return tomorrow, Brian headed home to Kenmore whilst I charged down into Glen Lochay on my mountain bike, the wild wind trying to unseat me on the hairpin bends. At the bottom I paused briefly to watch Brenda creeping her way safely down the bomb cratered road in the van, still high up the hill.

Then I was off again, biking on into the teeth of the gale and lashing rain to the upper reaches of the glen, where I passed Joan jogging along the same direction in order to collect my bike and take it back out for me, whilst I climbed directly over Beinn nan Imirean. The landrover track up the first part of the hill was straight forward enough, but the final north ridge to the summit was an epic! The wind howling through the bealach from the eastern corrie sounded like a fast train approaching and I tried to cower below the ridge line, but was still getting knocked about with ease. The Gaelic translation for Beinn Imirean is "Hill of the Ridge", and what a bloody ridge! Stumbling about like a drunk old man, I had to crawl on my hands and knee to the cairn and when I tried to stand, simply got barrelled over in the opposite direction! In fast failing daylight I needed to head off down the south-east ridge, but it was physically impossible and instead had to quickly retreat west for about 300ft of descent before I was able to traverse the south side of the mountain and across the final couple of miles of rough ground to Auchessan, in the last vestiges of light. Colin had been patiently waiting there for me in his car and as I changed out my sopping gear the interior turned into a steam room. It wasn't long until Brenda appeared down the road from Killin with Joan and my bike safely on board, along with Manuel & Duncan for the weekend, who had earlier been delivered by Brenda's sister Jennifer and partner, now husband, John. We bade farewell to Joan & Colin, our fantastic helpers and good company for the last couple of days and hoped to see them again later in the year, back at a hill race somewhere.

Colin & Joan blogged... *After being out for a while with Manny yesterday and experienced the operation first hand, we're even more in awe of how much focus & determination is being put into this project by both Manny & Brenda. Regardless of weather, driving conditions & road surfaces (potholes Brenda?) They just keep on going - keep it up folks! "By endurance you will conquer".*

Day 22 Saturday 16th May - Change of plan at Tyndrum
Foot 10.5 miles & 5,087ft, bike 14 miles (512ft), 3 Corbetts

Wet, again.

After last night's darkness finish we buggered about endlessly before finding a completely rubbish off-road lay-by in which we could park up for the night. Just as we woke in the morning we were all suddenly alarmed to hear a loud roaring clanking noise from outside, but collectively keeched ourselves when we raised the blinds and found a colossal truck and trailer, with a gargantuan sized digger on top, *squeeeezing* past the van with a good 3mm to spare!! It growled past doing about 10mph, but would have pulped us all to sausage meat if it had connected with us!

Days 22-23 Tyndrum

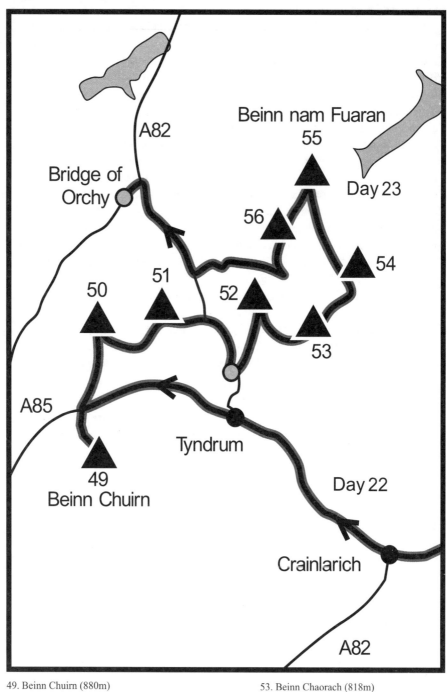

49. Beinn Chuirn (880m)
50. Beinn Udlaidh (840m)
51. Beinn Bhreac-liath (802m)
52. Beinn Odhar (901m)

53. Beinn Chaorach (818m)
54. Cam Chreag (885m)
55. Beinn nam Fuaran (806m)
56. Beinn a' Chaisteil (886m)

68

After that peculiar adrenaline rush to wake up with, it struck me that I was really, really knackered after yesterday's battering, and a rapid change of hill plan was needed - wimp.

Starting with the bloody awful A82 cycle up to Tyndrum, whizzzz, cars scuffing my elbows as they screamed past, and random blares on the horns like it's clever - ignorant bastards all of them! Soggy, and very crabbit, I arrived at our destination lay-by on the A85, just west of that now horrible little tourist bin, that not so long ago used to be a lovely wee village, Tyndrum. Thankfully Brian had turned up good to his word and led me moaning my way through the forestry and up into the thick mist hiding Beinn Chuirn. Two rather haphazard looking lassies that had set off twenty minutes in front of us had already stopped for a fag and a cup of tea, looking a bit dubious about continuing up into the clag – a bit like me.

Brian blogged... *This morning I turned up at Manny and Brenda's mobile home thinking that I was up for the Tyndrum 5... to my relief I discovered that Manny's last hill of the previous day had taken its toll and he needed something a bit easier... so how about just 3 Corbetts down Glen Lochy west of Tyndrum in 2 separate trips... 3 sounded better than 5, plus Manny still had to cycle along there so I could postpone the pain, so magic ! All too soon the Gorman fella had got there on the bike and we pushed off up Beinn Chuirn and found a nice wee route up ...and only got slightly wandered on the way off... great being able to keep up with Manny... amazing what 8000 feet the previous day in terrible conditions will do to your body. Back to the van in under 2 hours and time for some grub and also to admire Manny's impressive intake of calories mainly in liquid form. We'd got up and down the hill in dry conditions albeit in a howling gale of freezing wind at the top, but while we were in the van the heavens opened for about 30/40 mins. When it dried we started for the other 2, Beinn Udlaidh and Beinn Bhreac-liath, after about 500 feet of climb the rain started and 5 mins under trees proved it was going to stay on so out we came, put on gloves etc and plowtered on up the hill. It was fair to say that Manny's pessimistic genes were definitely on song and he had a right good going moan and rant for about half an hour. He thought I was trying to hurry up the hill but I was just trying to get out of earshot ....nae luck there .....but he calmed down and conditions improved to only drizzle as we got on to the summit plateau and then spied the summit with some sort of wrecked mobile aerial tower right beside the cairn .....a right mess ....Manny took a bearing and we were off heading for the bealach. Then miracle of miracles ....the skies cleared and we got magic views all round for the first time that day, and from then on we charged up the final hill and then down sharpish to the high point on the road north outside Tyndrum where we met up with Manny's kids and Brenda again. Cleaned up and time for a beer together in Tyndrum and then back home. A great day out with about 1600 metres of ascent according to my GPS... keep it going Manny and Brenda.*

Even though I had started the day on a low, Brian's relentless patter and tactless slagging had buoyed me back up again and I felt a bit of a fraud finishing so early in the afternoon and going for a pint; but the prospect of doing the next group of five Corbetts in one go while feeling so drained was too much. Stop Press – "Gorman discovers Common Sense!" In hindsight, it may have been a missed opportunity to drag back another day – instead I was almost giving away time that I had worked so hard to gain the previous day, but on the other hand I might have completely wrecked or injured myself by pushing on... och, who knows? Anyway, the beer was damn good and I was sorry to see Brian's wit leave again. The wet day had been a bit of a drag for the two boys and Brenda, stuck in the van other than a short walk from Tyndrum, but soon we parked-up down quiet Glen Orchy after a grand feed and more beer in the Bridge of Orchy Hotel. There, halfway through a life-or-death game of Monopoly with the boys (and yet more beer), we were joined by another camper van driven by fellow Westie and retired West Highland Way Race specialist, Donald Smith. I hadn't seen Donald for donkeys and it was great to catch up... over another beer, and still have time for a bit of Blog updating before bed, hic.

Day 23 Sunday 17th May - Auch Aye, It's The Tyndrum 5
Foot 10.5 miles & 6,442ft, bike 3 miles (82ft), mtb 3 miles (151ft), 5 Corbetts

A quick wheech in the van back up to the top of the A82 above Tyndrum found various Westies rooting about, looking for some morning Corbett action. After a soggy day yesterday we were able to persuade my boys to come up Beinn Odhar with us and although it was windy and cold at the top, they enjoyed the plod up and scampered over some big slabby rocks, before finally sprinting each other to the summit for some good photos – remarkably the only hill of 219 that the four of us got up together!

Johnston blogged... *Manny was aiming to cover the group of 5 Corbetts north of Tyndrum today and a breezy sunny morning saw the team head off to take the first summit, Beinn Odhar.*

Donald Smith had joined the party last night, and accompanied us on a gently paced ascent, with the full Gorman squad of Manuel, Duncan and Brenda out today. Graham Kelly and I had also made the early start from Glasgow for this one. I only found out the order of play at about 23:30 last night when I saw yesterday's blog entries, so decided to join in for the easier summit at the start of the day and go back to catch up on sleep later on. After taking in the fine views from the summit, Graham and Manny headed off to tackle the rest of the day's business, while Donald, Brenda, Manuel, Duncan and I descended back to our start point, with Donald staying around to assist on bike logistics for later in the day. I wrestled my iPhone back from Manuel jnr, and made a bolt for home.

Manny blogged... *I'll let Graham tell the story, but it's over!...kidding, KIDDING!!!*

Graham blogged... *Yup - Manny and I did discuss how much fun it would be to send out a false "I cannae go on any mair" post on the blog...but then again we did also discuss the fact that the bold boy only has 22 Munros to complete his round of those hills as well ...and how it would be good to continue onto that, following Ben Loyal!!!*

Manny's wee note... This proved to be a very poignant comment – although I didn't finish my Munros in the heroic manner Graham proposed, I did in fact finish them off with Graham's invaluable help in June 2011, in a very emotional sprint just before my magic Mum, Betty, died of cancer after a battle harder and longer than any rubbish Round of hills. It was my Mum's very last smiles and laughs that heard that I had finally completed the Munros using the Talisker sponsored Munros wall-chart she had given to me as a boy. I am indebted to Graham; it was an amazing couple of days for eleven Munros on Skye & Knoydart and then dash home to Kirkintilloch. Ultreia forever from Luinne Bheinn Mum x

Graham blogged... *Manny and I headed off from the summit of Beinn Odhar ...stopping almost immediately to check the map. Despite being perfectly clear, it was too long a day to make an "oops" at the start! The descent was not only long but steep down to the bealach and it seemed a shame to lose around 450m of height, but we agreed that section was far better being done early rather than at the end of the route. The climb up to Beinn Chaorach was actually alright ...steep enough to justify going slowly. Once on the summit we got a rather "iconic" photo on top of the trig point, and I mean on top of it. Think of the "Christ The Redeemer" above Rio De Janeiro or the "Angel of the North" just outside Newcastle and you will get the idea. But Rio has nothing on oor Manny - "Demon of the Corbetts"!*

We then moved onto the 3rd summit of the day and as we trotted down the ridge, I got the full story of "Manny vs the Borders Farmer" – I agree that we should have a club run on the same hill with multiple vehicles all legally parked close in the same lay-by. Arriving on the summit of Carn Chreag I managed to put a bit of doubt into the mind ..."were we at the right cairn?". We briefly headed along the southeast ridge before looking back and deciding we were correct after all! Quick retrace of the route before another long descent towards the watershed below Beinn nam Fuaran. One thing I have learned about the Corbetts is each mountain really is a separate mountain unlike many Munros where you sometimes can get multiple summits with minimal effort. It was here we met the only other folks out on the hill – a lovely older couple who commented that we had caught up with them rather quickly. They are obviously easily impressed since my legs were going into that loupin sair (Ed. translates as "affy sair") phase preventing anything like bold descending. The steep climb back up the other side exposed the lack of kCal and a wee piece / drink was in order. Manny had a brief sprint after a bar wrapper which had decided to head towards Ben Dorain – not what was needed at this point in the day. We arrived at the cairn and had some fun taking another summit pic via the self timer on the camera - funny what can go wrong in 10 seconds! If the ascent was steep, the descent was equally brutal but thankfully also fairly short. The last climb of the day to Beinn a Chaisteil was longer than necessary... not for any other reason than we were both getting tired (Ed. Actually, bonked out) but I had no excuse for feeling like this having done next to bugger all during the week. With the trudge over it was time for one last silly summit pic! Rather than risk an impromptu scramble through the crags of Creagan Liatha, we ran down the long grassy ridge before dropping down to the track where Donald was meeting us with Manny's mountain bike. Main topic of conversation coming down the ridge was campervans – I found myself for the second week in a row suffering from serious campervan envy, not helped by Donald's very smart VW complete with kayak and bike racks ....I NEED WAN! (Ed. Translates as "I would very much like one!") Donald had very kindly brought in cans of Fanta which certainly helped for the last few miles. Whilst Manny sped off into the distance to meet Brenda and a road bike for the last spin down Glen Orchy, Donald and I had a slow trot back out to his camper. I retrieved my car and we all headed to the Bridge of Orchy hotel for some rehydration. It seemed a shame to drive south... Don't know about anyone else but this blog is getting to be a bit addictive – kinda like Eastenders but for real! Maybe we should produce an omnibus edition to enjoy on a Sunday afternoon?!?!?

A wee note that on the way up the last hill, Beinn a'Chaisteil, I suffered what was to be one of only two major bonk-outs on the whole trip. For those who have never encountered this phenomenon, it creeps up quietly on you from behind, then whangs you over the back of the head with a sledge-hammer, laying your gutted corpse bare to the hill. Helpless, desperate, freezing. Food, drink and lying down can be the only recourse. I was lucky I had Graham there as a safety net. I'm not sure he ever realised just how bad I felt for that twenty minute stop by the burn, but still trying to hide behind a smile.

A superb day out with some great friends, although again a short one and a second night of revelry in the Bridge of Orchy Hotel, with my sons now convinced it was like this every night!

The "lovely older couple" passed us by without much notice at the time, but caught up with us again later on...

Anonymous blogged... *Hello again from the "old couple" (aka The Squires) you met en-route. We were doing it as a 70th birthday celebration, but I suspect in* *double your time. We could have done with your mountain bike at the end to get back to the car.*

Graham blogged... *Hello ! Congrats on the 70th birthday celebration trip - both Manny and myself hope we are still active on the hill in years to come (knees willing). It was good to meet you albeit briefly!*

Manny later blogged... *Ahh! The "lovely older couple"! How nice of you to comment - how the hell did you find the Blog?! Just as we were coming off the 3rd top we spotted you far below and I said to Graham that I would love to still be doing hills in any shape or form at your age, but the way I feel at the moment, sitting at the Kingshouse with a very sore leg, you will be celebrating your 80th with another mountain whilst I will be booked into the Grand View retirement home for crocked hill runners.*
Good luck to you both.

The Squires blogged... *Sorry to hear you are having to hop now: might just about slow you down to our pace. Watch those knees, reason husband descends so slowly is BAD KNEE, not age!*

Those five Corbetts at 70 years old was rather humbling and highlighted that I really ought to have been cracking on to do more hills that day, instead of going to the pub! Wee blasts of random encouragement like that from other hill folk really kept me going, and it slowly dawned on me how far reaching and entertaining the trip actually was via the on-line Blog! I had originally envisaged it merely as a means of keeping my support crews and friends up to date of progress, but it had quickly become a hill-soap for hundreds of people, with shouts of encouragement even coming internationally. Chris had done a great job in setting up an interesting format and was keeping it well updated with help from Johnston, Charlie and Archie.

Archie & Sandra blogged... *The blog is certainly addictive (unlike Eastenders!) but it's like watching it on Dave, you never know when the next episode is going to be on!!*

Day 24 Monday 18th May - White-water Rafting from Orchy to Creran Foot 16.5 miles & 8,447ft, bike 42 miles (840ft), mtb 4 miles (zero ft), 3 Corbetts

Low cloud, grey and wet, made for a less than enthusiastic late start at 10am! From the Bailey bridge over the lovely Falls of Orchy, a quick trot up a newly constructed footpath to the edge of the forest, out onto the open hillside of Beinn Mhic-Mhonaidh, and trudge up the heathery slopes into the thick mist. I kept a close eye on the compass and was glad to land straight on the pea-soup summit. It was freezing on top and I turned straight about and back down. I was glad to get

Days 24-28 Argyle to Loch Ossian

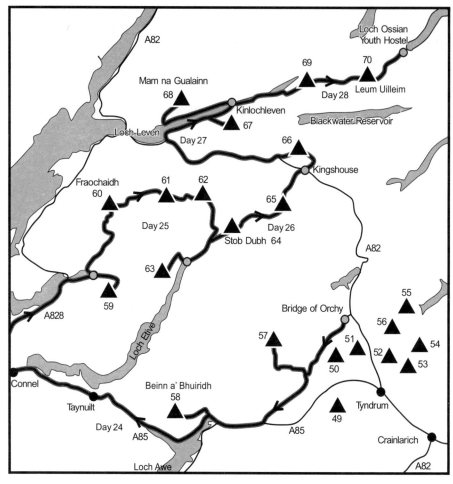

57. Beinn Mhic-Mhonaidh (796m)
58. Beinn a' Bhuiridh (897m)
59. Creach Bheinn (810m)
60. Fraochaidh (879m)
61. Meall Lighiche (772m)
62. Beinn Maol Chaluim (907m)
63. Beinn Trilleachan (840m)
64. Stob Dubh (883m)
65. Beinn Mhic Chasgaig (864m)
66. Beinn a' Chrulaiste (857m)
67. Garbh Bheinn (867m)
68. Mam na Gualainn (796m)
69. Glas Bheinn (792m)
70. Leum Uilleim (909m)

down with my frozen fingers and back to the forests' edge where Donald had taken my bike up for me, and I blasted down the winding trail back out to the van waiting at Eas Urchaidh. All these wee bike rides were cumulatively helping preserve my running legs for just a bit longer every day. Davy had arrived back, in between hill racing appointments, and was helping replenish the vans' water tanks from the river. After a good feed I was away on the road bike again, this time in full waterproofs for 9 miles through the freezing rain, down Glen Orchy and along the A85 past Dalmally to the end of Loch Awe. A complete change from sopping clothes into hill gear and then off across the fields towards the hill in now stair-rod rain. Yeuch.

The east ridge up Beinn a 'Bhuiridh was steep and fairly obvious, but I took a careful bearing once I hit the trig point on the minor top of Monadh Driseag to ensure I got up and down from the Corbett top without any problems in the solid clag. The top seemed to take eternity to arrive, but I guess it's not that surprising since it starts at sea level and rises to very nearly Munro status of 3,000ft, an irritating feature of west coast Corbetts! Disappointed not to get any of the spectacular views of Ben Cruachan and the corries I sploshed my way back down, listening to the roaring torrent of Allt Coire Ghlais far below. Back at the van, with rain drumming off the roof, for a huge lunch and yet more dry clothes with soggy waterproofs over the top, then onto the bike for a 27 mile haul on diabolical road surfaces west to Connel and north across the bridge over the Falls of Lora and up to Loch Creran.

Creag Bheinn is a close neighbour of the Munro Beinn Sgulaird which I had been up just a year before, so the ground was familiar to me. Davy had set off up the easy track ahead of me whilst I restocked my stomach with fuel and fluids. Brenda & Donald were to follow in my wake, taking turns to heave my mountain bike as far up Coire Buidhe as was practical. The evening rain had at last abated and the cloud lifted a good bit to give views out past Loch Creran and across to Mull, and this lifted my soggy spirits. I pushed long and hard up the hill to catch Davy who had taken a good short-cut across the floor of the corrie, and together we quickly climbed to find a big cairn in the mist. After almost forgetting that the actual top was a kilometre beyond this cairn, we recovered and trotted further on to the proper summit. We had a careful run back down in slippy conditions to meet Brenda & Donald at roughly the 300m contour, which made for a very exciting and fast final descent for me on my mountain bike, yeeha! Nearly coming to high-speed grief on a few bends, I finally popped out onto the road at the bottom, and there with its back and bushy tail to me, walking down the middle of the road was large Polecat! I just rolled quietly to a stop and he didn't see me for about a minute, just ambling slowly on. However, once I was spotted he leapt off into the dense undergrowth, but what a treat to see a creature as elusive as a Polecat so close up. I was still grinning from the buzz of the fast biking and from seeing the cat, when I realised the sky had suddenly gone very, very dark – black in fact. I was whizzing about to get the bike secured onto the rack just as the first gigantic drops of rain exploded onto the road, and within seconds a wall of water and noise hit the van as I dived in the door. I had had enough soakings for the day already thank you very much, and I was already supping a lovely cup of hot tea when the others appeared back, looking like shipwrecks, half floating down the road! At last today, the roles were reversed.

We enjoyed the evening parked up in a favourite spot by Loch Creran, eating and drinking after a long day, but unfortunately no signal for blog updates. With the legs stiffening up I noticed a bit of pain developing in my left leg...

Day 25 Tuesday 19th May - Two Glens, Creran to Etive
Foot 14.5 miles & 8,078ft, bike 7 miles (236ft), 3 Corbetts

A dry start and an easy couple of miles biking up Glen Creran to Elleric car park where we met up with Paul Raistrick, his famous dreadlocks and his giant dog, Dubh. Paul, a Scottish international for long distance mountain races, was able to squeeze in a half day running with me and we set off up the wooded slopes of Glen Creran, with Dubh conveniently towing his master through the thick brush. Layers of last years' dead bracken mixed with springs' fast sprouting new shoots made for hellish, tiring, leg-lifting work for about 600ft of hard climb, until we at last popped out onto the open hillside. A bit more climbing and we were on the broad, rough grassy ridge that now forms part of Lochaber Athletic Clubs' Two Inns hill race; a 15 mile/5,800ft route between the Creagan and Clachaig Inns. This proved to be a handy wee bit of unplanned reconnaissance for me, as I was able to recall this days' view of the hill to help me win the inaugural Two Inns in 2010. The good craic with Paul was interspersed with protracted bouts of shouting and bawling after his hound, "Dubh... DUBH... *DUBH FUCKING HELL!!!"*, as he repeatedly vanished off into the distance chasing imaginary deer, or perhaps a scent in the wind. Paul reverted to his secret weapon, a shock-box, zapper type gadget, strapped to his dogs collar, which when the frustrated master pressed a remote button, gave the poor beast a sharp electric shock to bring him round. Dubh was lucky it wasn't on his bollocks that day! Paul pointed out that the dog was only following his natural instincts to chase things, but at the same time he didn't want him unnecessarily harming wildlife, or worse, getting shot by an angry stalker or shepherd. With poor old zapped Dubh back in check we enjoyed topping the Corbett, Fraochaidh, then trotted along the ridge for another few miles before Paul and his hound had to drop back into the Glen Creran forest and back to his car.

I had to carry on though, and within minutes of Paul leaving was engulfed in rain as I headed over fiddly, rough ground towards Meall Lighiche. The rain was freezing and the mist thick as I climbed steeply to the top, where to my delight I found Donald Smith was still patiently waiting for me, huddled down out the wind, even though I was well down on my estimated arrival time. Donald fed me life-saving hot coffee and sandwiches before we both headed off south-east to the bealach below the Munro, Sgurr na h-Ulaidh. I thanked Donald for his help and waved farewell, as he was heading back to Glasgow once he was down, but hoped to catch up with us again further north in the journey. Meanwhile I had an awkward contour around the mountains' craggy northern corrie and climb up to the narrow ridge of Aonach Dubh a'Ghlinne, then forced to hike higher over the minor Munro top of Stob an Fhuarain, to be able to drop west towards Beinn Maol Chaluim. Once I had carefully slithered out of the mist, down some very nervy wet slopes and slabs, I was confronted by an impossible looking crag face, blocking my last Corbett of the day. From the col floor I had to traverse far to the right where I was able to climb 1,000ft of extremely steep wet grass until the slope finally relented, and another near-3,000ft summit was in the bag. The heavy rain had at last stopped and a welcome gap in the clag opened enough to allow a few photos of the top and of the south side of towering Bidean nam Bian in the background. A long ridge and broken misty descent into Glen Etive brought me to the road at a gap in the forestry, overlooking a small lochan. There was action in the water below – two otters were playing in the water and I sat and watched them while I ate everything I had left in my pack and took a fill of water from a burn. A bit of sunshine had broken through – heat, heaven! I was knackered and had taken another plastering on the hill, and my left leg really hurt now. Where was the van –mmm? I suddenly became concerned that the team were in the wrong place or maybe something had happened en-route? A quick look over the brow of the hill, back up the glen, and I spied the van about a quarter of a mile away, tucked in at the side of the narrow road. Phew.

Dot had now returned, along with Frank the dog. After a brief scoff and a hot drink I had a quick 4 mile downhill bike ride in the now surprisingly pleasant evening weather, to the new car park at the head of Loch Etive. In the van Brenda prepared a fantastic meal for us all, while I sat on a log by the shore of the loch with a bottle of superb Cairngorm Brewery Tradewinds ale and watched a group of kayakers paddle ashore. It was a magic scene, with moody Ben Starav on the other side of the loch and the massive Cruachan group further south. The evening passed pleasantly with a brilliant big dinner, good company with several more beers, double Ibuprofen for dessert, and once in bed I massaged my legs until unconscio.....zzz

Paul's diary... *Falling into the 'pussy-footing' category of 'mountain runner' it was with a degree of trepidation that Manny's invite to support his Round was accepted – knowing that blood, boulder, crag and hag could rank highly. Manny is*

no stranger to the hardships and loneliness of multiday running wild mountain journeys. His epic Cairngorms National Park (Badenoch & Strathspey)boundary run in 2006 is testament to his mountain skill, mental toughness, resolve and bloody mindedness. Manny's modesty meant that his unrepeated high altitude watershed run has gone mostly un-noticed. To the wild, pathless hag and boulder day in question... he appears on the bike having pedalled from his overnight camp. He looks leaner than I have ever seen him (my first intro to Manny was after Lochaber's Meall an t-Suidhe (Melantee) race in 1999. I was amazed that a man could drink alcohol so quickly after crossing the finishing line - he had the fastest beer belly in Scotland at that stage in his career. Hundreds of miles had honed that torso to that of a "Men's Health" model (or at least to "a bird cage on sticks" as Geoff Simpson described it later) in spite of his Cairngorm Brewery sponsorship. Many runners would aspire to a top running company's support for kit, but Manny had trumped them all with an unlimited supply of some of Scotland's finest ales. Steep bluebell oak woods give way to brackened ground and we arrive on the first section of high pathless hag. Cloud shrouds the tops. Manny's mental Corbett map moves up a gear and his sense of direction pull us cleanly up to the summit of Fraochaidh. Beyond there is a fine ridge to the North and the swirling cloud allows a fine brief glimpse... as Manny fires off at a fast pace down and into the mire I capture the image both digitally and mentally just a snippet of Manny's thousands of miles and hours on the tops. Little did he know that he would be running the same line in winning the inaugural 2 Inns Race just a year later. I reflect on my descent whether Manny was a Tarahumara Indian in his last life but then remember that he is just Glaswegian!

Davy reminisced... *Brenda and I set off from Glen Etive to intercept Manny on the hill. We were worried he may pass us in the mist so we separated, just keeping each other in sight, hoping to have more chance of meeting him. In the end we gave up and returned to the warmth of the van, Manny finally turning up about an hour later.*

Day 26 Wednesday 20th May - Glen Bloody Etive
Foot 12.5 miles & 8,693ft, bike 5 miles (317ft), mtb 1 mile (64ft), 3 Corbetts

Manny blogged... *So far my attempt to swim the Corbetts has been successful but I think my aqua endurance is now getting very low! The morning was greeted with monsoon rain lashing off the roof of the van, and I spat the dummy well out! First delayed - because I was on strike - and then a predictably very wet and slow flog up & down an incredibly slippy Beinn Trilleachan in 2 hours 40 minutes was not a good start to the day, but thankfully done with Davy who kept me going at a reasonable pace and with good chat to distract me.*

I found the going up & down the lower part of hill very hard in deep tussock grass and very rough ground, with the famous rock surface higher up extremely slippy in the wet conditions. Typically I would nail any hill in about 90 mins, up & down, so at 2hrs 40mins I was moving very slowly. Things weren't helped when we got to the top in thick clag and, after having a bar and photo/natter, realised that we couldn't tell which way we had come up, and neither of us had a map or compass! A brief sortie to the edge of an abyss had us retreat to the cairn and try a different way off, thankfully correct.

Brenny sensed that morale was dangerously low, so on our return it was a delight to find sausage, bacon & eggs on the go!! Even now I can still feel that immense lift from total dejection to slavering apprehension! I had a much extended break to dry out and feed like there was no tomorrow, as wave after wave of filthy weather poured over the van. God! Davy had to leave us again for Bog & Burn racing tonight in Perth and I eventually had to get my backside out the van and bike up the road a wee bit, before tackling steep Stob Dubh & Beinn Mhic Chasgaig with another heavy shower pouring down my neck. Thankfully the clouds slowly lifted and I even managed to get my shirt off for twenty minutes to air my fish-scales during a sunny interlude. Brenda and Dot managed to squeeze in a trip to Glencoe for shopping, returning in time for me to flounder off those two smashing big hills, and at last a nice view almost all around, if not for the bigger Munros.

A slithering drop north off the second hill for a refreshing wade across the River Etive, only just avoiding a complete dooking, let me finish the day with a short ride to Kingshouse, to have dinner and beer in comfort. Ken and Claire Rumgay from Kinlochleven joined us for a few hours to plot the next couple of days and possible medical/vet treatment for me. A very large bag of ice was procured from the bar, which is strapped to my now swollen left leg. I will have to re-jig the next couple of days to suit leg/logistics/weather…
Night night.

My leg was really giving me jip now and tendonitis was my suspicion. Drugs, ice and excessive ale were the only practical hope but Ken & Claire knew their local Doc in Kinlochleven was into sports crocks like me in a big way, so hoped to line me up as a good specimen for him the following day.

Archie & Sandra blogged… *As we said on day 11 "come on you big Jessie get on with it"!! I've got Rafferty's number (The local vet in Kingussie!) Remember you're only a couple of days away from a decent nights kip in your now house, at least the rain shouldn't be so noisy on the roof there.*

Stateside Swaz blogged… *Nice one, Manda - was the Kingshouse serving steak and ale pie?? Glad you're still alive!*

Charlie blogged… *Well done mucka, the swimming is going well. Don't let the weather get to you, just keep the hood up, the head down, and plod on - the sunny* *days will come. Plan in some 'easier' days and gub the ibuprofen, and hopefully it will give the leg a break (no pun intended) Bag on...*

bob @ sandstone blogged... *Keep going, Manny. Get through this bit and it's downhill the rest of the way. Okay - it will just feel like downhill, but that's enough.*

Stevie McLoone blogged... *Well done Manny - keep it going!!! . But why are you complaining? It's only 1 leg that's hurting.*

Brenda blogged... *What he means by "shopping" is food & drink for his daily intake... I really do wish I was shopping, I do feel a good shopping spree ahead, but not for food & drink...£££££*

Dot's diary... *Manny's motivation to get out in the morning was directly related to the weather – the harder the rain was hammering down on the roof of the van, the more likely he would have to be forcibly ejected to start his day's quota of hills.*

The web soap was growing and its comments would jab me into recovery with support being posted at ridiculous times of the day from all quarters of the globe, even Greenock, which some might suggest was on a different planet altogether!

Day 27 Thursday 21ˢᵗ May - News from the Hood
Foot 11.5 miles & 7,297ft, bike 28 miles (646ft), 3 Corbetts

I had my resignation head on this morning and accepted my lot as a bad one as I went through the motions on the rain-swept first hill, utterly forgettable.

Manny blogged... *Hello bath chums!*
I took my rubber duck up Beinn a Chrulaiste this morning and we had fun rafting back down to Altnafeadh at the head of Glencoe for a nice cup of tea, and bread for the duck.
A dangerous road bike with surface water and traffic down the Rio Coe and along Loch Leven-side to Caolasnacon, and what's this... SUN!!! Ken Rumgay of Lochaber AC had now joined the Magic Roundabout and was given a good talking to by Miss Brenda on full van instructions and how to go shopping in the brief interludes between hills. Then Dot whisked Brenny away home to sort out some other business (actually a job interview, which proved successful, but in vain as will be explained later...) for a few days whilst I enjoyed a warm, yes warm, ascent of Garbh Bheinn and lots of lovely views and photos on the summit - HURRAY! Wait... what's that black thing fast approaching? Oh Christ! Run down like there's only one pint left in the pub... too late, SPLOOSH!!
In a biblical downpour, I floated gentled back to Noah/Ken in the ark/van and paddled my bike around the loch and changed out of the umpteenth set of clothes. However, the last hill, Mam na Gualainn was an absolute pleasure. Good

company and blethers with Ken, more views, and a good run-off made it a good day after all, even if splunging wet.

A mad-fast cycle back to Kinlochleven to see the Doc about the duff leg, and the boy was genuinely interested in a running injury! A rarity in GP's! He's the Doc who does the bloodletting on the West Highland Wayers to check for life, (WHW racers, not walkers... it is run as an annual race mid-June, and the current record for the 95 miles & 12,000 foot of undulating ascent, is a knee-crumbling 15 hours 39 mins... most walkers take a full week) so he knows his stuff. The Doc has written various medical papers specifically on endurance running, one of them focussed on fluid intake and in particular the dangers of too much fluids which can lead to serious kidney damage, and in extreme cases, death.

However, it looks like a wee strapping and stopping for four weeks should cure me nicely. On the other hand I am planning flogging 14 wet boggy miles and over two hills to Loch Ossian tomorrow to meet the fast approaching - but always bloody late - Dave Rogers, and possibly my crocked-back Dad, who admits that he may have got slightly carried away with his latest comeback gentle training run from Lennoxtown, up over the famous Crow Road, to Fintry... and back again! (16 miles & 1,500ft) Yes, we share genetic stupidity! Stopping at Loch Ossian means another slight fall back in timescale, but given my leg is about to fall off, it is unavoidable. I can swim them but not hop them, sorry.

A lovely meal, washing, and BATH, BATH, BATH staying at Ken & Claire's house in Kinlochleven and beer & ice pack to cap it nicely.

See ya Bloggers!

Manny's note... The Doc was so impressed at my tendonitis that he asked if he could take a photo of it for his wee "Sick Book", a record of various exceptional ailments and conditions. Fame at last!

Brenda blogged... *Yes, I made it home tonight after Dot kindly dropped me off for what I thought was going to be a nice relaxing couple of days rest, but it started all over again. I had to start on the washing, 2nd load in the machine just now. I spent a couple of hours cleaning the house after the workmen had left, and I tried to empty a few boxes after our 6 months of staying in rented accommodation while the house was getting an extension, which we abandoned at the start of the run. Not long ago I sat down on the floor in the dining room to have my tea, (carry out) and then realised I had no plates, cups, knives, forks etc so I had to eat it out of the container. No chair to sit on and no bed......... I wish I was back in the campervan... luxury...*

The last few days have been hard going with the rain, and hope that he takes the next few days easy. Ken, it is all over to you until I return on Saturday, or maybe I will just get a one way ticket to the sun instead...

Dot blogged... *After a couple of wet days with Manny the rain magnet & Brenda, I* *arrived home with a pile of sodden camping gear to find it had been dry the whole time here (Carrbridge). Your talents are wasted Manny - you should be hiring your services to African countries with drought problems. Keep up the swimming/hopping.*

Charlie Campbell blogged... *Enjoy Loch Ossian Manny, and Warden Nick reading the Hostel rule book to you... again... and go steady on the old peg leg - you're almost back into your own stomping ground.*

Chris blogged... *Hang on in their Manny, and don't go messing with the saucepan handles or fire at Loch Ossian YH. Just tough out the next few days and I'm sure better weather is on the way.*

Day 28 Friday 22nd - May Loch Ossian
Foot 14 miles & 5,159ft, 2 Corbetts

The original plan was to do three Corbetts, going straight past Loch Ossian and out south near Rannoch Station in one big mileage push, but the gammy leg was complaining bitterly and if I didn't give it a rest here I might well grind to a complete halt in a few days. I had experienced the frustration of this type of failure before on big runs and have learned to respect the warning signs enough to know that it was time to ease off.

Loch Ossian Youth Hostel is a favourite spot of mine and also the location for the Westies annual hill/drinking/partying end of season event, so it was a natural choice for splitting a long day, with a few quick phone calls to arrange my Dad and Dave Rogers to meet me there with supplies.

After a good breakfast and my morning Ibuprofen intake, Ken escorted me up and out of Kinlochleven through his local hills on generally good stalkers paths past Loch Eilde Mor. Certain sections were chewed into small lochs of impassable, thigh deep mud, the result of the recent Lochaber Six Day Trials for trials bikes which had passed this way. We cut off the path, bearing north for the top of Glas Bheinn, a rough lump of a hill with not much in the way of distinguishing features. Ken held me to a steady tempo and we made good time to the top of the hill in clear conditions and great views of the Mamores, Grey Corries and Glencoe Munros. We headed down to the west and to Chiarain Bothy by the loch of the same name. This attractive wee cottage was built as a replacement to house the family living in the original Chiarain House, which was submerged by the rising Blackwater Reservoir in the early 1900s. After a mooch about inside and a bite to eat Ken started off back to Kinlochleven, but all things being well we would meet again on Friday afternoon by Rannoch Station. I managed to leap the loch's deep intake burn and marched up the next hill, Leum Uilleim – the hill shown in the hit movie Trainspotting, in the famous scene where the boys get off the train at desolate Corrour Station and Renton exclaims, "It's shite being Scottish!" From high on the hill, a view down into Coir' a'Bhric Mor showed a terrifying expanse of peat hags, bogs and the roughest ground imaginable, which leads off into the reservoir; beyond, the bleak wilderness of Rannoch Moor, where a century ago many a unsuspecting navvy vanished without trace whilst trying to walk to the Blackwater Dam construction site – it is recorded that in some cases even the people who went searching for lost navvies were themselves lost or drowned. I think I'll stick to hills.

It was a pleasant jog to the top of this hill which I had been up twice before in clag, but this time I got fantastic views all around and the warm sun dried out the rain from my soul. I ran off the northeast ridge towards Corrour Station and half way down spotted a train coming up the line from the south, which I hoped my Dad was aboard. When the train finally halted at the platform I carefully spied the vehicle track leading away down to the Youth Hostel, but as the train left there was no movement of any walkers – he must have missed the train! Disappointed I sat down on a grassy knoll on the ridge and had lunch, eating everything I had left in my bag - apple, bars, rolls, jelly babies, and a Complan to drink. I even dozed off for a brief but welcome snooze lying in the sunshine, before trotting down the rest of ridge and across the short section of bog towards the railway track and station gate. What's this? A figure on the platform - in a cowboy hat and holding a... pint! BEER! Auld Ricky had done the sensible thing and gone straight to the station bar and was enjoying the sun and view from the platform, but his dodgy eyesight took a while to focus on me jogging across the moor and into the station, almost taking him by surprise. My delight at finding Dad there turned to dismay when we discovered that the station wifey had unbelievably just shut for lunch! No one else for 20 miles in any direction and with Dad already there as a willing customer, she closed for lunch… only in Scotland. Still, we were not in any rush now and it was only gone three o'clock, so we hung about until she opened up again the made the most of the two Cairngorm Brewery ales on tap, Tradewinds & The Howler, magic! We had good craic with the lady for an extended stay before wobbling off down to the hostel.

The evening was passed eating and blethering with the few other hostellers, or standing gawping in silence at the gobsmacking scenery down mirror calm Loch Ossian in the evening sun… you had to be there.

Dave bumbled into town rather randomly, just in time for one of the bottles of beer that Dad had humfed in his colossal pack and carrier bags. We plotted the next day's assault on the hills and caught up on news.

A memorable couple in the hostel were a mum and teenage son "Fae Glesgae" who had come up here on the train for a few days to escape the madness. Chatting to the mum she explained that she wanted to keep her boy out of the rife local trouble, and was trying to give him a taste of "the other side". She was quite passionate and determined that he wouldn't end up like so many other kids of his age, trapped in drink, drugs and courts. She was a diamond. To talk to her boy sounded just like the classic wee Glasgow Ned stereotype, complete with nasal speech impediment and skip cap; but in fact was really a nice young guy, very sociable and full of genuine enthusiasm and excitement about the hills and these awesome surroundings. He clicked with it and understood it; he was gagging for tomorrow when his "Maw" would take him up Beinn na Lap. It is a bright light to come across characters like that, and just shows how much some us may take our outdoors lifestyle for granted without maybe fully appreciating its worth after a while.

I picked my regular bunk space and slept well, despite Dave's internationally famous snoring.

Ken blogged... *Hi ya - loved the trip over to Chiarain - quality sky and great views. Thanks for sticking to my pace. You have survived the Lochaber rain and Clare's chilli so you can survive anything now. You have a great weight of good people behind you on this- go Manny.*

Mike Cumming blogged... *Hi Manny, after weeks of computer meltdown I have just spent the last 3 hours catching up with your blog and photos so far on your amazing journey. Having moved back to Orkney 3 years ago I'm limited for any good hill running (apart from Hoy!) It seems a long time since we raced against each other and just reading about your adventure makes me feel more ferry crossings should be made!*
Good luck to you, Brenda, family and support crew. I look forward to following your progress.

Day 29 Saturday 23rd May - Just A Rannoch Double
Foot 16 miles & 4,303ft, bike 30 miles (328ft), mtb 2 miles (30ft), 2 Corbetts

This was always going to be a tricky day with the single Corbetts in this area scattered all over the place, generally in the middle of nowhere. The first one, Meall na Meoig, requiring in excess of 10 rough miles to cover the ground and get out south to the van by Loch Eigheach, on the Rannoch Station road. We had set off from Loch Ossian Hostel with my Dad and Dave humfing all the gear, along the old muddy Road to the Isles, but parting company with auld Ricky to head for the top with Dave, akin to part of the LAMM (Lowe Alpine Mountain Marathon) 2001 route I did with Jim Hall. Dave was carrying a bloody huge pack and still managing to make me work hard uphill to the summit, finally trotting off the misty hill to a sizeable welcoming committee which was waiting for us at the track-end with bikes. Ken had successfully made it the very long way around from Kinlochleven in the van, and Brenda was back from her brief excursion home, regaining control of logistics; we had been joined by Davy & Christine's van and numerous cars for Dave, Chris, Ellie, Johnston, Sandra & Archie and Emma

Days 29-31 Loch Ossian to Glen Feshie

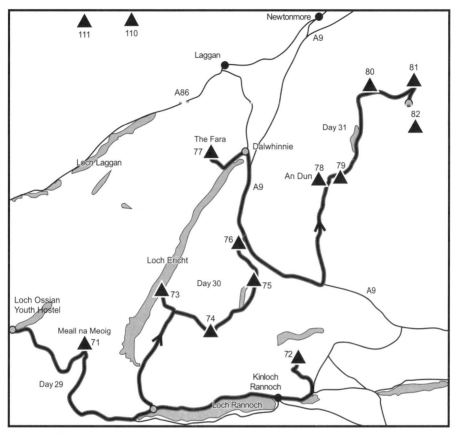

71. Meall na Meoig (868m)
72. Beinn a' Chuallaich (892m)
73. Stob an Aonaich Mhoir (855m)
74. Beinn Mholach (841m)
75. Meall na Leitreach (775m)
76. The Sow of Atholl (803m)

77. The Fara (911m)
78. An Dun (827m)
79. A' Chaoirnich (875m)
80. Meallach Mhor (769m)
81. Carn Dearg Mor (857m)

O'Shea! By the time I scooted out to the road on my bike, my Dad had already left, legging it 2 miles up the tarmac to the station to get a train back to Glasgow. I was disappointed that he hadn't stayed to watch the well oiled Corbett machinery in action – I had hoped he would wait a while or even have a night in the van, or there were certainly plenty of lifts back home to Kirkintilloch in the evening. Ho hum. I said thanks and farewell to Ken & Claire for great company, hospitality and vital help over the last few days, and they set off home on the long drive back around Rannoch Moor.

A ludicrous series of calamities suddenly unfolded within minutes of arriving at the van: Dad had just left which was already bugging me; one of my bike wheel bearings had just packed in and required emergency wheel replacement by Archie; while this was going on, the life-giving teapot had fractured and bled to death; the glass oven door, with lunch within, had inexplicably and frighteningly exploded into a zillion tiny pieces all over the interior; the van's electrical power had suddenly gone off for no apparent reason - thinking there might have been a gas problem to the oven, I quickly opened up the bottle compartment and the regulator fell off in my hand with pressurised gas spraying out!! The consequences of this happening un-noticed could have been devastating! After checking all the fuses and outlets, we eventually traced the power fault to simply a switch having been accidently pressed during the glass clean-up and the gas regulator was refitted as tightly as possible!

By this time my head was total mince; I couldn't, and didn't even want to, try handling all this domestic chaos anymore! All I wanted was to get out of there as quickly as possible – I just grabbed my road bike and rode away from the utter madness, leaving everyone else to sort out the mess. They had to get on with that, and I had to get on with hills. Having decided I would alter the planned route slightly to bag the awkward outlier of Beinn a' Chuallaich, I started with a 17 mile ride just past Kinloch Rannoch to the foot of the hill, and get back in the groove. I hammered down the road, holding 20mph all the way, but still enjoying the twisty, narrow road in the loch-side wooded setting with views across to Schiehallion. One by one the support vehicles caught me up and passed me and we all came together again within minutes at Druimglas farm. Local boy Brian Brennan had appeared too, having already done a couple of hours LAMM training that morning. This "hill of the herding" was just for the Westies herd – me, a grumpy Dave, Johnston, Ellie, Brian and Chris headed up at good pace into the mist. According to Johnston's blog, I was still a bit crabbit, *"Again Brian generously took the brunt of Manny's misanthropic tirade on the ascent."* After photos at the giant cairn the others enjoyed a fast blast down the good grassy track back to the vans, whilst I ambled down conservatively at a jog. A bite to eat, cup of tea and then back on the bike, retracing the road 12 miles back along Loch Rannoch-side to Bridge of Ericht, again trying to keep my 20mph average going. Archie &

Sandra passed me in their car, having returned from hunting a new oven door for us. When I got to the day's end at the bridge Archie pointed out the obvious, that there was absolutely no benefit from flaying myself on the bike – I ought to be using the time to spin the legs out and recover, certainly not working hard between hills. Mmm – I had jogged slowly down the last hill only to push hard on the bike? What he said made sense and I resolved to change my approach.

Despite the earlier domestic apocalypse and grumpiness I had enjoyed the day immensely, with so much company from clubmates and friends there to help out in any way that was required to keep my moaning backside moving along. A few of the crew headed for home, but after a quick shower we repaired to the Tummel Inn for a fine dinner and beer with Dave, Brian, Sandra & Archie. A great evening to finish the day, with the others pulling a childish prank of hiding and pretending they had left the car park without me, just long enough for me to spit the dummy well out, highlighting that my fuse was still rather short!

Snore.

Davy reminisced... *At the van we were catering for various supporters with tea etc. and even called in a cheery but weary looking chap just passing out on the road – it turned out to be Manny's dad!*

Up on "The Road to the Isles" track Manny duly appeared with Dave Rogers; Manny with a wee rucksack and Dave with a huge one, like the weight of Satan on his shoulders! Having a bike I took Dave's rucksack, which he was surprisingly reluctant to give up – not only was it large but extremely heavy – I was a bit saddle sore by the time I got back, so I don't know how he managed to carry it over the hills

Swaz blogged... *I had to look up "misanthropic".*

Johnston reminisced... *Dave Rogers had pitched up for a long stint, and with Brian Brennan around, the banter was flying. I found it hilarious that Brian got so much moaning, grief and general abuse from you - no-one else fulfilled the role of walking/running punch-bag quite as ably as Brian - he really took a pounding! You weren't for being cheered up that day - I asked you for highlights to date - seeing a golden eagle so close by, perhaps? "Aye, maybe... not many highlights really." I tried again, and finally got a grudging "I liked the boat (Finlandia)." Miserable git!*

Day 30 Sunday 24th May - Into Badenoch
Foot 17 miles & 6,143ft, bike 6 miles (50ft), mtb 11 miles (1,424ft), 5 Corbetts

It started a nice day, but breezy. Brenda & Dave headed off north on foot, up the 7 miles of tarmac that lead past the dam at the south end of Loch Ericht and deep into the hills, ascending all the time to over 2,000ft. Sandra, Archie and I chortled as they set off and Dave's notoriously fast walking pace had Brenda's wee short legs jogging just to keep up! I had a leisurely feed and prepared my days kit and mountain bike, whilst we gave them a thirty minute head start, before Archie & Sandra accompanied me on bikes at a relaxed, low gear pace.

The timing was near perfect as we all arrived at the road summit within a few minutes. It was blowing a hooley at the bealach and we didn't linger before heading up the short climb to the top of Aonaich Stob an Mhor, with stunning views the length of Loch Ericht and across to Ben Alder. Unfortunately Sandra's injured leg from the sailing had still not fully healed and she didn't make it to the top, instead retreating early with Archie to the bikes. Once we returned from the summit, Dave and I headed off south-east into the rough, broken high moorland, whilst the other three took the bikes whizzing downhill for the 7 miles back to the vehicles – great fun!

Dave's a good slave-driver to have on your case when you're feeling knackered, and usually spot on with his navigation too, so it was good to switch off a wee bit, knowing that I was in safe company. We made very good time across this really rough ground and topped remote Beinn Mholach in a gale, with Dave climbing the towering round cairn, risking being airborne for a photo. With dark skies and rain now threatening, we charged down north east towards Loch Garry and a well-earned lunch break in Duinish Bothy. I got quite chilled whilst hanging about reading the bothy book, and we bailed out just as two dottery old walkers arrived at the front door, jogging off across the grassy flood plain as heavy freezing rain began to fall. A quick splash through the river and up the steep hillside into the thick mist shrouding the heathery slopes and, after some compass fidgeting, onto the top of Meall na Leitreach. As we approached the cairn a pair of figures loomed out the mist – one with two legs and another with four. Dot the Doughnut Queen and her pooch Frank had just summited too and it was great to meet her there, with precision timing. A quick gab and photos before we trotted off towards Dalnaspidal Lodge at the north end of Loch Garry, then across the river once more and up The Sow of Atholl – Meall an Dodhrachan, a familiar hill to me as I regularly include it and its neighbour, The Boar of Badenoch, in a training round of the four western Drumochter Munros. Progress started to slow somewhat in the cold mist, and I realised Dave had suddenly dropped off the back and was looking totally shagged out; perhaps understandably since he had done the first 7 miles of the day on foot, while I got to gently bike in. We stopped briefly to emergency refuel, then bashed straight over the manky Sow's top without stopping and quickly dropped down the steep slopes to the big lay-by on the A9 at Drumochter Pass summit.

We enjoyed a good feed and drink before I jumped onto the road bike with a fluorescent vest and lights to do battle with the deadly traffic on the busy trunk road. There was a welcome change in the weather again as the clouds parted revealing the sun, but the wind had also risen considerably, fortunately for me as a tail wind. I knew I shouldn't have, but it was irresistible to blast down the road, out of the saddle in top gear, doing about 40mph – yeeeha! The 6 miles passed in minutes, whizzing into the metropolis of Dalwhinnie. There are two interesting things about Dalwhinnie - one is its distillery and fantastic malt whisky, the other is that Field Marshal Montgomery once stayed there briefly. He was so unimpressed that he decided to move to the continent, albeit he took the entire Allied invasion fleet with him – D Day was planned in Dalwhinnie, probably because of the good supply of malt, and no German spies (or anyone else for that matter) would ever think of looking there!

At the road turning-circle next to the railway level crossing, I was about to load the road bike onto the van-rack when a car appeared and turned, with some haggard old witch cackling out the passenger window "I hope you are not going to be parking there!" Brenda wisely took instant control of the situation by cutting me off and reassuring the old bag that we were only dropping-off. I wonder if Montgomery had the same problem here, or in Normandy? "I hope you're not going to park that tank there young man?" Also riled, Dave tried out his finest diplomatic skills by picking up a giant traffic cone and megaphoning down the tumble-weed street towards the witch, *"WARNING, WARNING, NO PARKING IN DALWHINIE, NO PARKING IN DALWHINNIE!!"* Oh God, time to leave...

Brenda politely parked elsewhere whilst Dave and I had a short mtb ride along Loch Ericht-side, then straight up the very steep face of The Fara; strangely for a hill so close to home it was my first trip up to this colossal stone cairn. It was blowing a gale at the top but the views were great, looking back south down Loch Ericht to where we had started the day. Dave was done in now but I was feeling not too bad for such a big C5 day. On our return to the van he tried hard to persuade me to get back on the bike and ride back through Drumochter for a head-start on tomorrows agenda, but my mind was already focussed firmly on a huge dinner and the fine ales at the Glen Hotel in Newtonmore! Dave headed home to Edinburgh at the end of a long day, and we met my boys Manuel & Duncan in the pub for drinks and to catch up on their news, which was a welcome shot in the arm for me. Afterwards we headed home to Kingussie for my first night home (a complete midden of unpacked boxes and thick stoor) since exactly a month ago when the Round had started in Harris!

Day 31 Monday 25th May – Gaick, Tromie, Feshie
Foot 8.5 miles & 4,866ft, bike 14 miles (371ft), mtb 15 miles (942ft), 4 Corbetts

Manny blogged... *A knackered, late start again on the road bike, south down the dreadful A9 in minging rain and worse... the wind. Happy days! It improved a bit after Drumochter when I snuck up on a John O'Groats to Lands Ender, also on a* *bike but with full panniers. In the racket of the wind, rain and constant traffic he didn't hear me and I gratefully stole about a mile and a half of drafting behind him until we hit the relative safety of the dual carriageway. I knew that since he was unaware of me there was no easy way past, so I shouted "Hello!" rather than just whiz past. The poor man filled his pants! He leapt out the saddle, both his feet unclipped and he did a major high-speed wobble across the road with the fright!! Somehow he just held it together and we enjoyed the next 6 miles of chit chat, exchanging of hopes for our different adventures. I never caught his name (The Birmingham Biker), but good luck to you on your travels.*

At the Trinafour/Dalnacardoch turn off I had a brief feed and change of bikes to the mountain variety, then it was north through the Gaick Pass, now with a tailwind and abating rain. On two wheels I quickly covered the ground to Loch an Dun, and whizzed up & down the very steep An Dun in thick mist, then some lovely single-track biking to the other end of the loch to climb a near vertical wall of grass to the most disappointingly tiny cairn of A' Chaoirnich on completely flat and utterly featureless ground in the clag. Another good run on the bike down the Pass, and a surprise to find Archie pointing his 300mm (lens) at me from Gaick Lodge. Great, company for the last two hills. Sadly our friends Davie & Cherie McGibbon were not at home in the remote Keepers Cottage when we passed, but thank you for allowing us to take our entourage of vehicles in & out the estate. (Can you freeze & post the lasagne Cherie?) Shortly after, Brenda arrived in the van and I had a feed and drinks, before Archie and I set off up heathery Meallach Mhor and Carn Dearg Mor just as the rain & thick mist set in again, and we got a hearty soaking in "warm" water from the east - or was it north-west? mmm? Anyway, it was good to be on very familiar local hills again, with a friend to blether to as we made very short work of them, descending at an enjoyable trot (yes, even Archie ran, albeit in the style of "Funky Chicken") to a high hill track in Glen Feshie Estate to meet Davy Duncan & Brenda, having borrowed running friend Alan Smith's jeep, and that is where I will start tomorrow's trot south to Blair Atholl.

The evening was spent enjoying the sorely missed Suie Hotel bar in Kincraig, for a few drinks and a magic dinner. Great draught Cairngorm Ales, great food and a fine host, Mike Welding. Try it if you are ever passing folks, you won't be disappointed.

It was then off to Nethy Bridge next to see my ever-patient physio, Alison Robb – a woman with dangerous fingers! "Oh God!" is not something she has said to me before in the many previous times I have visited with my varied aches and pains, but the sight of my angry red leg was enough on this occasion. After much rubbing, "ouching", and zapping, I was taped up like a Blue Peter Christmas surprise and sent home to ice, ice, ice!!! Alison gave me the honest view that a rest day may well be required very soon to give the leg a chance, before it does not work at all, and possibly occasionally in the future too. It will be better to skip a day or two rather than not finish the route but I will do tomorrow as it as relatively short, and assess how the strapping does for the leg.

Archie blogged... *I joined him for the last 2, Meallach Mhor and Carn Dearg Mor and despite more peeing rain he was in good form and going strong. He was last spotted in the Suie Hotel scoffing yet more grub washed down with a couple of pints of Trade Winds in preparation for heading off for a hard time by his favourite physio to see if he can get his gammy leg sorted out.*
I must say that having read reports of his leg "hinging aff" I was a bit unimpressed by the lack of limping that has been going on over the last couple of days. However when I suggested that the condition be officially downgraded to "a bit sair" I was told it merited at least a ranking of "affy sair".

Graham Benny blogged... *Good going Manny, you've now done more Corbetts in a month than I have managed in 48 years!*

Alec Keith blogged... *Sounds like time for a wee breather Manny - a fantastic effort to date, the days are long enough and the weather's been pretty cruel to you. Don't jeopardise all the hard work by utterly trashing yourself just yet - save it till the last couple of days! Anyway I'm looking forward to joining in and observing the suffering first hand when you get further north, so please don't wreck yourself until I've given you a good kicking. Just for once, try listening to your physio before rather than after the point of self-destruction...*

Cherie McGibbon blogged... *The Lasagne was yummy! Will try and salvage the leftovers for the freezer! Sorry to have missed you both - would have been great to catch up on your crazy activities! Sounds as though you should take it easy, get rested then keep going!*

Physio, Alison Robb's account... *Manny arrives for an emergency appointment as he's "done something pretty bad" to his left leg. He's been over West and proceeds to tell me (somewhat proudly) that he saw a Doctor over there who actually took photographs for his records as he'd never seen tendonitis quite like it. Manny slumps his leg onto the treatment couch to show me. Oooooh, yeah, this would be great if you were doing an anatomy lesson! Here we had Peroneus Longus (muscle on outside of calf) with its tendon shining out brightly from beneath the skin for about 2-3 inches, red, inflamed and a perfect outline.*
I need to give some history now on my relationship with Manny. By this time Manny had been coming to me for physio on and off for 5 years. I knew all that was at stake here; I was expected to do some magic and set him on his way, no time wasted. Typically he would listen to what I said, would nod his head, say "yeah, I know what you're saying", but only take what advice really fitted into the overall plan of things. So I'd come to realise long before, that what I needed to do

was fix him up the best I could to make it possible for him to carry on, minimising further risk to his body as much as humanly possible. I've also come to believe that when Manny starts exercising, his body must produce an extraordinary large amount of endorphin or some such substance that gives him some crazy determination. So, with this in mind, I administered to his tendon, showed him how to strap it to try and give it a break, and told him that it would be really sensible to have a day or two off, but if he really had to, maybe he could struggle up one Corbett slowly.

Manny stopped surprising me long ago by what he managed to do against the odds, and so when I read on the blog the next night that he had managed 5!, I just had to smile and wonder!

Stuart Simpson, Ochil Hill Runners, blogged... *You're an idiot but a truly inspirational one, enjoy the rest of your pain and suffering!*

Day 32 Tuesday 26th May - Farewell Suie Hotel, Hello Moulin Inn!
Foot 26 miles & 7,500ft, bike 3 miles (80ft), mtb 9 miles (200ft), 5 Corbetts

I woke up and felt like a bus had hit me, from the waist down. My legs groaned and creaked as I tried to get out of bed and stretch out Alison's massage from the previous night. It took a lot of muscles twanging like tent guy-ropes, and drugs as varied as a tube of Smarties to get me moving in time to meet up with Davy in the jeep to take me back into Glen Feshie to my finish/start point for 9am. On the bright side, it was a gorgeous start to the day with sun, well broken clouds and blue sky, but a freezing cold wind from the north-west. I marched off up the huge land-rover track to get warm, but not even trying to run the first hill, Leathad Taobhain, to give the poor legs a chance to warm up and settle down. From the trig summit the views were magic over to home in Kingussie, the Monadhliaths, the Cairngorms and the Atholl hills – wow! What a lift. I trotted off south into really wild and remote country with nothing man-made anywhere to be seen in the landscape ahead of me.

Manny blogged... *I came over the brow of a wee hummock and there were two eagles on the ground right in front of me – massive big things! I was scared they were going to set about me but they lumbered into the sky seemingly not too bothered by my intrusion and watched me for a while, probably deciding I didn't have enough meat left to make a decent snack.*

What a magic moment that was, but a shame I didn't think to take out the camera - I was so gobsmacked at their proximity for those brief moments before they scanned me then soared away in the blink of an eye. Despite my duff-leg pain, I moved steadily over the heather, bog and tussock surface, ticking off Beinn Bhreac and a 3 mile traverse over to Beinn Mheadhonach. The last three Corbetts are all just a fraction under Munro status which allowed great views of their

Days 32-33 Glens Feshie to Clova

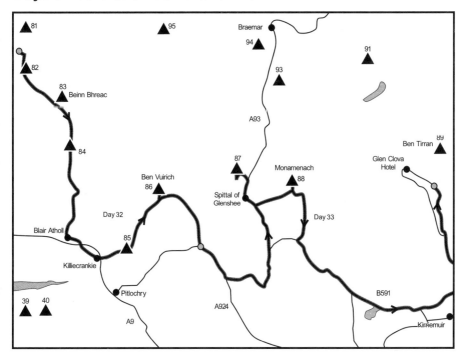

82. Leathad an Taobhain (912m)
83. Beinn Bhreac (912m)
84. Beinn Mheadhonach (901m)
85. Ben Vrackie (841m)

86. Ben Vuirich (903m)
87. Ben Gulabin (806m)
88. Monamenach (807m)

bigger cousins all around in Glenshee and Lyon, with dark rain showers just avoiding me on all sides! I was now going really well, and buzzed down the long runable ridge 2,000ft into Glen Tilt and Gilberts Bridge to meet Brenda and Davy with the mountain bikes.

The ride out to the centre of Blair Atholl was fun, and I knew with the time only 3.15pm I was going to keep going to Ben Vrackie. A brief road bike south whilst belting out the famous Corries song "...And the Deil's at Killiecrankie O..." to meet the van again, and once more bumped into Emma O'Shea and her wee dug going for a walk. Brenda and Davy joined me walking up the first steep tarmac section of track, before I pushed on alone over the coarse western slopes of this popular Corbett, rather than the usual motorway style footpath that has been constructed to the summit from the south. A surprise thump of thunder from behind gave me a jolt, and I lifted my pace to get up and over the top without hanging about in the cold wind. I had already decided I would make the most of this improved weather day and dropped off north, toward Ben Vuirich, nearly 5 miles distant.

Manny blogged... *Mistake. It was only half way across this rough route I realised the folly - it was now 7pm and the Moulin Inn may stop serving grub at 8.30!!! Emergency text to Brenda instructing advanced food order while I proceeded to set the heather on fire with an insane race-pace climb and descent of Ben Vuirich, absolutely eyeballs out! Crazy, just what I needed after 20 plus miles... I met Brenda, Davy and Aidy "King of the Bens" Davis (fresh from winning the famous Scottish Island Peaks Race) on the east side at Daldhu with a mtb for the mad 5 mile dash to the van at the road-end at Straloch, then whizz to the Moulin Inn just in time for grub – turns out it was 9.30 last orders for grub, and just as well because I had been hallucinating steak & ale pie with an Atholl Ale chaser for the last two hours. A good day, though I think I may suffer for it tomorrow, but at least with some new company promised for the hill.*
I'm away to cuddle a large Glengoyne before my coma.
Night night Blogites.

Two of my favourite pubs in twenty-four hours, with a dry day and five Corbetts in between – pure magic!

Davy reminisced... *We pushed the bikes up the west side of the River Tilt and met Manny coming off full of enthusiasm for the hill and the views. Then down to Killiecrankie where we met Emma O'Shea again with her dog Moss, working as a Ranger for the National Trust for Scotland. I don't know if Emma was suitably inspired, but she shortly went on to take up running and very quickly become one of the best lady hill runners in Scotland!*

Archie & Sandra blogged... *Manny, you're a blithering idiot! Why the hell do you have to take such stupid risks? OK, I can see the point in knocking off Ben*

Vrackie, but heading off to Ben Vuirich was utter folly which might well have ended in disaster, You could so, so easily have missed that steak and ale pie!! Make sure you know when last orders are in future. Well done sir.

Lyn & Kevin friends blogged... *Well Manny, now I know you're MAD. I can't believe how addictive your blog is... you are doing fantastically well. The book that you write after this will help pay for the extension on the house!!!! (Ed–sadly not, unless everyone in Europe buys it!)*

Jason biking buddy blogged... *Can you stay over in the East this weekend and keep your rain cloud with you as there are a few of us doing Ten under the Ben (endurance mtb race) and we would like a dry day! Keep up the good work.*

Day 33 Wednesday 27th May - Tricky into Angus
Foot 7 miles & 2,752ft, bike 50 miles (1,385ft), mtb 2 miles (393ft), 2 Corbetts

The morning was monsoon wet while eating breakfast in the van - *CRASH!!!...*what the f...!? Right outside, a bread delivery truck and a pick-up van had just blootered each other head on – nae rolls in Rattray today then! Thankfully there was just enough space left on the road for Davy's and our vans to squeeze past thus avoiding a long diversion back through Pitlochry, whilst I made reasonable headway against the tide on my paddle-bike once more. Wearing full heavy-duty waterproofs and very slow, I was suffering badly from yesterday's big day, and the day before's big day, and the day before that...

15 wet miles around to Spittal of Glenshee to meet up with Aidy, and a blast from the past – Tricky Dicky, aka Richard Speirs, a good friend of Charlie Campbell's I had last met in Glen Shiel during the famous record breaking Munros Round in 2000. Tricky was memorable for the appallingly gaudy leggings he'd wore, and he hadn't changed much, still wearing something peculiarly 80's today!! Boggin' leggings or not, I was delighted he had made the effort to come along and together the three of us (along with Aidy's mutt Ailsa) plodded and blethered up Ben Gulabin, easily bagged from the side of the road. Brenda had promised to follow behind us and humf my mtb up the big track as far as she could, in order to save my affy sair leg as much as possible on the descent, but we were actually back down at the van, just as she was taking the bike off the rack, much to her dismay!

Thankfully the rain had stopped and the clouds lifted enough to see the tops again, and we had a quick whiz 2 miles back down the road to then cut east through Westerton of Runavey farm, me on the mtb and Tricky & Aidy on foot. The supposed track was vague and rough though, and I would have been better off just jogging. After less than 2 miles the gradient steepened and I had to dump the wheels, which Tricky then took back out and locked to a gate by the road for pick-up later. I carried on with Aidy & pooch Ailsa heading straight for Monamenach summit, where a few minutes were spent enjoying the views and clarifying to Aidy the north & south points of the compass (or arse from elbow!) Navigation resolved, we headed south onto a good track down into Glen Isla and the steading of Auchavan, which had recently been converted into attractive self-catering accommodation. I had a good feed of the usual Complans and whatever else Brenda had cooked up before heading off on the road bike, for 30 miles of delightful cycling through wee back roads to get to Wheen in Glen Clova. Tricky had now driven around and was taking Aidy back to his car in Glen Shee before heading home. Brenny followed me afterwards, but stuck to the faster main roads in the van to get to the chemist in Kirriemuir for various potions and ointments for me. I had been flying along with a good tailwind in lovely weather for a couple of hours and popped out at a T-junction, turning right onto a very familiar looking leafy section of road only to find Brenda in the van heading straight towards me!? I had taken my first wrong turn on the trip and only gone 100 yards when Brenny, tooting the horn and waving, took great delight in pointing out the error of my ways, travelling out from Kirriemuir on the more well know B955 into the glen.

Soon at Wheen farm, I cycled straight past my official stopping point and the few extra miles up to the lovely Glen Clova Hotel, where Brenny already had the water heater on for a welcome shower, and was sitting in a deck chair enjoying the evening sun. After a shower we retired to the bar for a huge dinner and plenty of good beer in the bar with Aidy (now back with my retrieved bike) whilst watching Manchester United get totally outplayed 2-0 by a breathtaking Barcelona side in the Champions League Final.

Only two easy hills today but a lot of fun with friends and biking in the process, and a hopeful turn in the weather for a much bigger day tomorrow.

Brenny blogged... *I stopped, and yes it was Manny going the wrong way; he came to the end of the road and there was no road sign so he went right instead of left. I then drove away with a rather big grin and pleased that it was not me...*

Tricky reminisced... *Sadly, although I managed almost a week with Charlie on his Munros round back in 2000, I only got to join you for one day. Good luck with the book idea Manny, you might even beat Charlie to the publishers at this rate....!*

Day 34 Thursday 28th May - Clova to Muick
Foot 29.5 miles & 7,464ft, bike 17 miles (617ft), mtb 7 miles (560ft),
3 Corbetts

It was a grey and very low cloudy morning to set off up Ben Tirran from Wheen with Aidy and Westies clubmate Brian Bonnyman, a local from Forfar. Quite soon after heading up into the mist and lots of shouting & bawling by Aidy at a wayward Ailsa, there was a rammy out of sight in the clag, a bark then a squawk,

Day 50: Bambi on Sgurr an Utha (MG)

Day 50: Climbing Sgurr Mhurlagain (Chris Upson)

Day 51: Trotting up Sgurr an Fhuarain with Munro, Sgurr Mor behind (Chris Upson)

Day 51: Viewing Sgurr na h-Aide, Knoydart (Chris Upson)

Day 52: Beinn Bhuidhe, Knoydart. Rum still in sight (MG)

Day 55: Peter Bennet & Brenda join me on filthy Am Bathach (Dorothy Carse)

Day 54: Respite from the rain in Suardalan Bothy (Dorothy Carse)

Day 58: Fabulous Fuar Tholl (Dave Rogers)

Day 55: 1 Fast descent into Strath Croe (Dorothy Carse)

Day 60: Twenty winks on Baosbheinn (Scott Kennedy)

Day 60: Just Magic! (MG)

Day 62: Dave Riach on Domestique duty (BP)

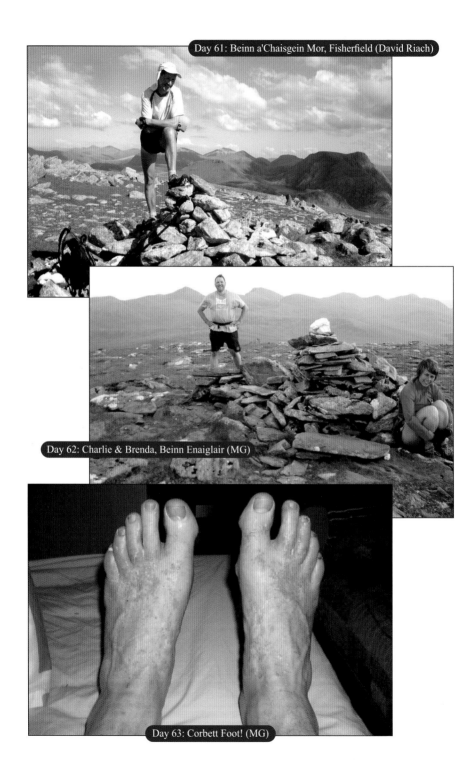

Day 61: Beinn a'Chaisgein Mor, Fisherfield (David Riach)

Day 62: Charlie & Brenda, Beinn Enaiglair (MG)

Day 63: Corbett Foot! (MG)

Day 65: Elsie & Peter Baxter escorting me to Meall a'Ghrianain (MG)

Day 65: My f@cking shoes!!! (Johnston Orr)

Day 66: Climbing Cul Beag, Cul Mor awaits (Chris Upson)

Day 66: Leaving Cul Beag behind (Chris Upson)

Day 66: Sadly by-passing Suilven (Chris Upson)

Day 66: Descending from heaven, Suilven & Canisp (Chris Upson)

Day 66: Flying off Breabag! (Chris Upson)

Day 67: Geoff, Don and Manny on Spidean Coinich (Chris Upson)

Day 67: Airy view point, Quinag (Chris Upson)

Day 67: Warming up for ACDC at Hampden! (Chris Upson)

Day 67: Traversing Quinag, Spidean Coinich behind (Chris Upson)

Day 68: Glas Bheinn. Hello, Mr Gorman's office... Quiniag behind (Chris Upson)

Day 68: Chasing after Chris (Chris Upson)

Day 68: Totally bonked out on Beinn Leoid (Chris Upson)

Day 68: The Paparazi await (Chris Upson)

Day 69: Westies Dave Calder & Donald Smith, before epic Arkle & Foinaven (John Donnelly)

Day 69: A hard days night... (Chris Upson)

Day70: Reluctantly finishing Cranstackie & Beinn Spionnaidh, with Mindy MacLeod (John Donnelly)

"At the head of the Kyle of Tongue stands one of the world's greatest mountains, Ben Loyal" (John Allen)

Day 70: Radio Scotland Interview. Ben Loyal awaits behind (Chris Upson)

Day 70: Manuel & Duncan hold me up on the final summit (Archie Lang)

110

Day 70: Three generations of twits! (Chris Upson)

Day 70: Three cheers for Brenda!!! (Charlie Campbell)

39 Days Later - Brenda does Ben Loyal !

December 2009 Westies annual dinner,
presented with the Fell Runners Association Long Distance Award,
Chris Upson 2003, Manny Gorman 2009, Charlie Campbell 2000 (BP)

Days 34-37 Glen Clova to Tomintoul

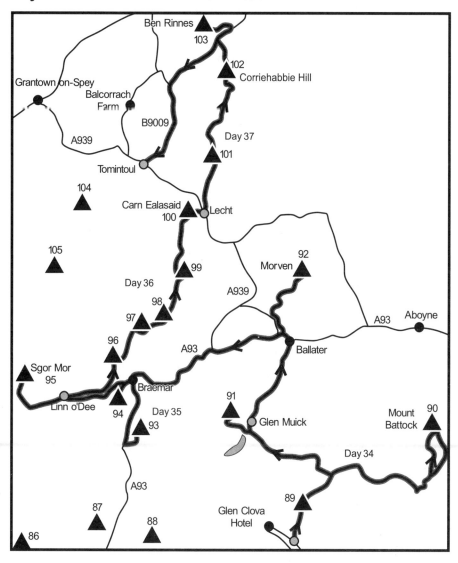

89. Ben Tirran (896m)
90. Mount Battock (778m)
91. Conachcraig (865m)
92. Morven (872m)
93. Creag nan Gabhar (834m)
94. Morrone (859m)
95. Sgor Mor (813m)
96. Carn na Drochaide (818m)

97. Carn Liath (862m)
98. Culardoch (900m)
99. Brown Cow Hill (829m)
100. Carn Ealasaid (792m)
101. Carn Mor (804m)
102. Corryhabbie Hill (781m)
103. Ben Rinnes (840m)

before the hound re-appeared out the mist to proudly present her professional ecologist master with a nice fresh grouse! Not ten minutes had passed before there was a blood-curdling squeal from the clag and the killing machine returned, this time with a mountain hare by the throat!! Christ, was the dog going to spend its day slaughtering the local wildlife? Thankfully Aidy had had enough and stuck a lead on the butcher.

A bit quieter now, we climbed well to a cairn in the mist, lazily presuming it to be the top. Brian was heading back down to take his car around to Glen Lee for logistics, while Aidy stayed with me in the murk. Brian wasn't away long when I suddenly realised there ought to have been a trig point at the summit; a quick bit of relocating on the map and a further slight rise led us to the actual top of "The Goet". Phew! If I had missed it with such a simple error, I would have been gutted when I downloaded the GPS reading later to discover the mistake! Vowing to avoid complacency and always check the map in future, Aidy led me well through the thick mist and across some rough featureless ground into Glen Lee as planned. Brenny had been warned not to hang about in Clova and drive the long way around in good time to deliver my mtb to the west end of Loch Lee for me coming off the hill. In almost perfect choreography, we saw her drop the bike when we were only a few minutes away, descending the heathery hill to Inchgrundle. I had a quick whizz back to van on two wheels and got a head start on eating, drinking and changing, ready to bike the 7 road miles east to Milden Lodge to meet Brian again. There was only a brief stop to admire and photograph the superbly well preserved ruin of Invermark Castle, a classic Scottish keep from around 1526.

The clag had taken until lunchtime to dissipate to blazing sunshine, and the heat was tremendous as the three of us again set off, up the track aiming at Mount Battock. We were all stripped to the waist and I tried to keep my trotting as relaxed as possible to control the unaccustomed heat build-up as we steadily plodded up the hill. I wasn't expecting a track as good as this, and regretted not taking the mtb to rest the running legs and for a fast descent. We bagged the top in fantastic heat, the novelty of which I would never complain about after some of the grim weather I had endured to date. Running off the top, we trotted down a ridge on the other side of the glen to make a loop back to the van, where Brenda as always had drinks and grub ready. I had enjoyed the guys company and was sorry to see them head away to get Aidy's car away back in Clova, but I still had a lot to do to finish the day in Glen Muick.

First, I returned the 7 miles back up the glen by bike to eat and drink as much as possible while Brenda ran off in advance, into the upper reaches of Glen Lee to the Stables of Lee (and judging by the amount of horse poo, still used as such). Now wearing a long-sleeved white Helly to protect against the sun, I biked in against a strong breeze and was surprised how long it took me to catch up with her – she must be getting fitter, or perhaps me more knackered!? We met up near the

Stables for a brief rummage about in the bothy there, before Brenny cycled out on my bike and I carried on by foot. I was careful to drink gallons of water from any burn I crossed, as it was still hot and dehydration can creep up and destroy you before you realise your mistake. Tired, I made a mess of the line to the bothy at Shielin of Mark, passing too far to the north (and oddly finding a single brand new training shoe sitting on the heather in the open moor!), before correcting my line down the magic wee gorge of the Allt Darrarie that leads to Spittal of Glen Muick. As I was trotting down there I was thinking that any stay in the bothy would require fuel for the fire, such as coal, to be lugged in the 2.5 miles over the hill. At that precise moment I stepped over a single piece of coal sitting on the narrow trod... weird coincidence: I put it in my bum bag for luck! I trotted into the Spittal feeling tired but exhilarated.

Brenda had a huge drive around the hills in the van which would take at least a few hours, so I figured in the good weather that carrying on to bash Conachcraig was the sensible thing to do. I made steady work of it, knowing there was no rush. The views from the now cool top were absolutely superb across Lochnagar and northeast to Morven. I took a while to soak it up, take photos and send a few update texts, correctly guessing that there would be no mobile reception in the Glen from the van later. As I was trotting gently back down I spied the van driving up the glen and disappearing into the car park trees at the Spittal. I didn't notice at the time, but somewhere on the run down I dropped from my pack webbing a brand new, unworn, Nike technical t-shirt that had been given as a very expensive present by Brenny – she wasn't impressed when I told her it was lost! Once the gravity of the descent had stopped working in my favour, my legs suddenly started to seize up. It had been a long hot day and they were saying "STOP!" I crawled back along the endless flat kilometre of track to the visitor centre. Brenda already had dinner on the go, but had removed my road bike from the rack in case I might want to go on. I was totally buggered, but as there was "No Overnight Parking" in the car park, I decided to very gently spin down the road just a few miles to one of the big lay-bys there, and save having to return in the morning.

Dinner and beer hardly touched the sides as it fell down my throat, before massaging my legs and applying sun cream to a burnt neckline. A great day out, with three isolated and potentially tricky hills in the bag on one big push. Pure brilliant.

Zonko.

Archie blogged... *Just to keep all Blog Addicts up to date since Manny seems to have better things to do - anyone would think he was busy rather than just swanning about the countryside.*
I've recently had a report that he is standing on top of Conachcraig having had sunshine all day. So that's another 5 in the bag since his last post.

Day 35 Friday 29th May - Smith Country, Deeside
Foot 13.5 miles & 5,546ft, bike 47 miles (1,371ft), mtb 13 miles (721ft), 4 Corbetts

Clear morning skies - it's going to be a roaster! I scoffed a quick breakfast and cup of tea, then out the door onto the road bike for an exciting - but perhaps a bit too exciting - descent down the tight Glen Muick road. There wasn't a car on the road until just at the wee narrow bridge, on a right hand bend at Brochdhu, a bloody great ten ton tipper truck appeared and stopped on the bridge taking up the entire width. Oh shite! I was flying down the hill far too fast to turn left into the farm, and nowhere else to go... TWANG! Rather than face planting into the truck, I chose a short section of ramshackled wire fence dead-ahead, and it only just held me up on my front wheel, without catapulting over the top and down into the burn and rocks! It all happened in a split second and was so close to disaster, but I "got out of jail free" - not even a mark on the bike. The truck driver had a quick look to see I was ok and drove on, but it certainly wasn't his fault – I was going too fast.

I recovered and rode into Ballater rather sheepishly, stopping at the van just beyond at Bridge of Gairn. Here we were to meet up with good friend and Gairnside loon Alan Smith of Deeside Runners, on his local stomping ground, for company over the next few days. But he hadn't appeared yet and this gave me time for a feeding frenzy. Brenda had made an inspired purchase of ice lollies for starters, and lying in the grass we sooked them down in minutes as they melted down our arms in glorious sunshine. For afters we had sausage rolls & beans, and cakes & tea... then Alan turns up with pots of stovies! Feeling like a circus elephant, I somehow pedalled my giant stomach up the hilly wee road to Lary, and changed to the mountain bike for the 3 miles of hill track to the slopes of Morven. We cycled slowly in the heat and blethered about the racing scene, which I was missing out on for the time being. Suddenly Alan shouted "ADDER!" and I looked down just as my two wheels ran over a bloody great snake - I nearly keeched my shorts! Sunbathing snakey was very pissed off with me and he re-coiled on the track, vainly hoping I would come back; I stopped but before I could get a photo, he slithered off into the long grass, and I wasn't for going looking! It had been quite a morning and I hadn't even done a hill yet!

Now totally paranoid about serpents I was watching every footstep through the short grass and heather, especially after Smithy recited his "getting bit as a loon" story, where he had a lengthy coma and nearly lost a leg! "Aye, this area is hooching wi' Adders" didn't help me any, but I think this was Alan's idea of humour...? At last the top of Morven arrived, in perfect blue sky, and we took a few photos before reversing our route, but twice as fast with the help of gravity. Back at the van Brenny had pulled the awning out, enjoying her book and hiding from the burning sun for a change. We had gallons to drink then onto the road bikes for a 23 mile ride north on the A93 past Braemar. There was a ridiculous strong headwind all the way and we ended up in single file for most of it, with me in front and Alan drafting! To be fair he did try and pass me a few times, but couldn't get by in the wind and against my strong biking - not that we were being competitive at all, but every time he tried to take the lead I would up the pace until he fell back again! Even in hill races there's something about being passed by Smithy - I never liked it and try my best never to allow it! We finally pulled up to the parked van on a lovely grassy verge in Glen Clunie, and we both collapsed off the bikes with exhaustion, crumpled, wheezing and laughing like old bags. Alan Smith crawling on his hands and knees is not something you see often, so Brenda took a photo of our carcasses as evidence!

It took us half an hour to recover, cool down and drink pints of juice, before setting off more sedately straight up Creag nan Gabhar. Quick and easy on mixed rock and heather, we were back at the van in just fifty minutes, including a good summit stop to enjoy the view. On a high now, I biked downwind back into Braemar, to quickly drop into the Youth Hostel where fellow hill runner Ali Hubbard was the manager, and we borrowed a mountain bike for Alan (his own was left back at his van in Ballater after Morven, and our van rack would be full when we ran over to Lecht tomorrow, making logistics more difficult for Brenda). From near the famous royal highland games field Alan led me up Morrone, on the footpath which forms the lucrative (for the winners at least) Braemar Games hill race, which he has fought out for many years battling for the prized "first local". No Queen Betty watching today as we plodded up in the early evening sun, still surprisingly fresh, and enjoying amazing panoramas. Flying back downhill to the van, we wasted no time and jumped on the bikes for the 8 miles around to Linn of Dee, on the way waving down a distinctive car belonging to hill running pal Laurie Anderson of Fife AC, along with Alan Graham of Lomond HR, who were heading into the Cairngorms for some weekend running and bothying.

It was well into the evening now, but still very warm. At the car park Brenda already had the mountain bikes off and we had a good feed before the three of us rode off west up the side of the River Dee to White Bridge, then turning north as far as the very inviting waterfall at Chest of Dee. Dumping the bikes in the heather and resisting the tempting river to cool off, we trotted on for another couple of miles before striking up the burnt heather slopes of Sgor Mor. The sun was sinking lower with every step and running directly into it needed quick feet for hidden rocks. It was heaven as we sauntered onto the summit table with only a few minutes of sun left, and the burning colours all around the deeply shadowed hills were just amazing. It was 9.30pm. As the northwest sun finally dipped behind The Devil's Point & Cairn Toul, the heat of the evening finally relented to welcome cool air. Many photos were taken of the scene before trotting back off to the bikes, buzzing with the kind of adrenaline that makes being in our mountains so special. It was gone 11 o'clock and almost dark before we got back to the van for a quick dinner, beer and drams then heavenly bed; everyone is smiles after a fifteen hour day in the heat.

Day 36 Saturday 30th May - North to The Lecht
Foot 20 miles & 6,794ft, bike 4 miles (55ft), 5 Corbetts

Groan… "Get up" poked Brenda. Groan again.

I was feeling like a bus had not quite hit me – more like parked on top of me. I was stiff, sore and absolutely knackered. Not nearly enough rest and sleep after yesterday's big day, and now I had another huge push north in the hot sun again. After creaking out of bed I investigated the hullabaloo going on outside to find friends from Newtonmore, the Forrest clan, were there and getting ready with support crew to set off for Devil's Point as a final Munro trip for faither Donald. What day for it! I recovered enough to get out and wish them well with a good dram to take to the top for the celebrations, otherwise I was very slow getting my act together and eventually got underway with a short bike ride to Linn of Quoich where Alan was waiting, and Brian Brennan had returned to the fray with more bags full of BA Business Class complimentary goodies. The morning sun was already blistering hot and we applied liberal amounts of sun cream to all exposed skin, wearing skip caps and long-sleeved tops.

The first Corbett of the day, Carn na Drochaide, was an absolute drag for me. Tired limbs were reluctant to do the work and I was struggling to keep up with the other pair. The only thing that kept me going, and my mind diverted from feeling rough, was the great weather and the incredible clear views all around, in particular the stunning view over the top of Braemar to the backdrop of Lochnagar. Brian gave me a relentless slagging with his usual banter as I lagged behind. With a good water/food stop in a shaded gully I moved slightly better up to Carn Liath's twin tops, and the short hop over to Culardoch passed quickly, passing an alien looking scientific heather research site along the way. Sadly Brian was taking his wit home again, but first required a long return run to Allanaquoich to his car.

Alan and I continued north into deep heathery countryside and a slog up onto Brown Cow Hill, easily the dullest Corbett summit of all. Almost completely flat and covered in haggy heather, it required careful attention to gain the actual top, and we were very thankful that it was a clear day as mist could easily have meant missing it. One to go, but a long trek and big drop were needed first, with a pleasant paddle through the upper reaches of the River Don. Finally, another landmark was reached - Corbett number 100, Carn Ealasaid. It gave me a shot in the arm. It had been a tough day on zero energy levels, but a short drop down to the Lecht Ski Centre, and then we were heading back to Alan's farm near Tomintoul to spend a well earned evening in the hot tub, drinking beer and eating until I burst. Bliss.

Brenda blogged... *Archie & Sandra managed to track me down at The Lecht while Archie swapped wheels on bikes and sorted us again after having a visit to the bike shop. Sandra brought some more Cherry cake which is going down a treat.*

Day 37 Sunday 31st May - A Foray into Moray
Foot 15.5 miles & 3,779ft, bike 19 miles (787ft), mtb 6 miles (918ft), 3 Corbetts

Manny blogged... *Greetings from the toaster Bloggers!*
What a magic day!! Sunny and hot from the start, and I was feeling surprisingly spritely after three very hard days on the trot, and feeling totally rubbish yesterday. Again I was joined in the hills by Alan, and a herd of Westies, some fresh from the Slioch hill race yesterday - Ellie, JD, Chris, Neil & Elizabeth. We headed north away from the Lecht, very quickly over to Carn Mor trig point, running all the way to the top and feeling surprisingly good. Great views all around! We dropped north off the heathery hill and Alan & I picked up the mtb's brought in by Chris & Neil for the 5 miles to the foot of Corriehabbie Hill while the rest of the gang ran along the same route, before we made short work to the top, while the bikes were taken back out again. A slight hiccup in concentration and direction led to the group being split up in Glen Rinnes, before me & JD recalculated and found the camper van parked in exactly the right spot. It was roasting hot now and plenty food and cold drinks were noshed down before the short road bike to the foot of Ben Rinnes where a pack of runners including Brenda, Chris, Ellie, Tilly & Alan enjoyed the scamper up the Ben in glorious sunshine to linger on the summit tors taking in the Moray coast views - magic.

Alan & I rounded the day off by road-biking 16 miles back to Tomintoul, with only one brief stop to articulate our opinions of a particularly bad drivers' errors to him and his missus, before an outrageously good feed of Soay sausages and lamb mince washed down with fantastic Cairngorm Ales. Another good day promises tomorrow and a run with an old Westies chum, Luke Arnott, back from a few years working in New Zealand.
103 in the bag, nearly halfway...

JD blogged... *It was indeed a fantastic day Manny. 2 new Corbetts for me (only 39 left!) and great company. And an hour and a half peaceful sunbathing and reading while you lot bashed up Ben Rinnes. Well done everybody, keep up the fantastic work Manny and Brenda.*

Ranald blogged... *Manny, at long last I have found your blog and glad to read that you have had a good couple of days. How is the leg holding up? Have to say that you were not getting a lot of sympathy in the Silverfjord on Wednesday night (Ed. my mountain biking crew) but you probably wouldn't expect any more!! Keep going and keep up the good work Brenda. Best of luck, Ranald.*

Elizabeth reminisced... *I arrived at the Lecht ski centre thinking that maybe we should be offering to carry your bag for you or something; instead, we could hardly catch you as you bounded off over the hills. The logistics were crazily complicated - I couldn't believe you managed to string it all together and make something so amazing, with bikes, meet-points, drop-off points etc. I got a marmalade cheesecake ice-cream in Tomintoul as a brilliant reward for the hottest run I've ever done in Scotland!*

Day 38 Monday 1ˢᵗ June - A Queen's View to Meall a' Bhuachaille
Foot 20 miles & 4,390ft, bike 7 miles (265ft), mtb 3 miles (452ft), 3 Corbetts

Manny blogged... *Another scorcher, great!*

After a delayed start, me and Luke set off west from the Queen's View car park, Tomintoul, on mtb's for 3 miles then on foot over rough ground to the top of Geal Charn in about two hours. A good feed and synchronised timer photos of us on the cairn before heading down, with Luke not feeling 100% (or even 50% I suspect) after only just flying in from NZ the day before, and not having done any running for about six weeks. Luke headed west to Ryvoan bothy, whilst I ran south across what must be one of the great untouched wildernesses in Scotland towards Creag Mhor. I dare any of you to try and link these two hills to find out... Not a trace of human hand to be seen or heard, utterly still, and boiling hot. Every peat hag would reveal new wildlife hiding from the sun. Grouse exploding from my feet every five minutes and flapping away with fake injuries to lure me away from their clutch of tiny chicks, deer lying down in the shade, curlews crying in the air, newts scampering for cover, fish diving for cover in the river. A special, but desperately rough, place.

At last, another two hour flog including a twisted right ankle with much whinging and punching of the heather, I finally fought my way to the top of Creag Mhor where the chunky summit tors allowed superb views north into Glen Avon, Bynack Mor, Cairngorm etc etc. I had my chit on the top and soaked up the scenery. A fast descent, climb & descent again over the Bynack path led me to a fast ascending Alan Smith. The cunning plan of shoving his bike up the path as far

Days 38-39 Strathspey

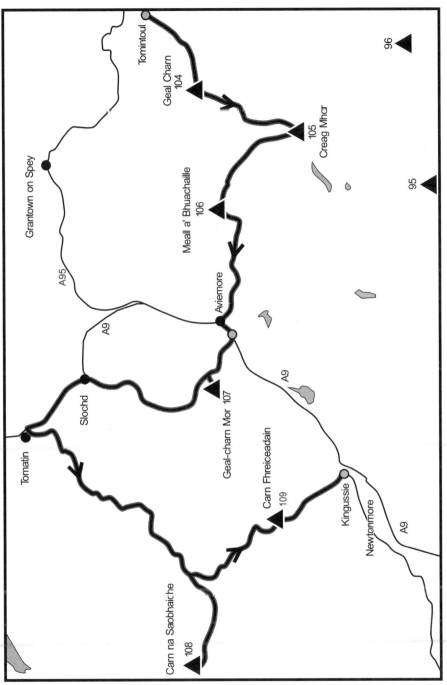

104. Geal Charn (821m)
105. Creag Mhor (895m)
106. Meall a' Bhuachaille (810m)

107. Geal-charn Mor (824m)
108. Carn na Saobhaidhe (811m)
109. Carn an Fhreiceadain (878m)

as possible for me had come unstuck when his rear mechanism had somehow got damaged and fallen off! So a slightly longer trot and very brief but exciting downhill free-wheel on his un-driveable bike led me to Ryvoan bothy to meet up with Brenda, Luke, Davy Duncan and Dave & Val Machin from Cairngorm Runners, and a sweaty but ever chirpy Peter Porteous and his mate Keith Bootle. We enjoyed a very relaxed plod up Meall a' Bhuachaille to the summit before a gentle jog back down to Allan & Tilly Smith's Reindeer House for drinks and food. I nipped off to finish the day with a fast 8 mile bike ride to Lynwilg junction outside Aviemore, then whizzed back to Glenmore Lodge in the van to get a long overdue massage by the ever patient Kirsty Wright - a woman who can knead your legs to dough... as long as you remember to bring your own bite stick! Thanks Kirsty. Friends Judy & Will Carey had arrived at Reindeer House to wish us well, sorry I had to dash off, thanks for the wine, nibbles & cakes. Thanks to Aidy for making tea, and a cracking couple of pints were had later in the world famous Suie Hotel, Kincraig, before retiring to bed for a bit of bloggercise - Brenda is now snoring.

Short day tomorrow; hopefully catch up with two handsome sons!?

Swaz blogged... *Ah yes - Aviemore – I lost all kinds of things there...*
Great job, Manda - Hopefully the weather is going to stick around a little longer... Does anybody know why it's called "The Burma Road"??

Archie & Sandra blogged... *Hi Swaz, You've never heard the legend of the infamous Burma Road?? Over the last 20 years 143 people have perished whilst trying to cycle over this perilous pass. Most have succumbed to heatstroke and exhaustion due to the severity of the incline and the fact that it faces directly into the sun. Many others have come to grief on the mad, fast, very scary descent on the other side. We can only sit and wait to see if our hero ever makes contact again!! Tune in next week for the next thrilling instalment!*

Swaz blogged... *Righto... does anybody want to explain what Burma has to do with Aviemore ??*

Archie & Sandra blogged... *Ok Swaz, I might have been telling a few porkies to try to create a bit of drama. After all we've been missing out on monsoons, hurricanes and plagues of locusts for at least a week now.*
A quick Google suggests that the Burma Road was built by prisoners of war in the 1940s so presumably that's how it got its name. Mind you, you don't want to believe everything you read on the internet!

Day 39 Tuesday 2nd June - Halfway home!
Foot 10 miles & 2,175ft, bike 13 miles (459ft), mtb 33 miles (3,295ft),
3 Corbetts

Manny blogged... *By the time we organised bikes and faffed about, it was gone 10am when Luke, Peter Porteous and I set off on our mtb's, grunting up the infamous Burma Road from Lynwilg Junction at Aviemore. A grinding 2 mile climb of about 1,700ft, then a quick walk up & down the remainder of Geal Charn. Peter's determination to keep using his biking shoes from the 1800's came back to haunt him when the sole fell off at the summit and he had to return direct to Lynwilg instead of following me & Luke down the fabulously fast & potentially dangerous descent on the other side to the River Dulnain, and on to meet Brenda and Dot at Slochd car park. This was great stuff - I was on familiar home ground and the weather was still superb. A very fast whizz on the road bike for 13 miles into Coignafearn Estate where some twitchers with giant scopes were spying a newly fledged Peregrine chick on a cliff-edge nest, and let me have a wee peek – magic! Still suffering jet-lag, Luke departed south to start his new job (night shift!) in Brighton the next day, but I was glad he had caught up with me and shared a couple of good days on the hill.*

Back on the mtb solo again for a long ride and climb most of the way into Carn na Saobhaidhe, one of the most remote and wild Corbetts of all, isolated in the centre of the Monadhliath Mountains. Then the last mile or so on foot in baking heat. It really was an overwhelming sort of still heat, and dripping with sweat I stripped off completely - shorts an' all – for a scuddy trot to the top! Slightly hazy views - perhaps just as well - from the beautifully desolate top, a place now embroiled in eco-politics. From the tiny summit cairn I took a series of photos showing the 360 degree panorama of a fabulous wild landscape, with virtually nothing man-made to be seen in any direction.

   Now as I write this just a few short years later, some of the adjoining greedy estates in conjunction with one of the many queued-up, money driven, publicly subsidised, ethically delinquent, renewable developers, wishes to erect thirty-one giant wind turbines slap-bang in the centre of this magnificent landscape, right on the doorstep of the Cairngorms National Park - the scandalous Allt Duine project. With the backing of the cash hungry local community councils such as Kincraig, to name but one partner-in-crime, desperate to get their hands on promised golden bribes, any possible refusal in local planning is certain to be over-turned by a desperately ill-informed Scottish Government, maybe after a token gesture public enquiry. If it goes ahead, it would be a crime of epic proportions, to sit nicely alongside the 20,000+ ignored objections to the Beauly to Denny pylon scheme. Wind-factories have their place I am certain, but it is not here.

Re-donning my clothes I enjoyed a fantastically shakey, fast mtb descent and out almost to the big lodge, then turned south up another dead-end track for a few miles before meeting up with Dot who was taking the bike out again while I dashed off on foot over rough ground, across the watershed to the upper Dulnain and the wee bothy that sits there.

A fast pull up from the end of the track, then cut onto the top of Carn an Fhreiceadain; hill number 110 and halfway at last! One of my neighbours, Russell Jones, had left his very expensive new Whyte mtb unlocked on the summit, after driving it up that morning in his 4x4 vehicle on the Pitmain Estate shooting track. Unknown to me at the time, another local running friend from Kingussie, Steve Myerscough, had also shoved his mtb 5 miles & 2,000ft up the hill for me to pick up, and I laughed when I imagined the scene as he discovered Russell's bike already there – at least he had a nice ride back down!! The weather had turned much colder from the north in the last hour and it was freezing on the summit so I was grateful for a very fast and smooth ride down on a superb bike all the way back to our house - what a treat!

A real team effort today; thanks to friends Finlay Binnie for a loan of his good mtb for Luke, Russell for his bike on the last top, Brenny for a lot of driving in the heat and especially to Dot the Doughnut Queen, not only for taking my bike out from the back of beyond, but for the priceless tips on the tracks in Coignafearn which are not marked on any OS maps! A great day for us finished off with the good company of my two handsome sons Manuel & Duncan for dinner/beer & pool in the Glen Hotel, Newtonmore.

The Doughnut Queen blogged... *Manny set off up the Burma Road on mtb's to Geal Charn Mor. By the time he arrived at Slochd he was minus Peter P who had to turn back due to the sole coming off one of his cycling shoes. Then a fast road cycle to Coignafearn Old Lodge passing huge herds of deer cooling off in the Findhorn. He was able to cover most of the Carn na Saobhaidhe to Carn an Fhreiceadain area by mtb on tracks which aren't all on the map, though it still took longer than he anticipated, leaving no time to do the road cycle to Garva Bridge which will be the start for tomorrow.*

Archie & Sandra blogged... *Yet another sole lost on the Burma Road!*

Skipper Johns' 1ˢᵗ Mate Anne blogged... *Was this lost sole a former partner of some chips; perhaps a 'solo mio'; a sole attempt at punning or maybe just a lost soul in the wastelands of the Burma Road? Finlandia's crew is still following Manny's enterprise with interest and a lot of sympathy.*
The First Mate (Finlandia)

Day 40 Wednesday 3nd June - A Burning in Glen Roy
Foot 24 miles & 7,200ft, bike 18 miles (688ft), 5 Corbetts

Manny blogged... *Jeeezuz it was hot today!*
*The morning started cool enough, and early cloud gave the impression of good
conditions for a long 24 mile hill day. Not so. After an hour's 18 mile bike ride to
Garva Bridge, Brenda & I wandered up the first hill Meall na h-Airse and it got
progressively warmer until it was hot hot hot! There were fine views all around
but we had to part company, with Brenda going back to the van for chores and me
for the alleged easy option... four more Corbetts & 20 miles whilst running
through an oven.*

*I actually felt really strong running across the very rough ground that separates
the first hill from Gairbeinn, then Carn Chuilinn, though admittedly a lot of the
bogs and peat troughs were well on their way to total drought. In the bottom of
deep Glen Tarff, looking upstream I could see the shiny new dam of the ill-fated
Glen Doe hydro electric scheme, and I was careful not to drink from the water
running directly from that massive concrete construction site. The views from the
tops today were stunning with not so much haze as yesterday, and getting closer to
the west coast again gave very dramatic shading with layer upon layer of
mountains to try and identify - the Nevis group, Ardgour, Lochy Munros, Glen
Shiel, it went on... Then it all started to go badly wrong. I had a good descent west
towards the Corrieyairack track, but after pulling myself away from the
temptations of a swim in the river, I noticed I was the colour of a large Alvie
strawberry! For the first time I had forgotten to sun-cream-up before going out,
and I had paid the price big time! Running with burnt red legs through deep
heather is something exquisite indeed... I took a bad route choice to the main
track and then a nightmare 3 mile flogging across long grass, bog and tussocks to
get to Carn Dearg. Knackered, sore and crabbit. Some comfort eating and the fine
views kept me going though and the last top, another Carn Dearg, was only thirty
minutes away. The final drop into Glen Roy was hellish rough and I got messed up
in some steep gullies, another tired mistake.*

*I was glad to see the van, and Brenda was a superstar once more to have dinner
ready to eat when I arrived! Ahh, food galore, beers, pain killers and after-sun
cream – what else does one need after a day like that? Well, a couple of big
Glenlivet drams, courtesy of Finlay Binnie – Slàinte!*

Graham K blogged... *Aye the classic west of Scotland tan salmon pink then
flaky skin!*

Ian Charters blogged... *Well done Manny. Just wanted to let you know we are
with you every step of the way - OK maybe not every step but certainly every word
of the way.*

Days 40-41 Kingussie to The Great Glen

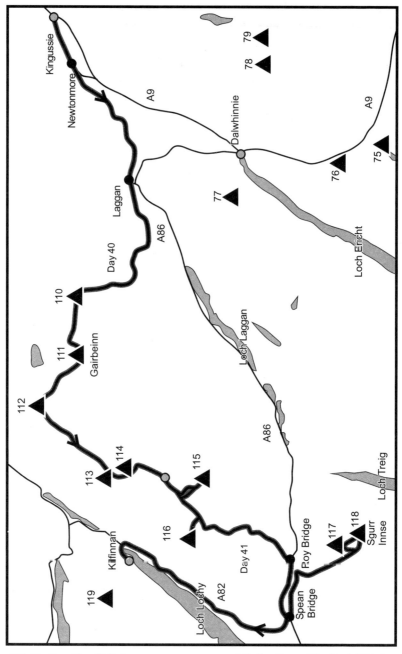

110. Meall na-Aisre (862m)

111. Gairbeinn (896m)

112. Carn a' Chuilinn (816m)

113. Carn Dearg (N) (817m)

114. Carn Dearg (S) (768m)

115. Carn Dearg (Glen Roy) (834m)

116. Beinn Iaruinn (800m)

117. Cruach Innse (857m)

118. Sgurr Innse (809m)

Stevie McLoone blogged... *you're going well Manny, - some people will do anything rather than go to their work!!!*

Day 41 Thursday 4th June - Glen Roy to Kilfinnan
Foot 10 miles & 5,873ft, bike 29 miles (7,96ft), mtb 9 miles (1,377ft),
4 Corbetts

I was just creaking out of bed with sunburnt skin stinging on my arms, legs and neck when we heard a car pull up outside. It was our local rag, the "Strathy", being delivered by our paperboy Archie, on his way to work in Fort William! After the usual scintillating read about the going's-on in Badenoch & Strathspey, Brenny joined me up the first hill of the day, yet another Carn Dearg – the third in a row! I noted how much fitter she had become in the last few weeks as we cruised to the top and enjoyed views across to the Nevis range. After an enjoyable trot down and a second large breakfast, I biked just a few miles down the glen before bashing up and down the extremely steep grassy side of Beinn Iaruinn. Although not as burning as yesterday it was still another hot day, and I was carefully clad in a long sleeved top and my cap with neck flap, with any remaining exposed skin slabbered in factor 60 sun cream just to be safe. Dot had rejoined us with fresh goodie supplies and her camera poised at every opportunity for a good shot.

It was an easy, relaxed ride downhill to Roy Bridge then Spean, before heading down the south bank of the River Spean to team up with Archie, who'd finally escaped from work. We rode our mtb's about 5 miles south, up into the Lairig Leacach at the east end of the Grey Corries. After we had dumped the bikes in the heather the climb up Cruach Innse was particularly enjoyable, choosing to take the craggiest, steepest route possible so that I could enjoy a wee bit of scrambling and rock hopping, while poor Archie followed on valiantly, with knocking knees and a squeaky bum! It needed some gentle persuasion to get him to join me for the second short climb up Sgurr Innse, but it worked and we were rewarded on both tops with fantastic views along the much bigger Munro range to the west. A rubbish, rough line off the Sgurr by me had us both muttering before we got back to the bikes, but it was quickly forgotten as the very fast downhill ride back to the van had our eyes watering!

Archie headed home to Boat of Garten happy whilst I pushed on with the road bike along Loch Lochy-side on the busy A82 to Laggan Locks, then hopped over the Caledonian Canal lock to Kilfinnan. At the road end turning circle I was getting showered and changed when a local dodgy character approached the van. Dot had pre-warned me about this notorious moron trying to extort money for parking on the public road, so I was ready for him. He knocked on the door and I threw it open with "*YES!*" Rather startled he mumbled about sometimes charging

£5 for overnight parking. I told him rather shortly that I wasn't overnight parking so that would be that! He muttered something again and began to slink away just as I slammed the door on him. If we hadn't been in a rush to catch last food orders at the Stronlossit Hotel back in Roy Bridge, I might have enjoyed the argument with the idiot, and possibly called the Police too.

Manny blogged... *That's me finished this side of the Great Glen!*
My apologies for any rubbish spelling and attention to detail, but my 14oz sirloin steak has just arrived at the table in the fine Stronlossit Hotel, with a superb pint of Atlas Brewery's Equinox, so must dash.
Love to all
Manny
XX

bob @ sandstone blogged... *You are fairly tucking away the grub, Manny. At least you won't wear away.*

6. NORTH OF THE GREAT GLEN
DAYS 42 – 70

Day 42 Friday 5th June - Four Seasons in 15 minutes!
Foot 24 miles & 9,611ft, bike 11 miles (495ft), mtb (3 miles (90ft), 3 Corbetts
Manny blogged... *Hi all, just catching up on a missing day with Don Reid acting as pacer and counselor at the same time - with a distinct turn back to colder weather and heavy showers my head took it bad, real bad. The heavy showers were easy to spot rolling in but this didn't help when they hit hard & cold. We set not a bad pace over rough ground and topped out Ben Tee in quick time, before a steep slippy drop west off the back and traversed over very coarse ground to reach Meall na h-Eilde, and a tough climb to lose the soft ground behind. Once on the ridge Don looked back to say something, but instead looked past me and exclaimed "OH FUCK!". I turned to follow his gaze and saw a jet black wall approaching us at high speed. Within minutes we were enveloped in thick clag, and hail started to fall in huge sweeps. The temperature plummeted and the hail changed to thick heavy snow, sticking to everything. After what seemed an eternity to my frozen toes, it cleared and as the next patch of blue sky whizzed over, the temperature soared again and the inch of lying snow vanished as quickly as it had fallen! After a thankfully brief nip up Geal Charn (rather appropriately translates as White Cairn!) we had a steady track descent back to the van on Loch Arkaig-side for a big feed and drinks supplied by Brenny & Dot as more heavy showers swept over. I opted to change the planned route a wee bit here by taking a longer road bike into Glen Loy for a slightly shorter but well-trodden climb up Beinn Bhan. Then followed a seemingly never-ending 6 mile hike to Meall a' Phubuill in howling winds and freezing cold! Testing our now exhausted patience, a quick map check revealed we almost missed the proper top and so had to plod down and up yet another wee lump to finally bag it. We sploshed our way down for a quick look into a favourite place of mine, Glensulaig bothy, before I mtb'd back to the van, while Don trotted out the final 3 miles, totally knackered. A great effort Don, we moved a lot better in the afternoon, thanks for keeping me going there. My Mum & Dad had arrived having ferried the boys to us from Newtonmore full of sweeties, fish & chips and fizzy pop!*

It's funny how time quickly eased the pain. I typed up that blog post just a few days after the event, but it conveniently does not mention what an utterly miserable sod I was that day, and how poor Don copped the lot. I was in a foul mood, short tempered and could hardly even speak to my companion, even though he was out in that pishy weather just to keep me going! I guess that a combination of built-up tiredness along with the breaking weather turned the screw, but on

Days 42-53 Lochaber, Ardgour, Knoydart

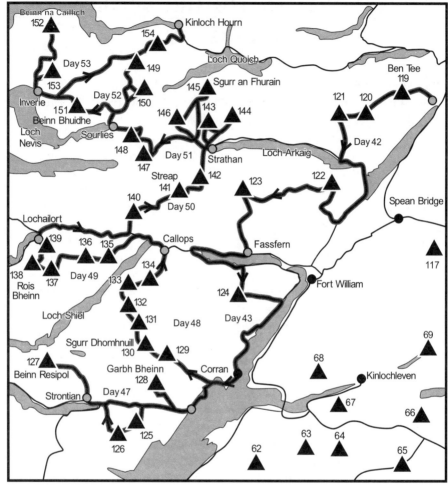

119. Ben Tee (904m)
120. Meall na h-Eilde (838m)
121. Geal Charn (804m)
122. Beinn Bhan (796m)
123. Meall a' Phubuill (774m)
124. Stob Coire a' Chearcaill (771m)
125. Creach Bheinn (853m)
126. Fuar Bheinn (766m)
127. Beinn Resipol (845m)
128. Garbh Bheinn (885m)
129. Beinn na h-Uamha (762m)
130. Sgurr Dhomhnuill (888m)
131. Carn na Nathrach (786m)
132. Stob a' Bhealach an Sgriodain (770m)
133. Sgurr Ghiubhsachain (849m)
134. Sgorr Craobh a' Chaorainn (775m)
135. Beinn Odhar Bheag (882m)
136. Beinn Mhic Cedidh (783m)

137. Sgurr na Ba Glaise (874m)
138. Rois-Bheinn (882m)
139. An Stac (814m)
140. Sgurr an Utha (796m)
141. Streap (909m)
142. Braigh nan Uamhachan (765m)
143. Fraoch Bheinn (858m)
144. Sgurr Mhurlagain (880m)
145. Sgurr an Fhuarain (901m)
146. Sgurr Cos na Breachd-laoigh (835m)
147. Carn Mor (829m)
148. Bidean a' Chabair (867m)
149. Sgurr a' Choire-bheithe (913m)
150. Ben Aden (887m)
151. Beinn Bhuidhe (855m)
152. Beinn na Caillich (785m)
153. Sgurr Coire Choinnichean (796m)
154. Sgurr nan Eugallt (894m)

several occasions that I was in that frame of mind, it was hard to focus on anything better... like the last week of stunning warm weather I had just enjoyed! On many days the mornings were hardest, but I reckon I really opted for that short solo biking diversion in order to get my head sorted, along with a massive lunch to put me back on track; thankfully Don hadn't told me to shove-it by then, because we had a much better afternoon's running, even in the grim weather. Thanks Don. I was still crabbit even when we got back to the van at Fassfern, where my Mum & Dad, the boys, Brenda and Dot, were all crammed inside, hiding from the man-eating clouds of midges. The heat inside was horrendous, steamy and stinking of fish & chips, and I think people bailed out pretty quickly when they saw how even-more grumpy I was getting! I really regret that now, because it was the only time my Mum made it along on the trip, but I reckon she was probably well used to me being grumpy by then!

Day 43 Saturday 6ᵗʰ June - Manny's Flying Circus comes to Strontian!
Foot 23.5 miles & 9,429ft, bike 30 miles (967ft), mtb 1 mile (zero ft), 4 Corbetts

Manny blogged... *It's the weekend again, so a large tribe of Westies had gathered by Loch Eil-side as I road biked around the west-end to start up Stob Coire a-Chearcaill across seemingly endless bog myrtle and soft ground. Before the top was conquered Donald Smith, Stevie Bell, Dave Rogers, Chris, Johnston, Ellie, JD and Don were all well spread out across the hill, with Shona Robertson and Brenda on van duties far below. I maybe lingered a bit too long on the windy top for photos & blethering, and got really cold before trotting off into Gleann Sron a' Chreagain, meeting Manuel & Duncan playing in a burn and the van by Loch Linnhe. A communal feeding frenzy ensued before I once more took to the road bike with a good easterly tail wind helping me along. I got a great surprise at the mouth of Cona Glen, Inverscaddle Bay, where Westies Dave "Snake" Riach and Steffan "Herr" Gorgas were lying asleep on the grassy road verge! Great company, they kept me going down into Ardgour, Steffan in particular tramping along on quite a clunky mtb that we nicknamed "The Panzer" and hauled up that last big hill – thanks for the beer Steff!*

After considerable faffing about which was the optimum route, we climbed one of my favourite hills, Creach Bheinn, with epic views up & down Loch Linnhe. A quick down & up to Fuar Bheinn on grassy trods then off towards Strontian, with Brenny having cleverly suggested that she would get JD to humf my mtb up a zig-ziggy track that seemed to go well up the hill. Great, that would save my once-again aching left leg from a hard jarring descent. After a very rough flog to find the track-end, I set off down on the bike with the gradient rapidly becoming much steeper and extremely loose! I had thankfully killed my speed by the first hairpin bend but as Ellie & Chris, who had ran on ahead, stepped aside and turned to let me pass, my front wheel turned right-angles in the gravel and I went straight over the bars Superman style! It all seemed to happen in super-slow-mo and only ended when I landed with an almighty crunch and a muffled, "Ouch, that hurt a bit". Chris had been just about to take a photo of me riding past, instead his mouth opened in stunned silence as I crashed out and he forgot to press the button, missing a great disaster photo! My left knee was completely mashed. Blood oozing from various scratches and feeling totally nauseous with the pain. I slowly got up and slumped back onto the bike and freewheeled cautiously down the rest of the hill back to the van, before a very painful mile to the Strontian shops.

My knee was swelling rapidly and hurt like hell, but with a good handful of various painkilling drugs and some more food I set off very slowly up Beinn Resipol with Stevie, Chris, Dave, Ellie, Brenny & Donald. Under such circumstances I would never normally have considered even trying it, but this was Chris's last Corbett which he had carefully factored in to completing during our journey. He had already made so much effort to help us out at every opportunity along the way, I had to at least try and get up with him. I took forever hobbling uphill in agony and was dreading the descent, unable to bend my knee! With a dram, tea & cake to celebrate his finale, the view from the summit to mark Chris's last Corbett was special. A low sun across Eigg and Rum; Harris & Skye in the distance; evening shadows cast over all the Ardgour hills and the length of Loch Shiel, WOW! Those are the nights you remember forever; unfortunately I will also forever remember it as the most painful, slow walks I have ever endured - five hours!! Stevie and Dave stayed to watch me hobble down, grinding my teeth in pain, while the others all ran down the hill at speed. At the road I picked up Donald's bike for a non-pedalling freewheel back to the shops, finally getting to the bottom around 11.30pm under a full moon.

We trundled off in the van to a wee lay-by just outside Strontian for the night. Utterly depressed and angry for such a stupid (but for me on a bike, predictable) mistake - very sore, food, beer, bed.

Not looking good all of a sudden!

Johnston's reminisced... *I don't think the full severity of the Superman-into-ditch mishap was immediately clear. I remember you arriving at the foot of the track looking pretty grumpy - no great surprise there. A long stop at the van ensued, time ticking on. The damage started to make itself known on the cycle down to Strontian. Further long wait at Strontian, with much banter from Stevie Bell as Dave Roger's rucsack hits the ground with a (flask) loud metallic clonk – I asked What's that?,"Stevie replied "That was the morale".*

Days 44, 45, 46 - 7th, 8th, 9th June - Bugger all and Beyond

After a restless night of pain and bad dreams I woke up and groaned. There were was absolutely no chance of a hill today. Just getting out of bed, with my leg as straight as a board and in sickening pain, was a battle. We drove back into Strontian to meet up with the gang in the wee cafe there, to break the news that at the very least there was going to have to be a time-out, possibly worse... maybe game over? I just didn't know the extent of the damage yet, but looking at my rugby ball kneecap it did not inspire confidence!

I could feel their disappointment. They had all been geared-up for the big seven hills of Ardgour, in stunning weather, and now it was off. We all comforted ourselves in huge fried breakfasts, before they wished me luck with the pending diagnosis, and all headed off up Garbh Bheinn by way of consolation.

Manuel and Duncan were not too upset – they got the whole morning to play on the beach at Inversanda Bay, without having to be dragged away to a next check point! I sat on a deck chair, eating, drinking beer and pondering.

After a few hours chilling out we drove up to Fort Bill to pay a visit to the Belford Hospital, and after some prodding the Doc confirmed (without an x-ray) that nothing was broken, but see a physio asap, which I already knew. So we trundled back to Badenoch for an emergency appointment with Alison Robb once again – at least the knee had taken my mind off the tendonitis on the other leg! Ali said ice, beer, massage, beer, drugs, beer, compression, beer... and keep repeating – ok, she didn't suggest the beer, but it was absolutely essential for morale and extra carbs! Crucially, Ali didn't think I was finished off just yet, but needed at least a few more days of complete rest and to follow her treatment to the letter. A glimmer of hope...?

We made a surprise visit to Sandra & Archie in Boat of Garten, and it was certainly a shock when they saw the massive strapping on my knee! After yet more life-giving beer, we headed back to all the comforts of our building-site home and an uncomfortable night on a mattress on the floor – we would retreat to Glen Feshie in our cumfy van the next night! Archie completed a strangely memorable day by posting a blog update, with some very nifty photo-shop decals on our camper van, now turned into a fine ambulance!

Two more full days of rest and Ali's treatments were definitely doing the job. The swelling was receding fast, although I wasn't risking any form of trial until I had to. I knew from past experience of other ultra long distance routes that my body would be in over-drive to repair itself. I don't know the science of it, metabolism and all that stuff, but I do know that when you are as super-fit as I was then, the body can deal with otherwise crippling problems and recover incredibly quickly – I was banking on it! However three days off was now enough for my head – I knew I had to try again tomorrow or it really was all over and the constant messages of support willed me forward.

Graham K blogged... *If I learnt one thing in that sandy madness (Marathon de Sable) I did last year, it was that when it really hurts ...take drugs. If the pain continues then take more (or better ones if anyone has any). Get sorted and get back tae it.*

Charlie blogged... *Graham, so true - you can't beat basic drugs for easing the strife. A huge coffee to get you going in the morning, then lots of aspirin / ibuprofen to try and keep the niggles at bay during the day, and then God's own medicine of a beer or two at night, as a relaxant and anaesthetic...*

Don blogged... *Hi Manny, look on the bright side, if your finish is delayed by a couple of days, Elma and I can council you up Ben Loyal. Stay strong and focused. It also gives Brenda a break from playing tea lady to Westies (she's the real star here!) see you in the far North.*

Swaz blogged... *Hang in there, Man-power - try to look at the enforced rest as breathing space allowing everything to recharge. Won't be long...*

Adrian Davis blogged... *Hoping to get out and join you again start of next week for a day or two so let me know where you are and I'll bring whatever appendages, bandages or herbages you need, all legal of course. All the best and remember the hot and cold tub philosophy. If it hurts freeze it! Then warm it up again. Go*

Physio, Alison Robb's account... *Oh Dear! Brenda had just phoned from the West. Manny and his bike had had another parting of their ways and he'd hurt his knee- pretty badly it would seem, and could they drive over and see if I could help? He was learning though; he'd been to the Belford to get checked over and apparently two Doctors had had a look and were sure it was just soft tissue. That was good news...wasn't it??!*

I felt a great expectation coming on and it was mildly concerning for two reasons. Firstly, he wouldn't be coming all this way if it wasn't pretty serious, and secondly, I knew for a fact that he was running out of precious time. How fast could this be fixed? When I thought about it, I knew better than to doubt him finishing for even a second. He would crawl it if he had to.

A few hours later, in they both came, Brenda looking fit and tanned and absolutely great, Manny looking like a skinned rabbit with an absolutely massively swollen, inflamed, grazed and angry left knee.

I caught up with the craic, and it was all really impressive - they'd been doing really well. His Tendinitis had settled and boy he could have done with staying on that bike! But, hey ho- these things happen.

After gathering all the history and examining the knee, I managed to satisfy myself that he'd not torn any tendons or ligaments and that the joint was stable (not easy or entirely conclusive I must add, what with all that swelling about), and I was relieved. The high velocity impact on his knee though had resulted in horrible bruising and a lot of inflammation and fluid, as well as skin grazing. He was finding it difficult to move it or take his full weight on it.

First priority was to get the swelling down or the knee was just not going to function, so after some tissue work and electrotherapy, specific exercises to try and get the appropriate muscles firing again and to help reduce swelling, I opted for a good old fashioned compression bandage. My reasons for this were two-fold; it would help reduce swelling, but also stop him using it at all until I saw him the next day. I taught Brenda how to reapply it so he could ice regularly, and away they went with the leg looking four times the normal size and Manny feeling like a proper invalid!

A lot of the conversation we had been having was on the topic of time. He was quickly running out of leave from work and would need to ask for a bit more time off, and so, bearing in mind this is Manny we are talking about, when he arrived back the next day, I wasn't entirely surprised when he suggested starting again later that day!!! "Absolutely no way!" was my response. I mean there's crazy and there's CRAZY!!! I managed to convince him to give it another day, as even 24 hours at this stage makes a difference, and even Manny realised the importance here.

On his arrival the next day he proudly demonstrated the improvement in his flexion and extension and the fact that he could weight bear with the help from his walking sticks. I resigned myself to the fact that he was going to do a hill that day, as it was make or break time and he needed to go now if he was going to finish this adventure. I gathered some rolls of tape, showed Brenda how to strap up his knee cap, and off they went to Ardgour to do a single hill.

I crossed my fingers for them-they needed a bit of luck on their side now.

No-one seemed to have any doubt that I would get going again, but I did opt to avoid doing a single hill later that day and instead accepted putting it off until the following day.

Day 47 Wednesday 10th June - Still Game
Foot 5 miles & 3,023ft, bike 9 miles (360ft), 1 Corbett

Manny blogged... *Well, hello again in the Blogosphere.*
Rumours of my final demise are unfounded, (only just) after all it's only pain – it will stop eventually... It's been an interesting three days. Physio, sleep, drugs, physio, eat, physio, ice, physio... and put beer between all of those items.

Me and bikes never did get on very well and it's no surprise that a stupid mistake on my mtb nearly cost me the whole run. Early indications seem to imply large and painful bruising to the whole left patella, and hopefully nothing more sinister underneath.

After the wonderful Alison Robb of Nethybridge worked on my leg for three sessions and with lots of ice and rest, I very tentatively got on my road bike this morning in Strontian, with clubmate The Right Horrible Al Campbell as my domestique. It was make or break as I turned the pedals for the first time, and thankfully the knee was not too painful. The next test was 2 miles later on the first climb in the road but even under stress the joint held its own, albeit very slowly and in the small gear rings. After warming up, we got a steady crawl up the hill and enjoyed the whizz down the far side to the east foot of Garbh Bheinn, one of my favourite Scottish mountains.

The weather looked good with broken high clouds, and with the good company of Brenda, Big Al, Isobel Coombs, Charlie Campbell and his sister June, with their indomitable pooch Stella as back-up, we enjoyed a slow but steady climb up the steep slopes with only one small shower, but otherwise warm all the way up. My defection to the use of walking poles or "cheating sticks" is only temporary, whilst the knee (hopefully) settles down again, but there is no doubt they helped take the weight off on the way up, but more importantly on the way down. My biggest worry about using sticks is that they make me go so slow it even made Al Campbell look fast! It was fantastic to get the views of those spectacular northern crags and then from the summit for lunch. A slow but steady stick-assisted descent got us back to the van with the knee sore but not progressively so. Then it was into Loch Linnhe for twenty minutes to chill the legs down whilst Al & Isobel took the full plunge!! Tea, buns & beer were enjoyed in the van away from the ever increasing midge population before the usual frustrations of trying to blog-on with poor connection signal.

Tomorrow I plan to try and get back into the run properly again by doing the other six tops to the north, leading to Callop – I reckon my knee only needs a bit of exercise now...

Don & Elma blogged... *Great to hear you're on the move again Manny, we were starting to miss your entertaining daily blog.*

Johnston blogged... *Great stuff, Manny! Hope tomorrow goes well.*

Chris blogged... *Manny, great to hear you are back out on the hill. You've had us all worried. Good luck with that tough set of 6 tomorrow.*

The Doughnut Queen blogged... *Manny you have gone to extraordinary lengths to ensure you retain the "Stabilisers" for another year. (Ed. My local mountain biking group have a trophy, the "Golden Stabilisers" awarded annually to the year's winning rider "for outstanding recklessness and dynamic instability") Graham Hall must have assumed a broken collar bone was enough to take them away from you! Good luck today and don't do anything daft (well dafter than usual).*

Malcolm Paterson blogged... *That's brilliant news, Manny. Hope you can slowly build back up to full strength, taking all the time you need - "Pole, Pole" as they would say on Kilimanjaro (or An Caisteal!).*

Skipper John said... *Well done Manny - glad to see you are back - Finlandia is at Loch Torridon - making her way to Loch Erribol to give you a lift back in style when you finish (Stugeron will be provided)*

Day 48 Thursday 11ᵗʰ June - Manny Hits a Sweet 6!
Foot 17 miles & 9,427ft, mtb 7 miles (276ft), 6 Corbetts

Manny blogged... *And so came to an end one of the finest days on the hills I ever had.*

Morning was beautiful once again and with my stiff knee I very gently cycled down the road and into Glen Gour to be met by a stunning view down the mirror calm loch and the first of the day's hills, Beinn na h-Uamha. I dropped the bike after a few miles on the rough footpath to be picked up later by Charlie and June. With my poles I started up the first big climb, taking it very slowly to let my legs warm up and assess the pain level in my knee. It was sore, but did not get worse as I continued upwards, although the breakfast of ibuprofen and paracetamol probably helped mask it considerably. There were a few dark clouds scudding about with just an occasional light shower, but not even worth stopping to put on a waterproof. The first steep descent needed concentration to get a good poling technique working. I quickly established that it was worth an extra bit of faffing about to alter the stick lengths each time I moved up or down. My skinny wee arms were aching from the unknown effort and I had to learn to relax and accept that I couldn't take most my body weight off my legs, just easing some of it off would do.

Once in the groove though I moved steadily over Sgurr Dhomhnuill and Carn na Nathrach before a huge, steep drop into the upper reaches of Glen Hurich at Mam Beathaig. Here forestry planting had chewed the ground into a hideously rough hell; fenced off and ungrazed for years the ground had now over-grown into a man-eating trap. I floundered about for ages trying to escape by climbing directly up the far side, but there was little respite before the 600m contour, by which time I was totally knackered. In the sun I took a time out by a wee burn and had a good feed, topping up on drugs.

Revived, I made short work of Stob a' Bhealach an Sgriodain and then enjoyed a lovely high ridge traverse above Loch Shiel for a few miles around to Sgurr Ghiubhsachain. I was buzzing now – I knew I had cracked the most important and committing day so far, and soaked up the scenery with adrenaline blocking any tiredness or pain. As I moved over to the sixth and final top of Sgorr Craobh a' Chaorainn the view south back to the day's first hill was incredible, having covered the 17 miles and 9,500ft of ascent in just ten hours, considering my wrecked knee.

I sat at the big summit cairn drinking in the evening scene over Glenfinnan and looking across to tomorrow's hills, when Brenda's head popped above the horizon! This was really quite adventurous for her as navigation is not one of her strong points, but as it was a lovely day so she just went for it and I was delighted she had made it up before I had left – we could so easily have missed each other! We trotted north off the hill together to pick up a horrendous new track, unsympathetically butchered into the hillside, for servicing a new mini-hydro scheme. Charlie met us there with my mtb to allow me an easy free-wheel back to the van at Callop, bang on 8pm.

A dash for a bar meal in Fort William was in vain as everywhere oddly seemed to have stopped serving before 9pm, so we made a successful late bid for the Stronlossit Inn at Roy Bridge, where I devoured the tried and tested huge steak platter, washed down with copious fine ales. We headed back to Callop to park-up for the night and a well earned night-cap.

Game on again, phew!

Archie & Sandra blogged... *Excellent job today, glad to hear the skint knee is still working. As I said before you dived off your bike, you're obviously getting into your stride. Crank it up and make the most of the good days, you're a lot stronger than you give yourself credit for. But caw canny on the mountain bike, you've always been rubbish on that (downhill anyway).*

Charlie Coull blogged... *Manny, good to see you on the go again. Enjoying the blogs.*

bob @ sandstone blogged... *How I envy you this big Ardgour day. Not that I'm fit enough to tackle it! With luck I will wave to you as you swoosh past the Little Wyvis cairn. Your nautical pal, John Allen, did a great gig at the Nairn Book and Arts Festival yesterday.*

Luke blogged... *Hey Manny, Really glad to hear you are back in action. Hopefully you'll enjoy another classic day on the Rois Bheinn ridge. Keep going.*

Tom Smith blogged... *Some boy Manny, keep it lit!*

Jason blogged... *Tis is an epic read Manny and you sound like it is still fun not just a miserable challenge which is amazing to hold on to. Keep up the good work, you are so near.*

Day 49 Friday 12th June - Moidart
Foot 15 miles & 8,165ft, bike 5 miles (462ft), 5 Corbetts

Originally I had planned to link today's first two hills by dropping north to Loch Eilt-side, then a 6 mile road bike to access the Rois Bheinn three. It was Luke Arnott who had tipped me off about the Druim Fiaclach ridge which is a bit longer on foot, but the going is on lovely short grass and saves a considerable amount of height loss. So after a very slow start and a 5 mile morning warm up on the road bike from Callop, it was off up the steep bracken covered side of Beinn Odhar Mhor. After about a thousand feet of climbing in the early hot sun, I heard a familiar and favourite sound in the distance and getting closer... chuff, chuff, chuff... the sounds echoing off the walls of the surrounding glens made for the type of sound effects that Harry Potter could only dream of! By the time the Hogwarts Express (aka The Jacobite) pulled into view at the foot of the hill, the sound was an incredible cacophony of chuffing steam and a screaming whistle. It was a magnificent visual and audio spectacle! At the top something didn't fit in... a check of the map told me the Corbett summit was the neighbouring top of Beinn Odhar Bheag, about a mile to the south. The views from there were superb: with Ben Nevis and it's large summer snow patches clinging on away to the east; the deep blue of Loch Shiel to the south, with Beinn Resipol prominent; Rum and Eigg glittering in the sun to the west; and daunting Knoydart waiting for me to the north. It was now a blistering hot afternoon and I was glad to be staying high in the slight breeze.

A brief trot north-west to Bealach a' Choire Bhuidhe and I passed a couple of silent walkers coming off my next target, Beinn Mhic Cedidh. Luke's advice was spot on; from here it was obvious to keep the height of the next ridge, along to the tight wee knot of three Corbetts of Rois-Bheinn. A soaring Golden Eagle and a small herd of red deer, disturbed from wallowing in a mud hole, kept me interested in my close surroundings. I took on a load of water before starting along the ridge, which isn't that long but it was very warm, so much so that I took the opportunity of a half hours' snooze in the warm grass, bliss. It's days like this that set hill running apart from any other sport – it's not just about the effort and hard work to attain a top or the reckless descents, but it's the deafening silence with epic views all around; the wildlife close up in its natural habitat; being able to cover so much ground quickly and lightweight, with minimal impact; ultimately total escapism, that wonderful feeling of solitude in a truly wild place.

Despite my painful knee slowing me down, I still felt in fantastic form and steadily knocked off Sgurr na Ba Glaise, Rois-Bheinn and finally headed for An Stac. I could see several figures on the top and correctly guessed it would be Brenda, Charlie and June, with poor old Stella puffing away lying on the grass. We enjoyed a sociable walk off to the vans at Inverailort, then parked up at the roadside of the A861 overlooking the Sound of Arisaig. We scoffed down another brilliant Brenda dinner in the van and were washing it down with a few Cairngorm ales as the most incredible sunset unfolded across the Sound. I lowered myself into the sea to chill my legs as the sun dropped low. It first back-lit some low cloud bright gold; then as it dropped further, up-lit the clouds to a fireball of red, reflected perfectly off the sea. The colour intensity increased over half an hour, with Skye and Arisaig swathed in crimson as we all watched silently with a beer in hand - an unforgettable moment of beauty.

Day 50 Saturday 13th June - Loch Eilt to Glen Dessary
Foot 21 miles & 11,510ft, bike 8 miles (460ft), mtb 2 miles (98ft), 5 Corbetts

The day started badly as I reversed the van into an earth bank and took a lump out of the rear bumper. Brenda was mildly amused after all the lecturing I had given her about how to be careful when manoeuvring the van!

The good weather couldn't last forever and it was back to dreich for the 8 mile bike ride past Loch Eilt and the first big slow climb of the day, into wet clag. In the thick mist I hit the summit of Sgurr an Utha without a problem, pausing only for a token photo of the rocky cairn, before plunging off the north side into Glen Donn, leading east to Glenfinnan Lodge. About halfway down the steep wet slope I rounded a large rock and there lying before me was a new-born deer calf. Still wet with afterbirth and utterly helpless lying in the heather, there was no sign of Mum, the noise of me approaching perhaps having scared her off? Very apt that I find such a beautiful thing on Sgurr an Utha – "hill of the udder", but I was careful not to touch the wee babe in case I scented it, causing it to be rejected by the mother on her return. I stayed only a minute to take a photo and short video shot before running down and away, hopefully for Mum to return soon after.

At the bottom of the glen I popped my head into Corryhully bothy, a new one for me, and was surprised to find it has electricity with a 50p meter! Brilliant – I must come back here with a lamp and kettle, just for the novelty value! Jogging steadily and feeling good after a big lunch, I startled a group of Munro-bound walkers when I ran up behind them, then shot off up the very steep sides of Streap – also appropriately named as "the climbing hill" - and back into the mist, now thankfully just starting to break up. I have run Streap on several occasions in the past and it's a smashing hill, with lovely ridges and scrambling rocks giving it great character and fantastic views, but unfortunately not today.

A quick trot over the subsidiary top of Streap Comhlaidh and I was descending with a fine view of my next Corbett, Braigh nan Uamhachan, and it's bigger Munro cousin, Gulvain, towering behind. I probably pushed too hard uphill and was feeling a bit done-in at the top, but cheery enough to have been travelling so well with the poles now second nature, and working well for my gammy knee. I paused at the summit, feeling a marked decrease in temperature and increase in the wind from behind, and a glance told me I was in for a pasting by a fast approaching black cloud. A thump of thunder was the starter's gun and I tore off down the grassy hill as fast as was sensible - I really don't like being the only thing sticking up when there's lightning about! Sure enough, within a few minutes I was absolutely clobbered by an enormous hail shower, with thunder and lightning blasting around me. After a nervous ten minutes the hail changed to freezing heavy rain and, sopping wet, I crossed Glean Camgharaidh, dropping towards Strathan at the very remote west end of Loch Arkaig. Brenda had thoughtfully put my mtb out for me; it was only a mile from the van, but I was very grateful for it now I was tired, soaked and frozen. I was glad to get into the warm van to get changed and get a huge hot pasta feed in me. I enjoyed lounging for a long while, having a snooze and recharging my batteries a bit, before seeing the evening weather was improving all the time and deciding that I ought to be out doing another couple of tops.

I biked the half mile of tar along to the start of the hill track up Dearg Allt, and enjoyed a leisurely plod up the south ridge of Fraoch Bheinn in the evening sunshine. It was lovely having no time pressure and no deadlines to get back to the van, just soaking up the scenery looking into the heart of Knoydart. Even with some ominous black clouds still scudding about the landscape, I was shirtless and had forgotten the earlier soakings. I dropped directly east to the bealach leading to Sgurr Mhurlagain, and on the way across I spotted a couple of tiny figures on the opposite skyline. Whoever they were, I guessed that they had to be out looking for me, so headed for them as they climbed. As I got closer I saw it was Chris and Ellie. They explained they had come up north to combine the long Lochy Munros hill race, taking place earlier in the day at the opposite end of Loch Arkaig, along with a few Corbetts – a real bonus for me as I hadn't been expecting company. We blethered as we climbed in the warm sun and a great view opened up a long way down Loch Arkaig. A few photos at the top and the dark clouds to the south produced a lovely rainbow over the top of the mornings' Glenfinnan hills. We enjoyed a soft grassy descent back to the track then returned to the van for dinner and some fine Glenfinnan Ales, courtesy of the Lochy Munros race sponsors, to finish a very enjoyable five Corbett day.

Day 51 Sunday 14ᵗʰ June - Sourlies
Foot 19 miles & 10,249ft, mtb 6 miles (322ft), 4 Corbetts

There was a big day ahead, and having Chris around made sure I was up and out by 8am in the cool morning mist that hung in layers through Glendessarry. I biked the track to Glendessary Lodge gates before taking to the walking poles up and through Feith a' Chicheanais, with Chris and Ellie keeping me good pace. By the time we reached the River Kingie at 9.30am the temperature had soared and we were taking on plenty of water and stripping off layers of Helly. We aimed at the bealach separating the Munro of Sgurr Mor and the Corbett, Sgurr an Fhuarain. The grassy gradient was brutally steep going, 500m of climb in a little over a vertical kilometre. Once at the bealach we were on a well worn Munro-motorway and the trot to the high 901m top was a doddle, with the wild west-coast views made even more dramatic by the fast dissolving morning mist, clinging vainly to the sides of only the highest tops and ridges. Our traversing descent back into Glen Kingie was fast on soft steep grass, but instantly reversed for another very steep climb up a rocky chute to attain the short west ridge of Sgurr Cos na Breachd-laoidh. The vistas here were breathtaking, and in particular my next two Corbetts Carn Mor and Bidean a' Chabair, on the edge of Knoydart, where I wouldn't be standing until nearly ten hours later! While I paused for a loo stop, Chris and Ellie ran on ahead taking a much faster line off the hill back to the lodge while I had the relief of my mtb, and all arrived back at the van at the same time. There were a few cleggs flying about delivering their painful bites with only a moments warning, making lingering in the sun quite uncomfortable. It had been great having company over these remote hills, and after lunch we wished Chris and Ellie well on their return to Glasgow.

I had to concentrate on packing for a couple of days and nights in Knoydart, and knew I was fast running short of time to complete the next two hills in daylight. At 6pm I set off again on the mtb to the cottage at Upper Glendessarry, where Brenda met me to take the bike back out as I continued on foot. Brenda had some important logistics to arrange once she got out the glen and into a mobile signal. I had at the last minute decided that a bike would be very useful around Knoydart, and we were hoping Davy Duncan might be able to oblige at such late notice? This was also the only section of the whole trip where I would need to stay away from the van overnight, carrying everything I needed for two days in my Kimmsac, and the gammy knee appeared to be coping with the extra weight with no pain. I trudged on upwards and got the top of Carn Mor just as a low flying black cloud hit the hill and turned to freezing rain which was a bit of a shock! I took a few quick photos then bailed out on a really long, rough and steep drop north, before once again facing an immediate huge and steep re-ascent of over 2,200ft. At least the rain had stopped and I climbed well, hitting the summit of Bidean a' Chabair just after 10pm, in time to watch a spectacular sunset over Knoydart with mist blowing up out the corries, giving the scene a ghostly atmosphere. I had to move quickly now in the dying light, but in my haste I took a dire direct line down through steep, wet crags and too bloody hairy in places! All the time floundering about there I knew I ought to have taken the extra time to climb over the small subsidiary top of Sgurr na h-Aide and descend by the safe grassy slopes of Coire Dubh. Twit.

In the pitch black I eventually sprackled into Sourlies bothy about 11.30pm, surprising seven resident walkers from their slumber. They were good enough to stick a brew on for me straight away whilst I got unpacked and dinner prepared. Another made my night by pouring a huge dram into my cup! They naturally asked what I had done and where I had come from at this time of night, and when I told them the day's route they topped up my dram! Perhaps I should have told them about the whole Corbetts Round to date and kept the bottle?! After 1am and a bit of good craic by the fire with a couple of the guys, I wedged in between two of them on the wooden sleeping platform and fell into an all too brief coma.

Day 52 Monday 15th June - Into Knoydart
Foot 21 miles & 9,094ft, mtb 2 miles (262ft), 3 Corbetts

God, is it time to get up already...

In the gloom of the bothy, the fire was already sparking into life courtesy of Mike Pratt, a regular bothy goer whom I remember being described as a "bothy vagrant" and I had met at a few remote bothies in the past. Not a man of many words at the best of times, his only response to his billycan of porage oats spilling into the fire was "FUCK!" ...I bit my lip and quietly prepared my grub safely by gas burner on the table. Even the table itself bore many scars of cooking disasters over the years. One incident I recall from a previous visit was when an English couple from London, complete with entirely brand-new kit, misfired their petrol stove and it exploded all over the table, the whole surface ablaze before we doused it out! Standard high carb, lightweight bothy fodder for me consists of a big bowl of muesli, mixed into a pint of Birds powder custard, with a couple of pints of sweet tea and perhaps a lump of Genoa cake.

And so it was with creaking guts that I bid farewell to the other bothiers and set off along the stony shoreline of Loch Nevis and across the tidal flats to negotiate the rickety wire bridge at the ruin of Carnoch. Here I changed the original order of play, deciding to do Sgurr a' Choire-bheithe before Ben Aden. I hid most of my pack's heavier contents in the long grass then jogged on with just the bare essentials for the hill. Running the first couple of miles up the bank of the River Carnach in quick time, I then climbed steeply to gain Mam Unndalain, then steeply again onto the summit ridge to Sgurr Choire-bheithe - only a single metre short of the Munro barrier of 914m. It was only long after the trip had finished that I discovered one of my Westies clubmates, Chris Osmond, hoping to surprise me, had completed this as his final Corbett on 6th June - my original schedule date which was sadly now nine days adrift. After taking in the views down to Barrisdale, Ladhar Bheinn and Loch Quoich, I descended 2,500ft into the glen and had an extended break with my aching feet soaking in the young River Carnach. Although the weather was fine and the scenery still beautiful, I was feeling really down in the dumps here; I was very tired and made the mistake of concentrating on how far I still had to go that day. However, I knew there was no choice in the matter - like it or not, I had to get the finger out and get on with it. I had a scoff and plenty of water, and even closed my eyes for twenty minutes lying back in the sun, opening them only at the sound of faint scampering. I looked across to the other bank only two metres away, and there was stoat making his way along, quite happily out in the open and watching me, probably thinking I closely resembled a corpse, therefore no threat!

I got my shoes on again and headed slowly up Ben Aden, "hill of the face" - and mine was scunnered. I passed over the top with a few more photos and took my time on the descent as my knee had started to hurt once more. I popped a few pain killing pills and trotted back to my hidden gear at Carnoch for a brew-up with a hot salty packet soup and a comforting feed. I felt better and was off again, up the well worn stalkers path zigzagging 1,800ft to the top of Mam Meadail, then west for 2 miles along the lumpy ridge leading to Beinn Bhuidhe, and my spirits soared once more. The last hill of the day, stunning views out to Eigg, Rum and Skye, and with a confirmation text from Brenda – my bike was already waiting at the bottom and Davy waiting for me in Inverie! I was really chuffed the last minute logistics had worked out and I picked my way off the hill via a new woodland plantation, collecting up my bike at the pre-arranged point. I was glad to get off my feet for the last 2 miles into Inverie and headed straight to the Old Forge Inn for a couple of pints! No sign of Davy there, so after a quick call to Brenda to check in, I headed to the five-star Old Byre Lodge Bunkhouse which was strangely almost empty, other than Davy waiting on me. After a shower we wandered back to the pub for dinner, but whilst the ale was very good, the food was quite expensive and not as plentiful as I had hoped, and I still felt a bit peckish as we headed to bed after a few more pints. I had found today much harder than the previous few and was glad to get to bed early.

Davy reminisced... *The phone goes, it's Brenda... "Can you help out?" – no problem – "Good, I need you to go to Inverie" – never heard of it, where is it – "It's out on the west coast, just above Mallaig"...I'm beginning to have reservations about this...I don't see a road into there Brenda? – "There isn't one; you have to take the ferry from Mallaig!"*

Once I had dropped Manny's bike at the designated spot I went for a donder in the hills and ended up doing the two Munros to the east, Meall Buidhe and Luinne Bheinn. Next morning Manny gave me £30 to square up the bunkhouse, then on reflection made it £40, very generous I thought. Then I raided the fridge for other people's leftovers and found a couple of slices of bread – we left so early the shop wasn't even open. I trailed Manny on his bike and ran the Munro, Ladhar Bheinn, then dropped down to our meeting point at Loch an Dubh Lochain. Thank goodness for those pieces of bread – it was all I had all day! Heading back, the bunkhouse lady said "£28" – that wasn't bad I thought as I handed her £30, but she stood her ground and said "Each"!! I was shocked and she obviously saw it in my face but held out her hand for the money just the same - that was extortionate!

Brenda blogged... *I did not tell him until last night but the bunkhouse was £30pppn, he just about had a heart attack (no wonder it was empty!)*

Day 53 Tuesday 16th June - Knoydart to Kinloch Hourn
Foot 21 miles & 9,364ft, mtb 12 miles (748ft), 3 Corbetts

Brenda blogged... *Another 3 hills done - Beinn na Caillich, Sgurr Coire Choinnichean & Sgurr nan Eugallt. Another stunning day. I set off from Kingussie around midday to give enough time to drive down to Kinloch Hourn. It was a nice drive around to meet Manny, although I was not at the exact location.... I had stopped about a mile too early; I had thought I was in the right spot, so as you can guess I was not too popular when he came off the hill... I think he had visions that I had gone off the road or pranged the van, but once I served him with steak pie & beer it was fine and he came out of his strop. Ken & Claire from Lochaber met with Davy in Fort William to hand over the bike and his belongings before they headed up to meet me at Kinloch Hourn. Thanks to Davy, Ken & Claire for helping out over the last couple of days. It was a very windy night and he was not looking forward to another long day.*

I had a brilliant day compared to yesterday. After a good breakfast, the bike saved me an awful lot of footwork (12 miles all in) on the vehicle track out to Beinn na Caillich. The weather was great and I was feeling frisky again, whizzing out to the foot of the hill, a neighbour of my favourite Munro, spectacular Ladhar Bheinn. Running past a busy Scout camp at Easan Buidhe, I whizzed up and down easily in under an hour, but still had time to enjoy the view and take a few photos on my erratic camera, now in its slow death throws - too many dookings in the rain were taking their toll on the electronics, so dates and times were no longer dependable which was/still is annoying.

Returning by the same track I dismounted at the edge of the forest above Inverie and blasted up Sgurr Coire Choinnichean, dominating the village below with a huge deep slash of a gorge on its western side and the fabulous looking ridge of Aonach Sgoilte, leading towards Stob a' Chearcaill and Mam Barrisdale – my original on-foot plan. Vowing to return one day to do the ridge, I trotted back to my steed and rode into Inverie for an ice cream and Coke, sitting on the pier soaking up the atmosphere, ahhh...

Another four miles and I was at the end of Loch an Dubh-Lochan where Davy was waiting in the sun to ride my bike back to the ferry, and on to the mainland. I was indebted once again for his help in making all these logistics work. As most Scottish hill runners know, Davy very rarely misses any race, and there was a midweek Dog & Dun Championship race, Den Sheann in Strathyre, the following night, so he was keen not to miss the boat back as there wasn't another for a few days! He still had to drop the bike in Fort William for immediate courier by Ken & Clare Rumgay on to Brenda at Kinloch Hourn the same day – look at a map for that journey! I thanked him yet again and wished him well for the race.

I still had 11 miles with a big Corbett to go and it was now sweltering. I slabbered on some suncream as I took in the view from Mam Barrisdale, before trundling down the other side and cutting the path corner at the White House, into Glen Barrisdale. I checked the watch and was well ahead of time, so took a long break by the river to enjoy a refreshing skinny-dip in a deep pool, and dried off lying in the grass. I was very weary but happy as I climbed the final steep grassy slopes of Sgurr nan Eugallt, now with a chilly breeze, on the final ridge section to the round trig point. I ate everything I had left knowing the van was waiting below.

Elated with such a great long day, completing tricky Knoydart and an early finish, I ran down the brilliant sweeping stalkers path whooping out loud, shouting "WESTIES" and whistling hard into the glen below, thinking Brenda would hear me coming from miles away. I got to the road... no van. Bugger. We had reccied this point before the trip, so Brenda knew exactly where to wait – a huge, flat lay-by and small plantation above the Loch Coire Subh, the old ruined cottage of Coiresubh and the obvious stalkers path coming off the hill, easy...? I knew she wasn't short of time, so I could only guess that she had thought I had already passed through early and perhaps gone down to the car park at Kinloch Hourn? Slightly deflated I left a marker in the middle of the road in case she turned up after me, and trudged the mile and 500ft down the steep tarmac to the road-end at sea level... shit, still no van! Aargh! Hanging about for half an hour watching a tame red deer chewing grass only a few feet away, I was starting to get eaten alive by midges; bollocks, back up the hill again – wait, I hear a van coming!.. no, it's only a bloody delivery van - out here?!! Dragging back up the hill again there was still no van at the path; two options – she has crashed the van, in which case I am totally screwed in the middle of nowhere or, check the map – no... no, she couldn't possibly have mistaken that other tiny little lochan a mile up the road for the place to stop, surely? I could see the whole road winding above me except for one hidden corner, so plodded up the hill, now totally knackered and starving. "Fuck, fuck, fuck!!!", echoed off the glen walls! There it was, in a crappy lay-by on a steep slope that was nothing like what we reccied just a few months ago! I had been on the go for nearly two extra hours now and was totally fuming, verging mostly on the side of totally unreasonable! Brenda looked very sheepish as she spotted me and came out the back door... "What the fuck are you doing *here*?!" I raged from a few hundred metres away! As I cursed and spat my dummy out, Ken and Clare Rumgay stepped out of the van looking somewhat horrified at the scene! It dawned on me that they had driven a very long way from Kinlochleven, via Fort William, to bring my mtb back, and still had the drive back to face so I tried to change my tune, impolitely mumbling thanks whilst still boiling over, and went to hide in the van. Wisely, they made their polite excuses and retreated rapidly in their car. I couldn't speak - from tired, hungry, frustrated anger.

Brenny, initially upset and overwhelmingly apologetic for the simple mistake, took it in her stride to wear me down, and returned me to earth with the things closest to my heart – steak pie and beer. Don't you just love her! Common sense, calm and real ale prevailing once more, I had to acknowledge that it was the only really bad mistake in nearly two months, and was entirely understandable for someone unfamiliar with these remote west coast roads, or map reading; and of course it could have been much worse, it might have been raining!

There were no more mistakes!

Day 54 Wednesday 17ᵗʰ June - Start of the Monsoon and Shiel Bridge
Foot 25 miles & 9,706ft, mtb 3 miles (196ft), 4 Corbetts

By way of punishment for my toddler tantrum the evening before, the wind had blown up fiercely during the night and dragged in filthy weather from the Atlantic. It was blowing a hooley and lashing down with rain as I set off from Kinloch Hourn, but I consoled myself knowing that I had escaped Knoydart in such conditions. There were four Corbetts on today's menu, and for starters the unusual twin-topped, but single Corbett, of Buidhe Bheinn & Sgurr a' Bhac Chaolais. Both tops are the same height on the same ridge, separated by about a mile and a half, but there is not the mandatory 500ft drop between them, therefore they cannot both be classed as individual Corbetts. In order to claim the hill I would have to go along the ridge to both tops - not as easy as it sounds. By the time I flogged up the stalkers path to near the top of Buidhe Bheinn I was drenched to the bones and the howling wind was absolutely freezing, changing the rain to driving hail. I once heard a talk by Trossachs MRT where the speaker described that when analysed, a huge number of call-outs had their origins with the wind – whether it be by driving precipitation or its guiding force or the sheer noise, it invariably forces people to simply lose concentration and make rushed and poor decisions on the hills. I was very conscious of this in almost zero visibility as I was trying to take a careful bearing, with my back to the thundering gale and the noise within my hood deafening. The ridge was not obvious and I couldn't look up properly without getting my eyes raked with hailstones. I stumbled about trying to keep at least one eye on the compass, which I had tied to my wrist just in case I lost it with frozen fingers. There were only very vague sections of what appeared to be worn path in the broken rocky surface. I got wandered on a few occasions, seeming to take eternity to relocate, but probably actually only a few minutes. It was hard to tell in the maelstrom. With a gasp of relief I got to the second top of Sgurr a' Bhac Chaolais, then headed down to the bealach adjoining with the Munro, Sgurr Na Sgine.

I plummeted south-west down out of the wildest weather into the glen and picked up the good track leading north-west under a line of ugly electricity pylons. The rain just didn't stop, but with the wind much lessened and a good feed I was

Days 54-59 Loch Hourn to Torridon

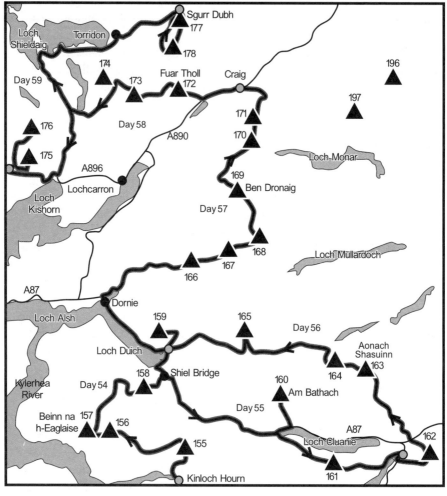

155. Buidhe Bheinn (& Sgurr a' Bhac Chaolais)(885m)
156. Beinn nan Caorach (774m)
157. Beinn na h-Eaglaise (805m)
158. Sgurr Mhic Bharraich (779m)
159. Sgurr an Airgid (841m)
160. Am Bathach (798m)
161. Beinn Loinne (790m)
162. Meall Dubh (788m)
163. Aonach Shasuinn (888m)
164. Carn a' Choire Ghairbh (865m)
165. Sgurr Gaorsaic (839m)
166. Sguman Coinntich (879m)

167. Faochaig (868m)
168. Aonach Buidhe (899m)
169. Beinn Dronaig (797m)
170. Beinn Tharsuinn (863m)
171. Sgurr na Feartaig (862m)
172. Fuar Tholl (907m)
173. An Ruadh-stac (892m)
174. Beinn Damh (903m)
175. Sgurr a' Chaorachain (792m)
176. Beinn Bhan (896m)
177. Sgurr Dubh (782m)
178. Sgorr nan Lochan Uaine (871m)

able to warm up again as I trotted on at a reasonable pace, eventually reaching Bealach Aoidhdailean. Despite being drookit I was in good fettle with two successive hills before me, Beinn nan Caorach and Beinn na h-Eaglaise, which I moved over quickly. The weather had given me brief respite and I had a view through gaps in the clouds. With another black cloud coming straight for me, I started to run off Beinn na h-Eaglaise at speed, but after a few hundred feet of descent realised that I had left my poles on the summit! Bugger - I walked back up to retrieve them just as the heavy shower hit me in the face. There was no point in stopping for a break in the heavy rain, I just had to keep moving in order to stay warm, and I covered the 4 miles through to Suardalan bothy in good time. As I neared the cottage I spied two approaching figures and a hound – it was Brenda and Dot with her dog Frank; what pleasant surprise. We took shelter in the bothy and I had food and read the bothy book entries, adding to it before we left. I had wisely not taken a camera with me today because of the weather, so Dot managed to get a few token shots before Brenda and I left to share the last hill, Sgurr Mhic Bharraich.

There was a welcome but brief spell of sun before the rain returned once more, and we walked steadily out of the forest and up the path from the west. After a bit of puffing we heaved up onto the broad summit ridge and were suddenly blasted with another storm of hail. We hid behind a rocky outcrop whilst I checked the map, then made an uncomfortable last bid for the summit cairn. There was a confusing mist about and I ran over a few wee tops and hummocks until I was sure I had the correct spot. "Right let's get out of here!" It felt an awfully long way back down to sea-level at Shiel Bridge, with tired legs and having being soaked for twelve hours; but a quick hot shower each and then along to Kintail Lodge for beers and dinner to recover, in the good company of Dot and now joined by a friend from Newtonmore, Jim Hall.

The weather didn't let up overnight but, appropriately parked at the Strath Croe cemetery, I slept like the dead.

Day 55 Thursday 18th June - Shiel Bridge to Bunloinn Forest
Foot 14 miles & 5,688ft, bike 14 miles (1,082ft), mtb 8 miles (781ft), 3 Corbetts

After a quick but wet 3 mile ride from Shiel Bridge back to the Strath Croe cemetery, I couldn't bring myself to go back out in the lashing rain. Dot and Brenda were downloading gps data of the route so far and I used this as an excuse to stay indoors. After delaying for thirty minutes, Brenda had had enough and chucked me out to climb Sgurr an Airgid. Jim had gone ahead and shoved my bike 1,000ft up the wee hill track as far as a deer gate. The rain stopped for a while and I enjoyed the climb up the well-worn path to the summit. I got a surprisingly good view down Loch Duich between the clouds, but didn't hang about as I could see the next deluge charging in. Sure enough, I got soaked as I descended but was glad to pick up the mtb and swoop down the bottom half of the track quickly, the last section with Frank the dog furiously chasing my back wheel!

At the bottom another feed and hot drinks, then off climbing up Glen Shiel on the road bike for 14 miles with a good tailwind, but still wet. I met up with the van again just past the Cluanie Inn where biking pal Peter Bennett had linked up with us to share a hill. He and Dot set off walking up Am Bathach in advance while I got changed out of sopping biking gear into already sopping running gear, and followed on with Brenda. The four of us converged near the top just as we were hit by the most horrendous shower imaginable. Freezing, near horizontal, stair rods of water lashed us as we paused and took photos for posterity! Brenny and I retreated back down at speed and got ready for the next episode of Water World. Again I had Peter for company on the mtb for 4 miles up the old road from Cluanie Inn which now ends abruptly in Loch Loyne, but I was cutting off early, east over Beinn Loinne and continuing to pick up another bike on the far side, careful pre-placed by Jim Hall. The traverse of the hill was hellish rough and in icy rain – utter misery. When I eventually found and rode the bike 3 miles out the east side to the forestry gate on the A87, I was totally caked in mud from the track and shaking all over with cold - hands and feet now useless frozen lumps of ice. It was only 7pm but there was no way I could do the intended Meall Dubh today. I was done in.

After many hot drinks and a hot shower to thaw out, we drove back to the Cluanie Inn with Jim and Dot for a well deserved big dinner and a few pints of the Skye Brewery's Red Cuillin. We enjoyed shelter from the wild wind beneath the Cluanie Dam for the night, where I applied ice to my niggling knee and tendonitis, and a handful of Ibuprofen for good measure.

Day 56 Friday 19th June - Back to Affric
Foot 23 miles & 10,665ft, mtb 10 miles (560ft), 4 Corbetts

Brenda blogged... *Up early this morning another windy day but it was not raining, to start with; he must only have been away 5 mins and then the rain started. He headed away to do Meall Dubh and Jim went to meet him for the last couple of miles with his mountain bike. Back at the van for bacon & egg rolls before heading away for his originally intended 20 miles. He was taking his bike 5 miles up the River Doe towards his next hill then Jim was collecting it and then taking it back around to Strath Croe forest for Manny to collect for the last 3 miles after his 4th hill tonight. Thanks to Jim for all his bike duties, as I would have struggled today getting the bike over the deer gates. The plan for today is Meall Dubh, Aonach Shasuinn, Carn a'Choire Ghairbh & Sgurr Gaorsaic, and I am meeting him at the Strath Croe cemetery car park at some point this evening. He is*

*away with his head torch so I am guessing it's going to be another late one today,
and not to start panicking and calling mountain rescue. Dot and I headed into
Broadford to get some shopping and managed to get some washing done. It was
nice and sunny that direction, then it started to rain as we headed back to Shiel
Bridge.*

An early but very slow start. Mind games – I missed a hill off yesterdays plan and
now had to try and stick it onto today's already long itinerary. Soon on the open
slopes of Meall Dubh the rain was hammering down and the visibility was poor. A
compass bearing took me across all sorts of rough heather and bog before
thankfully reaching the top in thick clag, with ghostly movements playing tricks
on my eyes. What the... windmills? A dreaded wind "farm", not marked on my
map, perched high on the west side of the mountain. I was suddenly glad of the
mist to hide the bloody awful things from my view. I dropped to the north and
quickly hit a forestry track where Jim was waiting with my bike for an easy mile
or so run back to the van at the main road.

After Brenny gave me a comforting big feed I headed up Glen Doe, hard work
riding on a track formed from huge cobbled boulders, but still quicker than
walking and easier on the legs than running. I dumped my bike after 5 miles for
Jim to pick up and set off up Carn a'Choire Bhuidhe. Checking my cut-out map,
something wasn't right... there was a higher top ahead? A quick text to Jim to
confirm, I had marked up my map wrongly; Aonach Shasuinn, a mile further on is
my target. Being on a ridge (Ridge of the Sassenach) I had to go over it anyway to
get to my next Corbett, but it was a useful lesson and I would be more careful to
check the SMC book before I left the van in future!

I contoured the north side of An Elric and quickly made Carn a'Choire Ghairbh,
with briefly clear weather for great views down Glen Affric. There followed a bit
of jiggery-pokery as I paused and guessed at the best line to the next hill, but
opted for the safe bridge crossing at Athnamulloch, where the dancing high river
made me feel better for choosing this slightly longer route. A long tiring trundle
west on the infamous Yellow Brick Road, past the Youth Hostel at Alltbeithe, and
soon after a gradual traversing rise north up the slopes of Sgurr Gaorsaic, the
"peak of horror"! Thankfully not so today, just more dull rain and mist. I was
starting to buzz a bit – I had almost knocked out a very big day and didn't feel too
bad. As I climbed into the mist of the very dramatic Bealach an Sgairne, I heard a
cry of "Westies!", and after a few more shouts from above I spied Jim huddled on
the hillside waiting on me. He had reccied a good wee route down the original old
zigzag drover path and into the forestry where my mtb was waiting. Yeehaa! I
whizzed down the big track at speed, hallucinating of food and beer. A couple of
deer gates to get the bike over then zoom down to Strath Croe where there was a
mad scramble from within the van. I had caught them all by surprise - they hadn't
been expecting me for a couple of hours yet.

Magic, I was back earlier that I had hoped, and very hungry. We had more company in Scott and Linda Kennedy of Bellahouston Road Runners, who had popped in from their But n' Ben at Inverinate to wish us well and offer showers and services from their house, but I chose to stay put and get showered quickly and stuck into the good hot grub Brenda had ready for me. I had been soaked all day and was now glad to be finished and put my itchy, red feet up with a beer.

Jim blogged... *I was along for the last couple of days because the schedule for day 56 promised 34,25,36; sadly this turned out to be just the map numbers! What a let-down. And with wind and hail, what a cold, wet couple of days it was too. But at least there were no midges. Luckily I was armed with a couple of running injury excuses to keep me off the clag-ridden hills, and I enjoyed visiting some of the odd, remote places where I had to leave or collect the bike. There's been so much rain, the waterfalls are awesome. So he's still plugging away (despite the advice from friends, relatives and experts in the field of physical health), triumphing over the Corbetts, hypothermia and trench foot through sheer determination. Well done Manny, and Brenda for the superb support.*

Day 57 Saturday 20ᵗʰ June - Another 6!
Foot 24 miles & 10,665ft, bike 13 miles (492ft), mtb 2 miles (160ft), 6 Corbetts

I started the day with a slow and wet 12 mile pedal to Killilan. Arriving just ahead of me, after a huge drive north the night before, were Johnston, Andy and Maria. Johnston kindly presented me with a very special bottle of Springbank Malt, drawn from one of his own connoisseur barrels - I very nearly went no further that day! However after their effort to come and join me, I thought I had better put on a show for the guys for the first half of the day's six hills.

Johnston blogged... *Passed Manny as he cycled along the road from Strath Croe to Killilan this morning, and met up with Brenda at the Killilan car park. After the usual excellent hospitality from Brenda's mobile tearoom - she's a star! - Manny then biked the extra mile from the public car park to Killilan to start the climb, while Dot the Doughnut Queen collected the bike.*

Manny's hill crew for today consisted of me, fellow Westie Andy Mott, and Andy's girlfriend Maria, who had all made the long journey north on Friday night for a big day out on the hills of the Killilan Forest on Saturday. First summit of the day was Sguman Coinntich, tackled via a steep climb from the Allt a'Choire Mhoir. Although Manny isn't as quick after his injury a couple of weeks ago, we did still manage a good jog across to Faochaig, with the weather still undecided on the cloud vs sun debate.

Andy and Maria dropped back at Faochaig, tackling it at a gentler pace before heading back down into Glen Elchaig. Manny and I descended via a stalker's path to consider an approach to Aonach Buidhe, again deciding on a steep and direct line. 3 large deer kept a watchful eye on us as we headed for the summit in conditions which were now pleasantly sunny (this cheered Manny up!). As my car was back at Killilan, we said our farewells and I headed down to Iron Lodge for the 8 mile jog back along Glen Elchaig, collecting Andy and Maria on the way to completing a 23-mile 3-Corbett day, which was nothing compared to Manny's efforts!

Manny went north to do Beinn Dronaig, Beinn Tharsuinn, and Sgurr na Feartaig before getting the MTB off the hill (brought in by Brenda), and finishing his 25-mile hill journey at around 10pm.

So that's another 6 hills completed for Manny, who is still grinding through the list at a relentless pace (leaving me wheezing behind him), despite injury slowing him down. Well over 75% complete now and fewer than 50 hills to go.

I'm just back in after the 4-hour drive home. Been a long day, folks. G'night.

It should be noted that Maria, Andy's lovely Russian girlfriend, had not heard of Munroskis far less Corbettskis, and had never before been up anything bigger or steeper than a flight of stairs. It is therefore testament to their true love that after reaching the top of Sguman Coinntich, an exhausted Maria did not chuck Andy off the crags, but instead carried on behind me & Johnston, to also do Faochaig; they later married and had lovely son, but I still wouldn't risk another big craggy hill Andy... even angels have a limit!

It was another huge day so after I wished Johnston well on his long return run to his car at Killilan, I made full use of the very remote Maol-bhuidhe bothy for a good time-out, feed and snooze. After lunch my rain-induced apprehension about crossing the out-flow from Loch Cruoshie was proven unfounded, and I sploshed across only thigh deep. I cruised up and over Beinn Dronaig, down to the good path near Bendronaig Lodge before trotting north and lugging more wearily up Beinn Thursuinn - a hill usually classed more as a nuisance than a Corbett, due to its blocking of two remote neighbouring Munros, Bidean a'Choire Sheasgaich and Lurg Mhor. I didn't care; I was at the top and only one more to go for the day, Sgurr na Feartaig. A quick wheech up from Bealach Bhearnais led me to the big rocky summit cairn, spectacularly crowned by shafts of low golden sun through broken clouds. A last feed from my pack and I started down the 2 miles of superb stalkers path – "Oooya!" my right calf was suddenly quite painful. Hobble, hobble, bugger. I was immediately reduced to a very slow shuffle off the hill, and far below I could see Brenda and Sandra were waiting for me with a bike in the wrong place! After some protracted long distance shouting, swearing and sign language they got the message and relocated to where I would actually be coming off the hill.

I was rather sore, tired and grumpy. My cause wasn't helped any when I realised they didn't have my own bike, but instead Brenda's x-small bike for x-small midgets. Grrrr! Having had all day to get to the rendezvous, via shops and pubs, they had come from Craig over the River Carron bridge, made the understandable error of mistaking right for left, then magically moulded the billion year-old rocky landscape of Alba to perfectly match their OS Landranger map whilst facing the wrong way, travelled for several miles under a thick cloud of blethering and securely locked my bike to a tree. On their return they must have paused for breath between yapping and suddenly realised that things didn't fit! Wading through a loch of gloopy mud, hurried waving and fluttering of eyelids at a hairy forestry worker driving a giant mechanical tree-muncher confirmed they should not be allowed outdoors without an adult, and my bike was most definitely in the wrong place... with the key miles away in the van! They left the poor guy unable to work with laughter, whilst Brenda franticly ran back to the van to collect her bike as a substitute and meet Sandra again now on the correct track - all just in the nick of time to meet me coming off the hill. If Carlsberg made Laurel & Hardy...

Thankful of even a tiny bike, I finally whizzed downhill back to the van in the midge hell that is Craig and threw myself in the door. The lassies appeared later, collected the bike-lock key and drove Sandra's 4x4 back across the railway level-crossing and into the dark forest to retrieve my bike from the tree. By the time they returned word of a free lunch had got round and the entire midge population were there to greet them! Brenda dived in and slammed the door whilst poor Sandra attempted to put up her tent in a black fog! It was like watching a sinking ship go down; between swatting, jumping, screams and the pegs bouncing off the iron-hard surface, it was doomed from the start. Highly entertaining as it was I couldn't watch anymore, and had to run out and help roll it all up like a giant ball of knitting and throw it into the back of her car. Safely back in the van we fly-sprayed the air and also Sandra's hair to kill millions of midges, and blocked up all the air vents. Sandra sadly had had enough and decided to retreat home scratching, but at least no longer attracting flies!

Dot's diary... *Everyone arriving at the camper van was immediately offered tea, Brenda must have made thousands of cups along the way – more mugs soon had to be acquired as word spread that Brenda's café was open. I took along a couple of bags of doughnuts on my first visit – they were eaten very quickly and I had to wait at the shop for more to be made the next day. After that I couldn't catch up with Manny and Brenda without bringing fresh supplies.*

Brenda blogged... *Dave Rogers arrived sometime in the middle of the night after having supported Stevie Bell do the West Highland Way Race. Stevie had a brilliant time of 19.56, well done. Dave is helping Manny out on Sunday, another long day ahead.*

Mark, Tracey & Hanna blogged... *Hi Manny, we've been keeping track of your Corbetts Run, awesome effort and (relatively) not far to go now! Hanna, who is two days younger than your Corbetts Round, did her first Corbett yesterday (Ben*

Ledi) and in fine Manny tradition it was p*shing rain. The sun did come out when we got to the bottom though! She passes on her best wishes, "coo woo wah" or something like that. All the best and keep it going!

Day 58 Sunday 21st June – Achnashellach
Foot 16 miles & 7,671ft, bike 13 miles (2,024ft), 3 Corbetts

Dave Rogers is a machine. He spends ludicrously long hours working as a high–heid civil servant in the Scottish Office, and as result rarely gets any regular training in. When time away from work and his busy family commitments do allow, he packs in as many hours, miles and climbs in the hills as he can possible squeeze, whether it be walking, running or racing. This weekend was no exception. He had just spent the last twenty-four hours supporting our old clubmate Stevie Bell do yet another West Highland Way Race, a tortuous race that Dave has completed many times himself. After Stevie had finished and without pausing for breath, he had driven the long way north overnight to help me out too, with the lure of another long day in the hills.

After a very slow start at 10am, I nipped down the two miles to Achnashellach on my road bike, before we struck out together on a direct line up Fuar Tholl, a fabulous rocky mountain and once more only a smidgin under the 3,000ft mark, climbed from almost sea level as is the west-coast humour. The weather was dry with thick cloud on the tops, but from scrambling on the lower craggy slopes the views up and down Loch & Glen Carron were superb. We enjoyed the steep rocky decent to the footpath separating the Corbett from the Munro, Sgorr Ruadh, then plummeted deep into the steep glen below and had a quick bite to eat by the burn.

We pushed on up the far side, past a group of slow walkers on the well worn footpath to Bealach a'Choire Ghairbh, and onto another cracking high hill, An Ruadh-Stac. Dave gave me a rolling education on the geology of the mountains as we travelled, and once again climbed into thick cloud, now slipping much lower and with drizzle. We dived off the knobbly top and traversed a path around the west side of Maol Chean-dearg and crossed a rough, lumpy corrie to the foot of Beinn Damh.

One of Dave's other qualities is precision navigation, having competed with distinction on countless mountain marathons and similar long distance mountain events. As we climbed up into the now very thick murk I didn't have to think, just follow Dave through a tricky line of crags, grass and more crags and we were suddenly at the top. I was cold and tired but Dave kept me trucking on when I might have messed about having food, and probably getting colder and slower. We trotted out on the Strath a' Bhathaich path leading to Kinloch Damph where I picked up my bike left by Brenda for the last mile riding on tarmac to the van.

Douglas Anderson, a biking friend, had driven over from Carrbridge but somehow we had just missed each other on the last hill where he had come up the path looking for us. I had a huge feed at the van, but was aware that time had marched on to 7pm and I still had two hills to do, with the weather deteriorating steadily. Dave had to depart home to Edinburgh, already very late, but promising to be back the following weekend. I got changed into dry biking gear and zipped down to the bottom of Beinn Bhan on the infamous Applecross road to re-assess. Nope, not tonight. It was now gone 8pm and the thick wet cloud was hanging a long way down the ridge; it looked totally minging up there and I was knackered. As Douglas had to return home for work the next day, I apologised for his wasted journey to miss doing a hill with me, but he hoped to perhaps return later in the trip - though ultimately couldn't. I still had one thing to do that might make tomorrows' hills a bit easier – cycle 2,000ft up to the Bealach na Ba! I had never cycled it before and perhaps having first done nine hours on the hill with three Corbetts wasn't the best preparation! However I was determined to do it without pause and plugged away, climbing up into really thick mist and drenching drizzle; my legs screamed, ears popped and eyes bled as the gradient constantly increased, and I nearly blew a gasket going round the final hairpins – but I made it, bang on 9pm, yeahaa! Dead chuffed and dead beat, I collapsed into the van for a shower. Brenda was heaving huge sighs of relief at making it up the very steep, narrow road in the van without incident or meeting any other vehicle in dire visibility. To celebrate another hard but successful day we had wine, beer and drams with a huge pasta dinner, overlooking a stupendous view - which was unfortunately totally obscured by pea-soup!

Swaz blogged... *Captain Epic strikes again - sounds like my kinda time-keeping. That road climb up na Ba is something else - there's a bike race goes round there every year - I swear half the field walk it - it's steep as daft !! Keep going heroes - and you Manda, ya valdaree-pole-wielding merchant. Much Love, Swanny & Jez*

Day 59 Monday 22nd June - Ba'heids in the Cloud
Foot 17 miles & 6,336ft, bike 25 miles (869ft), 4 Corbetts

Visibility nil; that is to say we could only just see the far side of the single track road!

There was no great rush to get out the door, but when we finally did it was indeed as horrible, cold and wet as it looked from the warm comfort of the van. The heavy mist seeped through our waterproofs and we kept as steady a walking pace as possible, whilst I kept one eye on the permanently raised compass and the other on the zillion boulders that covered the surface of the mountain. I had persuaded Brenda to come and bag Sgurr a' Chaorachain with me as it lay only a mile away, but I could sense her unease at being in these blind conditions with yawning drops hidden about us. We hit the top bang on, and returned along the ridge to the radio mast, but it had all seemed too easy and Brenda chose to come along for the wander to Beinn Bhan instead of returning to the van. Again we picked our way over the rocky landscape, but painfully slowly, the edge of the crag and ridge not just as obvious as I had hoped. I was relieved getting to Bealach nan Arr to get off the pathless rock and pick up the grassy foot trod to the summit. At the second top in over two hours, we were starving and only had a single banana to share, thinking we would have been much quicker back to the van. We returned by the Bealach and once again had to meander through the gloop, eventually hitting the tarmac road with a sigh after a tortuous four hours!

We changed into dry gear and poured gallons of tea and hot soup down our throats to thaw out, before Brenda had the daunting prospect of the drive back down the hair-pinned road in virtually no visibility, and me likewise ahead on the bike. I chose my mtb for this which would give much better tyre grip on the wet road surface, and allow me to hit stones or gravel at speed without puncturing; the mtb disc brakes were also much safer than my road bike brake-blocks in the wet conditions. After an exhilarating descent we met up again at the bottom where I changed to my road bike for the 20 mile undulating ride past Shieldaig into Glen Torridon to the Ling Hut car park.

The weather hadn't improved a jot. With less altitude there was certainly slightly more visability, but everything was soaking and wreathed in mist. Re-fed and recharged, I trotted off into the murk once again and was not looking forward to more slow navigation, which even the SMC Corbetts book warned could be tricky in such conditions. The Ling Hut is a popular base for Scottish Mountaineering Club members climbing in the area for several days, and there were a few in residence as I ran past and off into the maze of glacial moraine hummocks. I took a direct line straight up the side, weaving in and out of crags, and was pleased to hit the top first time. I sat down behind the cairn and had a roll and a biscuit, hidden from the wind. Then I got the map out and took a very careful bearing in the direction of Sgorr nan Lochan Uaine, stood up... and ran off in completely the wrong direction! I don't know what was going on in my head, but I didn't realise my mistake until the nice fast scree run I was on ended abruptly over a cliff! Having come to my senses and realising what my blooper was, I didn't want to climb back up to the top so instead tried to traverse to the right. Crags, big scary crags... the thin ledge I was following narrowed, then vanished. Mmm? I still wasn't 100% certain of my location so whipped out the GPS I carried in my bum bag and checked the grid. Sorted, I am exactly where I thought – the wrong place, so back up for a good bit then try again for a contour line. Hurray! I made it back on track, feeling a bit thick for such a simple error. GPS isn't a thing I normally use and this was only one of two occasions I used it in earnest on the trip, in laziness rather than requirement; it was horrible conditions, I was tired and wanted my dinner & beer as soon as possible. The GPS which Archie had lent me for the duration was useful in that it plotted my exact route wherever I carried it, and it not only confirmed I had done each top but also made totting up the final distance and ascent gains on the mountains much easier than doing it manually. I don't own one and probably never will; a map and compass is far more interesting and reliable than buttons, bleeps and flat batteries, or no signal...

The climb up Sgorr nan Lochan Uaine was again blind but straightforward, as was the descent and run-out on the sopping stalkers path via Coire a' Cheud-Chnoc, a fantastic jumbled glacial rubbish dump. Brenda was waiting on the road to cheer me back and sit me down to another proud dinner, well earned tonight!

Not surprisingly this is the only day of the trip where we have absolutely no photographic record, unless we were to hold up a sheet of white paper in front of our faces... and for the 3D effect, pour a bucket of cold water over the head.

Brenda blogged... *I headed off into Kinlochewe to get gas and water. While I was there I met Charlie & his folks - they are up to join us for a couple of days and David Riach turned up on his bike, he had cycled from Inverness. He was booked into the Kinlochewe Hotel for the night and is joining us for the next couple of days along with Scott Kennedy.*

Archie and Sandra blogged... *Nae luck with the weather Manny, it must be a real pain in the ass to be in such a spectacular hills with no views. Never mind, get on with the job and come back and do them again on a good day, the views will still be there. Good to hear that Charlie C is on hand to give you a sympathetic kick up the backside. I'll try to get out and join you later in the week as long as you promise to slow down a bit, (I still don't believe you're as crocked as you make out), Archie*

Kevin Doonan said... *Just checking Manny, I take it you are not going to see ac/dc... good luck.*

Swaz blogged... *AC/DC Concert?!! Are You Ready? Well I guess it's back down the Highway to Hell to Glasgow? Well we know Manny's endured plenty Stormy May Days that Shake your Foundations and got his schedule All Screwed Up, but even though It's a Long Way to the Top and you're probably running on Borrowed Time, you've definitely got Big Balls so Let's Make It through next Friday then Have A Drink On Me!*

Day 60 Tuesday 23rd June - Torridon, Flowerdale, Ben Eighe
Foot 25.5 miles & 11,886ft, bike 22 miles (579ft), 5 Corbetts

There couldn't have been a bigger contrast in the weather when we opened the blinds to a perfect blue sky, yeeha! After a quick breakfast, Dave Riach arrived at the van at 8am on his steed from Kinlochewe, and together we rode west back down Glen Torridon, through the village and up to the Coire Mhic Nobuil car

Days 60-62 Torridon through Fisherfield

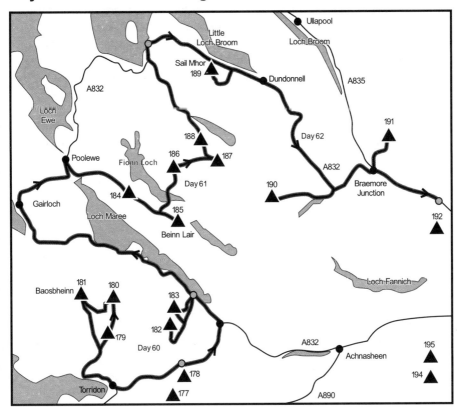

179. Beinn Dearg (914m)
180. Beinn an Eoin (855m)
181. Baosbheinn (875m)
182. Ruadh-stac Beag (896m)
183. Meall a' Ghiubhais (887m)
184. Beinn Airigh Charr (791m)
185. Beinn Lair (859m)

186. Beinn a' Chaisgein Mor (856m)
187. Beinn Dearg Mor (910m)
188. Beinn Dearg Bheag (820m)
189. Sail Mhor (767m)
190. Creag Rainich (807m)
191. Beinn Enaiglair (890m)

park, to meet up again with Scott Kennedy. After more grub I grabbed my hill-pack before the three of us headed off just after 9am for Beinn Dearg in the rapidly increasing heat.

Invigorated by the sunshine once more, the guys set me a good pace up the well constructed footpath and through some of the finest mountains in Scotland, heading just left of the nose of the dramatically shaped Beinn. It was a brutally steep climb straight onto the 2,999 foot summit where the views were simply jaw-dropping; surrounded west, south and north by the giants of Beinn Alligin, Liathach and Beinn Eighe, with our next two Corbetts in Flowerdale to the north. Take note, there is absolutely no point in going up this magnificent mountain in the mist! We lingered as long as we could before dragging ourselves reluctantly down into the corrie and crossed a long mile of moor and bog to the foot of Beinn an Eoin in now incredible heat.

My companions kept me going with pace and blethering, and I kept supping water and nibbling grub. However this next very steep climb in the heat had me toiling a bit, and at the top I took in the view briefly before lying down on the lovely soft grass with my cap over my face and zonking out for twenty minutes. Prodded back to life for a few photos we were off again, directly down to the Poca Buidhe Bothy at the head of Loch na h-Oidhche. Now here was a pleasant surprise, a neat wee bothy with a heap of spare grub, and a water cooled fridge in the burn, also stocked with bacon, eggs and... beer! There was no sign of anyone; no kit left, no one fishing on the loch, no walking gear. The book said a fishing party had been and left in the last few days so this must have been the remains of their stocks, all in-date, and how I wished we had more time for a slap-up feed; as it was we contented ourselves with a bottle of cold beer, magic!

A flog around the end of the loch then up onto the ridge leading to Baosbheinn, taking care to re-apply sun cream in the burning heat. Another ticked hill and we were heading back past Beinn Dearg via Bealach a' Chomhla. I was now tired and stumbling a bit, bashing my toes off various rocks, so was relieved to pick up the good access path again and trot back to the car park after a memorable eight hours on the hill. Here now was Charlie, with his parents, walking up to greet us back. Great stuff, Chuck always brings a smile to an occasion and I was delighted to see his folks along too, along with the rest of their family. Having been the major logistics cog in his epic Munro round, they wanted a wee taste of that again out on the road. It was appreciated and gave me a real boost. There was still work to do and in this sublime weather I had to make the most of it. I had a huge feed and umpteen drinks before thanking Scott as he headed home to Glasgow, whilst I road biked with Dave the 16 miles through Glen Torridon, for the third time, past Kinlochewe to the Glas Leitire car park by the shore of Loch Maree. Dave was continuing on to his booked digs in Poolewe where we would meet up again tomorrow.

It was gone 7pm but I was still planning another two Corbetts, although now in the cooler evening it was very tight for daylight. Feeling pumped up to race the time limit I blasted off up the mountain trail, where at it's summit cairn opened up an amazing view across the back of Beinn Eighe and to my first target Ruadh-stac Beag. Those who travel the hills at this time of evening know the special beauty it offers. The stillness, the softer low light, the contrasting shadows moving across the corries and slopes, and nothing stirring except me. Buzzing with adrenaline I flew across the rough ground above the northeast gully leading around the back of this rocky gem, a detached outlier of its famous parent ridge. Now easier to move in the cooler air I easily clambered up the huge loose blocks of rock on the south ridge, with every other slope well protected by impenetrable crags. I enjoyed the summit for five minutes, and looking back across the glen I could see Brenda and Charlie slowly climbing Meall a' Ghiuthais, hoping to soon meet me on the top, so I had to get a shift on! Hopping quickly between the big boulders I started to descend but froze still in an instant.

There, not five metres away, perched proudly on a rock with his back to me, was a Golden Eagle! I didn't even breathe, but silently adjusted my feet and hunkered down low behind a large rock just in front of me. Could this day get any better!? I sat there and watched him scanning the corrie for prey, even risking the dreaded Velcro strap ripping open to get my camera out and get a few photos of him. Wow, what a privilege. After ten minutes I could feel my legs stiffening up in that crouched position and I knew I couldn't sit there all night, as much as I would have liked to. I stood up and took half dozen silent steps even closer, with the camera ready for the inevitable... whoosh, up he went in an instant, effortless, majestic, maybe even slightly insulted that a great spud like me could sneak up on him. It didn't matter, he soared away to safety and I got my shot, and have an etched memory of something very special indeed.

Bloody hell, look at the time now! Belting down the rocks I retraced my steps off the hill, down the gully, then bore north up the ridiculously steep grassy slope of Meall a' Ghiuthais. I grunted my way upwards to find Brenda and Charlie on their way down, trying to warm up after waiting for me on the top for too long in the cold wind. I said I would try and catch them on the way down and clambered on up. The day did get even better – bang on 10.30pm, the golden ball of sun was just about to dip below the horizon, beyond the end of Loch Maree and Poolewe, in the light fantastic. Chittering with cold I stayed for five minutes to soak up the scene, to soak up the whole fabulous day.

Down I flew, at racing pace. Hurtling down the steep grass for a thousand feet, then a short bog hop before the final charge down the rough rocky mountain path in fast dying light, all the way back to the Glas Leitire car park hoping vainly to catch the other two in front. I took a minor wrong turn on one of the nature trails and as a result just missed catching Brenda and Charlie by thirty seconds; they had jogged down the whole trail too - what a buzz! Within seconds of being greeted back by Charlie's folks in the car park it was clear that standing about was risking a painful death by midge, so everyone wished each other goodnight and in a flash dived into their vehicles! It was 11.15pm.

Time for a beer and dinner, and perhaps another beer to toast one of my best days ever on the hill.

Geoff Simpson & Ali Johnson blogged... *Hi Manny & Brenda, we're following your exploits with incredulity - I hope you're not sitting at home in your new house making this all up!*

Day 61 Wednesday 24th June - Big Day Out in Letterewe
Foot 22 miles & 9,677ft, bike 23 miles (1,230ft), mtb 8 miles (538ft), 5 Corbetts

The scheduled plan was huge; six Corbetts over 26 miles, plus 15 miles of biking, but now I was starting with an additional 22 mile bike ride through Gairloch to Poolewe. Feeling a bit bleary after yesterday's efforts and late finish I took it easy on the bike to get warmed up and let the body come awake, and the big climb on the A832 through Slattadale Forest was a real toil. The weather was the same again, the cool morning about to be overtaken by roasting heat. It was pleasant to roll down into Gairloch and a shame not to be stopping at The Old Inn for a good pint, but I pressed on and over into Poolewe, where Brenda was waiting on the far side of the bridge with food & drinks ready, and Dave set for a big day on the hill. Whilst I got changed into running gear and had a feed, Brenda and Dave set off on foot in advance, down the private track to Kernsary farm where I caught up with them on the mtb. Brenda took my bike out again and Dave carried my day-pack with loads of grub. Because of my road biking prologue I didn't set off from the van until after 11am and the heat was now fierce, with our running slow by necessity.

Even as soon as we turned off the good footpath, up the first steep slope of Beinn Airigh Charr, we hugged tight to the bottom edge of a sheer crag face that offered just one hundred meters of welcome shade, grateful of everything we could get! The climb was sweltering and the summit brought a reduction in temperature, and this pattern would be repeated for the next twelve hours. Dave led me a good line around the bottom of the Graham, Meall Mheinnidh, and we dropped our packs at Bealach Mheinnidh before nipping up Beinn Lair to it's fabulous huge round cairn with a superb view across to Slioch. We lingered on the sunny top before another hour took us back to the bealach and trotting down the stalkers path to the iconic causeway across the middle of Fionn Loch and Dubh Loch, for a spot of lunch by the stream at Carnmore.

Grudgingly we hauled ourselves back to our feet and headed up for the direct, very steep gully leading to Carn Mor, and ultimately the Corbett, Beinn a'

Chaisgein Mor. Hands on were required over a few steeper rocky shelves and we baked with the hot sun directly on our backs all the way up. The top was again tremendous with views straight into the dramatic craggy corries of Munros, Ruadh Stac Mor and A' Mhaighdean. We ran east then slightly north, steeply dropping into Strath Beinn Dearg, a classic glaciated glen with a million hummocks and strewn with discarded boulders. At the bottom having a drink from the river, Dave decided he was now feeling a bit weary and opted out of the first of the twin peaks, Beinn Dearg Mor, and instead would meet me again on the second, Beinn Dearg Bheag. I scoffed a filled roll and we headed off in V formation for our respective tops. I had not long realised that time was fast marching on and that I still had a long way to go to reach my proposed last hill, Sail Mor, so I upped my pace considerably and beasted hard up the final 1,000ft of loose rock, only to undo any time gained by stopping dead in my tracks at the summit, stunned by the awesome vista before me. The pin-sharp An Teallach ridge was laid out across a deep blue Loch na Sealga, with every crag and crack highlighted sharply by the slight shadow cast by the slowly lowering sun in the west. To my right a knee trembling drop into a vertical gully and my own shadow cast perfectly against the rock wall opposite. After a few photos of the scene I turned and descended fast back to the col, then climbed hard again to gain Beinn Dearg Bheag with Dave happily sitting on the cairn. Five more Corbetts now in the bag today, great!

Despite pushing the pace I had severe reservations about reaching Sail Mor. It sat directly to the north, almost 5 miles as an eagle would fly, but Loch na Sealga separated it from me, so reality meant 7 miles over unknown ground and another 2 miles off the hill, with the real prospect of finishing in the dark without a head torch. It was now 8pm… no, time for a bit of common sense here. A quick look at the map for plan B options then I pulled out my mobile and called Brenda, but only got her voicemail. Damn it - she would be waiting in the van on the far side of the mountain by the side of Little Loch Broom and probably didn't have a signal. Plan B/1 – I called Charlie who was still having a few days off in the north, and explained the situation to him. I was going to bin Sail Mor today and bail out west, along the good track from the end of Loch na Sealga to the roadside at Gruinard; Brenda would have to pick us up there, or better still, bring my mtb down the track to save me 5 miles of track on my tired legs/knee/tendonitis etc. Charlie would just keep trying her phone until he hopefully made contact, as I would certainly lose all signal as soon as we dropped off the hill. With fingers crossed, me and Dave made our way off the top and along what is a superb long scrambling ridge and tremendous fun. Within minutes I had already justified my route alteration as the going was very slow and extremely steep in places, with no room for hurried errors. The pace didn't get much better when we moved into a morass of bog myrtle, heather and ditches for nearly 2 miles to the end of the loch, and we were both reduced to a trudge with tired legs being shredded by the harsh undergrowth. There is no way I would have got to Sail Mor in daylight, never mind getting off safely. With sighs of relief we were happy just to reach the track-end and stopped to rest and take in the stunning view. An Teallach was now bathed red in the low sun and at last we were in cool shade. I took both packs while Dave ran off at pace down the track and I started walking out at a slow tired plod.

Meanwhile Brenda at last received a phone call from Charlie outlining the new requirements, which was all fine apart from one small problem - Brenda was already most of the way up Sail Mor expecting to meet us! Being such a stunning evening and having plenty of spare time after domestic duties, she had rightly opted to get herself up the hill. What to do now? Should she go to the top first or head straight down; Charlie promised not to tell me, and said if it had been the other way round, I would certainly have completed the hill first - he was correct! Brenda continued to the top and briefly enjoyed the view before belting down again, faster than she would ever run any race, then drove the van like a Ferrari around to Gruinard before whizzing down the track on my mtb, passing two puzzled elderly cyclists going in the other direction in now fading light. Soon after she met Dave running out - they swopped roles and Dave returned to me with my bike whilst Brenda ran back out again. As she caught and again passed the two older cyclists, now pushing up a wee hill, one of them said "Brenda...?" which in her surprise brought her to a screeching halt! By pure chance it turned out to be our blog-friends "the lovely old couple" aka, the Squires, from back at the Tyndrum 5. Remarkably having never met Brenda, they correctly guessed that a young woman zipping down a remote glen at dusk, on an mtb that was too big for her, and reappearing soon after at a run could only mean one thing... it just had to be Brenda delivering a bike for Manny!

Dave had arrived back with me and I was relieved to sit on the bike and start pedalling, with poor Dave relegated to having to repeat his run out! In my ignorance I quickly caught and screamed past the Squires, biking to the van as fast as possible in the now gathering clouds of midges; it was only once there that Brenda explained who they were, but there was little time to linger as I scrambled to get the bike onto the rack whilst being sucked dry of blood by a zillion mini-vampires. We had a brief but welcome blether with the Squires who again had showed me up; they had also just completed Beinn Dearg Mor and Bheag, having first flogged in through all the rough ground before returning all the way along the loch side. I admired their determination to get their final remote Corbetts finished, with their age having very little effect on the results! (As I type this, three years after the event, they are both now on the verge of also completing all the Grahams; an inspirational and remarkable pair.) After driving Dave to his booked accommodation at the Dundonnell Hotel, we retreated to the huge lay-by high overlooking Little Loch Broom, now dark apart from that special mid-summer glow. We prepared dinner at midnight.

Brenda blogged… *A grand total of 26 miles today. Poor David was carrying all the food today. They are away with a dozen rolls, pork pies, cakes, biscuits etc… but I am sure with Manny being around they will all be demolished by the end of the day. I had a lovely afternoon in Gairloch, had a walk around the harbour, and got to laundry facilities, which was well overdue. At present I am overlooking Little Loch Broom having an ice cream…*

Archie & Sandra blogged… *Manny, I've just had a look at my best guess at your route for today on Memory Map. It confirms that you are totally mental! Brilliant job if you pull this off, although I don't really see any obvious plan B! Top marks to David for doing it whilst lugging around 100 kilos of pork pies!*

Don & Elma blogged… *Fantastic effort Manny, watch out for the Goml ("Get of my land!") on little Wyvis. It would add some symmetry to your trip if you had a fight at the beginning and one at the end!*

Katherine & Keith blogged… *Ah Little Loch Broom and an ice cream Brenda - those were the days for me many years ago, must go up there soon. Glad to hear you're eating well Manny. Not too long to go now!*

Ellie blogged… *I'm so excited that you're so close to the end and enormously frustrated that I can't be there with you for the finale - as I sit here in sticky, muggy Glasgow cussing my work diary. Sending lots of Tunnocks inspired sentiments for the final bash. Take good care of each other this week… no scrambling down scree on bikes now Manny!*

Day 62 Thursday 25th June – Flying bikes to Braemore Junction
Foot 15 miles & 6,731ft, bike 30 miles (2,131ft), 3 Corbetts

We got up about 7.30am, both feeling a bit jaded. I went outside for a pee and the view across the loch to Beinn Ghobhlach was stunning. The north and east sides of the mountain were cloaked in mist, but west and south were warming to the early morning sunshine. The midges chased me back in for breakfast. Muesli with bran flakes and a Complan poured over the top, followed by several slices of toast and a banana, all drowned with endless cups of tea. I prepared my day's kit as I munched, before Brenda drove us back to my finishing point from the night before, then started with an 8 mile road bike from Gruinard round to Ardessie to attack Sail Mor. I enjoyed a gentle ride in the morning to loosen the legs up, but the 600ft climb up Druim nam Fuath came a bit too soon and my legs burned painfully to keep the pedals going. The whiz down the other side brought me back to the van which was precariously squeezed onto the road verge, and I admired Brenda's close parking skills. A quick change of shoes and I was off up Sail Mor, realising that I would not have enjoyed descending this horrible "path" in the dark last night, with its many washed out and hidden gullies, every one a potential ankle breaker. I took a steep direct line up, between loose rock and crag, and was on the top in forty-five minutes. Looking south back across to the Beinn Dearg pair was frustrating - so close. Toasting in the sun, I watched the Calmac ferry pull out of Loch Broom headed for Lewis, then peeled off back down the steep grass and tiptoed my way through the potholed path to the van.

Dave had arrived back on his bike and after elevenses escorted me east past Dundonnell, 1,000ft up the Corrie Hallie pass into a strong easterly headwind and along "Destitution Road". We met up with the van again at the popular parking spot for accessing the Fannich Munros, on the tight road bend and track leading to Loch a' Bhraoin. We sat in the van out of the sun and wind for lunch and I got changed into running gear. I decided the van was not level enough to be comfortable and reversed it about 20 yards onto a flatter area. Fed and almost ready to leave, Brenda got up to step out the van, with me and Dave just getting out our seats when there was a tremendous roar as a motorbike screamed past; a split second later a second roar, then silence... an instant later Brenda screamed and for a moment I couldn't understand what I had just seen! A spinning motorbike had just flown past the van window at roof height, with no rider; Brenda had just put her head out the doorway when the rider went flying past her and landed with a crump on the tarmac of the parking area! Bloody hell! We jumped out and ran over to the rider who was motionless on his back and I shouted to Brenda to phone an ambulance straight away. I was grateful on several counts – on checking the rider over, miraculously he appeared to have got away with nothing more than a hell of a clatter and badly shocked, but in any case I still made him lie totally still until paramedics could check him over; and more importantly, where he had landed would have been in the back window of the camper van had I not moved it just ten minutes previously, almost certainly causing death to himself and our van! His precious bike had fared rather less well – it had come out of orbit and returned to earth at an almost vertical angle, stopped from travelling any further by the back end of a parked car, whose poor owner was probably enjoying their day in Fannichs and about to be spoiled on their return. The first bike had now returned and his girlfriend (in order to paint the picture, I like to imagine her name was Hagar the Horrible) was ranting and cursing the Highland Council upside down, for having recently laid a new surface of custard and breadcrumbs on the bend of the road. "We wur'nae canin' it or onythin' – wi wur only daen' aboot seeventy (on a sharp bend) - it wur thae bloody loose stanes!" I quietly had a look for myself and whilst she was right about a newly laid surface, the only loose stones were actually on the very outside edge of the road, and if his bike wheels were out there, then he was already in serious trouble. In a Keystone Cops moment, I was waving down the expected police car, approaching at high speed with lights blazing... and it whizzed straight past the unmisable scene of carnage, heading off towards Dundonnell!

Nothing more could be done until the ambulance arrived, or the police officers came to their senses and returned, so Dave and I headed off leaving a slightly shaken, but not stirred, Brenda to give Hagar a cup of tea and make sure that the fallen rider didn't move or try to take his helmet off. Buzzing from the incident, we mtb'd down the track and along the loch side, where we hid the bikes at an old shieling before trotting up the grassy slopes of Creag Rainich. It was a grind in the heat, and at the summit we found the biggest sheep I have ever seen, obviously overheating and trying to get cool in the summit breeze. By the look of it, the poor beast hadn't been sheared for years and it took all its strength just to get to its feet. We huddled behind the trig point out the wind to enjoy the view of At Teallach and the Fisherfield Munros and munched a roll. It was a swift run off and return to the van, to find only the dead motorbike left from the crash. Brenda filled us in on the details; the rather embarrassed police had finally returned and she had recognised one of the officers, Mike Anderson, from his previous posting in Aviemore and we had a good laugh at their expense. When the ambulance turned up from Ullapool one of the paramedics recognised my name when she was giving details to the police - it was Steve Worsley of Highland Hill Runners. After a brief chat with him, the rider was carted away and the bike abandoned to be recovered later, all quiet again.

Dave rode with me one last time to Braemore Junction, before heading back to Inverness and a train home to Glasgow. It had been three superb days we had shared in the hills and on the bikes. Charlie had returned and met the van at the junction, then he and Brenda had walked off ahead of me aiming for Beinn Enaiglair. I enjoyed a leisurely cup of tea and goodies before chasing after the pair, hoping to catch them before the summit. I figured they would head to the bealach before the big pull north to the top, so I sneakily cut a corner but ended up on the top about fifteen minutes before them, and got cold waiting. They finally puffed up and we enjoyed the view for just a few minutes before trotting off, reversing the route. I ran ahead to get organised for my last bike ride of the evening, and bumped into Archie & Sandra walking up the path to meet us; Sandra using all her willpower to overcome her horsey-phobia to get past a pair of clapped-out, but clearly intimidating…, highland ponies. Archie jumped on his road bike to take the lead in the easterly headwind and allowed me to draft the 6 miles to the side of Loch Glascarnoch where we would call it a day. It was a strangely early finish being only about 9pm and with such a short hill next on the list, but the mere suggestion of fish & chips in Ullapool was overpowering to my slavering senses! After a fast blast into town in Archie's car, the hot deep-fried food caked in salt and grease all washed down with good ale was absolute heaven, not having tasted anything like it for two months!

Day 63 Friday 26th June - The Naked Ramblers
Foot 14.5 miles & 7,021ft, bike 32 miles (789ft), 4 Corbetts

Days 63-65 Strathconnon to Alladale

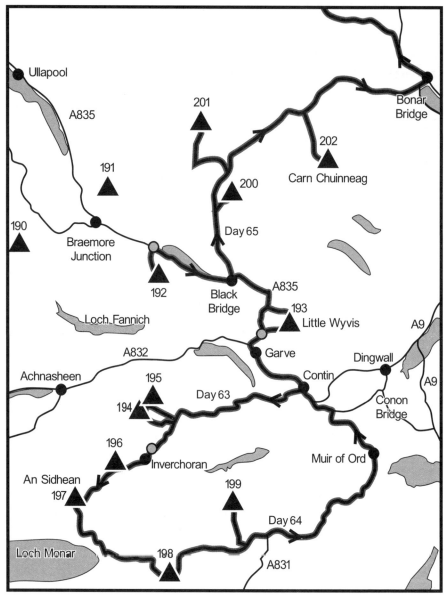

192. Beinn Liath Mhor a' Ghiubhais Li (766m)

193. Little Wyvis (763m)

194. Meallan nan Uan (838m)

195. Sgurr a' Mhuilinn (879m)

196. Bac an Eich (849m)

197. An Sidhean (814m)

198. Sgorr na Diollaid (818m)

199. Beinn a' Bha'ach Ard (862m)

200. Beinn a' Chaisteil (787m)

201. Carn Ban (842m)

202. Carn Chuinneag (838m)

Another gorgeous morning and Brenda accompanied me up the Gaelic mouthful of Beinn Liath Mhor a' Ghiubhais Li. Within a few hundred metres the sweat was dripping off us and I whipped off my T-shirt before it got soaked. Not be outdone, and claiming sexual discrimination, she whipped hers off too. Set free from civilisation and feeling all caveman, I upped the stakes and wheeched my shorts off, once more Brenda reciprocated, claiming liberation, and we marched up to the summit like Tarzan and Jane but without elephants or loin cloths! Proclaiming a draw, and a chilly wind at the top, we pulled our kegs back on and trotted back down, chuffed that the first hill of the day was in the bag before second breakfast-time.

A feature of the last week had been the almost constant easterly wind; not strong, but enough to make you try a bit harder when you were riding your bike into it, like now as I headed down the side of Loch Glascarnoch towards Garbat, the access to Little Wyvis. With an unfriendly height restrictor preventing access to the car park, and with the van teetering on the edge of the high-speed main road, I did a quick Superman change into my hill gear and took off up the path. Brenda would meet me again at the big tourist car park just two miles further south. I enjoyed a pleasant plod straight up the well-constructed Ben Wyvis footpath until I cleared the forest, then cut off, sharp right across the burn and up the steep north side of Little Wyvis, following a line of old rusty fence posts in deep heather. The top came quickly and I messed about for a few self timer-photos on the final ridge, with Ben Wyvis in the background. I started the easy run down the huge bulldozed track that scars the face of this hill, but stopped to admire the previous landowner/deer farmer's idiotic printed warning "DANGER – please be aware of farmed red deer stags and wild red deer stags. They are very dangerous and could cause serious harm. You enter this area at your own risk. It is also advisable not to enter with dogs. We do not accept and any responsibility for any physical and or mental injury to you or your pets or valuables" Don Reid's blog warning about this garbage just other day was still fresh in my head, but with no need for confrontation now, as it was clear there were no longer any deer in this massive enclosure and the operation had thankfully ceased to exist. I met Brenda sunning herself on the bridge over the falls, baking in the sun, and we retired to the van for a huge lunch.

More biking, this time turning right at Contin and south for the first time in many weeks into Strathconon, nipping along the tight wee back roads that led to the tiny settlement of Strathmore. My dad had re-appeared and had brought Manuel & Duncan with him for the weekend. However, I had two more Corbetts to bash before I could relax, so Brenda and I set off together up Meallan nan Uan. About halfway up I decided to push on ahead as Brenda was only planning one hill, but I also had Sgurr a' Mhuilinn to pick off. It was another lovely evening and once on the high ridge the running was great on grassy trods. It was a short but steep drop and climb out on smashing short grass, and a few photos from the top were in order before plummeting back down. As I dodged a few craggy sections an eagle soared up in front of me, and climbed away without any effort, scanning me carefully. I was too slow to get the camera out and only managed a poor effort of a photo; still, it was bonus to have seen it close up. Back down at the van the midges were making their presence felt, and my Dad quickly made tracks to find himself a B&B, while I finished the day with a short 3 mile ride down the glen to Inverchoran. We parked up, had dinner with the boys and caught up on their news before settling down for the night, disturbed only when Dave Rogers parked up next to us in the early hours of the morning, having driven up from Edinburgh with Mary and their two girls Helen and Ruth. After much stage whispering and arguing about tent poles or sleeping bags and clunking of doors then cursing midges, silence descended once more.

Day 64 Saturday 27th June - The Strathconon Loop
Foot 21 miles & 8,218ft, bike 39 miles (837ft), mtb 3 miles (458ft), 4 Corbetts

A 9am start, I biked the first mile and half on the track past Inverchoran Farm with Dave, leaving the respective families to recover the bikes. We plodded down Gleann Chorainn before bearing west and up into some thick clag, but thankfully still dry. I was happy and confident to switch off leaving Dave to navigate, something he is excellent at. It was good to have the craic and catch up on news whilst meandering through the gloop up to Bac an Eich trig point. A four mile traverse on a broad ridge to An Sidhean needed to be careful and efficient, but with Dave on the compass we made good time trotting along. In thick mist it was only at the summit that I realised I had been on this hill before; visited during my 1998 Munro run from Ben Hope to Lomond, but not realising then that it was a Corbett - I had been traversing from Maoile Lunndaidh east towards the Strathfarrar Munros. With the clouds starting to break up and a hot sun burning through, we cut a good line of descent out of the mist to the loch-side footpath that led us quickly to the Monar dam and Brenda with the van.

To Dave's annoyance I had an extended break eating and drinking, enjoying the views over the dam wall with the boys. Mary and the girls had already headed off to explore and camp elsewhere, while cycling pal Peter Bennett had rejoined us to catch up on progress and the brief bike ride 4 miles down the glen, before I set off up Sgorr na Diollaid with Dave - getting grumpier by the minute with all my faffing about. His grumpiness was not improved any as we flogged steeply up the first 1,000ft slope, pock-marked by cattle hooves and covered in stinking dung. The temperature had rocketed in the sunshine and made the climb hard going. After a while in silence, I looked around and there was no sign of Dave. Assuming he had simply taken a different line I continued up, but when I looked back again and saw him far below I realised he had run out of steam! He was plodding up very slowly after me so I continued to the pointy wee summit and had a bite to eat in the sun while I waited. Finally he appeared, covered in salt and slavers, not saying much other than unpleasant grumbles and slumped in a heap on the grass just below me. I threw a bag of jelly-babies on top of him which were dispatched quickly. With Dave somewhat revived after a spell, we started down aiming for the bridge at Cambussorray, but quickly found ourselves wallowing in chest deep heather, hidden broken rocks and nasty drops. It was horrendous going but Dave found new legs and led the way through the jungle. I note that the SMC Corbetts book describes climbing the hill from the south side – now I know why! After a tortuous hour we stumbled out onto the track, and a fast transition was required to bike 6 miles east to the power station. We had to get the van out the Glen Strathfarrar private access gate before closing time at 8pm, so a knackered Dave would drive the van, whilst Brenda opted to do the final hill of the day.

From the hydro station, a short mtb ride up an access track, then hit the hill for a speedy ascent; I left Brenda behind to plod up at her own pace. It was a beautiful warm evening with lovely clear views from the top, but I had to get back down quickly and prepare to finish the day with a thirty mile road section. With Dave waiting on Brenda returning, I had a good head start on them but was horrified when they finally passed me on the narrow roads near Marybank to see that the toilet window was propped wide open; it was a miracle it hadn't already been ripped off by a passing vehicle. Thankfully I had my mobile with me and a quick call prevented an expensive disaster. It was nearly dark now and my lights were on as well as the fluorescent vest, but I was pretty knackered and fast running out of energy. Another call to Brenda and I arranged that we would call it a day, slightly short, at the Little Wyvis car park where we could get the van well off the main road for dinner and peace & quiet, now about 11pm.

Geoff Simpson & Ali Johnston reminisced... *We arrived on the Saturday evening, parked the car at Black Bridge at the foot of Strath Vaich and sat down to enjoy a beer and watch the sun going down. Five minutes later a car came screaming down the Strath and the driver appeared like a whirlwind – told us we were "in his parking space... no, it doesn't matter, would you like a dram?", "Well maybe just a wee..." – whereupon he produced a 40oz bottle of Whyte & Mackay, poured me a half pint, thrust a can of beer into my hand, gulped his back and chucked the rest in the boot of his car just before another car screeched to a halt on the main road, he jumped in and they were off to the Aultguish Inn - I just hoped that the next couple of days would be less frantic!*

Day 65 Sunday 28th June - Knockin' on to Knockan Crag

Days 65-68 Assynt

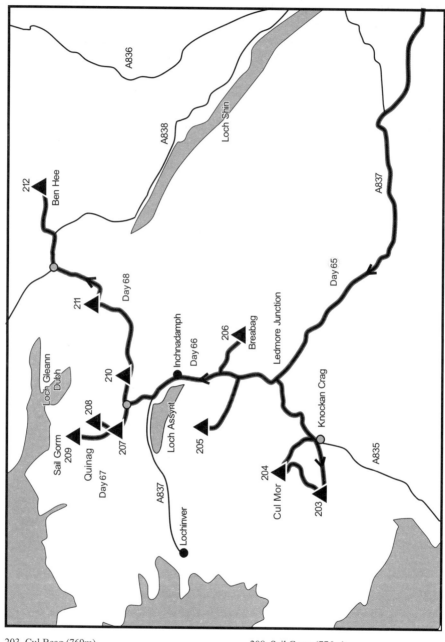

203. Cul Beag (769m)
204. Cul Mor (849m)
205. Canisp (847m)
206. Breabag (815m)
207. Spidean Coinich (764m)

208. Sail Gorm (776m)
209. Sail Gharbh (808m)
210. Glas Bheinn (776m)
211. Beinn Leoid (792m)
212. Ben Hee (873m)

Foot 14 miles & 5,351ft, bike 53 miles (1,793ft), mtb 28 miles (1,164ft), 3 Corbetts

Straight after breakfast I finished off the 7 miles of A835 road to Black Bridge. There Dad was waiting, along with Hunters Bog Trotters Geoff Simpson & Ali Johnson, and fellow Westies Pete & Elsie Baxter. After much dithering and switching bikes, blethering etc, a posse of seven riders, The Magnificent Seven, set off along the good track to Loch Vaich. It was already a warm day and a herd of Heilan' Coos were standing in the river to cool off, eyeing us with indifference as we took obligatory photos. I suddenly realised that I had set off in the wrong footwear. I had forgotten to change from my road biking trainers, which hurt my Achilles too much to be of any use as hill shoes, for my tried and well tested trail shoes. Rather than return miles to the van, I still had a signal so called and left young Manuel with clear and concise instructions that my running shoes had to be taken in to me by Johnston Orr and Andy Mott, who I knew were going to be following us in on foot very shortly. Impatient as ever with all the faffing about, Dave had blazed off in front but took a wrong turn, having to double back and slink his way back into the rear of the pack, much to the delight of everyone else. Halfway along the loch side at Lubachlaggan we dumped the bikes and set off on foot up Beinn a' Chaisteil. It was a cracker of a day and the view from the top was superb, although it was nearly eclipsed when Pete took his top off and his belly unfolded! Once we all had a breather on top of Corbett number 200, we trotted off back towards the bikes and met Johnston and Andy, having run in, on their way up the hill. I watched them approach… the answer was clear before I asked, "Have you got my shoes?" "Shoes? Ahh… shoes! Oops, eh, mmm sorry, no we didn't realise, emm… did you want them?" "AAARGH! I needed those fucking shoes!!!!!" I spat the dummy so far out it landed in the loch about a mile away. I was in an instant rage and stormed off down the hill trying not to speak to anyone in case I would later regret it in court! I was now committed to wearing these crappy shoes, that were already hurting my feet, for the next two Corbetts, but what really irritated me was that it could and should have been avoided... grrrr!

I calmed down again during the 6 miles of biking to the foot of the next hill, but Brenda and Ali were heading back to the van, reducing us to five. After an initial steep climb the plod up Carn Ban was quite straight forward and was another hill I had forgotten that I had climbed years previously, with Dave in filthy weather from Corrie Mor bothy to the west. This time there were terrific views across to the neighbouring Beinn Dearg group. We dropped off the hill and a short double-back was required on the bikes before bidding farewell to Pete & Elsie. And then there were three…

Another 10 miles of bumpy mtb'ing east down Gleann Mor into Alladale, which offered some lovely riding by the river, with an occasional stop to ease now tender hind parts for some. It was clear when we had reached the boundaries of Alladale Estate with its ridiculous intimidating electrified fencing, apparently to safely enclose proposed wild animals such at wolves, bears and dinosaurs... aye right! To date there are none, but the fences remain.

At last we popped out onto the road at Glencalvie Lodge, where as always Brenda was waiting patiently, with the boys and my Dad. Mary and the girls had returned to pick up Dave after a few good hard days out with me, which were much appreciated as he always pushed me on that wee bit harder each time. Geoff and I biked up Glen Calvie, chasing an advanced party of Johnston, Andy and Cat Millar who had managed to track us down in time to do the last hill of the day, Carn Chuinneag. When we finally biked up to them at the foot of a stalkers track, I suddenly felt rather stupid and embarrassed. Having already run 13 miles in & out from Beinn a' Chaisteil and the infamous "shoe" episode, Johnston & Andy had risen above my childlike strop and driven a very long way around from Black Bridge with my hill shoes and brought them into the foot of the last hill for me! They were too polite to say "Here's your *fucking shoes*" you twat", but they were certainly entitled too after the way I had behaved earlier.

Correct shoes now donned and my humble pie eaten, we set off up the hill on a very good stalkers path that zig-zagged its way through deep heather, some of it freshly burnt. I was buzzing a bit and took the lead, striding out fast and hard. Cat kept pace right on my heels, almost pushing, with Geoff next in line revelling in revisiting a favourite hill of his from his time living in the area previously. Johnston and Andy couldn't believe the pace we were running at, after over thirty miles of mountain biking and two Corbetts. We regrouped at the top, all puffing away madly but exhilarated. We had earned a few extra minutes on the summit, enjoying the evening view and munching various goodies, then the descent which was as furious as the climb. I dropped off the back to get a few photos of them all tearing down the hill. To catch up again, Geoff and I cut out a few zig-zags through the burnt sooty heather, leaving our bare legs looking like a tattoo artist had etched crazy Celtic patterns up to our knees! A very fast mtb whizz back to the van and quick change into road biking gear, along with a good feed and fluids. Dad was taking the boys back to Newtonmore again, but hopefully all returning for the finale in a few days time. Geoff and Ali were off to camp for the night whilst I thanked Andy, Johnston and Cat for their help and company, bidding them farewell as they headed home to Glasgow.

I set off on a 50 mile ride from the east coast to the west. It was a defining moment and marked the start of the end; the final push. Once I warmed up on the bike and got spinning, I lifted the pace and rode off into a stunning red sunset. Brenda had driven ahead and I met her halfway for a fresh water bottle. I hadn't been sure if I would manage the full cycle distance tonight but my tail was up and the adrenaline pumping, so there was no stopping me. On the long climb out of Oykel Bridge I was in second from top gear and dancing on the pedals to make it go faster! Flies and bugs were pinging off my glasses like bullets and sweat trickling off my nose. I heard a shout and there was Geoff and Ali waving at me, camped up well off the road by the river, enjoying a beer and the epic sunset. I flew into Assynt, one of the most spectacular areas of Scotland, at Ledmore Junction and hung sharp left for the final effort, the big climb up to Knockan Crag Visitor Centre. I was running out of steam fast, but buried myself to nail the steep hill, out the saddle with quads smoking with pain to keep going. Finally, finally, the top, and Brenda out to cheer me home. What an truly amazing day out. 11pm and dinner time.

Johnston blogged... *A logistical cock-up meant we didn't have Manny's fave fell shoes to replace the trainers he uses mostly for biking. The fell shoes were thereafter referred to loudly as "my fucking shoes!!!" Oops.*
After the long run back out, I just had enough time for the 90-min drive to Glencalvie, where the infamous shoes were successfully transported up the glen. The 3rd Corbett of the day was another super-fast ascent - fitness clearly back to 100% after the Ardgour crash all those days ago. At least he was happy to be reunited with the footwear! Today was yet another illustration of how busy Brenda is and what a great job she does in keeping Manny on the road.
202 Corbetts done, 17 to go...

Geoff & Ali's diary... *****! said Manny, exploding in an amazing tantrum, stamping his feet and thumping his poles in the ground, sending deer scampering for cover in all directions. Manny was showing no signs of caution on the bike despite having recently fallen off and "broken" his leg - flying down any descent, probably still fuelled by rage at having the 'wrong shoes'. I was shattered by the time we dropped the bikes at the foot of Carn Chuinneag and was looking forward to a gentle jaunt up and down the hill but Manny had other ideas. Before we joined in on the Corbetts Round Ali had asked me if she would be able to do some of the hills or would she hold Manny up. I assured her that the pace would be fairly moderate especially as Manny would be pretty weary by now. However, Manny shot off up the hill, aided by his cheating sticks, leaving the rest of us struggling in his wake! After finishing and a welcoming cup of tea, I was looking forward to a leisurely drive round to Ledmore Junction and then crawling into my tent. Incredibly, Manny still had a 50 mile cycle ahead of him before the day was done. Unfortunately fortunately, I hadn't brought my road bike! We found an idyllic spot to pitch our tent, just south of Ledmore Junction. We had only just settled down to have a beer and enjoy the sunset when we heard a whoop as Manny flew past on his bike on his way to Knockan Crags...*

Bob @ sandstone blogged... *Reads like you and your team are completely on top* *of things, Manny. Now you are entering a unique landscape that is also the best of Corbett Country. The weather also looks as if it is going to cooperate in a great finish. No stopping you now!*

Lyn and Kev blogged... *If your last Corbett is Friday does this mean you and Bren will be competing in the Corrieyairack Challenge? ONLY JOKING... we will be waiting at the finish line in Kincraig with a Cairngorm Beer just in case. xx*

Brenda blogged... *Not going to make the Corrieyairack this year but will make it to the Suie for a pint on the way home on Saturday.*

Steve Wall blogged... *Not doing the Corrieyairack??? Why ever not, you will be hill-fit and in with a chance!! Seriously, well done Brenda; Manny would never have done so well without a good girl by his side and supporting him, we at Cairngorm Runners are very proud of you both. As a mountaineer I know exactly what Manny has bitten off and am so impressed with his amazing efforts thus far - come on almost there. Truly amazing.*

Manny's note... I *was* actually starting to consider the Corrieyairack Challenge the day after we finished. It's a great duathlon event of 18 miles running on General Wade's road over the famous Corrieyairack Pass from Fort Augustus, followed by 30 miles of fast road biking finishing in the village fete of Kincraig, just 6 miles from our home... it would have been a nice warm-down, but fate had other plans for the finish...

Day 66 Monday 29th June - Amazing Assynt
Foot 23.5 miles & 9,492ft, bike 15 miles (778ft), 4 Corbetts

It was a grey morning with huge licks of highland mist wrapped around the individual peaks of Assynt, some with their tops sticking out, some obscured. But it was clear that it was going to burn off quickly and the air was already warm and sticky with humidity. I was very tired from the big finish of the night before. There was no spring in my step as Geoff and Chris accompanied me across the moor toward Cul Beag, with a new enemy to contend with – cleggs, millions of them! They were homing in on us in squadrons, and you would have only a split second to slap the swine once they landed before they could deliver their painful bites, even through our t-shirts. As the ferocity of the attacks ebbed and flowed we took to slapping each other if we spotted one land on another's back. From a distance we must have looked like one of the more bizarre Monty Python sketches!! Geoff and Chris were blethering away quite the thing but I was in a tired grump with the world, though kept it to myself while my legs creaked and groaned into life for their daily battering. With my head down and them yapping, we all missed the opportunity to contour around the side of the unnecessary wee bump Meall Dearg, costing me an extra few hundred feet of climb; now I was *really* grumpy! Again I kept it in, I knew I was knackered and had learned to read the signs. However as soon as we hit the top, the mist evaporated around us and my foul mood with it. It took a new top to drag me up.

We tried to enjoy the tremendous views of Coigach opening up around us in among the relentless kamikaze cleggs, but cut our stay short to escape off the very steep north side. It took concentration to get down the steep tussocky grass safely into Gleann Laoigh, and the line 2,500ft up Cul Mor looked daunting. Even though this is described in the SMC guidebook, I guess there can't be too many people who try this rough line to join these two fantastic mountains? After a few hundred feet of slogging up the side, we came to Lochan Dearg a' Chuil Mhoir with a breathtaking view of Stac Pollaidh across a beautiful sandy beach and crystal clear water; this was paradise! Chris was leaping about all over the place trying to photograph the scene from every possible angle, while Geoff and I, tired of feeding colonies of cleggs, leapt into the cold water to drown them! At last on our way again we climbed for the top, the last wisps of mist fizzling away and blue skies allowing a burning sun to get through to us. We hit the top in great spirits now, with truly epic vistas all around and a surprise waiting on top. Sitting on the trig point was a small bag of sweeties, and below scratched onto a flat rock were mysterious messages "I love Geoff" and "Manny ♥ xx" We didn't have to think very hard to figure out who our secret admirers were. Lingering, we soaked up the heat and the view, but got fed up of swatting cleggs. We jogged off, slowly gaining pace, with dramatic Suilven tantalisingly near but not reaching the Corbett 762m mark, sadly to be bypassed. We gathered pace on the way down and soon were haring along and having a real blast. My walking poles were a nuisance now and I folded them away; as I did so I knew it was for the last time. My knee felt fully mended and I was super-fit again – I didn't want to finish the last few days using the poles, but was forever converted to their importance for those still wanting to get out on the hills, even after the legs want to stop! I still use poles for walking, particularly when carrying our small but fast growing daughter Maisy, or a heavy pack, for balance and to ease the strain on the knees, but never since for running. As we neared the end of the track by the road a familiar face was waiting to greet us; Don Reid was back along with his wife Elma for few days, great!

We got back to the van and drank, ate and blethered updates with Don & Elma, whilst we were aware of huge black clouds boiling up in the sky. I had an easy 7 mile ride on the bike, past Ledmore Junction onto the A837 at Loch Awe, and got ready for running up Canisp. Brenda, Ali and Elma had set off thirty minutes in advance so that we could all meet on the summit, but just as Don, Geoff, Chris and I were about to step out of the van in pursuit, a colossal wall of rain crashed down with a terrific noise! In seconds there was thunder and lightning and the road flooded in a few minutes with the sheer volume of rainwater. I turned to the lads and asked "Cup tea anyone?" We all chuckled long and hard as the monsoon thrashed the van and we thought of the girls out in the middle of it, floating gently along! It lasted long enough to boil the kettle and have a cuppa and Chris took a couple of video clips to remind us just how loud the rain was – deafening! It stopped as suddenly as it had started and the air was clean and fresh again. The hill burns had all burst into gurgling life and we hoped that all the cleggs had drowned. We made good time up the hill, taking turns in front, trying to make up for the lost time on the girls. We caught them bang-on the summit and had a good laugh at their soggy misfortune, but given the heat of the day, they had actually quite enjoyed their dousing - except the close lightning. Swirls of mist hugged the sides of Canisp and made the windows of scenery even more atmospheric, especially with a few distant rumbles of thunder. We enjoyed an extended stop for goodies and photos before splitting forces once more, with the boys tearing off down the hill, and the girls walking off together. It worked well, as by the time they came off the hill I had refuelled and was getting on my bike for the very short hop north to the famous Bone Caves car park at the foot of Breabag.

Everyone was buzzing a now. At the Bone Caves car park, Geoff & Chris were going to come up Breabag with me and the others were going to get booked into Inchnadamph bunkhouse, then get a bar meal in the hotel. They were under instruction to make sure I had food ordered up if it looked like I might miss last orders. With the black thunder clouds now receding to the east, leaving us bathed in glorious sunshine, we ran and walked up the glen past the bizarre sight of Allt nan Uamh which pours fiercely straight out the bedrock to instantly become a fast flowing river. The caves were tempting but we marched past at good pace and up the heathery, mossy hillside, heading through the prominent craggy face straight onto the summit. All the time the sun had been lowering and the scene from the top was spellbinding. We sat on big flat quartzite blocks at the cairn and fell quiet to soak up one of the most beautiful evenings I have seen in Scotland. The sea shimmered in the sunlight with a hint of pink, whilst all the classic individual mountains of Assynt stood out as silhouetted satellites. There were odd wisps of cloud left lingering from the thunderstorm and the was air clean and still. Silence. Finally we had to move, and after a flurry of photographs of the picture-postcard scenery we reluctantly headed down the slope, stopping at every vague excuse to have another look west. I twisted my ankle slightly and abruptly realised I still had a job to do! We finished the run past the caves and back to the van. We were all flying with excitement and adrenaline, but I still had to finish the day with a bike ride up the hill from Skiag Bridge. I had been told that bar meals were on a time limit so had to beast the ride hard, nearly blowing a gasket by the top of the hill, before jumping into the van back to the Inchnadamph Hotel for dinner and a few pints. Thankfully Don had spoken to the barman and explained my predicament, who although the kitchen was now closed, had my meal kept warm in the oven for my arrival, and with a nice touch donated me a pint of fine ale to wash it down with! What a great night and a few more beers with the team capped it perfectly. The barman, whilst clearing some of our glasses away, dropped into the conversation that he had heard that tomorrow night's huge AC/DC concert in Glasgow had been cancelled; for a second I bristled, then caught his eye and realised he had been put up to it by one of my lot - Brenda and I were due to be going to the gig the following day!

Newtonmore Primary School P5-7 Gaelic Class (Duncan's class) blogged.... *Hey Manny, well done on getting this far. We hope you complete all the hills and have fun doing it!*

Geoff & Ali's diary... *Running with Chris is like being out with your dog. He must have covered about 3 times the distance of the rest of us as he dropped back to take pictures of us from behind; then you would see him off to your left or right; and as you came up to the crest of a rise, remarkably there he would be waiting in front of you to take more pictures! We climbed Cul Beag & Mor whilst slapping ourselves and each other to fend off the biting enemy clegs; it was a bit like some demented German folk dance. Thankfully we reached Lochan Dearg a 'Chuil Mhoir into which Manny and I immediately plunged (Chris was about 2 miles out to the West taking more pics!). Not only was this a great way to escape the clegs, it was absolutely bliss on such a hot day. From the top majestic Suilven, just to the North, looked close enough to touch; it's hard to believe it's not even a Corbett! On the summit of Breabag at around 7:30 pm we sat in the sunshine admiring the islands out to the west and a golden eagle circling overhead... I would have slept anywhere I was so tired and, I was overwhelmed with the thought of how Manny had been doing this for the last 60+ days; I was knackered after 2!*

As a wee side issue, and only after the Round was long finished, I found out that everyone who stayed in the bunkhouse that night became very ill soon after. Chris's diabolical symptoms kicked in forty-eight hours later; Don & Elma both also got clobbered, Don in particular being ill for weeks after; Geoff and Ali had what they described as "twenty-fours hours of living hell" a few days later, even convincing themselves that they might have Swine Flu! I later learned that it was an airborne virus that they had picked up, and nothing what-so-ever to do with the hygiene of the accommodation, which they all agreed, was a smashing place. It was just really bad luck, but I was extremely grateful that we had slept in our van!

Day 67 Tuesday 30th June – Quinag, a Highway to Hell
Foot 8.5 miles & 3,801ft, 3 Corbetts

When AC/DC first announced they would be playing a gig in Glasgow in June 2009 I was already well advanced in planning the Round, and a quick look at my 60 day schedule told me that even with a few hiccups, I should still be finished in plenty of time to be able to swan down to the Big Smoke to take in the best live rock n' roll band in the world tearing up their Scottish/Glaswegian roots, along with 40,000 other like-minded souls; what a fantastic way to finish the trip I thought! However, falling off my bike back in Ardgour was never part of the plan, which all told, had cost me four precious days; the knock-on effect being that the gig now fell still with a few days of the Round left, while we were located at just about the furthest away point north possible! In the lead-up to this day no-one really believed that we would actually go to the gig, but then, they had probably never seen AC/DC play live! I had seen them four times before and there was absolutely no way I was going to miss them this time.

The morning was already burning hot as my posse trotted off up this brilliant knot of three Corbetts. Quinag is the collective name for this stand-alone massif, which by the luck of ancient glacial erosion, contains Spidean Coinich, Sail Ghorm and Sail Gharbh, all attainable within a few short hours effort. The lassies had chosen to follow on at a walk up the first top, whilst we clattered ahead around the whole group. Don was leading us at fine pace, with Geoff and Chris keeping the conversation going about the stunning evening the night before. We were on top of Spidean Coinich in no time, enjoying the epic views. The run off north was steep, rocky and technical, but great fun. We were all nudging each other on faster and faster. A brief stop for photos while standing out on a very high and narrow sandstone finger with yawning drops on three sides, then running on with the shirts off towards Sail Ghorm. We touched the top and moved on past the stone summit cairn to the edge of the massive crags and sat down. It's funny how no-one needed to say anything to know that we all wanted a stop here for a while - we all just chilled out and gawped at the scene in silence. I lay back and shut my eyes for a few minutes, and felt the gorgeous heat of the sun cooking my skin. Twenty minutes rolled by, but felt like seconds, before we grudgingly got to our feet to double-back along the ridge. The final climb up Sail Gharbh felt effortless. The more mundane top, with its freshly vandalised concrete trig point, failed to do justice to the mountain whose northern cliffs are so spectacular and most imposing when viewed from the Kylesku road. Only a brief stop for food and a slurp to drink then we were off again, cutting down the steep grass and rocky slope into the huge corrie below, like a giant cauldron full of baking heat. We all hammered down the stalkers path and were back at the car park in jig time, all dripping with sweat and grinning like a herd of cats. Brenda had left Elma and Ali to walk out after the first hill, and carried on herself to run Sail Gharbh, and must have made good time because we never saw her on the hill at any point. Her fitness had improved incredibly over the last few weeks, now picking off as many Corbetts as possible between domestic or travel duties, always one or perhaps two a day as the opportunity arose. It hadn't been voiced publicly, but it was clear that there was an unofficial competition going on between Brenda and Chris to see who could manage the second largest collection of tops during the trip - it was going to be close!

It was only about midday, but this day's Corbetteering was at a premature end – we were off to Glasgow. We got ourselves changed, fed & watered and after a quick Angus Young (AC/DC's enigmatic guitarist) impersonation around the car park, we were ready for the long drag back to Kingussie in the campervan, to then pick up our car for the drive south. We had a great laugh with the others about this madness but all the time Chris was quiet about it; although he never mentioned it, I sensed he was utterly dismayed and could understand his thinking. All the effort of the huge days and late finishes, only to throw away two half days in stunning weather, just to go on a crazy 500 mile round trip for a concert! But this was the whole essence of the Round. Ok, the gig wasn't meant to happen like this, but it had, and we were out to have fun - first and foremost, to have fun. This was simply part of it and very memorable it was. As we set off I think Chris was still hoping we would stop and say "Only joking!" Unfortunately we did have to stop, just down the road a few miles, when I noticed in the mirror that the bike rack was wobbling about rather a lot. On closer inspection the weight of the three bikes (sometimes four, for supporters) was in danger of ripping the rack out of the bodywork by the fixing bolts! There was nothing I could do about it here so I put my mountain bike inside the van to ease the strain on the bolts until we got back to Kingussie. The drive in the heat was torture, but we were now really looking forward to the gig; a brief stop at our home to swap vehicles then south at a much faster pace in the car, getting to Glasgow and meeting up with my brother Richard in perfect time for the concert.

The streets around Hampden Park were heaving with people as the 40,000 tickets had sold out in a few hours many months ago, and most of them seemed to have been drinking since lunchtime, or earlier! There were denim and leather clad bodies lying on grass verges or slumped on the pavements all over the place; it resembled a war zone! The atmosphere inside the stadium was electric, with dozens of vendors still feeding the natives yet more crap, expensive lager from back-pack bowsers, the result being drunken fights breaking out all over the place. Thankfully we had raised seats in the terraces and a great view across the heaving pitch to the stage. The band came on with their first track "Runaway Train" and the crowd completely erupted. It was absolutely sensational. A few tracks in and there was a sudden surge in the crowd just to our left and an exclusion zone instantly opened up around an unconscious individual slumped in his seat. Super-greasy long hair, big bushy beard, dressed in a manky old leather jacket and shredded jeans, he had thrown up, pissed himself and fallen unconscious all in one majestic movement, and the smell had everyone within a ten seat radius gagging for fresh air! The poor First Aiders, wearing Marigolds, carried him away for treatment, probably hospital, whilst AC/DC continued to smash out "Hell Ain't A Bad Place To Be"… It's the only hard rock gig I've ever been at where the cleaners came in during the show!

Finally, thoroughly entertained and completely hoarse from singing and cheering we bid farewell to Richard and headed back north for Kingussie. As the adrenaline of the foot stomping music wore off, the exhaustion of the running, heat and the driving kicked in and dangerous sleepiness was racing up on me. Now very late, we stopped at Perth for coffee and Red Bull at the 24-hour garage there, and found most of the Highland population inside also returning from the concert, including Jane & Beth from the Cairngorm Brewery - my fabulous sponsors, still bouncing after the gig! We struggled back home, my eyes screaming to close, finally doing so around 3am. Tick, tick, tick…

Geoff & Ali's diary… *Quinag is a wonderful day out and on another glorious day like today it was all over too quickly. Don, Manny and I trotted along at an even pace whilst Chris did his manic photographer/sheepdog thing before all descending back to the car park for lunch. Sadly, Ali & I had to depart at this point and we left to the sight of Manny strutting Angus Young-like round the car park with a wig-mop of black hair on his head, in preparation for the AC/DC concert in Glasgow that night. As if the logistics weren't hard enough!*

Day 68 Wednesday 1ˢᵗ July - Back In Business
Foot 18 miles & 6,376ft, mtb 5 miles (426ft), 3 Corbetts

BEEP BEEP BEEP… oh no!

Death came to visit us; it was time to get up. Neither of us could move, paralysed with tiredness. I dozed off then groaned awake again and managed to roll over enough to throw the duvet off. Piece by piece we started to move, slowly. A life-giving cup of tea before a few last minute items of re-packing, including leaving behind Brenda's mountain bike to help take the weight off the creaking bike rack, then we were off on the road again. It was 8am. Brenda managed to get some sleep on the way north but I struggled to keep my concentration. It was another brilliant day of sunshine, and yesterday's journey now a surreal memory. We drove back into the car park beneath Quinag around midday and found our supporters already waiting on our return, keen to get us going again, certainly keener than us.

Chris was our fresh pacer as we set off up Glas Bheinn, Brenda determined not to lose ground in the unspoken battle for second place. The heat was tremendous, the ground initially very steep and we were both knackered, but feeling better for the exercise and the blood pumping again. We plodded on up, Brenda fielding calls from supporters on the mobile as we moved, "Hello, Mr Gorman's office…" At the top I breathed a sigh of relief to be back in the game, and Chris took some good photos of Brenda and I. Brenny headed straight down again, but I had a 6 mile section of remote upland ground to cover to get Beinn Leoid. John Donnelly had rejoined the circus and was heading up the same hill, but from the north side, and didn't know if we would meet up. Inspired again after Glas Bheinn, Chris and I made great time across the moor, trying to follow a vague stalkers path for as long as possible. The obligatory afternoon thunderclouds were building up and the heat oppressive. It wasn't long before we got a solid dousing and the temperature plummeted, our lightweight wind-proofs little defense against the freezing rain, with white flashes and thumps of thunder echoing all around us. I had run quite strongly for the last hour, but I could suddenly feel myself weakening dramatically and started to pop jelly babies into my mouth. Chris strode effortlessly away from me, but I managed to continue at a trundle as far as the summit cairn and trig. Once I stopped I started feeling quite ill. Shattered with tiredness, last night's journey and very late night were starting to punish me. I ate more and had a drink, but all in vain, I was dying. There was no sign of JD anywhere; he had been and left much earlier. I knew we had to get moving and at least the initial big descent was easier to cope with, with gravity doing most of the work, but on the flatter stalkers path by Loch Dubh my wheels finally fell off. I couldn't run anymore, but only stumble about roughly in a forward motion, Chris coaxing me onwards all the time. I had to stop and take in more water and food, but my body was crying out for sleep with my eyes and head feeling very heavy. I was bonked out in a big way. Feeling like death, Chris managed to nudge me onto the final zigzag stalkers path that would lead us down to the roadside and the van. I had already decided that I couldn't do the next planned hill for today. I was creeping along whilst Chris shot off down out of sight. What a relief to hit the road and shuffle in misery the final few hundred metres to the van, straight past the waiting Paparazzi of Brenda, Don, Elma, Chris and Donald straight inside to slump onto the cumfy bench cushions, out-cold in an instant.

Brenda let me sleep in a coma for half an hour then forced me awake, pushing a plate of food under my nose and demanding I eat; then came a Complan and a can of coke, along with a pudding and a cup of tea with biscuits and crisps then sweets... I wanted to throw up but wasn't allowed; quite rightly she bullied me into action again. Within half an hour I was feeling fine again and thinking about the next hill, Ben Hee; I had to push on. A 2 mile bike ride on the road, then up a track for a further mile to meet up with Chris once more and shoot off up the Allt Coir' a' Chruiteir at a cracking pace. Brenda was following behind with Donald Smith at a walk/jog, but we were now belting up the hill at almost racing pace, daring each other to push harder. By the misty top we were in an all out sprint for the summit trig, Chris winning by just enough to still have time to whip out his camera for a photo of me. We laughed in-between gaps for oxygen! Two hours previous I felt like I was about to meet my end, and here I was now, thrashing up Ben Hee at full pelt – it's just amazing how quickly the body can recover so quickly with a bit of grub, a drink and a wee sleep! We descended a good bit slower and more carefully, knowing that we were finished for the day, and met Brenda and Donald still plodding upwards. I jumped on the bike and retraced my route to the van, even daring to think I might carry on to do another Corbett, but quickly came to my senses, realising I was pushing my luck as it was. A good dinner and an earlier bed than usual were in order to recharge the batteries for another full-on day tomorrow.

Donald's VW van was parked-up tight next to ours, hosting Chris and JD. Suddenly in the dead of night we awoke when there was a shout and scramble from next door, "Oh fuck, oh fuck…!" then the sliding door being thrown open in a hurry and a dreadful retching noise as Chris spewed his guts into the grass, and again, and again, and again. It was terrible to listen to. Finally his pitiful groans receded back into the van…

Day 69 Thursday 2nd July - The Mother of all Storms
Foot 22 miles & 8,680ft, mtb 6 miles (492ft), 4 Corbetts

Chris was blaming his night of hell on some cold meat that he had eaten the day before. Brenda disagreed, as although the meat hadn't been kept chilled he had only purchased it that day and was kept in the cool boot of his car. It was hard to identify any other reason for it at the time, not knowing until weeks later about the bunkhouse airborne virus that would also strike down Ali, Geoff, Don and Elma; but in any case, he looked utterly wretched and felt miserable. Sadly he could not be involved in any hills today. JD would accompany me up the first couple of tops; him on foot with a head start around Loch More, and me chasing after him by mtb, Brenda to pick it up again. Donald would meet us later in the day at a pre-arranged point high in the hills. Just as I met up with JD and was dumping the bike, a golden flash streaked down the track towards us at high speed – well, high-ish speed – it was Dave Calder, Westies clubmate and frequent cross-dresser, with an occasional hokey-cokey habit usually on platforms... Fresh back from China, he had whizzed north to get in on the last minute Corbett action and of course the final glory legs, which were better than his own milky-white limbs. He wasn't quite ready to go straight out on the morning session with me and JD, but would take my bike back out to Brenda at the van, then walk in with Donald and meet us later in the hills for the afternoon stint.

JD and I made good steady pace over the fantastically named Meallan Liath Coire Mhic Dhughaill or "The Grey Hill of MacDougall's Corrie", again in brilliant sun with a great view of Ben Stack to the west, and Arkle waiting on me further to the north. Before that we had a 4 mile high-level trek to nail Meall Horn, a new hill for both of us. It was a short but steep descent to the Allt Horn footpath, where we could see Donald and Dave waiting on us from the top of the hill. We

Days 69-70 Loch Stack to Ben Loyal

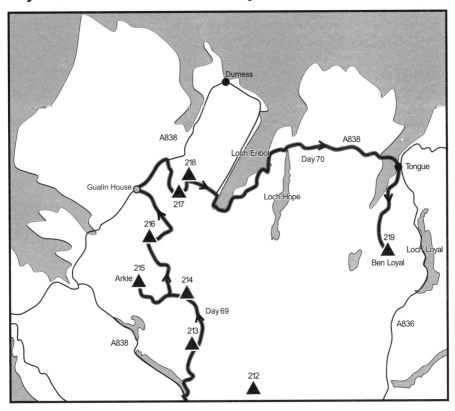

213. Meallan Liath Coire Mhic Dhughaill (801m)
214. Meall Horn (777m)
215. Arkle (787m)
216. Foinaven (911m)

217. Cranstackie (800m)
218. Beinn Spionnaidh (772m)
219, Ben Loyal (764m)

enjoyed a good break for lunch and blethers, relaxing in the sun before it became apparent that the afternoon thunderclouds were already brewing up to the south.

JD headed off down the track to his car by Loch Stack, while the other two escorted me towards Arkle. Quite soon after setting off, and looking at the ominous black clouds, Donald told Dave and me to push on ahead which we gratefully did. Once on the first top, we could see a jet-black storm heading our way and sinister rumbles told us it meant business. We still had to cross the narrow rocky spine to get to the main summit and then return before it arrived. We legged it as fast as we could, all the time the dark curtain closing in. We touched the cairn and turned without stopping, hammering back along the ridge, past Donald who looked a bit resigned to his fate as he still headed upwards. I knew if we managed to get back over the subsidiary top and start down the other side we would be fine, but almost as we were about to get off the narrow ridge it happened. It was like being hit by a train; a solid wall of hail, wind and deafening noise crashed into us with terrific force. Day turned to night in an instant and as we tried to push up and over it was almost impossible to think straight, never mind navigate. All sense of direction was obliterated and lightening started to smash down around us; it was absolutely terrifying. Other than poor Donald, we were the only things sticking up above the ground – we had to get out of there fast, so with a bit of sign language we dived off the top in any direction and down into some extremely steep broken ground to hide like rabbits in a dip behind a big rock. The maelstrom continued for twenty minutes, with lightening all around, soaked and frozen and wishing we were somewhere else. The hailstones were big and painful on bare skin, leaving a carpet on the ground. After an eternity, it eased off to merely dreadful and we made a dash for it, having to first relocate before running down the hill and wondering if Donald was okay? With thunder still ringing around all the rocky corries, we nursed our jangling nerves down to Lochan na Faoileige and a had a brief break for food and recovery. Phew!

We pressed on, and warmed up as we started the new climb in the direction of Foinaven. Unlike previous afternoon storms, the clouds didn't clear away, and distant flashes and bangs continued. However the spectacular scrambly ridge towards the Corbett summit of Ganu Mor was clear and breathtaking with the dramatic weather backdrop. The amazing rock spur of A' Cheir Ghorm looked like an alien landscape, perhaps Mars, and we enjoyed the sprackle over the steep loose ground. BOOM! It was starting again - a second wave. Once more we were taking a pounding, with lightening flashing around us, exposed on a knife edge ridge, we hid again and stayed put. Thankfully this time it was shorter lived and we had just started to move on when my phone rang. It was Brenda calling. "She'll be checking to see if we are still alive after that lot!" I said to Dave as I pressed the button.

Brenda said "Hello, it's me, I've had a wee incident" – instantly I was thinking

"Oh no, there's been a disaster with the van" or such-like. "I think I've broken my arm" Oh shit, now that was a bit more serious. Straight away my mind started to race, thinking of the final day tomorrow, and all the logistics - how to get Brenda's arm x-rayed, plastered and get her back in time... yikes! She explained she had fallen off my bike when trying to ride it 3 miles down Strath Dionard to drop me at the foot of the hill; she had come off on a bend into some rocks. Chris, still recovering from illness, was with her. "Ok, you'll just have to go and get it seen to and get back as soon as you can tonight." Without much more discussion, Chris, still suffering from his own illness, was going to cart her off to Durness and let a local doctor see it first. I was hoping for a sling, or at worst, having to go down to Raigmore Hospital in Inverness to get it x-rayed and plastered. Bugger. My Dad was heading up with Manuel and Duncan, due to arrive soon. I had to get off the hill and find out what was going on.

We soon topped Ganu Mor, with the sky finally starting to clear and the storm receding. Unfortunately the descent down Glas-Coire Granda was tedious, tricky underfoot and we were both knackered. When we eventually hit the track in the glen floor, my bike was exactly where it should have been. Before heading off and obviously in lot of pain, Brenda had still managed to make sure my bike was put in place, taken in by JD who was now back at the van entertaining the boys who had been dropped off by Grampa. Given the unfolding circumstances and even though it was now late, I had considered continuing over the next two hills (the second and third last) and biking all the way to Tongue tonight, leaving just Ben Loyal for the morning - hopefully with Brenda back. Dave told me to stop talking rubbish. "What would it really achieve?" He was right, I had to get out and find out how and where Brenda was, so I whizzed out fast on the bike to the van parked near Gualin House, leaving Dave to trot out behind. At the van JD confirmed Chris had driven Brenda first to Durness, then the long way south to Raigmore in Inverness. It was good to see the boys again and we had a long hug, then quickly onto the phone to speak to Brenda.

It was Chris who answered and the news was bad, very bad. She hadn't just broken her arm. She had also exploded her shoulder joint into many pieces with catastrophic damage. She wasn't going anywhere except an operating theatre – tomorrow! My head fell apart in an instant. From being focussed on just one thing for so long, then labelling it meaningless, mentally tearing it up and discarding it was devastating. I only wanted to be with Brenda now, which was all that really mattered. With that news the guys could see my pain and quickly bailed out to Donald's van to leave me alone with Manuel and Duncan. They were the only ones I could look at, and the only reason I didn't take off down to Inverness there and then. They had just travelled north for four hours with my Dad who, unaware of what had happened, was now away to a B&B and un-contactable; it was already late and I couldn't really put them through hours more driving and starving. I was stuck there. I marched up and down the quiet single track road, calling Charlie and talking through all the ifs, buts and maybes, gnashing my teeth and swearing at the sheep.

Charlie's diary… *Manny phones at 11.30pm. Really upset on the phone 'cos Brenda had fall from a bike and badly smashed her shoulder and away to Raigmore – FUCK! Try to calm him down and tell him he needs to finish tomorrow…*

I really didn't know what to do next, but I knew what I definitely didn't want to do next – any more Corbetts.

I called Archie for advice, but unexpectedly it was my great old boss and mutual friend Michael Hamilton that answered Archie's phone in his usual big cheerful voice and it completely cracked me up. I couldn't really speak and Archie had to call me back a while later when I could make sense. He reiterated what Charlie had said, all good calm common sense; I was hearing what they were saying but it wasn't sinking in. I retreated to the van with the boys, made us all a very late dinner and played monopoly with them, trying to take my mind elsewhere and deflect the stress, occasionally having to stifle blubbering and snotters. My phone rang again, it was Brenny calling from her hospital bed. There was no question, she instructed, I absolutely had to get up tomorrow and finish it off. She wouldn't accept anything else, and certainly didn't want to see me at the hospital until it was done. Still seeing herself as "on duty" even in the ward, she had arranged emergency accommodation for Chris with a friend, Alison MacBeath, in Inverness, now completely wrecked from his illness and an epic auto-pilot drive south, occasionally up the road verges during micro-sleeps! Hindsight says there really ought to have been an ambulance called by the useless Durness doctor, but I was extremely grateful for a good friend to have been with Brenda at that time.

Davy reminisced… *We were making our way north past Inverness and up & over the Struie road, having a happy sing-song along to Bob Dylan, when a car passed the other direction with what looked like Chris & Brenda inside?!? A little later we phoned Manny to be told the bad news about Brenda. We arrived to an atmosphere of gloom and doom. Manny had shut himself away in his van and we all just hung about waiting to see what happened next? Brenda saved the day from her hospital bed…*

Manny blogged… *I was completely crushed on Thursday night with Brenda's news. I wasn't going to do the final day, it was all very dark. Hills didn't matter then… but they do. They get your head straight again, they clear the cobwebs away and flush the mind clean. I hid in the van that night not wanting to face anyone except my two boys, and after the head spinning for hours and virtually no sleep I just had to do what Brenda wanted me to do - finish it.*

Day 70 Friday 3rd July - Pushed Over The Line
Foot 9 miles & 5,602ft, bike 21 miles (1,344ft), mtb 3 miles (zeroft), 3 Corbetts

The only reason I stepped out of the van the next morning was for Brenda. I hadn't slept, my head was mince and I just wanted to be in Inverness at the hospital with her, but I wasn't allowed to do that. My loyal team were all still there, waiting apprehensively to see if I continued forward – I couldn't let them down either. So many people had contributed so much to this journey, it would have been wrong to end it there, even in such circumstances.

During the course of the night and morning other friends and clubmates had arrived for the final scene. Murdo Macleod who had helped me with logistics away back on the first day on Harris, would see me over Cranstackie and Beinn Spionnaidh, and I was relieved to be in such familiar company. Davy Duncan and Christine had also arrived, and Christine would drive our campervan around to Loch Eriboll with the others to meet us off the hill at Polla. What a great team. I had a quick 4 mile whizz on my mtb to the foot of the hill at Rhigolter where I dumped the bike, then Murdo and I set off up the steep grassy slope. It was all a bit of a blur. Higher up I blasted off up through the rocks in anger and greetin' with frustration at the crappy scenario, leaving poor Murdo trailing well behind. I waited at the top of Cranstackie and calmed down again, making sure we stuck together for the second hill, Beinn Spionnaidh, the "hill of strength", which was slightly ironic when I started to run out of steam halfway up! I had to stop, sit down and take on a good feed; I perhaps hadn't eaten properly that morning, because Brenda hadn't been there to force feed me the usual huge breakfast. We summited the rocky cairn taking our time to enjoy the penultimate Corbett scenery. Only one to go. Mindy led me down a direct route and kept a steady pace for me to hang onto at trot, otherwise I would have just trudged down. He was bang-on line and a fleet of vehicles were waiting on us.

Cleggs were swarming around us all and Manuel and Duncan were having fun chasing them with the mini-hoover from the van. It was scorching hot yet again. I made sure I had a good feed and plenty to drink, and prepared my road bike for the final time. I was looking forward to the twenty-odd mile ride to Tongue, with time alone to think and chill out before the last hill. It wasn't going to be easy though; it was blowing a strong easterly and the road is undulating to say the least. The guys all wished me good luck as I set off, and then soon passed me in their vehicles heading for Ribigill to meet me. There had been no sign of my Dad this morning and I thought someone said he would be picked up from the Tongue Hotel, so expected I would see him later on the hill. I spun the pedals and enjoyed the big climbs in the road. The views were great as I reflected on the whole trip and the unimaginable finish. Somewhere along the A838, on one of the long straight moor sections, and now struggling against the relentless headwind, I spotted a lone figure cycling towards me, like a mirage… a brown one. It was Alec

Keith of HBT, from Inverness. After a morning phone call to Brenda lying in hospital, but not knowing my exact timings for the final hill, he had travelled from Inverness more in hope of bumping into me, and succeeded. Unfortunately he was on a very tight time limit to be home for a family gathering and dinner or risk his wife Gilly's wrath, so would not be able to go to the summit. He took the front, into the wind, and let me draft behind. His bike I had noted was of the rusting steel scaffold-tube variety, and to change gears required a violent hand-haul directly on one of the cables, as the thumbs shifts had clearly long ceased functioning. Alec has equipment still in use that only the late Cpt. Scott would know how to operate. I once witnessed him put up a tent that I was sure he had pinched from the film set of Monty Python and The Holy Grail. The poles were of three inch timber and nine feet high! Anyway, he did me a sterling service by dragging me through Tongue at a pace I could barely hang on to, and finally to Ribigill Farm.

As we crossed the causeway I recalled a passage from Skipper John's book, *Cairngorm John*, *"At the head of the Kyle of Tongue in the north-west Highlands stands one of the world's greatest mountains, which is also one of its greatest viewpoints. Ben Loyal has several tops that project almost like a goat's horns around the summit. It is not high, at 764m falling well short of Munro status. The mountains of West Sutherland, all unique and fascinating sculptures, range across the landward sides. To the north though, the observer looks down the long stretch of the Kyle to a cluster of rocky islands inhabited only by seals."*

Some of the supporter posse, including the boys, had already set off up the hill at a walk; indeed some were already on the top. Donald had unfortunately injured his ankle and had to stay put in the car park. I took my time and changed, drank and ate, eventually leaving the farm last, with Alec for a pacer initially. Soon on the way we met some of my Aviemore biking pals, Graham & Margaret Hall and Peter Bennett, who not knowing my timings had guessed too early and were now almost back at the farm! We ran well in the heat and quickly caught the others as the steeper climb started. However, Alec's time limit was up and he had to retreat to Inverness, but I was grateful for his effort of coming so far north to help.

I noticed a few people missing I had expected to be there – Dad, Charlie and his folks, Alan & Tilly Smith… maybe they were in the group already at the top? A bit further on and my phone rang – it was Bill Whiteford from BBC Radio Scotland wanting a live interview for the Newsdrive program. Bill told me he had called Brenda to set up the interview and was shocked to find she was taking the call from a hospital trolley, fully prepped for surgery in just a few minutes! She quickly told Bill that I probably wouldn't want to do the interview under the circumstances, but to tell me that she had instructed me to do it! Murdo, who works for the Beeb, had arranged this a few days before with Brenda, and although my heart wasn't in it, I hid behind a big boulder out of the strong wind to do a short blether with Bill. My head was birlin' and I didn't remember a word of what I had been asked or replied, and only heard the interview weeks later, noticing that I referred to the Corbetts as Munros – confirmation that my head was totally mince! Interview over, we marched for the top.

Manny blogged... *With Manuel & Duncan by my side, and a lump in my throat, I walked up onto the lovely top of An Caisteal, on Ben Loyal and it was over. Brenda was there with me just the same.*

Davy, Christine, Dave, JD, Archie, Sandra, Hamilton, Mindy, and of course Chris were there to cheer me home. A few drams, Cairngorm Brewery ales and champers were had in the howling wind, along with loads of photos.

Phone calls & texts to a few folk including my Mum to confirm arrival. A few moments alone. Gulp!

After 70 days I was standing on top of the last Corbett, and Brenda had just started five hours of surgery.

Alec reminisced.... *Loyalty knows no bounds. Manny's last day was a belter, sunny and breezy, a day of big skies, a great day for having a party just for being alive. As I'd missed all of the dirty work supporting Manny's inspired lunacy, but had followed the whole nerve wracking injury-strewn car crash of a trip on his blog, it only seemed right to front up for the good bit. I got on my bike and let the wind blow me up the hill and away westwards, eventually to meet Manny pedalling steadily east towards his goal. On first viewing the wheels were turning but the hamster was dead; he looked tired and withdrawn, no wonder, and had physically shrunk over the last couple of months. There was more muscle and grit than before, but the personality hadn't improved much! He was glad to take what little shelter he could find behind his newly arrived domestique. We pedalled across the vastness of the A' Mhoine headland then down through Tongue village to Ribigill Farm where the masses had relocated themselves, waiting for the prophet to lead them to the mountain. One refreshing beer later and he was off up the peaty path at a pace far quicker than most of the team could manage, his focus not on the summit festivities but purely on how fast he could get back off the hill and away to Raigmore to see Brenda.*

Johnston blogged... *Breaking news - Day 70 - Completion on Ben Loyal! Manny reached the summit of Ben Loyal today at around 16:30, thereby completing all 219 Corbetts in an incredible 70 days. CONGRATULATIONS MANNY!!!!!!!!!!!!!*

Bob @ sandstone blogged... *Congratulations, Manny! Sympathy to Brenda. He wouldn't have done it without you. It has been a privilege to log in day after day and see you taking the rough with the smooth. What 'smooth' you might ask. Okay,* *the rain and the shine and the sore leg. You are (all) inspiring. Brilliantly done.*

Don & Elma blogged... *Well done Manny, a tremendous achievement. Very few people could do what you have just done (I saw the state of you on Wed afternoon and know how hard you had to dig in to keep going!)*

Gibson Fleming blogged... *Well done Manny it took me 35 years from my first to last Corbett not 69 days. Best wishes to Brenda*

Ken & Clare blogged... *A huge well done. The AC/DC concert 2 days from the finish was an inspired touch. Congratulations to you both. Awesome achievement.*

Graham Kelly blogged... *Simply awesome! Congrats on a fantastic achievement ~ it was a privilege to have shared a couple of days. All the best to the two of you.*

Scott & Linda blogged... *Fantastic achievement Manny! Really sorry to hear about Brenda's woes... all the best to her for a speedy recovery. Feel privileged to have accompanied you on even the smallest part of your journey - it was a special day in Torridon, complete with the discovery of the best bothy in the World! Enjoy the rest and recover well. And enjoy the beers and a proper hangover!!!*

Alec Keith blogged... *Congratulations Manny on your fantastic effort, sorry to have to abort 1/2 way up Ben Loyal. While you take the headlines, the real hero is of course Brenda for sticking with you through all this madness, and picking up the pieces masquerading as your body. Everybody's thinking about her and wishing her a good recovery. Payback time now, boy. And well done to all your pacers and supporters, particularly Chris on what must have been one hell of a final week. A top man to have on your side!*

Squiz (aka the Squires) blogged... *Many congratulations. We have been plodding round the Corbetts, hoping to finish them this year... or next, so have been overtaken by Manny on the Auch Five, and again coming off Beinn Dearg Mor and Bheag. We were mightily impressed by the way he powered over these (to us) gruelling hills. I think this is a feat that won't be out-done for many years. Hope Brenda's shoulder will regain full function... Manny wasn't the only one to overtake our bikes en-route to the motorhome. Brenda did too... and she was on foot. Best wishes.*

Ellie blogged... *Well done Manny and Brenda - you're an amazing team - and thank you for the multiple opportunities to play around in the hills with you. Rest and recover well. x*

Archie & Sandra blogged... *Well done both of you! Like so many others have said it has been a real privilege for us both to be involved in this crazy journey. From the start at the Tarbert Hardware Emporium, through the doldrums of Rum,* *the snows of Ben an Lochain, the midges of Achnashellach to the summit of Ben Loyal. It has been great to have been a part of it and meet up with all those great folk that have helped you out along the way.*

Fantastic achievement by the Gormanator and his Coordinator.

Bruce Smith blogged... *Congratulations Manny - that is an incredible achievement and one that will stand for a very long time. Sorry to hear about Brenda's fall - I'm sure you'll look after her as well as she's looked after you for the past 70 days, although from following the blog that's going to be some effort.*

Skipper and First Mate, John & Anne on Finlandia blogged... *Mixed feelings when reading all this news - delighted for Manny of course - well done - we really wondered if you had taken on too great a challenge - a fantastic achievement in often very difficult conditions. So sorry to hear about Brenda's accident - that is really the worst of luck so close to the finish! - But it doesn't diminish your input one bit so congratulations to you too and our best wishes for a speedy recovery.*

Chris blogged... *We all thought Manny was mad, and he has proved us correct by today completing his astonishing self- and wind-propelled round of Corbetts in 70 days. From the eve of London Marathon on 25th April, until Wimbledon men's semi-final day on 3rd July, Manny has been relentlessly chasing his dream right through the months of May and June. The only 'rest' days in the whole 10 week epic came due to getting stormbound between Jura and Arran at the end of the first week, and then much later 3 days R&R were needed after crashing off his bike just before Strontian. The first weeks saw some of the coldest wettest windiest early May weather on record, with Manny getting repeated batterings during his progress through Galloway, Moffat and Arrochar. The tide finally turned for the epic trip through from Loch Lomond to Ben Ledi, and the scene was set for a mighty sweeping move north through the southern and central highlands. But of course Manny was only half the team, and Brenda has been working overtime the past 10 weeks keeping Manny fed, watered and motivated through the countless ups and downs. And just when the finish appeared to be within grasp on the penultimate day, the story saw one final cruel twist with Brenda crashing off Manny's bike. Once again, a massive well done to Manny and Brenda on a truly remarkable achievement, and I hope Brenda is soon up and about and making a speedy recovery.*

POSTSCRIPT

Après Corbetts

Everyone did their best to help out a bit with Brenda missing on the final day, but no single person really took control, and as a result my Dad was left sitting in the Tongue Hotel wondering where everyone was, until finally twigging that no-one was coming for him. He finally made his own way to the farm, then with no map or any idea where he was going, headed up the first hill he could see - the wrong one. Chris spotted him as we all descended Ben Loyal and shouted and bawled to him, eventually drawing him over. I was gutted he had missed the top but after a dram he insisted we continue down as he went up, eventually returning to the farm with a gigantic summit rock in his bum-bag as a memento for me! Alan & Tilly had also suffered the result of Brenda's absence by not knowing the correct meeting place, and failed to find us despite scanning the hillside with binoculars for hours! Charlie and his folks completely mistimed their drive from Glasgow and only arrived long after we had left for the top. There were nearly as many friends left at the bottom as there were on top! Afterwards I headed for Inverness in the campervan, fighting to stay awake and relieved to finally arrive. The nurses were all fully primed on the whole story by Brenda, and very kindly allowed me in for an hour even though it was well after 11pm.

Another unfortunate consequence of Brenda's crash and severe injury was that she was unable to take up her new employment post which she had left the trip to successfully negotiate, away back on Day 27.

Manny (now drunk and pondering in the campervan at Kincraig Fair, Saturday 4th July) blogged... *It's all a bit odd.*

From the best views in the world to spending the night parked up in Inverness, Raigmore Hospital car park, then sitting in Tesco's watching the crazy world go about its inane business. Looking forward to a very long lie in bed, I of course woke up at 7am, the body still thinking it was about to get its daily punishment! Not today legs! However, I'm completely knackered mentally & physically and have spent the day doing a frustrating nothing other than seeing Brenny for an hour this morning and again this afternoon - I wish I had just headed off and done a wee hill this morning.

Anyway, many thanks to everyone for the best wishes and kind thoughts for Brenny - needless to say we were both absolutely shattered when she could not get to Ben Loyal. There is absolutely no way I could have achieved the Corbett Round if Brenda had not been there every step of the way to push me out in the rain, feed me, move the van, arrange all the supporters, come up hills with me, washing, cleaning, cooking, wipe my brow etc...

I didn't do the Corbetts on my own and could never have made it without the help of so many of my clubmates and friends and my parents - from the wonderful week long sailing trip with John & Anne Allen, and the 2 crew shifts, to the hell of the Borders alone with Brenda, through the gruesome west coast with all sorts of Westies & friends, out east with Davy & Donald, back west for more tough weather and mind games but Dots doughnuts to keep me going, big pulls east again with Ken & Clare for urgent help and good hill company, to Allan & Tilly and more Westies, and then the massive pull north from beautiful Ardgour with our own Charlie Campbell, all be it after nearly ending the trip with a disastrous bike fall, the days growing longer and longer all the time – 12 & 14 hours being the norm; beautiful Knoydart for 3 days, Manuel & Duncan being ferried back & forth to us for weekends, huge days through Torridon, and Poolewe with Dave Riach & Scott Kennedy, and constant encouragement from Archie & Sandra, Brenda bagging more hills every day, and the indomitable Mr Rogers to shove me around Straths Connon & Farrar, and the relief of getting to Assynt after great hills with Geoff, Ali, Pete, Elsie, the ever-present Johnston, Andy and Cat, the AC/DC gig as an insane sideshow, and constantly juggling the schedule to suit 14 hour days.

I guess it would have been boring if the story didn't have a final cruel twist.

A tough few days with Don, Elma, and Dave Calder, including the extraordinary venture across Arkle & Foinaven in a thunderstorm, led to the end of Brenda's journey in hellish circumstances, again whilst still trying to help me with a bike delivery.

I started it just for me, plain selfish me – but in the end I finished it for Brenda and for every single one of the dozens of friends who helped or supported along the way, even just on the blog, or with a text.

It wasn't just about the hills but the people too.

Thank you all for making it, we both enjoyed every minute.

Lots of love

Manny & Brenda

Xx

12th August, 39 Days Later - Brenda does Ben Loyal

Brenda blogged… *We made our way up to Tongue with lots of cups of tea stops, a bit of reading and taking in the scenery. This was very different to what I was last used to, as every stop normally revolved around making tea, rolls, Complan, pasta etc. I'm getting used to having everything done for me; Manny driving, cooking, washing, cleaning, shopping – well just about everything, while I just sit back & relax! We finally got to the top where the views were magnificent and then we hid out of the wind and had a bite to eat.*

Thanks to all who joined us on the trip, all who followed the blog & all who turned up for the surprise party, it was a very memorable trip & I am just pleased now that I made it up Ben Loyal & on road to recovery.
Thank you all once again. Brenda x

The Stats

I have been as careful as I could in measuring and re-measuring the whopping distances & ascents throughout the journey, with only very minor alterations here or there to the final "on foot" figures, mostly determined by Archie's accurate GPS which lived in my bum-bag or back-pack, recording as we travelled. However, although the biking mileages were very accurate, I was never comfortable with the initial staggering ascent figures for road & mountain biking of 91,324ft & 31,645ft respectively, which proved wholly inaccurate. It was perhaps a basic error to focus on the mountain sections and not carry the GPS on the many biking legs too, as it would have saved a colossal amount of time and grief to finally come up with an acceptable set of numbers. Archie again came to my aid by putting me onto some biking-specific software which gave far more realistic numbers, although still not perfect. Some importance still has to be placed on the major biking climbs with several mountains such as Geal Charn Mor, Carn na Saobhaidhe, Beinn Bhan and Sgurr a 'Chaorachain to name but a few, easily accessible on foot after the majority of height first being gained on two wheels.

Without printing every last gory detail here, here are a few wee nuggets to chew on...

After painstaking scrutiny the final figures are as follows.

On foot 1,001.5 miles & 420,658ft of ascent.

On bike 1,132 miles & 44,077ft of ascent.

On mtb 276 miles & 19,373ft of ascent.

Sailing approx 200 miles.

Total journey of 2,609.5 miles & 484,108ft of ascent – not bad for Scotland!

If it matters to anyone, the actual time taken was 69 days & 2.5 hours; 70 is just easier for description.

In answer to Archie's question back on day 1 onboard Calmac's "Hebrides" sailing to Harris, I had approximately 160 views from the summits.

The week from days 48 to 54 saw daily averages of 20+ miles & 10,000ft, covering 30 Corbetts, from Ardgour up the lumpy west coast to Shiel Bridge.

The biggest days in terms of - *mileage on foot* was just under 30 miles with 7,500ft on day 34 from Glens Clova to Muick; *ascent on foot* with 11,886ft over

25 miles on day 60 through Torridon to Loch Maree; *on road & mountain bikes* was 81miles with approx 3,000ft of ascent, along with 14 miles & 5,300ft on foot, on day 65 from Blackbridge to Knockan Crag.

There were 7 days without any tops being reached due to sailing or injury, and 5 days with just a single Corbett, for the same reasons. 3 other days were halved into 6 due to injury or AC/DC. There were a few other days where I simply finished a bit early and went to the pub! So there is plenty of scope for taking a huge chunk of time out of the record if anyone is that way inclined, and I'll gladly give tips and advice if it's needed.

For all that, it was never about numbers or a record - it was all about the journey.

Manny

Acknowledgments

This book would never have been possible of my own accord.

Sincere thanks go to many people,

Brenda, Maisy, Manuel and Duncan for their love and patience to see me through endless late nights, non-attendance at many moments, and often frustration and much crabbitness.

Fiona Newman for her painstaking proof reading and advice.

To clubmate Scott McKendrick of Advertising Direct for last gasp help with mapping design. Fifteen minutes my arse...!

John Allen and Bob Davidson at Sandstone Press for excerpts from *Cairngorm John*.

Each and every contributor.

My loyal Corbetts Round team, who provided me with an amazing record of five thousand photographs from which to choose. I have credited these as best as I can remember, so apologies if I got an odd one wrong.

Ian Grover of Groverprint & Design, Newtonmore, for his advice, patience, skill and good craic.

Hamish Brown and Heavy Whalley - two men who not only understand our mountains, but why people need to roam there - for their advice, encouragement and generous words.

2009, 219 Corbett Index, in running order

Islands

Day 1
1. An Clisham (799m)
Day 3
2. Glamaig (775m)
3. Garbh-bheinn (808m)
Day 4
4. Askival (812m)
5. Ainshval (781m)
Day 5
6. Dun da Ghaoithe (785m)
Day 6
7. Beinn an Oir (785m)
Day 9
8. Caisteal Abhail (847m)
9. Beinn Tarsuinn (826m)
10. Cir Mhor (799m)
11. Goatfell (874m)

Borders

Day 11
12. Shalloch on Minnoch (775m)
13. The Merrick (843m)
14. Corserine (814m)
Day 12
15. Cairnsmore of Carsphairn (797m)
16. Hart Fell (808m)
17. White Coomb (821m)
Day 13
18. Broad Law (840m)

South of the Great Glen

Day 14
19. The Brack (787m)
20. Ben Donich (847m)
Day 15
21. Beinn Bheula (779m)

22. Beinn an Lochain (901m)
23. Stob Coire Creagach (817m)
Day 16
24. Beinn Luibhean (858m)
25. The Cobbler (884m)
26. Meall an Fhudair (764m)
Day 17
27. Beinn a' Choin (770m)
28. Stob a' Choin (869m)
29. Beinn Stacath (771m)
30. Benvane (821m)
31. Ben Ledi (879m)
Day 18
32. Beinn Each (813m)
33. Meall na Fearna (809m)
34. Meall an t-Seallaidh (852m)
35. Creag Mac Ranaich (809m)
Day 19
36. Auchnafree Hill (789m)
37. Creag Uchdag (879m)
38. Creagan na Beinne (888m)
Day 20
39. Meall Tairneachan (787m)
40. Farragon Hill (783m)
41. Beinn Dearg (830m)
42. Cam Chreag (862m)
43. Meall nam Maigheach (779m)
Day 21
44. Beinn nan Oighreag (909m)
45. Sron a'Choire Chnapanich (837m)
46. Meall Buidhe (910m)
47. Meall nan Subh (806m)
48. Beinn nan Imirean (849m)
Day 22
49. Beinn Chuirn (880m)
50. Beinn Udlaidh (840m)
51. Beinn Bhreac-liath (802m)

Day 23
52. Beinn Odhar (901m)
53. Beinn Chaorach (818m)
54. Cam Chreag (885m)
55. Beinn nam Fuaran (806m)
56. Beinn a' Chaisteil (886m)
Day 24
57. Beinn Mhic-Mhonaidh (796m)
58. Beinn a' Bhuiridh (897m)
59. Creach Bheinn (810m)
Day 25
60. Fraochaidh (879m)
61. Meall Lighiche (772m)
62. Beinn Maol Chaluim (907m)
Day 26
63. Beinn Trilleachan (840m)
64. Stob Dubh (883m)
65. Beinn Mhic Chasgaig (864m)
Day 27
66. Beinn a' Chrulaiste (857m)
67. Garbh Bheinn (867m)
68. Mam na Gualainn (796m)
Day 28
69. Glas Bheinn (792m)
70. Leum Uilleim (909m)
Day 29
71. Meall na Meoig (868m)
72. Beinn a' Chuallaich (892m)
Day 30
73. Stob an Aonaich Mhoir (855m)
74. Beinn Mholach (841m)
75. Meall na Leitreach (775m)
76. The Sow of Atholl (803m)
77. The Fara (911m)
Day 31
78. An Dun (827m)
79. A' Chaoirnich (875m)
80. Meallach Mhor (769m)

81. Carn Dearg Mor (857m)
Day 32
82. Leathad an Taobhain (912m)
83. Beinn Bhreac (912m)
84. Beinn Mheadhonach (901m)
85. Ben Vrackie (841m)
86. Ben Vuirich (903m)
Day 33
87. Ben Gulabin (806m)
88. Monamenach (807m)
Day 34
89. Ben Tirran (896m)
90. Mount Battock (778m)
91. Conachcraig (865m)
Day 35
92. Morven (872m)
93. Creag nan Gabhar (834m)
94. Morrone (859m)
95. Sgor Mor (813m)
Day 36
96. Carn na Drochaide (818m)
97. Carn Liath (862m)
98. Culardoch (900m)
99. Brown Cow Hill (829m)
100. Carn Ealasaid (792m)
Day 37
101. Carn Mor (804m)
102. Corryhabbie Hill (781m)
103. Ben Rinnes (840m)
Day 38
104. Geal Charn (821m)
105. Creag Mhor (895m)
106. Meall a' Bhuachaille (810m)
Day 39
107. Geal-charn Mor (824m)
108. Carn na Saobhaidhe (811m)
109. Carn an Fhreiceadain (878m)

Day 40
110. Meall na-Aisre (862m)
111. Gairbeinn (896m)
112. Carn a' Chuilinn (816m)
113. Carn Dearg (N) (817m)
114. Carn Dearg (S) (768m)
Day 41
115. Carn Dearg (Glen Roy) (834m)
116. Beinn Iaruinn (800m)
117. Cruach Innse (857m)
118. Sgurr Innse (809m)

North of the Great Glen
Day 42
119. Ben Tee (904m)
120. Meall na h-Eilde (838m)
121. Geal Charn (804m)
122. Beinn Bhan (796m)
123. Meall a' Phubuill (774m)
Day 43
124. Stob Coire a' Chearcaill (771m)
125. Creach Bheinn (853m)
126. Fuar Bheinn (766m)
127. Beinn Resipol (845m)
Day 47
128. Garbh Bheinn (885m)
Day 48
129. Beinn na h-Uamha (762m)
130. Sgurr Dhomhnuill (888m)
131. Carn na Nathrach (786m)
132. Stob a' Bhealach an Sgriodain (770m)
133. Sgurr Ghiubhsachain (849m)
134. Sgorr Craobh a' Chaorainn (775m)
Day 49
135. Beinn Odhar Bheag (882m)
136. Beinn Mhic Cedidh (783m)
137. Sgurr na Ba Glaise (874m)

138. Rois-Bheinn (882m)
139. An Stac (814m)
Day 50
140. Sgurr an Utha (796m)
141. Streap (909m)
142. Braigh nan Uamhachan (765m)
143. Fraoch Bheinn (858m)
144. Sgurr Mhurlagain (880m)
Day 51
145. Sgurr an Fhuarain (901m)
146. Sgurr Cos na Breachd-laoigh (835m)
147. Carn Mor (829m)
148. Bidean a' Chabair (867m)
Day 52
149. Sgurr a' Choire-bheithe (913m)
150. Ben Aden (887m)
151. Beinn Bhuidhe (855m)
Day 53
152. Beinn na Caillich (785m)
153. Sgurr Coire Choinnichean (796m)
154. Sgurr nan Eugallt (894m)
Day 54
155. Buidhe Bheinn (& Sgurr a' Bhac Chaolais)(885m)
156. Beinn nan Caorach (774m)
157. Beinn na h-Eaglaise (805m)
158. Sgurr Mhic Bharraich (779m)
Day 55
159. Sgurr an Airgid (841m)
160. Am Bathach (798m)
161. Beinn Loinne (790m)
Day 56
162. Meall Dubh (788m)
163. Aonach Shasuinn (888m)
164. Carn a' Choire Ghairbh (865m)
165. Sgurr Gaorsaic (839m)

Day 57
166. Sguman Coinntich (879m)
167. Faochaig (868m)
168. Aonach Buidhe (899m)
169. Beinn Dronaig (797m)
170. Beinn Tharsuinn (863m)
171. Sgurr na Feartaig (862m)
Day 58
172. Fuar Tholl (907m)
173. An Ruadh-stac (892m)
174. Beinn Damh (903m)
Day 59
175. Sgurr a' Chaorachain (792m)
176. Beinn Bhan (896m)
177. Sgurr Dubh (782m)
178. Sgorr nan Lochan Uaine (871m)
Day 60
179. Beinn Dearg (914m)
180. Beinn an Eoin (855m)
181. Baosbheinn (875m)
182. Ruadh-stac Beag (896m)
183. Meall a' Ghiubhais (887m)
Day 61
184. Beinn Airigh Charr (791m)
185. Beinn Lair (859m)
186. Beinn a' Chaisgein Mor (856m)
187. Beinn Dearg Mor (910m)
188. Beinn Dearg Bheag (820m)
Day 62
189. Sail Mhor (767m)
190. Creag Rainich (807m)
191. Beinn Enaiglair (890m)
Day 63
192. Beinn Liath Mhor a' Ghiubhais Li (766m)
193. Little Wyvis (763m)
194. Meallan nan Uan (838m)
195. Sgurr a' Mhuilinn (879m)

Day 64
196. Bac an Eich (849m)
197. An Sidhean (814m)
198. Sgorr na Diollaid (818m)
199. Beinn a' Bha'ach Ard (862m)
Day 65
200. Beinn a' Chaisteil (787m)
201. Carn Ban (842m)
202. Carn Chuinneag (838m)
Day 66
203. Cul Beag (769m)
204. Cul Mor (849m)
205. Canisp (847m)
206. Breabag (815m)
Day 67
207. Spidean Coinich (764m)
208. Sail Gorm (776m)
209. Sail Gharbh (808m)
Day 68
210. Glas Bheinn (776m)
211. Beinn Leoid (792m)
212. Ben Hee (873m)
Day 69
213. Meallan Liath Coire Mhic Dhughaill (801m)
214. Meall Horn (777m)
215. Arkle (787m)
216. Foinaven (911m)
Day 70
217. Cranstackie (800m)
218. Beinn Spionnaidh (772m)
219. Ben Loyal (764m)

Current 221 Corbett Index

Cairnsmore of Carsphairn (797m) Day12
Caisteal Abhail (847m) Day9
Cam Chreag (Auch)(885m) Day23
Cam Chreag (Glen Lyon)(862m) Day20
Canisp (847m) Day66
Carn a' Choire Ghairbh (865m) Day56
Carn an Fhreiceadain (878m) Day39
Carn Ban (842m) Day65
Carn a' Chuilinn (816m) Day40
Carn Chuinneag (838m) Day65
Carn Dearg (East Glen Roy) (834m) Day41
Carn Dearg (North G Eachach)(817m) Day40
Carn Dearg (South G Eachach)(768m) Day40
Carn Dearg Mor (857m) Day31
Carn Ealasaid (792m) Day36
Carn Liath (862m) Day36
Carn Mor (Lecht)(804m) Day37
Carn Mor (Glen Dessary)(829m) Day51
Carn na Drochaide (818m) Day36
Carn na Nathrach (786m) Day48
Carn na Saobhaidhe (811m) Day39
Cir Mhor (799m) Day9
Cobbler, The (884m) Day16
Conachcraig (865m) Day34
Corryhabbie Hill (781m) Day37
Corserine (814m) Day11
Cranstackie (800m) Day70
Creach Bheinn (Morven)(853m) Day43
Creach Bheinn (Benderloch)(810m) Day24
Creagan na Beinne (888m) Day19
Creag Mac Ranaich (809m) Day18
Creag Mhor (895m) Day38
Creag nan Gabhar (834m) Day35
Creag Rainich (807m) Day62
Creag Uchdag (879m) Day19
Cruach Innse (857m) Day41
Culardoch (900m) Day36
Cul Beag (769m) Day66
Cul Mor (849m) Day66

Dun da Ghaoithe (785m) Day5

Faochaig (868m) Day57
Fara, The (911m) Day30
Farragon Hill (783m) Day20
Foinaven (911m) Day69
Fraoch Bheinn (858m) Day50

Fraochaidh (879m) Day25
Fuar Bheinn (766m) Day43
Fuar Tholl (907m) Day58

Gairbeinn (896m) Day40
Garbh Bheinn (Ardgour)(885m) Day47
Garbh Bheinn (Loch Leven)(867m) Day27
Garbh-bheinn (Skye)(808m) Day3
Geal Charn (Loch Arkaig)(804m) Day42
Geal Charn (Cairngorms)(821m) Day38
Geal-charn Mor (824m) Day39
Glamaig (Skye) (775m) Day3
Glas Bheinn (Mamores) (792m) Day28
Glas Bheinn (Assynt)(776m) Day68
Goatfell (874m) Day9

Hart Fell (808m) Day12

Leathad an Taobhain (912m) Day32
Leum Uilleim (909m) Day28
Little Wyvis (763m) Day63

Mam na Gualainn (796m) Day27
Meall a' Bhuachaille (810m) Day38
Meall a' Ghiubhais (887m) Day60
Meall a' Phubuill (774m) Day42
Meall an Fhudair (764m) Day16
Meall an t-Seallaidh (852m) Day18
Meall Buidhe (910m) Day21
Meall Dubh (788m) Day56
Meall Horn (777m) Day69
Meall Lighiche (772m) Day25
Meall na Fearna (809m) Day18
Meall na h-Aisre (862m) Day40
Meall na h-Eilde (838m) Day42
Meall na Leitreach (775m) Day30
Meall na Meoig (868m) Day29
Meall nam Maigheach (779m) Day20
Meall nan Subh (806m) Day21
Meall Tairneachan (787m) Day20
Meallach Mhor (769m) Day31
Meallan-L-C-MhicDhughaill(801m)Day69
Meallan nan Uan (838m) Day63
Merrick, The (843m) Day11
Monamenach (807m) Day33
Morrone (859m) Day35
Morven (872m) Day35
Mount Battock (778m) Day34

Rois-Bheinn (882m) Day49
Ruadh-stac Beag (896m) Day60

Sail Gharbh, Quinag (808m) Day67
Sail Gorm, Quinag (776m) Day67
Sail Mhor (767m) Day62
Sgor Mor (813m) Day35
Sgorr nan Lochan Uaine (871m) Day59
Sgorr Craobh a' Chaorainn (775m) Day48
Sgorr na Diollaid (818m) Day64
Sguman Coinntich (879m) Day57
Sgurr a' Bhac Chaolais (885m)removed 2012
Sgurr a' Chaorachain (792m) Day59
Sgurr a'Choire-bheithe (913m) Day52
Sgurr a' Mhuilinn (879m) Day63
Sgurr an Airgid (841m) Day55
Sgurr an Fhuarain (901m) Day51
Sgurr an Utha (796m) Day50
Sgurr Coire Choinnichean (796m) Day53
Sgurr Cos na Breachd-laoidh (835m) Day51
Sgurr Dhomhnuill (888m) Day48
Sgurr Dubh (782m) Day59
Sgurr Gaorsaic (839m) Day56

Sgurr Ghiubhsachain (849m) Day48
Sgurr Innse (809m) Day41
Sgurr Mhic Bharraich (779m) Day54
Sgurr Mhurlagain (880m) Day50
Sgurr na Ba Glaise (874m) Day49
Sgurr na Feartaig (862m) Day57
*Sgurr nan Ceanaichean (913m)2009
Sgurr nan Eugallt (894m) Day53
Shalloch on Minnoch (775m) Day11
Sow of Atholl, The (803m) Day30
Spidean Coinich, Quinag (764m) Day67
Sron a' Choire Chnapanich (837m) Day21
Stob a' Bhealach an Sgriodain (770m) Day48
Stob a' Choin (869m) Day17
Stob an Aonaich Mhoir (855m) Day30
Stob Coire a' Chearcaill (771m) Day43
Stob Coire Creagach (817m) Day15
Stob Dubh (883m) Day26
Streap (909m) Day50

White Coomb (821m) Day12

Police

and

Policing

An Introduction

Police Ethics
~ Seumus Miller, John Blackler, Andrew Alexandra

- One of the leading books on policing across the globe
- In regular use by colleges and institutions, libraries and senior police officers
- A 'bible' of ethical principles
- Incorporates peacekeeping, community policing and anti-terrorism

2nd Ed. | 304 pages | 2006 | ISBN 978-1-904380-26-9

Covert Human Intelligence Sources
The 'Unlovely' Face of Police Work
~ Editor Roger Billingsley

A unique insight into the hidden world of informers and related aspects of covert policing.

Edited by Roger Billingsley, head of the Covert Policing Standards Unit at New Scotland Yard, this book is the first to look behind the scenes of undercover police work since the authorities relaxed the rules on secrecy.

Jan 2009 | 192 pages | ISBN 978-1-904380-44-3

The New

Home Office An Introduction ~ Bryan Gibson

'Will prove invaluable for anyone trying to get their head around the 21st century new world of criminal justice': *Thames View*

'A sound and practical book that is useful for both the newcomer and the seasoned practitioner. For a small book, it is incredibly comprehensive and yet easy to read': *The Justices' Clerk*

'This is a book that should be read by everybody involved in the Criminal Justice System': *Internet Law Book Reviews*

2nd Ed. | 172 pages | July 2008 | ISBN 978-1-904380-36-8

Details and ordering **www.WatersidePress.co.uk**

☰ WATERSIDE PRESS

Police
and
Policing

An Introduction

Peter Villiers

PREFACE SIR HUGH ORDE OBE

≫ **WATERSIDE** PRESS

POLICE AND POLICING: AN INTRODUCTION
Peter Villiers

Published 2009 by
Waterside Press
Sherfield Gables
Sherfield on Loddon
Hook
Hampshire
United Kingdon RG27 0JG

Telephone +44(0)1256 882250 Low cost UK landline calls 0845 2300 733
E-mail enquiries@watersidepress.co.uk
Online catalogue www.WatersidePress.co.uk

ISBN 9781904380 467 (Paperback)

Cataloguing-In-Publication Data A catalogue record can be obtained from the British Library.

Cover design © 2009 Waterside Press.

Printed in Great Britain by the MPG Books Group, Bodmin and King's Lynn

North American distributor International Specialised Book Services (ISBS), 920 NE 58th Ave, Suite 300, Portland, Oregon, 97213-3786, USA
Tel: 1 800 944 6190 Fax 1 503 280 8832 orders@isbs.com www.isbs.com

e-book *Police and Policing: An Introduction* is available electronically at leading i-libraries and e-suppliers (e-book ISBN 9781906534752)

POLICE AND POLICING: AN INTRODUCTION

CONTENTS

Preface

I was pleased to be asked to write this introduction by an author whom I knew for many years at the Police Staff College, and whom I believe to know his subject.

The question is whether policing is an art or a science. Does it require a higher degree in mathematics for its completion? In many ways, it is a test of character as much as of theoretical competence. It is easy enough to work out what is the right thing to do when you are warm, dry and well-rested. Most police challenges, however, do not arise under those circumstances!

Whether future or current police officers, we should learn as much as we can about our difficult and demanding profession. That is why a book like this is invaluable, for in its deceptively simple style, it contains a great deal of useful information, and it asks the right questions about policing; the enduring ones. The police service is a disciplined organization, with a clear purpose: to help people. We must use an informed discretion in deciding how best to do so. We must accept responsibility for our choices, and admit when we are wrong. And we are still entitled to take a pride in belonging to the finest service in the world; a service that gains from its mistakes as well as its successes, and is never too proud to learn—or to teach.

Sir Hugh Orde OBE
Chief Constable, Police Service of Northern Ireland

January 2009

Introduction and Acknowledgements

Policing is a universal concept. However, the detail in this book is primarily about the police and policing in England and Wales, although Scotland and Northern Ireland are also mentioned, and comparisons made with foreign police services on occasion. No attempt has been made to explore every nook and cranny of the police service, as this would subvert the overall purpose—which is to draw a clear and balanced picture, showing how the police service has developed from its fresh start in 1829, and moving from past to present with a guess or two about the future.

Readers may, however, find the *Glossary of Words, Phrases, Acronyms and Abbreviations* at the end of this work helpful in understanding some of the more basic and everyday matters affecting the police and as a guide to the language of policing. Similarly, the *Timeline* at the end of the book will help them to place various matters mentioned in different parts of the book into a wider perspective.

The appearance and organization of policing is subject to constant change, but its fundamental purposes alter much more slowly; and it is hoped that those who read this book, whether probationers, senior officers and experts in policing, or simply members of the public with an interest in the subject, will form a clearer understanding of those purposes, and of the means by which police designers, practitioners and reformers have attempted to seek their achievement.

TO DESCRIBE IS TO SELECT: TO SELECT IS TO ANALYSE

To describe is not necessarily to criticise, but this would be a very dull work if it simply listed the various aspects of policing as they exist, and left its readers to assess their validity and effectiveness unaided. The author has taken a middle view, and imagined his reader as someone with a strong interest in policing, who does not want to be blinded by official propaganda, but at the same time is not interested in disparagement for its own sake; and so we have asked the sort of questions which we imagine that any intelligent observer would ask, as we went along. In regard to the attempts to reform policing which are an inescapable part of its history, we have tended to take the same approach by asking:

- what was the intention of the reform; and
- what was the result in reality?

Ambiguous terms

Any commentator on policing soon discovers that terms in everyday use may have another use. Take, for example, 'community policing' and 'neighbourhood policing'.

We would suggest that these terms have intelligible meanings in everyday speech, which have no need for further explication. However, they are also part of police doctrine, and are items in the police modernisation programme in which New Labour has been engaged since it came to power in 1997. 'Neighbourhood policing', in this latter sense, is described in a government White Paper of 2004, 'Building Communities, Beating Crime', and thus has a special meaning. We reserve the right to use the Queen's English (and, incidentally, to use the word 'he' to mean 'he or she', exactly as in legislation, since there is no satisfactory alternative).

Police work has been compared to the labours of Sisyphus, who was condemned to roll the same stone up the same hill in perpetuity, for every time he reached the summit, the stone rolled down again. I believe this analogy to be misleading. Police work can be dull, and certainly repetitious; and its achievements are not necessarily consolidated. Crises occur, and mistakes are repeated; but the organization as a whole makes progress, and the quality of policing as a whole improves. The police are better at investigating crime, better at quelling riots, and better at policing a complex multi-racial society, than they used to be. They are more sophisticated, more open-minded, and at the same time more knowing. They may have lost something in the process—no achievement in human affairs is without any disadvantage—but the progress is indisputable.

As always when I finish a book and add the final touches to an introduction that I began so long ago, I wonder at my temerity in having attempted the task at all. I am not, and have never been, a police officer, and my knowledge is mainly theoretical. Moreover, my practical experience of policing was gained a long time ago in Northern Ireland, as a soldier at the height of The Troubles; and a police force under attack must concentrate its activities. But policing fascinated me, and still does; and I hope that this book will be judged by its merits and not the pedigree of its author. Does it present a balanced and comprehensive introduction? Does it say something useful about policing? Does it leave the reader wanting to learn more, or indeed to write a better book? If any of those objectives has been achieved, I shall be more than happy.

ACKNOWLEDGEMENTS

As with my first two books for Waterside Press, I am grateful to its director, the indefatigable Bryan Gibson, both for suggesting this book in the first place and offering many helpful hints towards its completion.

I am grateful to my former colleagues at the Police Staff College, Bramshill, and for the patience and good humour of the police officers whom I tutored. The latter included those who attended the Overseas Command Course, many of whom came from former British colonies, and who accepted British food, weather, and a sort of ingrained assumption of superiority which any post-colonial power must have difficulty in overcoming, with an extraordinary grace. They taught me more about policing than they ever learned from me, and I can only hope that their time in the United Kingdom proved worthwhile.

I am grateful to my long-term colleague and sometime co-editor, Dr Robert Adlam, whose intellectual insight was always far more acute than my own, and who treated policing seriously when for the majority of academics it was still seen as the province of uncouth artisans of stunted intellect and a deeply suspicious instinct towards authoritarianism—police officers who saw them, in their turn, as the residue of CND and other unworldly if not seditious causes. (Contemporary academics, of course, are quite the reverse, and have cosied up to the police quite remarkably: quite possibly because they no longer belong to CND, and have accepted not only the capitalist ethic, but the government's management of their own performance).

Professor John Kleinig of the Australian National University and of the John Jay College of Criminal Justice in New York is a long-term colleague who has constructively challenged my more facile assumptions in this text, and I am grateful to him.

I am obliged to my colleague Raymond Bell, for many years an omniscient tutor on IT at the Police Staff College and still an expert for Interpol, who has advised me with unflagging zeal on the mysteries of crime in cyberspace.

Marisa Silvestri of the University of East London has been kind enough to educate me on gender and policing, and I am indebted to her for her comments.

Barry Loveday, reader in police studies at the University of Portsmouth, has advised me on the implications of the government's 2008 Green Paper on policing, and is a respected commentator on police affairs of long standing, as well as an occasional tutor for the strategic command course at Bramshill.

Penultimately, I am grateful for the many comments and insights on policing which have been furnished to me by Commander Allan Gibson of the Metropolitan Police Service, during our lengthy period of collaboration in writing opinion pieces for *Police Review*, and in reviewing much of this work. He has been an invaluable consultant, whose discreet and tactful wisdom has improved both its accuracy and balance.

Finally, I am as always grateful to Carolyn, who has tolerated my love affair with the computer for so many years now, and who has never lost her belief in the improvability of human nature—possibly including my own. The mistakes that remain in this manuscript are mine, and the picture of policing that it conveys is undoubtedly my own. I remain a firm believer in policing by consent as a tangible and progressive doctrine. Long may it flourish!

Peter Villiers
January 2009

About the author

Peter Villiers is a police adviser and consultant, editor of the international website journal *Ethics in Policing* and an occasional columnist for *Police Review*. He lectured at the Police Staff College, Bramshill from 1986 to 2004 on ethics, leadership and human rights, including to police officers from across the United Kingdom and around the world. He has written two earlier books for Waterside Press: *Police Leadership in the 21st Century: Philosophy, Doctrine and Developments* (2003) and *Policing A Safe, Just and Tolerant Society: An International Model for Policing* (2003)(both with Dr. Robert Adlam). He is the author of a range of further works on policing, ethics, human rights and leadership. These include *Police Studies* (1991), Unison; *Better Police Ethics* (1997), Kogan Page; *The First Fifty Years: A History of the Police Staff College* (1998), Police Staff College and *Human Rights for Managers: A Practical Guide* (2001), Kogan Page. He has always sought to understand policing as a whole and remains a firm believer in policing by consent.

The author of the Preface

Hugh Stephen Orde joined London's Metropolitan Police Service in 1977 and was promoted through the ranks, becoming Deputy Assistant Commissioner in 1999. He was awarded the OBE in the New Year Honours List of 2001 for services to policing and a knighthood in 2005. He was appointed Chief Constable of the Police Service of Northern Ireland (PSNI) in 2002. A graduate of the FBI National Executive Institute, he also holds a degree in Public Administration and an honorary doctorate in Civil Law from the University of Kent. He was elected Vice-President of the Association of Chief Police Officers for England, Wales and Northern Ireland (ACPO) in 2006.

CHAPTER ONE

The Purposes of Policing

CHAPTER ONE

The Purposes of Policing

A community of any kind needs to find some means to police itself. By this, we mean that it needs to be able to deal with conflict, aggression, violence and disruptive non-conformity.

Family and tribe, the original forms of social cohesion, will have informal but highly effective means to deal with disruptive behaviour and enforce the will of the community, usually as interpreted by its elders.

Formal policing, we would argue, begins with the need of the sovereign power to keep control over his subjects within a larger community, no longer contained by the natural boundaries and bonds of family or tribe. Those subjects may need to be identified, mustered, counted, taxed, subjected to local or national service and punished or rewarded. The agency that carries out this service is at least in part a police service, whatever its official name or other duties. It may well combine police and military duties, and the separation between the two, so important to the later development of a civil society, may not exist at an earlier stage of social and political development.

In essence, then, the police service gathers information and uses force. The traditional role of a formal police service is to support the government in power, whether at a central, regional or local level; and although some idealists might like to argue that policing arises through the spontaneous agreement of the people, as a voluntary surrendering of autonomy in order that anarchy might be prevented, there seems no historical evidence that this is in fact what occurs. The modern practice of policing did not arise as a result of some sort of democratic cost-benefit analysis by a set community at a set time; and the social contract so beloved of 18th century constitutional theorists is a convenient myth.

Gradually, the role of the police has expanded and changed, and in a modern liberal democracy it is more service than force, accountable more to the people whom it serves than those who control the political system, and more open and honest in how it accounts for the proper use of the powers with which it has been entrusted.

Or is it? It might be argued that beneath the veneer of a modern society, with its language of egalitarianism and human rights, the role of the police remains what it has always been: to exercise power on behalf of the haves, over the have-nots. Despite the seductive appeal of this radical statement, we do not believe it to be entirely true; and in the course of this short introduction to policing we shall show how the police service has developed a professional ethos of its own, and has recognised that to police by force, and without the consent and cooperation of the majority of the public, is to make its task, if not impossible, then very much more difficult.

We shall argue that the origins of policing by consent are pragmatic, rather than ideological, and that that is the strongest reason why it has succeeded. Policing by consent *works*, in a way that other methods of policing do not; and that is the reason for its survival.

FORMATION OF THE METROPOLITAN POLICE SERVICE

Rather than continue to explore the origins of policing a settled community, let us examine the purposes and role of the police service as it has developed since 1829: a year that marks both the end of the industrial revolution, which had transformed traditional society, and the creation of the Metropolitan Police.

It was, perhaps, a mark of the genius of Sir Robert Peel that he set out to create his new force without undue fuss, and much of the rhetoric that accompanies any contemporary police service was conspicuous by its absence in 1829. Peel knew that the British public, and indeed the majority of his colleagues in Parliament, distrusted the whole idea of a police service, which they associated with continental spying and despotism: the chief of police under Napoleon had famously said that if three people were gathered together on a Parisian street, one of them was a police spy, and there was an element of truth in this picturesque exaggeration.[1]

But Peel also knew the need for a modern police service, for the London of his day was polluted by crime in a way which is difficult to imagine nowadays, when despite the outbreak of juvenile stabbings and the ever-present threat of terrorist outrages, the metropolis as a whole is comparatively peaceful and law-abiding.[2]

The Fabian socialists Beatrice and Sidney Webb noted that by 1829 London was the commercial and financial capital of the world, its busiest port, and its largest city. However, its condition was one of increasing lawlessness, and they 'confessed to despair of conveying any adequate picture of the lawless violence, the barbarous licentiousness, and the almost unlimited opportunities for pilfering and robbery offered by the unpoliced London streets... Whole districts were regarded by immemorial custom as sanctuaries in which thieves enjoyed complete immunity...'

---

1.   Despotic regimes maintain a large and well-funded secret police force: see, for example, the state security system (the Stasi) in the former East Germany, which employed a vast number of officials and ran a grotesquely inflated system of informers penetrating the whole of East German society. A main part of its purpose was to ensure that East Germans did not flee their socialist paradise, and to punish those who helped others to escape. The repercussions of this iniquitous system persist today for those accused of having been informers under communism, whether in East Germany, Poland or elsewhere. Should the past be buried and forgotten: or should people be brought to justice regardless?

2.   The British aversion to policing did not apply to the role and actions of the Royal Navy. '[It] acted as a global policeman, suppressing slavery and piracy, protecting trade routes and surveying the oceans.' (National Maritime Museum pamphlet: The Empire Lectures, July 2008). However, the international role of the Royal Navy protected the security and increased the prosperity of Britons at home, and did not interfere with their freedom—provided that they were not press-ganged into it.

(Critchley, 1967, *A History of the Police in England and Wales*).

What applied to London applied elsewhere, but Peel had first to concentrate his attention on the capital. His solution to this dilemma was to initiate the development of a new style of policing, which *would* be acceptable to the public of all classes; and to this end he set up, recruited and equipped a police service which was to be distinguished by its civility. Further developments in policing in London and elsewhere appear in the next chapter and in the *Timeline* at the end of the book.

The purpose of the New Police Service

Sir Charles Rowan and Richard Mayne, the original joint commissioners of the Metropolitan Police, described the purpose of the MPS as follows:

> The primary object of an efficient force is the prevention of crime; the next, that of the detection and apprehension of offenders when crime is committed. To these ends, all the efforts of the police must be directed. The protection of life and property, the preservation of public tranquillity and the absence of crime will alone prove whether the efforts of the police have been successful, and whether the objects for which the police were appointed have been attained.

> Every member of the force must remember that his duty is to protect and help members of the public, no less than to apprehend guilty persons. Consequently, whilst prompt to prevent crime and arrest criminals, he must look upon himself as the servant and guardian of the general public and treat all law-abiding citizens, irrespective of their social position, with unfailing patience, courtesy and good humour.

Comment

Sir Charles Rowan's strategically significant 'mission statement' articulates the primary role of the police with great clarity, and at the same time makes the point that how the police carry out their duties is of equivalent importance to what those duties are. This makes the role of the police service unique. We might accept the work of a surgeon who saved our life, even though his bedside manner was rude and overbearing: better a competent physician, we might say, than an incompetent well-wisher; but the analogy does not transfer to policing, where *how* the police carry out their duties is of crucial importance. (We might also note that the individual police officer is expected to have a wide range of skills at his disposal, and does not have the opportunity to specialise of, say, the medical consultant: a point to which we shall return later in this book).

Police work as craft

An experienced police officer will say that how a police officer deals with an emerging incident may lead either to a restoration of peace or a riot; and we would comment that what is needed on this and other occasions is craftsmanship (indeed, experience of policing by those who participate in it is frequently referred to as 'tradecraft'), the essence of which is the unfettered exercise of individual judgement and discretion, based on personal experience of the work in question. For the craftsperson, all challenges to his skill are unique, although all benefit from the exercise of accumulated experience and wisdom, which he may have obtained in part by discussion with his colleagues. We should not argue from this, that all police work is craftsmanship, nor that the lessons of police work cannot be analysed and synthesized so that no form of organized and collective training is possible. But we should argue, that the essence of policing remains neither art nor science, but a form of craft.

An evolving purpose

Royal Commissions are a useful source of evidence as to what the public expects from its police service, and they have occurred in response to periodic crises that have rocked public confidence in policing and given rise to sustained debate in Parliament.

The Royal Commission on the Police of 1960 (which reported in 1962) consolidated previously established expectations, and described police duties in England and Wales as being to:

- maintain law and order and protect persons and property;
- prevent crime; and
- detect criminals. In the course of interrogating suspected persons, the police have a part to play in the early stages of the judicial process.

Comment

The following points can be made thus far:

- since 1962 the role of the police in the judicial process has been clarified and categorised under The Police and Criminal Evidence Act 1984 (PACE);

- we might also notice the creation of the Crown Prosecution Service in 1985. The CPS has assumed the decision-making process once made by the police, in determining why and when to charge whom with what crime; and

- it might be argued that the Human Rights Act 1998 has made an impact on the role of the police in the criminal justice process, and we shall go on to explore the impact of this fact in a later chapter. For the time being, however, we shall simply assert that the impact of the 1998 Act has been less dramatic than the former two changes, although it has altered the language of policing.

The Royal Commission also stated that police duties included:

- controlling road traffic and advising local authorities on traffic questions; and
- carrying out certain duties for government departments.

Comment

This rather coy statement needs to be substantiated. Since its creation in 1829 the professional police service has acted as an extremely useful general purpose unit, carrying out duties which may have had little to do with its official purposes as listed above. The police were the first social service, and are still the only provider of a 24/7 response capability in that area.

Miscellaneous police activities have included carrying out the census, enforcing weights and measures legislation, coping with agricultural emergencies such as foot-and-mouth disease, and making enquiries about immigrants and aliens. New or evolving tasks, such as the creation and maintenance of a sex offenders' register, or of a National Database for DNA samples (maintained by the police), constantly arise as technology advances and social priorities change.

Offences such as credit card fraud could not have existed in 1829, for the very obvious reason that there were no credit cards; and the theft of mobile telephones would have been incomprehensible. Whilst some offences have now been made obsolete by the passage of time, we would suggest that the duties and responsibilities of the police have tended to increase rather than diminish over the same period. (So, of course, have their numbers, resources, and technical capabilities, but not necessarily in proportion to the increase in demand.)

Some of the traditional tasks of the police have now been taken over at least in part by other agencies, such as the UK Immigration Service (since 2007 part of the Border Agency or 'UK Borders'), which did not exist in 1829; but it would be a mistake to see the police as no longer involved. The police are the agency of last resort, and although they will sometimes query a new task, or question the need for their services in support of another agency—and certainly question its cost and the additional burden it will impose on what are always claimed to be already strained resources—they will very seldom say 'no'. Indeed, as the Royal Commission of 1960 also concluded:

- the police have by long tradition a duty to befriend anyone who needs their help, and they may at any time be called upon to cope with major or minor emergencies.

A word on policing in wartime

We should comment at this point that policing in wartime and civil emergency comes under a different regulatory system, and the role of the police in the Second World War, when we operated, in effect, with a national police service under central direction, is an exception to what is described in this short introduction. Policing in wartime involves the use of special powers which are only acceptable in time of war, and when the whole nation is in one way or another involved in the struggle. Does international terrorism create a state of war, and does it require special powers by the police, in order to deal with it? We shall return to this highly interesting and topical question in *Chapter 7*.

No subsequent overall re-examination of policing

There has been no further Royal Commission on Policing since 1960 (even if there have been a number of White Papers, Green Papers and as will appear from other parts of this book, significant reforms), and hence no further official and overall re-examination of the role and functions of the police; although since 1960 that role has changed very considerably, firstly by the addition of new responsibilities and secondly by the changing nature of society in an era of multi-racialism and multi-culturalism, partly the result of major commonwealth and wider immigration, which we explore further in our final chapter. The United Kingdom in 1960 was a relatively stable and homogeneous society. The UK today is neither, and there is a need for a new Royal Commission on policing to re-address its fundamental purpose and values—something which successive governments since 1960 have been accused of avoiding.

THE POLICE DEFINITION OF PURPOSE

The police themselves have clarified their purpose in various declarations. *The Principles of Policing and Guidance for Professional Behaviour,* commonly known as the Blue Book, was published by the MPS in 1985 and was a clear and inclusive analysis of the fundamental objectives of policing, which presaged the commitment to human rights later emphasised by the passage of the Human Rights Act in 1998. But the Blue Book was restricted to the MPS, and as it was not made part of a specific training programme had little impact.

The Statement of Common Purpose and Values (1990), as agreed and jointly published by the three main police representative associations, the Association of Chief Police Officers (ACPO), Superintendents Association and Police Federation reflects Rowan and Mayne's duality of emphasis on task and method, with a new acknowledgement of the need to respond to public priorities. It is both short and clear, and is worth quoting in full.

The Statement of Common Purpose and Values

The purpose of the police service is to uphold the law fairly and firmly; to prevent crime; to pursue and bring to justice those who break the law; to keep the Queen's Peace; to protect, help, and reassure the community; and to be seen to do all this with integrity, common sense and sound judgment.

We must be compassionate, courteous and patient, acting without fear or favour or prejudice to the rights of others. We need to be professional, calm and restrained in the face of violence and apply only that force which is necessary to accomplish our lawful duty.

> We must strive to reduce the fears of the public and so far as we can, reflect their priorities in the action we take. We must respond to well-founded criticism with a willingness to change.
>
> (ACPO, 23 October, 1990)

POLICING IN THE ERA OF HUMAN RIGHTS

As will also be discussed at various points in this book, in modern times, police across the European Union have been obliged to operate within the context of the European Convention On Human Rights and Fundamental Freedoms (ECHR). In terms of what are also sometimes called 'civil rights', it is interesting to look at the formation of one new police service in a part of the UK which has been affected by assertions of rights from both sides of a divided community, as well as from other sectors.

The formation of the Police Service of Northern Ireland

The Police Service of Northern Ireland (PSNI), created in November 2001, 172 years after the formation of the MPS, is a significant development for a number of reasons.

- it is a new police service, the result of a considered and deliberate act of creation, resulting from the Patten Commission;
- it polices an entire province;
- it is accountable to a highly critical populace, from both sides of the traditional divide; and
- it replaced the Royal Ulster Constabulary (RUC), hundreds of whose officers had been murdered by the IRA and other organizations, and thousands of whose lives had been shattered by terrorism: which was regarded at best as policing by authority and not by consent.

The reputation of the RUC

Its republican critics had often stated that the RUC was not impartial, and it had been accused of collusion in loyalist killings and other illegal acts. Clearly, the RUC was not policing a normal part of the UK by normal means, and given the violent origins of the province of Northern Ireland, its officers had never had the same opportunity as their colleagues across the Irish Sea, to police unarmed and by consent. Some of its members had done their best to police without fear or favour, throughout the province; but any sustained move towards 'civil' policing had broken down in the late-1960s.

After 30 years of violence and under the impetus of the Good Friday Agreement (also known as the Belfast Agreement), there was an overwhelming recognition of the need for a new beginning. The base chosen was human rights, in accordance with the influence of the Patten Commission upon the ideas of which the new police service was founded. Patten stated that:

> ...the fundamental purpose of policing should be...the protection and vindication of the human rights of all... ...There should be no conflict between human rights and policing. Policing means protecting human rights.

Patten further recommended, *inter alia,* that:

- all police officers were to swear a new oath expressing an explicit commitment to upholding human rights;
- a new Code of Ethics should replace the existing, largely procedural code, integrating the European Convention On Human Rights (ECHR) into police practice. Codes of practice on all aspects of policing, including covert law enforcement techniques, should be strictly in accordance with the ECHR;
- all police officers, and police civilians, should be trained (and updated as required) in the fundamental principles and standards of human rights and the practical implications for policing. The human rights dimension should be integrated into every module of police training; and
- awareness of human rights issues and respect for human rights in the performance of duty should be an important element in the appraisal of individuals in the police service.

Comment

We would suggest that these are not one-off objectives to be achieved once and for all, for example by the creation of a felicitous mission statement, but constants, to be revisited by both PSNI and those to whom it is accountable on a regular basis. Police reform is not a single objective, but a continuing process.

In summary, then, the fundamental purpose of the new service was to protect human rights, beginning with the right to life and including all the rights enumerated under the ECHR and its additional protocols. The PSNI thus committed itself, not only to protecting the lives and property of those whom it policed, and their rights to freedom from torture or mistreatment and abuse of civil liberties: it also set out to protect their rights as citizens of what the Council of Europe describes as a democratic society, by which it means a pluralistic democracy. This means, for example, that a right such as the right to demonstration and (peaceful) protest must be upheld and indeed be facilitated by the police service.

Is all this really new? By no means; but it is an explicit commitment to a policy which previous police forces might have recognised by one means or another, but which was not spelled out for them in an official constitution. If the PSNI is successful in creating a new police service for a new society in Northern Ireland, then the advancement of the protection of human rights to the front of that agenda will be part of that process; and that achievement will have a wider significance than simply for the six of the nine counties of the historical province of Ulster which became Northern Ireland.

CIVIL AND MILITARY MODELS OF POLICING

The MPS is a civil police force. It is not part of the army and is not subject to military discipline. As we have seen, Sir Robert Peel set out to emphasize the non-military features of his new force, down to the details of its uniform and ranks. If policing had once been part of the military's duties, whether by the regular army or the militia, he wished to emphasize that that was no longer the case.

There is, however, an alternative and sustainable model of policing, and that is the military one.[3] France, for a very good example, has two systems of policing co-existing within the same administration: the civil and the military. The civil police are the Police Nationale, who report to the Ministry of the Interior. The other police service is the Gendarmerie Nationale, which is officially part of the army and belongs to the Ministry of Defence. The gendarmerie, whose origins go back to the 14th Century, are commanded by regular army officers and are stationed in rural

---

3. Some police historians would argue that Sir Robert Peel established both systems, as far as the traditions of policing the British Isles are concerned; since before founding the MPS in London, he had previously set up what went on to become the Irish Constabulary: a paramilitary force.

France, policing the countryside and small towns (as well as the armed services); whereas the Police Nationale are essentially an urban force who have no military role, although they possess formidable paramilitary resources in case of a major breakdown in public order.

The Police Nationale is a national force and corresponds to one of our larger urban forces, magnified to a national scale. The gendarmerie, however, has no equivalent in Great Britain, although variations are to be found in Spain (the Guardia Civil), Italy (the Carabinieri) and elsewhere. Police systems evolve as part of national history, and French national history has produced two national police services of equal legitimacy, both of which police by authority.

POLICING AS A PRAGMATIC ACTIVITY

We have seen that the purpose(s) of policing may be articulated by its founding fathers, or by the government, or by the police service itself—and nowadays in the increasing academic literature on policing. We have further noted that any police service tends to accumulate responsibilities, some of which cannot be easily reconciled with its official purpose. The Royal Commission of 1960, for example, refers to the traditional role of the police as 'a friend in need.' Is this a residue of Victorian paternalism? Does it have any real meaning? Should it be included in the contemporary concept of policing? We would suggest that it should and does still apply, and that much of what the police do, if not precisely providing 'a friend in need', cannot easily be reconciled with straightforward law enforcement, the prevention and detection of crime, and so on. There is a moral aspect to policing, and the police do see themselves as there at least in part to help the more vulnerable elements of society.

They are not, as they say themselves, social workers: but some of what they do is akin to social work. It is a paradox of modern society that the police both enforce the law, for example by ensuring the deportation of an illegal resident who may also have family responsibilities in the United Kingdom; and will also make every effort to find that illegal resident's missing child, a task which calls for the same resolution and purpose, but poses no humanitarian dilemma.

Why welfare?
We would suggest that the reason why the police provide a service, at least on occasion, that seems to go beyond the formal limits and boundaries to their official duties, is fourfold:

- it is in the tradition of British policing, and is therefore, at least to some, in no further need of justification;
- no other organization is set up to provide the service needed, on a 24/7 basis, and

the police may therefore take a legitimate pride in the service that they provide, and the opportunity afforded to exercise and test their skills for use in emergency;

- it is a source of positive relations between police and public which means that help, cooperation and information will be forthcoming when needed, from the public to the police; and
- women joined the police service during the Great War, against immense opposition, partly at least to expand the capacity of that service to provide welfare for women and children.

The enduring need for policing: care in the community?

There is a paradox in policing: for it may be that the need for policing is greatest where it is least apparent.

It could be argued that small, settled communities do not need the same sort of policing as larger ones. They have mechanisms for policing themselves which are not available to new residential areas in which people do not even know their neighbours, or some housing estates notorious for vandalism and anti-social behaviour: and heavily urbanised areas do, on the whole, present more crime.

However, whilst a settled and virtually self-policing community may have some appeal as an ideal, we must offer these comments:

- settled, bounded, definite communities are rapidly becoming a thing of the past, and society is unlikely to return to this sort of community in the future, in what has become the era of globalisation;
- many issues with which the police, on behalf of society, need to deal, cross over established boundaries in any case; and
- small, settled communities may present problems of their own, where local traditions have proved ineffective and to which modern policing may be the preferable solution.

Examples of potential challenges for policing in remote areas

During the time we researched for this book, a major investigation has been taking place into alleged child abuse on the island of Jersey, in the English Channel. There has also recently been an investigation into sexual abuse on the island of Pitcairn, in the Pacific Ocean. Despite their widely separated locations, the two stories have something in common; for in both locations, the young and vulnerable would appear to have been abused within a settled community in which there is an established tradition of law and order.

Jersey

During 2007, a number of allegations of sexual abuse and other offences at a former children's home at Haut de la Garenne came to light, and an official investigation began. Had there been a series of breaches of the law in Jersey, covered up, dismissed or ignored by officialdom in the interests of preventing scandal? What was the relationship between local or voluntary and professional police in regard to this issue, and how did that relationship affect the investigation of the complaints of abuse?

Pitcairn Island

Pitcairn Island is about as remote as it is possible to be: a tiny island in the middle of the Pacific Ocean, unpopulated until the mutineers of 'The Bounty' chose to settle there with women who joined them from Tahiti, and whose descendants still populate the island now: Christian (after Fletcher Christian the leading mutineer) is the most common surname.

A sub-tropical paradise? Not really: as *Police Review* reported in depth in February and March 2008, such was the number of allegations of unlawful sexual intercourse and rape reported to have taken place on the island in which older men took advantage of younger women and girls, that in the end an official investigation was launched by an outside police service, culminating in trial and conviction in New Zealand (Given the small population of the island, those convicted had to build their own jail). An atypical example of behaviour in a small community? We hope so: but not a unique example of abuse behind closed doors. Any community is capable of breaking the law, and any citizen should have access to redress of grievance under the Rule of Law.

If authority rests in the hands of the elders of the community, then they are in a position either to enforce high moral standards, or to break them; and to create or sustain a culture in which such behaviour is accepted as the norm. We are arguing here for the Rule of Law, on Pitcairn as elsewhere, and a fair, objective and professional means to enforce it. Professional does not necessarily mean paid, nor full-time in all its aspects: special constables are perfectly capable of upholding and enforcing the law, but behind them should be a professional framework.

We should not expect law enforcement on an island such as Pitcairn, with its tiny population, nor on the States of Jersey, with their unique constitutional tradition, to be identical to law enforcement elsewhere. But there are certain principles of police organization and practice that must be respected, even if the police service in question consists of a total of one person.

POLICING BY CONSENT

Let us end this chapter on the purpose of policing, by linking it explicitly to policing by consent at which we can also take a closer look. As a colleague and I have written elsewhere (Adlam and Villiers, 2003) that doctrine has never been officially defined, and even the police themselves are not always in agreement as to its precise meaning. However, if we cannot refer to an official source document on policing by consent, we may easily recognise its opposite; and we may put forward some general thoughts towards a definition.

There are a number of key factors, a combination of which tends to suggest the presence of policing by consent, and an absence of a significant number of which may indicate or precipitate its withdrawal. Those factors are not necessarily constant over time, and nor are they determinate in number. However, there is what we might call a critical combination of successful factors, which good police leaders need to keep in mind if they are to be able to continue to police without force, or with only such force as is tactically necessary. Those factors include:

- upholding the Rule of Law, which means, most importantly, the police not seeing themselves as above the law;
- not acting as a political police, but preferring to deal with 'crimes ordinary';
- maintaining a visible presence in the community;
- remaining an unarmed and civil police, and not a paramilitary organization;
- preferring to use persuasion rather than coercion where possible;
- tending to use the official power of the law as a last resort;
- attempting to balance the rival interests at stake in any conflict, and find a common sense solution in which no-one is an absolute loser;
- emphasising the original authority[4] and discretion of the constable as an officer of the law—which means considerable variation in how problems are dealt with;
- playing a specific and constrained role in the criminal justice system
- defining its other duties inclusively rather than exclusively;
- not being directly accountable to central government, but recognising and applying the principle of accountability in everything that it does;
- attempting to be and remain locally recruited, representative, responsive and accountable; and
- showing that the idea of the police as a friend in need is not entirely mythical.

---

4. 'Original authority' is the Anglo-Australian doctrine that all police officers hold their powers by original authority, directly from the Crown, and not by delegation. Therefore, a senior police officer cannot direct a junior, how and when to enforce the law.

Policing by consent is a *renewable* doctrine. It implies that the police service engages in a *dialogue* with the public both as to its duties and *modus operandi*. That dialogue will, of course, include the propensity of the public to complain about the police. A functional complaints mechanism is a good thing, as it indicates that the complainant believes it to be both safe and worthwhile to make a complaint. The same logic applies to the police complaining about the public, for example in not volunteering information that would help to solve crimes.

Policing by consent is an *organic* doctrine. Its tenets cannot always be neatly separated into philosophy, doctrine or style; and it is not necessarily the case that top police leaders deal with policy, intermediate commanders with strategy, and more junior officers with tactics—although police training manuals would like to have us believe that this is so. In reality, policing by consent is an organic doctrine that cannot easily be separated into its constituent parts, nor applied by one section of a police service in isolation from its other parts.

Policing by consent is a *realistic* doctrine. One of the problems of the performance management culture, in its various manifestations, is the sometimes fantastic disparity between what the organization is supposed to be doing, according to its official policies, priorities and procedures, and what is actually going on. Our comments here are certainly not restricted to policing, but apply to other public sector organizations. We would suggest that what happens at street level is both the reality of policing, by definition, and more likely to correspond to the practice of policing by consent. Police officers are street-corner politicians, and their essential role is to negotiate between conflicting parties and find a way forward (Ker Muir, 1977). As my colleague Dr Robert Adlam and I have previously noted:

> The reality of policing by consent includes negative as well as positive factors. Policing by consent is not necessarily the best solution to any problem. It may not appear the most efficient way to make use of the resources available to the police; and it is bound to give rise to disparities between the apparent productivity of one force and another. We would argue, however, that improvements in efficiency do not necessarily lead to corresponding improvements in effectiveness; and that policing by consent is the most effective form of policing for the United Kingdom (Adlam and Villiers, 2003).

CONCLUSION

Some commentators have argued that there is a fundamental division of opinion as to the core role of the police. We refer to law and order, but in fact this convenient phrase needs further analysis. A senior Indian police officer stated to the author during a fundamental discussion at Bramshill, that one can have law *or* order, but not both. We would argue that the essential role of the police is to maintain order under law, and that upholding the law (i.e. any law which may be being broken) must come second to this if a choice has to be made.

A simple example will explain our point. Let us suppose that a riot is in progress. The first task of the police is to stop the riot, no matter what infractions of the law may be taking place. Law enforcement can take place at a later stage. The police may be able to gather evidence of law-breaking, for example by examining CCTV footage after the event, and use this for prosecution, for it is right that people should be aware that they cannot break or flout the law with impunity; but that is a secondary consideration. Public order is the priority; and public order should be seen within the broader context of public safety. One does not arrest the pilot of a passenger ship as he is about to bring his charge into a difficult harbour.

The police exist to fulfil more than one role and their ability to switch resources and change direction, on occasion in an instant response to a new demand, is not only desirable but necessary. Their roles are partly cast upon them and partly self-adopted; and both may change over time. All modern administrations seek to improve public services *and* reduce costs; and any government is constantly seeking ways to achieve this dual objective. Some police tasks can and have been taken on by other government departments, or have been offered to different categories of police officer, or put out to the private sector; and we shall have a good deal more to say about the privatisation of some police functions and its consequences, as this guide progresses. However, the role of the police in preserving the Queen's Peace is unlikely to be put out to contract by even the most ardent advocate of privatisation; and the police need to retain a degree of discretion in how they interpret that role.

A Short History of Policing

A Short History of Policing

We have explored in brief the purpose of policing, and now need to spend a little time exploring its evolution. In Anglo-Saxon times every citizen had a responsibility for maintaining law and order, and under the Statute of Winchester (1285) this principle was perpetuated by the Normans. As T A Critchley puts it (*A History of the Police in England and Wales*, Constable, London, 1967):

> The Statute of Winchester was the only general measure of any consequence enacted to regulate the policing of the country between the Norman Conquest and the Metropolitan Police Act 1829."
>
> Under [the Statute of Winchester]:
>
> - it was the duty of everyone to maintain the King's Peace, and it was open to any citizen to arrest an offender;
>
> - the unpaid part-time constable had a special duty to do so;
>
> - if the offender was not caught red-handed, the hue and cry was to be raised;
>
> - everyone was obliged to keep arms with which to follow the cry when required.
>
> - finally, the constable had a duty to present the offender at court… These arrangements… enlisted the whole community in what would nowadays be called the fight against crime, and penalised laxity by the imposition of a collective fine.

Commentary

It is remarkable how little the fundamental issues of policing have changed since this statute was passed. Clearly, everyone should have a responsibility to uphold the law, and the ideal of a self-policing community is a good one. Clearly, also, the principle of the Statute of Winchester cannot be applied to all crimes. The outraged shopkeeper whose goods have just been stolen or damaged, has every reason to raise the hue and cry. But what about crimes where there is no obvious single victim, such as some forms of fraud; or if the wronged person is too embarrassed, ashamed or fearful to raise a complaint, as may be the case with child abuse or rape? Under such circumstances, we begin to see the advantage of a professional and disinterested police service, which can carry out its inquiries in an objective and fair manner, searching for the truth without fear or favour.

Nevertheless, the idea of the hue and cry should not be abandoned, and such events still occur spontaneously, leading to a rebirth of good citizenship which might be taken further, as politicians sometimes comment. The goodwill of the ordinary citizen may be encouraged into his becoming a special constable, supporting the neighbourhood watch, or in some other way assisting the role of the regular police: but we are not aware of a modern state that recommends the return of the entire responsibility for policing to the community. There would be obvious hazards if such a policy were to be put in place, of which punishment beatings are a dramatic example. There is a difference between a police officer and a vigilante, and it must be preserved.

On the other hand, the moral enthusiasm which drives the ordinary citizen to help the police in searching for a missing child or helping in a fire, flood or any other emergency should continue to be harnessed and put to good use. The police officer is, or should be, a leader in the community, and should help to harness community spirit to good use.

THE RIGHT TO BEAR ARMS

The second amendment to the USA Constitution famously protects the right of the ordinary citizen to carry arms openly (but not concealed weapons). There is no such right in the UK, and we imagine that public opinion would be against it. However, a brief glance at history will remind us that in Great Britain the respectable (i.e. property owning classes) could and did carry arms, which they kept at home without a licence from any constabulary, until the Firearms Control Act 1920 breached this traditional liberty. Shotguns remained untouched until 1967. In the opinion of the Libertarian Alliance, which is, of course, hardly a disinterested party, the UK now has the most restrictive firearms control legislation in the western world. Criminal use of illegal firearms remains a major problem substantially unaffected by legislation, although penalties may be increased.

THE NEW POLICE

The New Police force in 1829 comprised just over 1,000 men, soon to be increased to 3,000. They were dressed in a non-military style, wore a sort of top hat in order that they might both be recognized and seen from a distance, and which was strong enough for them to stand on; and were largely unarmed. Constables carried truncheons. Inspectors might carry pocket pistols or cutlasses on occasion. The New Police was radical in its intent as well as its design. There was no Criminal Investigations Department (CID) or traffic department, and the number of clerks was negligible. Police officers were expected to be able to deal with anything, without help from any specialist department, and with a rudimentary knowledge of the law. Their overall purpose was to keep the peace—the Sovereign's Peace—and their primary objective was to prevent crime by acting as a visible deterrent to potential law-breakers.

How was the new force to keep the peace? They were to patrol set, interlocking beats on a regular basis and to deal with crime as it came their way. They were to support each other as necessary, and could attract each other's attention by using their whistles or truncheons, or even by beating their truncheons against the side of the pavement. They usually patrolled alone, and were expected to use their eyes and ears on patrol and to be both visible and communicative with the public, but not to engage in idle gossip.

The management structure of the new police

The New Police, soon to be officially known as the Metropolitan Police Service (MPS), were commanded by two commissioners who were of equal authority: a daring experiment by the Home Secretary which was to prove immensely valuable. The two men were a soldier and a solicitor, Charles Rowan and Richard Mayne. They were joined by another solicitor who was to act as head of finance and administration and was known as the receiver. His staff was originally a clerk or two and is now an enormous enterprise, but some problems inherent in the police design of 1829—for example were the clerical and support staff part of the police as a whole, or a separate organization altogether?—Have still not been resolved to this day.

Under the two commissioners, the original structure of the new police encompassed eight superintendents, 20 inspectors, 88 sergeants and 895 constables: i.e., about one sergeant for every ten constables, a much higher proportion of supervisory ranks than in the army, but in an organization with no lance-corporals or corporals to lessen the gap between the lowest rank and the first promotion. They were organized by division, section and beat, and the total number of police personnel was rapidly increased to over 3,000 men.

Its style of leadership and management

The New Police was led by gentlemen and managed—supervised might perhaps be a better word—by former non-commissioned officers (NCOs) and warrant officers from the armed services, who would be expected to know their place and concentrate on their ostensible duties. Peel did not want the new force to be officered by gentlemen and indeed turned down many such applications, whether because he thought that they were seeking a sinecure or because they would create the wrong relationship between force and public.

What was that relationship? The police had a subordinate role in Victorian society, and remained under the control of their 'betters'. It would be impossible to imagine a cash for honours scandal such as occurred in the UK in recent years, having taken place a century or more before. Firstly, of course, the relevant legislation did not exist, and therefore the offence of buying an honour had not as yet been created. Secondly, if there had been misgivings in the higher circles of government and administration as to one or another form of corruption, the police would not have been entrusted to deal with it. They were expected to know their place, and to concentrate on policing the 'dangerous' classes—in other words, the law-defying element of the urban poor. Until the development of the motor car, they were unlikely to enforce the law against the property-owning classes, and were seen as their protectors or even their servants.

COUNTY AND BOROUGH FORCES

Professional policing in the metropolitan style spread at an uneven pace throughout the United Kingdom, aided by government legislation culminating in the County and Borough Police Act 1856. It is not our intention, here or elsewhere in this brief introduction, to chart in detail the history of the development of the police. It is relevant to know, however, that from the creation of modern policing until the wholesale national reforms of 1964, there was a substantial difference between county and borough forces.

The borough forces, some of which were extremely small, were under the detailed control of the local watch committee, and the chief constable had no tradition of operational independence to rely upon. It was not a coincidence that borough forces tended to be commanded by professional police officers, promoted from within the ranks, whereas county forces were led by retired military officers of good social standing, who did not experience the same local scrutiny, but instead practised, at least in the better examples, a form of benevolent paternalism which was not unsuited to the spirit of the times. (It is interesting to note in this context that the novelist-to-be John Masters (1914-1983), who retired early from the regular army in 1947 as a substantive lieutenant colonel with a distinguished war record, considered himself perfectly well-suited to apply for the post of chief constable of the police in Cornwall, until he reflected that it would impose unacceptable constraints on his apparently bohemian social habits).

THE TRENCHARD SCHEME

Unlike the armed services, the British police service does not have and has never had an officer class (in fact, all police constables are called officers, as officers of the law; but they are not commissioned officers as in the armed services). All police officers join in the rank of constable, and all promotion is from there. As we have seen, historically, gentlemen were appointed to the highest ranks in the police service, but all other promotion was from within.

There was no attempt to create an officer class within the police service, and the Trenchard Scheme (1934-1939) is not an exception to this statement, despite the myths that used to surround it. Lord Trenchard, who was appointed to be MPS commissioner in 1931 after a long and distinguished career in the army and air force, described himself as 'an old man in a hurry.' He wished to improve police leadership and started a course at his new police college in Hendon in north London to train selected individuals for the highest ranks in the police service.

Trenchard set out to catch the most able young constables, by competitive entry or recommendation for accelerated promotion, and to recruit well-educated young men from public schools, colleges or universities, all with the promise of immediate appointment to the newly created rank of 'junior station inspector' after successful completion of a 15 month programme at Hendon. Thirty-five young men began the course, 21 of whom emerged from within the police service. The Trenchard Scheme persisted until the Second World War, although Lord Trenchard himself retired in 1935. According to his biographer, of its 197 graduates, nearly a third rose to the highest police ranks in the United Kingdom and Commonwealth, including the MPS Commissioner, Sir Joseph Simpson.

For a short-lived experiment, the scheme had remarkable results. Nevertheless, it did not create an officer class for the police service, and it is noteworthy that at least half of its intake came from within the police service and not as outside entrants. It could best be described as an accelerated promotion scheme: a title that was later used at Bramshill (q.v.)

THE CREATION OF THE POLICE STAFF COLLEGE IN 1948

The new Police College as set up in 1948 and its name officially changed to the Police Staff College in 1979. The main purpose of the new college was that the police service might develop or 'grow' its own leaders, rather than continue to appoint retired military officers as its provincial chief constables, and the design and curriculum of the new college—first located in Warwickshire and then at a former Jacobean Mansion, Bramshill House, in Hampshire—reflected this intention.

The Police Staff College is still in existence to-day, and remains a centre for higher police training, although its role and status has changed considerably since 1948. It is now part of the network of the National Policing Improvement Agency (NPIA), which has responsibility for police leadership training amongst many other things; and we shall be looking at the evolution of police leadership and management in theory and practice in a later chapter.

Current police commanders are in one way or another, responsible for the actions or inactions of different work groups, all of whom share some responsibility for the impact and effectiveness of the police service as a whole, and all of whom may be judged by the public at large as representing the police service. They are:

- police constables (PCs)
- police community support officers (PCSOs)
- special constables
- support staff.

We shall explore their roles further in the next chapter. In addition, the modern police commander has to work with other agencies, the voluntary sector and the private sector; either in joint task forces or in partnerships. Here the command structure may not be as clear as it is within the police service itself.

Comment

The modern police manager has to be able to work with a very wide range of people, some of whom are not under his command, and with whom he can at best use the skills of persuasion and example in order to influence their behaviour towards achieving an agreed common goal.

For this work, the quasi-military origins of the modern police service, its emphasis upon paternalistic direction and control, and its tradition of punishment should something be found to have gone wrong, are far from useful. Radical reformers have argued that the police service is in need of a complete re-design, and that its traditions and traditional working practices are detrimental to its true purpose, which is to be a service and not a force.

We would agree that the modern police service needs to be both flexible and adaptive, but the radical critique needs to take history into account. In our view, the police service needs to build on its origins rather than to discard them. It was set up for an honourable purpose, to keep the Queen's Peace; and it has a right to be proud of its traditions.

The view that any British police service (other than the Royal Military Police and its naval and air force equivalents) is a military or paramilitary organization is misleading, and a source of confusion for its reform. The similarity of the (British) police service to a military model of organization and command is both limited and superficial. The army is under the command of commissioned officers, is subject to military law, and exists to move and fight as government policy directs. Soldiering is a collective enterprise, and soldiers come armed, in boxes of ten. Soldiers are recruited, equipped and trained to make war. War is a fundamentally irrational activity in which one side aims to defeat another by the maximum use of force. The concept of proportionality in modern war does not preclude the threat or use of overwhelming force in order to prevent or end the war.

Policing is a 'different activity'

Policing is a fundamentally different activity. In reality, the origins of the New Police were both hybrid and eclectic, and its most important foundation stones were the advice given by both Sir Robert Peel and its first commissioners, in at least two regards:

- firstly, in terms of the sort of relationship which the new force needed to develop with the public if it were to police without constant coercion, the use or threat of force; and
- secondly, the qualities that this required of the individual constable.

Implicitly if not explicitly, police discretion was recognised as a necessary part of policing from the outset. The individual constable was recruited, trained, uniformed, and brought to a higher stage of physical fitness by the organization he had joined. His beat might be and was dictated to him, and he was not at liberty to vary from it; indeed, he was expected to be at a set place at a set time, and his sergeant or inspector might well check that he was there. But what the constable actually did on patrol was up to him. The observant, intelligent, motivated constable acted with discretion, keeping the fundamental purposes of the police service in mind. His opposite does not.

Police Organization: Identity and Control

CHAPTER THREE

Police Organization: Identity and Control

The United Kingdom has no national police service. There is thus no national police commissioner, as compared, say, with the Republic of Ireland, which has one such service, the Garda Siochana, commanded by a national commissioner and reporting to the Minister of Justice.

The UK is the exception to the rule, and all other European states, to the best of our knowledge, have national police services reporting to a government minister. Some, like France, have two national police services (see *Chapter 2*); and all or most will have specialised police services such as the military police. Many will also have some form of municipal police, which has local accountability. Those other forces, however, are in addition to the national police and are secondary to it in both status and power. Before we go on to make comparisons in more detail, let us explore further the situation at home.

POLICE FORCE ORGANIZATION IN THE BRITISH ISLES

Scotland has eight territorial police forces. England and Wales contain 43 'Home Office' forces, each of which has its own geographical territory to police, and of which the largest by far is the Metropolitan Police Service (MPS). The City of London retains its own police force, known as the City of London Police. Like the MPS, it is commanded by a commissioner; and its equivalent of a police authority is the Court of Common Council of the City of London.

The other police services in England and Wales vary enormously in size and manpower, and also in the volume of crime with which they tend to deal; it still being the case that urban areas generate more crime and require more policing per division; or put another way a comparatively small urban area may have far more crimes than a large rural area a crucial factor, seemingly, being density or concentration of population.

The Channel Islands and the Isle of Man (which are not part of the UK but part of Great Britain and the British Isles) have their own police forces; and the island of Ireland as a whole has two police forces, the Garda Siochana in the Republic of Ireland and the Police Service of Northern Ireland (PSNI) already described in *Chapter 1* in the 'six counties'.

Although the UK has no national police service as such, it has some police agencies with national responsibilities such as the Serious Organized Crime Agency (SOCA) and National Policing Improvement Agency (NPIA) which will be considered later. In Great Britain as a whole there is also a mixture of local forces with unspecified duties and general jurisdiction and national forces with specific responsibilities and circumscribed jurisdiction (sometimes referred to as 'non-geographic' forces). Thus Hampshire Constabulary polices the county of Hampshire, but there are also other police forces which operate within its boundaries, such as the British Transport Police (BTP), Ministry of Defence Police (MODP), Royal Military Police (RMP) and others. Their duties and responsibilities are specific and targeted on given areas of public life, whereas Hampshire's are general; and the two co-exist.

Neither is there a 'standard police force' in England and Wales. However, most 'Home Office' police forces have the following characteristics:

- they are commanded by a chief constable (CC), supported by a deputy chief constable (DCC), one or more assistant chief constables (ACCs), and headquarters and administrative staff;
- the police headquarters does not necessarily have any operational police officers working from its premises. However, it is usually a communications centre and may direct or control some operations;
- the next level of command is the division or 'basic command unit' (BCU), usually under a chief superintendent or superintendent of police. A BCU has its own Criminal Investigations department (CID) and other specialist functions, although the responsibility for road traffic police may not be delegated to this level;
- there may be sub-divisions between police divisions or BCUs and the lowest unit of police command, the police station;
- the police station is the hub of policing in its area. However, there are units such as CID and traffic police which operate only from a higher level; and it could be argued that the advent of centralised command and control systems and their associated arrangements (such as Altaris: see *Glossary*) has reduced the significance of the local police station, since the citizen may no longer be able to visit or telephone his local police station to report a crime, air suspicions about a neighbour, or indeed raise any other issue. However, as will be mentioned later, various important functions attach to a 'designated police station' (i.e. one that has been designated by the chief constable) for the purposes of the Police and Criminal Evidence Act 1984.

Neighbourhood policing: A new development?

Some police forces practise neighbourhood policing, mostly built around electoral wards, and involving the combination of police constables, police community support officers, and others. This is a result of governmental pressure and legislation, which we summarise in an appendix to this chapter as a siginificant development.

Police forces differ in their attitude towards the importance of local communication. However, there has been a general move towards the centralisation of police communications, and whilst the maintenance of local police stations is a hot topic for police authorities, and a major issue in police rhetoric, in reality the trend is for the closure of police stations, or their reduction to limited hours, and the centralisation of police resources in larger units.

Who controls the police is the issue underlying this, since the police service is generally concerned to make changes in the interests of efficiency and the better use of resources, which the public and its political representatives oppose because they want a local police service; and it is time we discussed the tripartite relationship.

THE TRIPARTITE RELATIONSHIP

The chief constable is answerable to the public and accountable both to national and local government under the tripartite relationship which has formed the constitutional basis for the control of policing since 1964. In essence this is the relationship between the chief constable, Home Secretary and the local police authority. We shall deal with them in reverse order.

Police authorities
Local police authorities would like more control over policing, but are probably the weakest element in the tripartite relationship, although they jealously guard the power to make all appointments at Association of Chief Officers of Police (ACPO) rank. Their association, the Association of Police Authorities (APA) has recognised that unity is strength and attempts to articulate a common policy on many issues. The MPS has its own Metropolitan Police Authority (MPA), which was created in July 2000; up till then, the MPS was unique in being directly accountable to the Home Secretary, who still appoints its commissioner and assesses its national contribution. The tensions inherent in this shift to a new arrangement remain to be fully worked out ,as was illustrated by the forced resignation of Sir Ian Blair in October 2008. The Home Secretary, Jacqui Smith, was quick to inform Boris Johnson, the elected Mayor of London and newly elected chairman of the MPA, that the appointment of a new commissioner was her responsibility and not his, although it was Johnson's expression of a lack of confidence in the commissioner which had led Sir Ian Blair to resign.

The Home Office
The Home Secretary in whom enormous powers in relation to the safety and security of the country reside, is supported by one of the oldest offices of State, the Home Office. That department is constantly seeking to increase its powers over local

forces, and is in a strong position to do so. It is, via The Treasury in reality the main source of police funding. Policing is officially classified as a local responsibility, paid for by local government, as every community charge payer is aware. However, it is a constitutional fiction that local government is paid for by locally-raised revenue such as the council tax. About 80 per cent of local government revenue comes from the national exchequer; and the Home Office has a responsibility for ensuring that policing represents value for money in terms of national expenditure. The Home Office is to the fore in many areas, not least the technical and scientific developments on which much modern-day policing ultimately depends.

The Home Office liaises closely with HM Iinspectrate of Constabulary (HMIC), which was traditionally responsible for ensuring that the police forces it inspected were efficient, and now has a larger role. It sets targets for police activity as part of the National Policing Plan (NPP), via performance indicators. Although target-setting is not officially intended to reduce the power and autonomy of chief constables, that is one of its effects. Some chief constables have declared that they are not prepared to continue with a 'performance measurement culture' in which they are directed to address nationally determined policing priorities which may not match local needs and wishes. The Government has moved some way towards chief constables by indicating that it will review and maybe end such targets, which have sometimes led to priorities being given to 'point scoring', e.g. by pursuing soft targets rather than automatically prioritising more serious incidents. This battle is part of a larger debate about how central government seeks to improve all public service activities within the UK, which we expect will continue long after this book is published.[1]

Chief constables

Twenty or thirty years ago, chief constables were commonly described as analogous to feudal barons: men (no woman chief constable was appointed until 1995) who were able to rule their forces as private fiefdoms. The analogy was exaggerated and never wholly true, but had an element of truth about it: and there were examples of chief constables who were able, in effect, to defy both central and local government in following their own agenda.

The last of the dinosaurs?

The chief constable of Merseyside, Sir Kenneth Oxford (in office from 1975 to 1989), took his own approach to central government's wishes, which he ignored when he disagreed with them: he also clashed with his police authority on operational matters, and was able on occasion to play off local against central government.

---

1. The powers of the Home Secretary have increased considerably, for example in regard to the appointment and dismissal of chief officers, as a result of the Police Reform Act of 2002 and other measures; and we recommend a sister volume to our readers for a full analysis. It is *The New Home Office: An Introduction*, by Bryan Gibson, Waterside Press, 2nd edn, 2008.

His attitude is uncharacteristic of his successors, who tend to be more subtle in their approach; but Sir Kenneth Oxford was not unique in his time, and his contemporary, the chief constable of the Greater Manchester Police Sir James Anderton (in office 1975 to 1991), probably achieved an even greater public notoriety for his comments on AIDS and its victims among other things.

Like the police authorities, chief constables have recognised that unity is strength, and both ACPO and ACPO(S) (see the *Glossary*) exercise a political influence by lobbying and other means. Chief constables are a highly educated and trained elite. They have the advantage of being at the seat of power, so that they have the best knowledge of what is happening in their force (as opposed to the Home Office or police authority, who can only gain their knowledge at second hand). Moreover, chief constables may claim the right to operational independence: in other words, not be subject to political interference on matters of professional policing.

It is debatable that the old arguments over the tripartite relationship are now becoming less relevant to contemporary policing, as:

- the Home Office has found new ways to increase its powers;
- the move towards regionalisation will render some police chief constables and their headquarters redundant; and
- under regionalisation, police chief superintendents and superintendents as BCU commanders will hold the key decision-making role in policing, as they are beginning to do already.

In our view, county chief constables are neither dead nor dying, and predictions of their demise in the near future are much exaggerated.

Changes in governance

What are sometimes called 'partnerships' between the police and other organizations did not exist in 1964. Organizations other than police authorities are now involved in policing through partnerships of various kinds, including Crime and Disorder Reduction Partnerships under the Crime and Disorder Act 1998. This is an important facet of modern day police work in which the voluntary sector or private sector may also play a part in bringing about crime prevention and crime reduction. Such activities cover everything from membership of advisory groups, to design out crime by improving the environment, to the provision of CCTV in shopping precincts and to the coordination of a number of watch schemes such as Neighbourhood Watch and the other variants of this method noted in the *Glossary*.

Partnership also exists at national, regional and area levels through police involvement in committees, schemes, initiatives and projects all of which traverse agencies or services so as to bring the strength of multi-agency strategies and tactics to bear on the problems of policing and crime and disorder generally. Examples include the Cabinet Committee on Crime and the Criminal Justice System (CCCCJS), Multi-Agency Public Protection Arrangements (MAPPAs), a National Criminal Justice Board and Local Criminal Justice Boards. In all such matters the police retain their own operational control, powers, duties and discretion but the picture is long way from what it was in 1964.

LOCAL POLICING: GOVERNMENT RECOMMENDATIONS

Community policing has already been mentioned in outline. In 2008 the Home Office published a Green Paper on the future of policing, 'From the Neighbourhood to the National: Policing Our Communities'.[2]

We are indebted to our colleague Dr Barry Loveday of the University of Portsmouth for the summary and appraisal that follows and for permission to publish it in an edited form.

Following the Casey Review an emphasis will be placed on encouraging community engagement and making a reality of the local delivery of policing. All of this is, of course, highly laudable and warrants public support. It is, however, the challenge of making the police more locally accountable that could prove to be the fatal flaw within the Green Paper.

Police Authorities

Drawing on the existing model of accountability the Green Paper emphasises the critical role of police authorities in the future and recommends that they be strengthened by way of direct election. In future the police authority will be made up of one third elected councillors, one third 'independents' and one third directly elected representatives. Direct election along with community empowerment over policing, it is argued, will provide a more robust system of accountability than currently pertains. Together it is expected that a [much needed] emphasis on 'customer care' along with embedding neighbourhood policing will be sustained by opportunities for direct action within the community which will be able, by way of public meetings, to identify their priorities for local policing.

It is certainly the case that if police authorities are to be retained their public profile would need to be enhanced. Very few people know what police authorities are or what they do. This in part is of course the direct result of the public profile currently adopted by police authorities, which can be best described as being akin to climbing into a ditch.

---

2. Cm 7448. Also known as 'The Casey Review'.

Elected Mayors

At the 2008 Local Government Association's conference at Bournemouth, David Cameron [the leader of the Tory Opposition] committed his party to establishing elected mayors for all of England's big cities. This was premised on the fact that the evidence suggested that voter turn out had proved to be much higher for mayoral elections. More significantly, Cameron was to state that mayors could in future be given responsibility for the police which would serve to emphasise his party's commitment to 'new localism' and to dismantling the central Whitehall control over ostensibly local services.

This interesting development reflects the success of the mayoral system in New York in relation to the NYPD and the direct accountability of the Chief of Police to the Mayor who appoints that officer. Building on this, it is apparent that should David Cameron win the next election then all current responsibilities exercised within the Home Office over the Metropolitan Police Service will be handed over to London's mayor.

This could have a number of very beneficial effects. City residents would for the first time have a very clear idea as to who was ultimately responsible for local police service delivery. Those responsible could also be made directly accountable for any evident failures at the ballot box. Additionally, direct mayoral engagement might begin to provide a degree of financial accountability within the big metropolitan police forces that to date has unfortunately often eluded them.

This would be of immediate application to the MPS where as the Morris Report highlighted, effective internal financial management appeared to be noticeable by its absence.

Variations on a theme

Cameron has made it clear that city mayors may be appropriate for the cities but would be out of place within smaller local authorities. Here the case is made for closer engagement with the existing local authority which would in future make the local police BCU commander accountable to scrutiny committees.

Comment

The control of British policing is embodied in a complex net of interlocking relationships, about which the only generalisation that one can make with some certainty, is that all generalisations are subject to exceptions; and it is time for some brief international comparisons.

INTERNATIONAL COMPARISONS

France

As we mentioned in *Chapter 1* in our delineation of civil and military or paramilitary models of policing, France has two entirely separate national police services, the Police Nationale and the Gendarmerie Nationale. The Police Nationale are the civil force, and police the major towns. The Gendarmerie, who are the military police as well as having civic responsibilities, are proud to claim that they police 90 per cent of the national territory and 50 per cent of the population.

Is it confusing to have two entirely separate national police forces? The simple answer is, that it can be; and whilst the French sometimes claim that to have two police services renders them both more accountable, since the performance of one can always be compared with that of the other, we suspect that this is a justification after the fact. The two national services are of separate historical origin: that is why they exist. We note that police reform is a major issue in contemporary French politics.

Spain

Like many other European States, Spain has a paramilitary as well as civil police. In Spain, the paramilitary force is somewhat confusingly entitled the Guardia Civil, and is easily recognised by its remarkable head-gear of a patent leather hat with an upright rear brim. Under Franco, the Guardia Civil maintained the dictatorship, and were stationed in barracks a long way from home, so as not to develop local loyalties (a different tradition to that of Great Britain, for example, where, other things being equal, it is considered an advantage if a police officer is locally recruited and posted).

Now that Spain is a democracy once again, regionalism is a powerful force in Spanish politics, and the domination of Castille is under increasing attack. The Basque region has sought to obtain its independence by armed struggle, which has led to a bloody and bitter campaign against the Spanish security forces. Catalonia has taken the democratic route, and there is now a regional Catalan police force which is attempting to increase its powers by negotiation and peaceful expression of the popular will.

Germany

As part of the de-Nazification programme which followed the defeat and collapse of the Third Reich at the end of the Second World War, West Germany received a federal constitution. Each of its 16 constituent states set up its own police force, and the powers of the central state were severely limited. Regionalism was seen as part of the answer in preventing the re-emergence of national socialism, and the German police were intended to forge a new identity, a new ethos, and a new relationship with the public. There was also then and since reunification a German federal police, which is increasing its powers in the age of global migration and terrorism. It is probably true to say that whilst the German police are both highly organized and professionally competent, they have been hampered by a history which does not encourage the public to volunteer information. Since reunification in 1989, problems of integrating two very different styles of policing have needed to be addressed, as we discuss further below.

Italy

Italy has both State and regional police and the carabinieri, a national paramilitary force of long tradition. It is remarkable in possessing, as a separate and well-equipped police service, the Guarda di Finanza, who are responsible both for financial policing in all its aspects, and for customs.

Former communist States

The former communist states of central and eastern Europe have had to reform their police services as one of the conditions for entry into the European Union, and a great deal of internationally provided police training has taken place as a result. This has been organized both by the Council of Europe, which was set up to promote European co-operation in 1949 and whose most significant achievement so far is the European Convention On Human Rights, and by the European Union itself.

The FBI Academy in Budapest, CEPOL, and other developments

The United States FBI set up its own police college, the International Law Enforcement Academy, in Hungary in 1995 (as well as creating other ILEAs in Bangkok and Botswana). A European Police College (CEPOL) has also been created, although regular funding remains a problem. CEPOL has a virtual existence in so far as member states can be persuaded to provide and host training and conferences, and it has a small reality in that there is a permanent administrative staff for CEPOL at the former police staff college for England, Wales and Northern Ireland at Bramshill in Hampshire which is now part of the National Policing Improvement Agency (NPIA). Interpol intends to create an International Anti-corruption Academy in Vienna.

Russia

It remains a moot point as to whether or not Russia is a western power, although it is certainly a power on the world stage, as is evidenced by its membership of G8 and its seat on the United Nations Security Council. Since the collapse of the Soviet Union in 1992 Russia has been subjected to a massive process of change, and it is unclear what sort of State it may eventually become. Having abandoned State socialism, it has embraced capitalism as a means of economic organization; but it has not at the same time miraculously become a liberal democracy. Russia remains a profoundly authoritarian and illiberal state, and we must assume that its police service will continue to reflect this tradition of continuing autocracy.

At the same time, international liaison is greater than it was during the Cold War, and it may be hoped that the various Russian police services will see the benefits of practising a style of policing more akin to policing by consent, than the style of policing traditionally favoured in the Soviet Union—or indeed in Tsarist Russia which was its immediate predecessor, and which was to some extent a police state. The Bolsheviks who seized power in 1917 created a new police service, the militia, since the role of the police was no longer to protect the bourgeousie. Aspects of the militia system remain active in Russia today, such as the emphasis on stationing police officers within the community to gather local intelligence and prevent crime. What cannot be doubted is that the Russian police services are led by a highly educated elite, who take a pride in their profession—although they may never have served on the beat.

Outside Europe

Countries which were once British colonies and may still be described as following common law traditions tend to have some other features in common.

Australia, which was formerly a British colony and then a dominion, has both State police and a federal police service.

New Zealand once experimented with a separate Maori Police Service, and may do so again: it has a national police service.

The *United States of America* has some similarities to Great Britain, as far as the organization of policing is concerned. Each state of the union has its own state police. There is also the FBI, which is not a police service but deals with federal crime, and has executive powers to do so; and there are about 16,000 local police services, which have jurisdiction in their areas and are locally accountable to the extent that the local chief of police is a straightforward political appointment and that local chiefs are expected to run for office. Surely, a British observer might commentate if he felt so inclined, this must lead to corruption, and perhaps it may do on occasion: but the Americans are very happy with their system, which they believe gives real local control over local policing.

Where some British towns and cities have begun to elect their mayors as figures of real rather than symbolic authority, those elected mayors have tended to take a strong interest in policing. In this context, it is relevant to note that the directly-elected mayor of Middlesborough in the North East of England is a former senior police officer; and that the Mayor of London, Boris Johnson, has asserted that he should have more control over policing within the metropolis [3]

Before we leave the USA, we must make two further points:

- the sheriff, so prominent a figure in so many American westerns, was a local appointee, whereas the marshall was a federal official. The posse, or *posse comitatus*, which the marshall could raise by enlisting anyone who was both suitable and willing to pursue, for example, a fleeing felon, is a tradition that can trace its origins back to the Statue of Winchester of 1285 and its hue and cry (see *Chapter 1*).
- the tradition of unarmed policing of which the UK is so proud is also a characteristic of the Republic of Ireland, but not of the continent of Europe where all police officers are trained to use firearms, and usually carry them. Unarmed policing would make no sense at all in the USA, where not only the police carry firearms, but so do private security guards, even on university campuses, and criminal justice personnel such as probation officers.

Canada has both local and State police, as well as a federal force, the world-famous Royal Canadian Mounted Police (RCMP)(founded 1920) which polices the whole territory as a federal force, and in many areas is also, by appointment, the local police. The Mounties have an international reputation and are part of Canada's national identity.

India has a national police service, the Indian Police Service (IPS), which provides leadership for policing at state level. IPS officers, who are selected by competitive national examination, are an elite corps and may be stationed anywhere in India. They may take charge of prisons as well as police forces, and it is noteworthy that the first woman to be commissioned into the IPS in 1972, Kiran Bedi, made her name internationally by carrying out a major prison reform programme when director of Tihar Jail, with 10,000 inmates, from 1993 to 1995. Kiran Bedi retired from the IPS in 2007.

India has a number of specialist police forces which have been set up at various times for various purposes, to address problems such as dacoitry (armed robbery and murder), cross-border incursions, and insurrection. The Indian police face the problems that all police forces must address, writ large; for India is the largest multi-religious democracy in the world. The Indian police are officially dedicated to serving the ideals of a secular republic, and one of their greatest difficulties is to police without fear or favour in a community with a long tradition of political interference in policing.

---

3. One practical effect of this has already been mentioned earlier in this chapter.

Colonial traditions and the limits of tolerance

India under British imperial rule was a balancing act, for the British Raj, which, even if it should have so wished, did not have the manpower or resources to rule India by force. Until 1948, much of India remained as princely states; and it took the democratically elected national leader Jawaharlal Nehru to incorporate them into India and bring them under a national administrative system.

Having crushed the Indian Mutiny of 1857 and ended the monopoly of power of the East India Company in 1858, the British administered (British) India through district officers who sought to practice religious and cultural tolerance in so far as it was compatible with the Rule of Law. The interpretation of what was tolerable and what was not presented what were sometimes testing issues. Was the practice of suttee, for example—the self-sacrifice by immolation of the grieving Hindu widow on her husband's funeral pyre—to be discouraged, tolerated at a distance, or viewed with approval as a long-established Hindu ritual? And if the widow was assisted in her suicide, what should be the fate of the assistant? Should his actions be approved, or at least tolerated? Or should he be charged under the Indian Penal Code so carefully drawn up by Lord Macaulay, with the crime of murder—or at the very least, assisting in a suicide? We shall come back to the issue of tolerance, in considering the realities of policing the diverse and multi-cultural society which is modern-day Britain.

PROBLEMS AND PATTERNS

A glance at policing, both globally and historically, enables us to identify some strategic factors in assessing the nature and quality of policing in a given area.

Recognition

A police force is, in our view, by definition a uniformed and disciplined body of men and women, and a uniform is necessary but not sufficient for good policing. However, whether in uniform or not, the police are usually easily recognised. In any totalitarian system they will tend to be generally known by the population at large, if only because of the aura of ruthless authority which they project; and they may be especially recognised by those under surveillance, which thus becomes an overt means for the suppression of dissident behaviour, rather than a covert means of intelligence-gathering by the State. The East German secret police assisted in this process by listing their telephone number in the telephone directory—unlike MI5 at the same time, in London (MI5 now has its own website[4] and openly advertises for recruits, targeting the widest of backgrounds).

---

4. mi5.gov.uk

Legitimacy and acceptance

Police forces do not necessarily police with the consent of the population at large, but tend to have some degree of acceptance in practice which may differ from their legitimacy in theory. For both theoretical and practical purposes, it is as well for their long-term survival if they are not seen as simply the force that keeps the current regime in power, but forge some sort of identity as a neutral and impartial body which may be of use to any government that operates under the Rule of Law.

Policing divided communities, or where the legitimacy of the State itself is in question, must present special difficulties: as the history of the United Kingdom makes clear; and many other examples could be offered of contexts in which such difficulties have arisen,

Northern Ireland

Northern Ireland came into existence in 1922 as a separate entity to the then Irish Free State, and set up its own police force, the Royal Ulster Constabulary (RUC), by descent from the Royal Irish Constabulary. By and large, the RUC was not accepted by the nationalist community in Northern Ireland, since they would have preferred to be living in a united Ireland. That did not mean that they necessarily supported the IRA or Sinn Fein. They might, on a day-to-day basis, have dealings with the local police officer on local issues: but there was an issue of the legitimacy of the police, and it did not make for better police relations with the minority community. This was at least in part because the police service did not represent that minority community, and the Protestant majority was profoundly suspicious of it.

Policing a divided community or disputed territory

The key questions to be asked are the following:

- does the police force have legitimacy, within an overall political context?; and
- how well does it perform its functions, within that context?

Before they can be judged for the quality of their performance, the police will have needed to establish their right to police in general. In a mature democracy like Great Britain, that right is pretty much unquestioned, and the issue becomes 'How well are the police policing?', rather than why are they policing at all. In a divided community or failed state, the achievement of any form of non-military, locally-related policing may be something to be welcomed; and the efficiency of the police service in its duties will not form the first criterion for assessment of its effectiveness. It remains the case that in many ways, policing is a symbolic activity.

The assessment of police performance: Efficiency and effectiveness

Issues which are seen as 'political' in some sense, such as the (British) national miners' strike of 1984, may poison police-community relationships in affected areas. From the government's point of view, it was essential that the police succeed in 'policing' the miners' strike to the extent that the miners should eventually fail; and it is interesting to note that in assessing police performance in this context, the key criterion was effectiveness rather than efficiency.

Human beings are not always consistent in their behaviour, and are quite capable of supporting something in practice whilst condemning it in theory: or *vice versa*. The wise police officer does not seek to be loved by the community, perhaps, so much as respected by it; and the quest of the police to find out who are the leaders of the community, which can give rise to difficulties on occasion, is nevertheless a legitimate quest.

The middle way?

The police need to be able to make contact with decision-makers in the community; and it is often the case that the older members of any community, who are, by and large, the people with spouses, families, property and businesses to protect, and children to educate or straighten out, will be the natural allies of the police service. Are we then arguing that the role of the police is to support what the press has been known to call middle England: the middle-aged, the middle-class and the middle of the road?

Are the police condemned to support only settled communities, and is the police move to include gays, lesbians, transsexuals and other groups, not an indication of the police moving out to embrace previously marginalised groups, but rather a sign that the groups themselves are moving in to becoming part of the bosom of the Establishment?

Not necessarily, for the challenges of policing are more subtle than that. The police will naturally support those who accept and obey the law and encourage others to do so; but laws may change.[5]

Hunting with dogs

When hunt saboteurs began to become a serious problem for the fox-hunting community, its leaders assumed that the police, in policing a hunt, were there to protect the hunters. They needed to be disabused of this belief. The role of the police at a hunt, just like the role of the Indian police during a religious confrontation leading to a riot, was to:

- keep, or restore, the peace;
- prevent illegal activities by either side, and to investigate them if they did occur; and

---

5. For example, adult male homosexuality in private was de-criminalised in 1967.

- remain vigorously impartial as to the merits of whatever activity had led to the problem, provided it was lawful.

The hunting example is a good one by means of which to explore the reality of policing, since after Parliament outlawed hunting with dogs in 2004, a previously legal pastime enjoyed by many of the great and the good as well as a substantial element of the rural population, became illegal. The police came under greater pressure to demonstrate impartiality, than when hunting with dogs had been legal. Some of them had hunted themselves, whereas we doubt that many had been active saboteurs; and the fox-hunting community included judges, barristers, land-owners and farmers whom the police would previously have seen as pillars of the community, but who might have now begun to feel the temptation to break the law themselves.

In this challenging situation, the police were entitled to weigh up what resources they should rightfully award to the successful enforcement of the prohibition of hunting with dogs, given the other demands for their services; and, as always, to use their discretion. We may note that very few huntsmen have been prosecuted, and none by the police via the Crown Prosecution Service; and that the *softly, softly* approach has so far prevailed.

LOCAL, NATIONAL AND INTERNATIONAL CO-OPERATION

Police officers go to considerable lengths to establish informal, personality-based relationships in order to get things done, rather than the formal and inevitably bureaucratic means by which both national and international police co-operation is officially achieved. Liaison is all, and a major reason why police officers attend courses, seminars and conferences both at home and abroad is to develop networks by means of which to overcome or circumvent official obstacles to co-operation—as, we suppose, with any other organization.

The ideal instrument of co-operation for the police officer is the unrecorded telephone conversation from one colleague to another, both of whom met on some previous occasion, and shared something of their personal as well as professional lives.

'Collegiality' is of especial importance in international police relations. Police officers like to feel that they have more in common with their professional colleagues overseas than what separates them. Whatever the constitutional and legal differences that separate State A from State B, the police officers working for both States, systems or regimes share common values and a common purpose. In reality, all police forces throughout the world share a partial agenda, based on a common agreement on fundamental right and wrong: although it is unusual for them to say so.

Crime special and crime ordinary

Police officers and services tend to differentiate between 'ordinary' and 'political' crime, and ordinary and political criminals. We would suggest that the majority of officers prefer dealing with ordinary criminals, rather than those offenders whom they see as extremists, deviants or fanatics. After all, the 'ordinary decent criminals' are people whose motives the ordinary police officer can understand. Those criminals tend to recognise the fundamental legitimacy of the system that locks them up, and do not necessarily feel a personal hatred for the officer who arrests them. They have an established role in an established system, and it is almost comforting to reflect that they will always be there.

Naturally, no-one apart from the criminal offender, wishes for crime: but nevertheless, a certain level of crime is inevitable, and the police culture is well able to treat its practice with a certain sardonic humour. Police forces therefore find it much easier to co-operate on crime ordinary than crime special, at any level. Indeed, Interpol, to which we now turn, made it an item of its constitution that it was *not* there to provide a means for cooperation on political crime; a decision whose repercussions are still reverberating today.

International Police Cooperation: Interpol

As the 20th century began, conferences were held on topics of international concern, such as white slavery (1904); pornographic publications (1910); and the opium trade (1912.) The first international police 'congress' took place in 1914. Interpol can claim to be the oldest mechanism for international police co-operation in the world, and its origins were pragmatic: Prince Albert of Monaco realised that there was a need to begin the means towards informal but effective international police co-operation, of which we have already described some of the characteristics. The first international conference on police co-operation in 1914 was a purely informal affair, with no official status or recognition. The name Interpol may imply an official international police organization, founded by governmental action, but that is not how it all began. We quote from research by Paul Swallow for part of what follows.

> Interpol can trace its origins to 1914, when Prince Albert I of Monaco called together the First International Police Congress. Rather than using the established protocol of governmental and diplomatic channels to do so, he contacted an eclectic mix of police officers, lawyers, magistrates and other interested people from 14 countries, on an almost random basis. In so doing, Prince Albert set the tone for the organization as being nothing more than an informal club of policing agencies, which at its heart Interpol is still to-day.

Dr Johann Schrober, the Austrian Police President, revived Interpol in 1923, advertising in newspapers for: "Any interested police officer or criminologist" to attend a new conference. The topics presented for discussion bear remarkable similarities to those still under discussion today. They were:

- firstly, the organization of rapid and direct means of intercourse between police authorities in all countries;
- secondly, the institution of a vigorous campaign against international criminals, to include fuller cooperation and the most modern methods of crime detection;
- thirdly, extradition and post-sentence expulsion;
- fourthly, the combating of drunkenness and the drug habit in so far as the matter came into the competence of police authorities; and finally
- the need for criminal signs, and especially criminal tactics and statistics, to be stored and collated for future exchange.

It was decided to set up the International Police Commission with its headquarters in Vienna, and by 1938 it had 34 member countries. (After the Nazi anschluss in Austria the Gestapo made much use of its records). In 1946 the 'International Criminal Police Commission' was re-established in Paris, and it moved to its present home in Lyons in 1989. It has five regional offices around the world, and opened an office at the UN in 2005.

Interpol today facilitates international police cooperation by providing a channel of communication between police forces and law enforcement agencies in 186 countries. In theory, it is the obvious platform for present and future international police cooperation. In practice, this does not always happen, and it may be that rival or alternative organizations will be preferred for future developments. Why? Commonplace criticisms of Interpol have been that it:

- is slow, cumbersome, and bureaucratic.
- has an unclear official status, and thus cannot be used for some purposes; and it is not democratically accountable.
- has a limited area of activity, and cannot change its constitution.

Article 3 of the Interpol Constitution forbids it from dealing with matters of a political, military, racial or religious nature, and in the past this has been taken to include terrorism. Interpol itself claims that in the current (post-September 11) climate of an increased international awareness of the dangers of terrorism, police cooperation on terrorism is improving. It has also made attempts to change the mindsets of those officers who use it, so that there is an increasing willingness to pool information packages. Also Interpol:

- has been misused (as is hardly surprising with a membership of 186 nations) and its officials have not always proved suitable.

Some cases have been more scandalous than others. In January 2008 the President of Interpol, South African police officer Jackie Selebi, resigned following accusations of corruption at home. Finally:

• Interpol is insecure.

It has been criticised for its insecurity over records and documents. Although its massive investment in new technology may cure that, it still has to gain trust. One memorable quip, hopefully now redundant, but making the point with telling precision was that 'many British police officers would as soon hand over their operational information to Interflora as to Interpol'.

Assessment

It may be time for a change of view towards Interpol, although at the moment, the jury is still out. There are many matters of a 'normal' criminal nature, or which attract universal condemnation, such as child pornography, on which cooperation is possible; and the investigation of internet-related crime (see also 'cyber-crime' in a later chapter) may prove to be an area suitable for Interpol in some regards. The fact that Interpol is neutral, has no official political agenda, and that one of its best functions is as a databank, may help to demonstrate its enduring usefulness.

Interpol has survived much since its eclectic origins in 1914. We believe that it will survive permanently, but not necessarily grow in power.

International Police Cooperation: Europol

The Treaty of Rome of 1957 created the Common Market, which evolved into the European Economic Community (EEC). This became the European Union (EU), as agreed in 1992 at Maastricht and ratified in 1994. European enthusiasts see the end result as full political union in a United States of Europe: sceptics and nationalists have other views.

The EU is increasingly interested in security, and has recognised the dangers that emerge from the dismantling of internal barriers: an issue that led to the Schengen Agreement following the Treaty of Amsterdam, and several other working agreements under various names, by means of which member states have sought to replace national by European security.

In 1991 Chancellor Helmut Kohl of Germany proposed the creation of a European Police Agency, Europol, which came into full existence eight years later at The Hague in Holland. Despite its name, the new creation was not a police force but an EU criminal intelligence agency, as Europol officials (unlike FBI special agents) have no executive powers. Europol comes into play only for serious international crimes when investigations are conducted by a criminal unit with an organised structure, and that affect two or more EU states. It has a complex command structure.

Europol deals with such crimes as terrorism, drugs-trafficking, human-trafficking, illegal immigration euro-counterfeiting, and financial/property crime; and its biggest unit provides tactical and strategic analyses for member States.

Comment

The success of Europol will no doubt relate at least in part to the general success of the EU in developing working and effective institutions. It would be natural to expect the UK to be a less enthusiastic participant in this process than some other member states such as Holland, which lack easily defined and defensible borders, and which have much more to gain, at least in the short term, from the creation of a secure and well-policed EU than has the UK; and in fact Europol is relatively understaffed from the UK. However, British participation in international policing is increasing, as we shall go on to explore; and we suspect that Europol will play an increasingly important role

Does the international community need both Interpol and Europol? It is possible to argue, as do both organizations, that they serve complementary purposes. If the hidden agenda that lay behind the creation of Europol, was to create a means for European police cooperation which meant that EU nations would no longer need to use Interpol, that has not in practice occurred; and indeed Europol is still far from playing a leading role in European policing. Police services are innately conservative and suspicious of change, and are by tradition extremely reluctant to share information of a sensitive nature. Any organization which is able to overcome this fear, is achieving a good deal; and we suspect that it will be judged pragmatically in its ability to achieve that objective.

Further international developments

Eurojust is a European Union body established in 2002 to enhance the effectiveness of the competent authorities within member States when they are dealing with the investigation and prosecution of serious cross-border and organized crime.

The Schengen Information System (SIS II) is a Europe-wide data system designed to allow access to 'alerts' issued by member States (effectively, connecting the Police National Computer to a European wanted/missing database). It is envisaged that the UK will participate in the law enforcement aspects of SIS II by late 2010. There were 504 arrests under the European arrest warrant in 2007, and this is likely to treble when the UK implements SIS II.

European Union member states have agreed on a system to speed up the transfer of evidence needed for criminal investigations, from one member state to another.

The agreement, reached on 1 June 2006, creates an 'evidence warrant'. This is an order that would be issued by a judicial authority in one member State and recognised in another. EU Justice Commissioner Franco Frattini praised this as a significant development.

International peace-keeping: an increasing role?

UK police continue to be involved in international peace-keeping work in different parts of the world at the request of the Foreign and Commonwealth Office (FCO) and Department for International Development (DFID), e.g. in Iraq, Kosovo and so on. British police officers are popular abroad. They know how to talk to people (which does not always rely upon a felicity for foreign languages) and they know what it means to police without firearms and by consent. Moreover, they are flexible, friendly and determined, for example in investigating allegations of war crimes:

> The FCO is conscious of the need to take a more coherent... approach to international policing. The *Strategic Task Force* has been set up to address that concern. It will seek to harmonise and enhance the interests and efforts of all stakeholders with a direct interest in international policing, identify how UK police forces can best add value, and produce workable recommendations for implementation from August 2005 onwards (House of Commons Select Committee on Defence, 2004).

CONCLUSION

Policing on an international basis is no longer simply desirable. It is necessary. Massive migration into and out of the UK has internationalised policing on a *de facto* basis. National boundaries are increasingly inconsequential to criminals, extremists and criminal networks that are operating supra-nationally, often in cyberspace. In an age of international terrorism and organized crime, global police co-operation can only increase

It is, perhaps, a paradox of British policing that a system that emphasises the importance of 'localism', and that still retains 43 separate territorial police forces in England and Wales, is able to participate successfully in international co-operation. Much of this is achieved, no doubt, under the auspices of the Metropolitan Police Service; but it is in effect a national effort. It seems doubtful whether the UK will create a national police service of its own. But it is predictable that the process of infinite adjustment will continue. The government, whether Labour or Conservative, is committed to the modernisation of the police service; but modernisation has more than one possible meaning.

Appendix to Chapter 3

Revitalised community policing For today's world

In 2004 the Home Office announced its intention to revitalise community policing (which embodies many of the features of policing by consent.) This was a significant development for both the organization and purposes of policing, by which the government was seeking to restore faith in the direct contact between police service and public which was perceived to have withered. How to do so? We quote from the 2004 White Paper in outlining government intentions, which were backed by a significant investment of money.

> Revitalised neighbourhood and community policing for the 21st century is central to the Government's approach. By 2008 we want every community to benefit from the level and style of neighbourhood policing that they need. This will involve dedicated teams of police officers, police community support officers and wardens providing a visible, reassuring presence, preventing and detecting crime and developing a constructive and lasting engagement with members of their community.
>
> **Neighbourhood policing teams**
>
> Fully trained officers using modern techniques and updated powers, working with PCSOs with a minimum set of powers, will make up neighbourhood policing teams. They will take an intelligence-led, proactive, problem-solving approach to enable them to focus on and tackle specific local issues (such as anti-social behaviour)' They will involve their local community in establishing and negotiating priorities for action and in identifying and implementing solutions. ...

The government expressed a need for:

- a dynamic, modern workforce
- leadership at all levels
- career development
- new powers for PCSOs.

We will strengthen the roles of police staff and introduce national standards and a minimum set of powers for police community support officers. These minimum powers will contribute towards freeing up police officers for front-line policing by including the power to issue a range of fixed penalty notices. Following a successful pilot in six forces, we will empower all forces to be able to give their PCSOs the power of detention. We are also committed to ensuring that the powers available to police officers themselves are up-to-date and effective – equipping them for the difficult and demanding range of tasks that we call on the police to perform

Police and local authorities

... The role of police authorities in ensuring effective delivery of policing will also be strengthened. They will oversee local consultation, including the relationship between Crime and Disorder Reduction Partnerships and neighbourhood bodies. We will also enhance their role in holding chief officers to account.

Comment

The effectiveness of the new system of policing is a matter of ongoing perception and review. Cynics may claim that the new PCSOs are inadequate substitutes for 'real' police officers, and that this is policing on the cheap. Realists will see it as a useful reform which was needed to maintain the contact between public and police which is the essence of British policing.

Police Leadership and Management

Police Leadership in the 21st Century

Philosophy, Doctrine and Developments
~ Editors **Robert Adlam** and **Peter Villiers**

The editors bring together a collection of authoritative and innovative contributions to show that:

Leadership is less of a mystery than is often supposed

Much mainstream leadership theory can be adapted to police leadership

The qualities required can be developed by education and training

There are 'Golden Rules' for police leaders

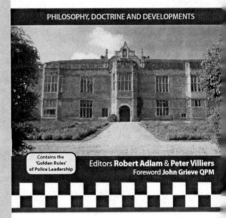

246 pages | Jan 2003 | ISBN 978-1-872870-24-3

‘ This is an important and timely book, not only because of the depth and breadth of the coverage of the issues but because it addresses the practical challenge of leadership at all levels . . . When the challenges come . . . an understanding of the underpinning principles and conflicting values of policing is vital for organizational survival ’

John Grieve QPM (from the Foreword)

Full details and ordering **WatersidePress.co.uk**

WATERSIDE PRESS

CHAPTER FOUR

Police Leadership and Management

We saw in *Chapter 2* that the police in 1829 adopted a model of 'leadership', if it might be so called, which emphasised the importance of strict and indeed relentless supervision. In essence, police constables were not to be trusted. If left to their own devices, they would drink, flirt, gossip and idle their time away; they must not be allowed to 'get away with it'. In other words, senior police officers saw their juniors in terms of theory X and not theory Y, in Macgregor's terms (see the *Annex* to this chapter); and set up a structure of management and supervision that reflected these pessimistic assumptions.

The tradition has persisted. Police management and supervision has been notorious for its lack of trust, and its attempts, which were largely unsuccessful, to regulate what was in practice impossible to regulate—what police officers actually did whilst on patrol, once they had left the observable location of the police station. Senior police officers, it seemed, were there to catch their juniors out and to punish them for any misdeeds, usually as a result of inquiry after the fact; and the presumption of innocence, or even the assumption that they had acted in good faith, did not tend to come into the equation with regard to the internal investigation of the conduct of police officers.

This 19th century style of management persisted for a long time. My colleague Dr Robert Adlam has referred to the 'infantilisation' of police officers which this culture engendered, and to the importance of the 'bollocking', or ritualised denigration of the work of the junior officer by his superior, which is not unknown today. In 2003 he and I charted the views of the police on leadership as practised in the police service as follows:

Leadership exists, but is under-developed in the police service

Police officers are more used to management or supervision than leadership, whether as recipients or practitioners.

Every officer is a leader

Having said that, there is a school of thought that argues that by virtue of their original authority, need for the proper use of discretion, and powers of influence in the community, all patrol officers exercise leadership. Consequently, leadership is not a characteristic that only senior officers need possess or acquire, but is needed by all ranks who go on patrol or respond to emergencies.

The 'military' style of leadership still exists

Whatever the reality of the demands of practical police decision-making on the streets, the police service has traditionally practised what it terms a 'military' style of leadership—in other words, autocracy.

In fact, what the police refer to as the military style of leadership would probably be rejected by the contemporary armed services as a caricature of rule by non-commissioned officers under national service, 50 years ago. However, the fact that a belief may be mistaken or distorted does not reduce the intensity with which it is held.

Leadership by example has been neglected

The police understanding, or rather misunderstanding, of what is meant by military leadership makes no reference to the leadership by example that one might expect the better type of military leader to display.

That ideal may be ignored because it is considered that leadership by example is usually impossible in the police service. Police commanders very rarely *lead* the men and women under their command, in any very obvious sense; and few are the opportunities for heroic leadership. Even during a riot, the police officers in charge are more likely to require a sort of stoical endurance than any dynamic capacity for leadership; and their fundamental role may be to restrain their officers from impetuous action.

Unheroic leadership

There are ample opportunities for the practice of leadership by example in such areas as not making improper use of privileges and benefits, or simply by the leaders showing themselves to be honest and dedicated police officers, who are prepared to listen and learn from those around them. These are not heroic activities, but very necessary ones; and their impact need not be confined to the leader's immediate circle.

The need for a new style of command

There is a general agreement that the autocratic style of leadership is outdated and counter-productive, and the modern police service requires a much more democratic and less dictatorial style. But the old style is extremely difficult to eradicate, and has so far survived all attempts to achieve its extirpation.

The blame culture

Time after time, the police have been described as having a blame culture, or a fault-finding culture, rather than one based on a respect for professionalism and the proper use of trust. Senior officers tend to allow, if anything, rather too much discretion to the officers supposedly under their command—until something goes wrong.

A culture of generalised cynicism

The police are on the whole a cynical culture: about the public, about themselves, about their leaders, and about the limits of what can be achieved by their organization.

Distrust of charisma

Paradoxically, although ruthless determination is admired, charisma is regarded with some suspicion, and a charismatic style of leadership is generally seen as neither necessary nor even desirable for police leaders. The police quite rightly point out that their authority rests upon the constitutional grounds of legality and tradition, rather than force of personality or religious or ideological conviction. The police must not take sides, cut corners, or interpret the will of society before it has been able to do so for itself; and the charismatic leader may be tempted to try all three.

A masculine culture

The majority of police officer and their leaders are men. Consequently, we do not know what a police service led by a proportionate representation of women police officers would be like, or what it could achieve. It might be a very different sort of organisation.

A culture of anti-leadership?

If the police are suspicious of charisma, we must further report our impression that they have mixed views about the whole notion of leadership as the display of authority. Senior police officers recognise that they have to provide leadership, and will find a means to do so. But they are much less comfortable with the idea of officership, which they would appear to associate with the supposedly class-ridden and rigid distinctions of the armed forces; and which may not in any case be easily reconciled with the original authority of the constable.

The contrast

Some police leaders set an excellent example. They manage to combine the ability to radiate warmth and a sense of unity with the person or group with whom they are interacting, *with* the need to pose some sort of challenge to its individual and collective capacities which is the essence of leadership; and they are admired for it. Whether their skills are innate or acquired, however, is a more difficult question to answer.

(Extracts from *Police Leadership in the 21st Century: Philosophy, Doctrine and Developments* (2003), Adlam R and Villiers P)

POLICE LEADERSHIP DEVELOPMENT: A BRIEF SURVEY

Concerns over the quality of police leadership are a prevailing characteristic of both new and mature democracies. Great Britain shares in this tradition, and it is noteworthy that even the supposedly golden age of policing of the 1950s and early 1960s was not in reality the period of happy acceptance of a benevolent and well-led police service that sentimentalists would have us believe. Senior police officers such as Sir Robert Mark (Metropolitan Police Commissioner, 1972-1977) and Sir Paul Condon (the same, 1993-2000) described the Police Service they joined as far from ideal, and there was clearly a considerable gap between the myth or fiction of policing and its reality. To understand where we are today, it is useful to briefly review the post-war history of leadership development in the Service.

The Creation of the Police Staff College
The creation of a national Police College for England and Wales in 1948—whose students were later to be joined by officers from Northern Ireland but not from

Scotland, where a Scottish Police College was set up at Tulliallan to cater for all Scottish police training—was a massive step forward in the development of police leadership in the United Kingdom, for the Bramshill approach to police leadership, whilst both pragmatic and incremental in its approach, broke new ground.

As noted in *Chapter 2,* the Police College was renamed the Police Staff College in 1979. It saw its task as twofold. Firstly, it needed to develop the police leaders of the future, so that the Police Service would no longer need to look to the armed services, or indeed anywhere outside its own ranks, for its top leaders. Secondly, the college saw the need to develop leadership in general within the Police Service and not just for its senior commanders.

Both tasks were addressed by the provision of residential command courses, laying particular emphasis on student participation by means of syndicate presentation and discussion.

Over the second half of the twentieth century Bramshill grew in size, scope and experience, and offered a wide range of courses for both British and overseas police officers, developing a close relationship with both the Royal Ulster Constabulary (RUC) and the Royal Hong Kong Police. In 1962 the Special Course and Senior Command Course were first offered and their successors continue today. Bramshill promoted both university scholarships and fellowship programmes to encourage higher education amongst police officers, a development which was much welcomed (The Royal Commission on the Police of 1960 could find no recent instance of a university graduate joining the Police Service: a very strong contrast to the situation to-day, when graduates number about 20 per cent).

In summary, Professor Robert Reiner of the London School of Economics was able to remark in his seminal study of the development of leading police officers in the British Police Service (Reiner, 1991) that the Association of Chief Police Officers (ACPO) itself was the product of Bramshill, since its members must have completed the Strategic Command Course, and many had attended a range of command or specialist courses at the Police Staff College.

Fundamental principles of democratic leadership

The autocratic police leadership culture which we described earlier in this chapter as archetypal to the police service is now officially under reform and a new doctrine of police leadership has emerged which is summarised in the Police Leadership Qualities Framework (PLQF). In essence the PLQF insists on the benefits of democratic leadership as a necessary practice, and advocates its extension to transformational leadership (TFL). Through this process three core qualities and values were identified to sit at the centre of the PLQF. These are:

- *self-awareness* Outstanding leaders have high levels of personal awareness that transcends self and includes an understanding of others and how others perceive them;

- *personal integrity* Outstanding leaders possess high integrity and moral courage which inspires trust and loyalty; and
- *passion for achievement* Outstanding leaders are driven by an inner desire to achieve objectives and to constantly improve.

The importance of democratic leadership

Michael Argyle, reader in social psychology at the University of Oxford, found in the course of his massive research into social behaviour that democratic leaders are more effective. Democratic leadership works for at least three reasons.

- first, a social style that moves between directing and consulting makes it easier for people to achieve—'to get the job done'—and to have their needs met for inclusion, belonging and support;
- second, participation in decision-making means that the members of the group are more likely to become committed to the action that is decided upon; and
- third, group discussion enhances understanding and this leads to greater cohesiveness and co-operation within the group.

Transformational leadership

Transformational leadership (TFL) is in favour in the contemporary police service, and is contrasted with its apparent opposite, transactional leadership, to the apparent disadvantage of the latter. What is TFL?

Leaders and followers

To James MacGregor Burns, transforming leadership 'is a relationship of mutual stimulation and elevation that converts followers into leaders and may convert leaders into 'moral agents''. The hypothesis here is that the transformational leader not only sets and maintains standards, but that the standards relate to a higher realm of endeavour. The transformational leader creates meaning which is defined in terms of a visionary purpose and a higher ideal which invokes greater commitment and effort by its attraction. Transformational leadership:

- is extremely challenging;
- is *not* the same as charismatic or heroic leadership;
- emphasises the moral obligations of the leader; and
- stresses the need for a positive relationship between leaders and followers and the need for two-way communication between them.

The practice of successful leadership is an art in which good leaders find what works for them. At the same time, as in any art, leadership evolves over time. Although transformational leadership is in favour, we must also recognise that leadership theory will continue to evolve.

Women as police leaders

The MPS of 1829 was an entirely masculine affair and women were not recruited into the police service under any terms until the Great War. They were then accepted reluctantly as a wartime necessity, treated with suspicion, and employed under unfavourable conditions (the first policewomen were unpaid and not even accorded the status of special constables who possessed powers of arrest). After the war they remained on sufferance, and their status was in dispute for decades. They were, eventually, recruited into the police service itself, but remained a separate part of the organization, restricted to the duties considered appropriate for their sex, such as dealing with women and children, and what would generally be regarded as welfare issues, until 1976. The climate of prejudice, whether active or passive, may be summarised as follows

- firstly, there was a traditional prejudice against the recruitment of women *per se*. The conventional assumption, from some women as well as men, was that women were too fragile, too delicate, even too emotional, it seemed, to be suited to any form of police work. If they were to be allowed to join the police service, their work must be carefully restricted to duties considered suitable for their sex. They were not to perform general duties such as street patrol; and as to riot control, or handling firearms: never!;
- secondly, they were breaching a masculine monopoly of labour; and we may note that after both the First World War and Second World War, women were encouraged to return to the home, having worked in factories and carried out similarly 'masculine' tasks throughout the hostilities. Both actions were promoted by official propaganda; and
- thirdly, women were perceived as a threat to masculinity itself in that they were capable of policing in a different style, with a different outlook and different priorities.

1976 and afterwards

A major change in women policing arose as an unintended consequence, or at least a not fully-anticipated consequence, of the Sex Discrimination Act 1976. Once this had become law, women's police departments were immediately abolished, and women left to sink or swim as best they could in a new environment that included many male officers who did not think that women were suited to 'real' police work and were unwilling to work with them.

A further consequence of this abrupt change was that women found promotion more difficult, since there were no longer any promotions guaranteed to them within the women's section, and they had not gained the experience necessary to compete on an equal footing with men for general promotions. It would take a new generation of policewomen to overcome this handicap, and it is perhaps not a coincidence that the first woman chief officer was not appointed until some 20 years later.

The current situation

Times have changed, but not to the level of equality. Women are now a substantial minority within the police service, and have achieved representation in its more active parts: there are women detectives, mounted policewomen, and women in armed police units and riot control. The RUC under Sir John Herman refused to arm policewomen until his policy was changed in court; but the RUC is now history, and the women of the Police Service of Northern Ireland are now armed (until the day when the service as a whole can become unarmed).

So far as we can tell, public attitudes have changed, and the public as a whole does not react against policewomen simply because they are women, and therefore employed in an inappropriate role. The situation may be very different in any community in which traditional male attitudes predominate, such as, we assume, within a traditional Islamic community. If a woman's place is in the home, how can she join the police service? And what real man would accept direction from a woman, in any case?

We suspect that here as elsewhere, practice may sometimes subvert theory. Some traditionalists will accept women police officers, especially as their children go through the state school system and are acclimatised to different attitudes. And whilst some police commanders may try harder than others to be sensitive to local 'attitudes', policewomen will still be used on occasion to police any area where policing is needed. Good policing will be accepted in practice, we hope, wherever it may be achieved.

Promotion and style

Women are still comparatively thin on the ground in the higher ranks, at one in nineteen (if we take all ranks, the figure is five out of twenty). The first woman chief officer, Pauline Clare, was appointed to be chief constable of Lancashire in 1995, retiring eight years later to become an executive coach. The police service is no longer a masculine preserve at any rank, and no longer as monolithic as it once was. Campaigns to improve the service and make it more user-friendly to women have at the same time benefited people from other disadvantaged groups, and *vice versa*. The male, white police officer has himself benefited from such reforms, for he also can take career breaks, return to work with the appropriate catch-up training, and so on.

It might be argued that the police service has now moved from one extreme to the other, in that women and members of what were once other disadvantaged groups are now treated with a sort of exaggerated caution, lest they sue the organization for unfair discrimination—a not impossible outcome in an organization that has never been noted for the subtlety of its internal conflict management.

The government wants to achieve proportionate representation for both women and ethnic minorities in all ranks and units of the police service as a whole; and we may note that the police service does offer the possibility of a full and rewarding career to women at the end of the first decade of the new millenium, which would barely have been dreamt of 100 years earlier. The police service is a pragmatic organization, and it does change over time; although we must conclude that the pace of change is not what officials hope for, and that full equality still lies ahead—for society as well as the police service.

The future: Women as a force for change?

Women are not substitute men, and whilst some of the women pioneers who managed to climb the greasy pole of the police promotion ladder, may have needed to adapt themselves to some aspects of the male culture, that is no longer the case for the high flier of today, who is able to be herself. People, men or women, seek to join the police service because they already have something in common, which sets them apart from the majority of the human race who do not choose to become police officers: but we do not share the view, if it were ever seriously argued, that men and women working in a professional role are or should be indistinguishable.

Conflict resolution

It is recognised that police women are less confrontational than men in resolving conflict, and their force may receive fewer complaints of the excessive use of force, with consequent costs in court if the force is found guilty or chooses to plead guilty. The National Centre of Women Police argues, indeed, that in the USA 'the average male police officer on a big city police agency costs the taxpayer (considerably) more than the average woman officer in excessive force liability lawsuit payouts'.

Style of leadership and managment

Silvestri (2007) argues that once they have reached a critical mass in senior management positions, women may be crucial in changing the police service for the better, because women are more suited to transformational leadership than men. 'Underpinned by the principles of participation, consultation and inclusion, those using such styles share power and information to reinforce open communication and create loyalty. They also encourage others to participate so that they feel they are part of the organization and enhance individuals' appreciation of the worth of others by giving them praise and recognition.'

Heidenson (1992) (as quoted by Silvestri) speculates that a feminisation of policing would lead to an increasing focus on crimes such as rape, domestic violence and child sex abuse. This might be seen as a partial return to the attitudes of 1914, but this time by choice rather than restriction. However, the assumption would still be wrong. To emphasise the need to address some offences which may traditionally have been neglected, and to find a means of doing so, does not mean that other offences will no longer be investigated. There are real difficulties in successfully prosecuting offenders for rape, domestic violence and child abuse, for a number of reasons. That does not mean that the police service should withdraw from the field, or assume defeat as inevitable. But it does mean that it should make its best effort in these areas as well as others.

The Gender Agenda

The Gender Agenda[1] was launched by the British Association for Women in Policing (BAWP) in 2000. Its aims are to:

- raise the awareness and understanding of issues affecting women within the police service;
- facilitate and contribute to discussions on issues of concern to all officers—providing wherever possible the female perspective;
- develop a network of professional and social contacts between officers nationally and internationally;
- facilitate the sharing of information on issues affecting the Service, and women in particular; and
- contribute to the continuous professional development of all members.

The Gender Agenda and the association that produced it show that women police officers, like the policemen before them who first took part in an international police conference in Monaco and went on to found Interpol (*Chapter 3*), are alive to the possibilities of formalised networking—an example that has followed by the Black Police Officers' Association and other interest groups. The modern police service accepts this, and is a plural occupation to an extent that would have been undreamt of in 1829, 1929 or even 1979 when the UK's first female prime minister came to power. Not all women are feminists, and not all feminists are women.

---

1. There is an Equal Opportunities Commission campaign of the same name

CONCLUSION

Notwithstanding the absence of a direct entry officer corps, the leadership of the police service is in practice a highly educated and trained elite. All members of ACPO must have completed the Strategic Command Course at Bramshill, an assessed course to which access is only available by national competition; and many members of ACPO are also graduates of the Special Course or its later incarnations, designed to help potential high flyers to reach the top of the police service when they are still young and fresh enough to wish to make changes for the better.

Many future members of ACPO will have entered the police service as graduate entrants, and have benefited by accelerated promotion; but neither is a necessary qualification for high command. Moreover, many superintendents and chief superintendents, who as borough, district or divisional commanders with their own budgets and areas are, it could be argued, of an equivalent importance to ACPO in terms of decision-making, have followed a less accelerated path to command.

Most senior police officers are both white and male, although this state of affairs is gradually changing; but that does not necessarily mean that they can easily be categorised in other ways. Nowadays, they may not be all police officers: the police service has long recognised that those in charge of finance and IT need not be police officers, and the principle is being taken further.

Are they cautious pragmatists, so well-moulded by the Home Office and Bramshill as to be incapable of independent thought and expression? We think not. Politically aware, they may be; but that is a necessary but not a sufficient quality for high command. The police service needs leadership of a high quality: discreet, subtle, self-reliant and effective. They are neither generals, nor captains of industry, nor all-purpose managers, interchangeable with other public sector functionaries: they are police officers. They need a clear sense of right and wrong. One may see it in their blogs, if they are so indiscreet as to publish them.

Annex to Chapter 4

Douglas McGregor's classic book *The Human Side of Enterprise* was published in 1960, and made an enormous impact. His view is still relevant to-day. McGregor's thesis is that leadership strategies are influenced by a leader's (or manager's) assumptions about human nature. As a result of his experience as a consultant, McGregor summarised two contrasting sets of assumptions made by managers in industry.

Theory X managers believe that:

1. the average human being has an inherent dislike of work and will avoid it if possible;

2. because of this human characteristic, most people must be coerced, controlled, directed, or threatened with punishment to get them to put forth adequate effort to achieve organisational objectives; and

3. the average human being prefers to be directed, wishes to avoid responsibility, has relatively little ambition, and wants security above all else.

Theory Y managers believe that:

1. the expenditure of physical and mental effort in work is as natural as play or rest, and the average human being, under proper conditions, learns not only to accept but also to seek responsibility;

2. people will exercise self-direction and self-control to achieve objectives to which they are committed;

3. the capacity to exercise a relatively high level of imagination, ingenuity, and creativity in the solution of organizational problems is widely, not narrowly, distributed in the population, and the intellectual potentialities of the average human being are only partially utilised under the conditions of modern industrial life.

A leader holding Theory X assumptions would prefer an autocratic style, whereas one holding Theory Y assumptions would prefer a more participative style.

Police Work

Police Work

The police service is the UK's premier and leading crime prevention and crime reduction agency. Among other things, it investigates crime and regulates traffic, although both tasks are now shared with other agencies. The police service provides a general presence and a wide-ranging response to the unforeseen perils of everyday life a such as accidents, emergencies, disasters and attacks on public safety. Its contemporary duties extend to dealing with anti-social behaviour using powers first introduced in the Crime and Disorder Act 1998 and extended by the Police Reform Act 2002. The rising use of 'summary justice', by issuing tickets and fixed penalty notices of various kinds mean that the ordinary police officer now deals with many minor offences on-the-spot. Police officers also deal with juvenile offenders and take part in youth offending teams, using a range of powers.[1]

POLICE POWERS

As noted in earlier chapters, the United Kingdom is not a police state and the powers of the police are not unlimited, but restricted by law: although there is no one law that prescribes their duties and powers *in toto*. Instead, there is a complex mass of legislation which it would be a mistake to over-simplify for the purposes of this short introduction, in which some broad comments are made.

It is worth noting from the outset that the power of the police to deprive a person of his liberty is one of their most important powers, and is absolutely essential as a means to effective policing. At the same time, it is potentially a source of great abuse. British police powers are governed both by legislation and Common Law, and are now expressed in the language of human rights. Before we go on to explore some police powers in more detail, we quote the relevant rights in full.

Universal Declaration of Human Rights, Article 3

Everyone has the right to life, liberty and security of person.

---

1. For this specialist area of police work readers should consult other texts.

Universal Declaration on Human Rights, Article 9

No one shall be subjected to arbitrary arrest, detention or exile.

European Convention On Human Rights, Article 5

1. Everyone has the right to liberty and security of person. No one shall be deprived of his liberty save in the following cases and in accordance with a procedure prescribed by law:

   a. the lawful detention of a person after conviction by a competent court;

   b. the lawful arrest or detention of a person for non-compliance with the lawful order of a court or in order to secure the fulfilment of any obligation prescribed by law;

   c. the lawful arrest or detention of a person effected for the purpose of bringing him before the competent legal authorities on reasonable suspicion of having committed an offence or when it is reasonably considered necessary to prevent his committing an offence or fleeing after having done so;

   d. the detention of a minor by lawful order for the purpose of educational supervision or his lawful detention for the purpose of bringing him before the competent legal authority;

   e. the lawful detention of a person for the prevention of the spreading of infectious diseases, of persons of unsound mind, alcoholics or drug addicts or vagrants;

   f. the lawful arrest or detention of a person to prevent his effecting an unauthorised entry into the country or of a person against whom action is being taken with a view to deportation or extradition.

2. Everyone arrested or detained in accordance with the provisions of paragraph 1(c) of this article shall be brought promptly before a judge or other officer authorised by law to exercise judicial power and shall be entitled to trial within a reasonable time or to release pending trial. Release may be conditioned by guarantees to appear for trial.

3. Everyone who is deprived of his liberty by arrest or detention shall be entitled to take proceedings by which the lawfulness of his detention shall be decided speedily by a court and his release ordered if the detention is not lawful.

4. Everyone who has been the victim of arrest or detention in contravention of the provisions of this article shall have an enforceable right to compensation.

Universal Declaration of Human Rights

The right to liberty and security of person is one of the most fundamental human rights, and it is protected with the right to life in Article 3 of the Universal Declaration. This right guarantees personal liberty in the form of freedom of movement and freedom from physical restrictions, and legal protection of that freedom. Security of person means physical security in the sense of freedom from arrest or detention.

The individual has a right to security from arbitrary deprivation of liberty by the state, and it is this right which is explicitly protected under Article 9 of the Declaration.

European Convention On Human Rights

Article 5 enshrines the right to liberty and security of person. Under paragraph 1 it provides protection from arbitrary arrest by setting out an exhaustive list of six permissible grounds for deprivation of liberty. Under paragraphs 2 to 5 it sets out procedural rights which must accompany any of the grounds for deprivation of liberty.

Whilst police may be involved in depriving people of liberty on any of the six grounds set out in paragraph 1, the grounds in sub-paragraph 1.c (arrest or detention on reasonable suspicion of having committed an offence, when necessary to prevent commission of an offence or fleeing after having done so) are the grounds of most relevance to police.

It is important to note that the three grounds for deprivation of liberty under paragraph 1.c are exhaustive, and that the provisions cannot be used for purposes not specified in the paragraph.

Arrest

The primary official means whereby a police constable exercises his powers is by making an arrest or warning someone that this could happen. We may describe police powers of arrest as falling under three categories. A police constable:

- has a general duty and power to keep the peace, and may need to act pre-emptively to do so. A police constable who sees A about to strike B, does not need to wait until the blow has been struck before arresting him (or in some other way preventing the commission of the offence).[2] In this case, the powers of the police constable are *preventative*;
- is entitled to make an arrest after the event, if he has reasonable suspicion that someone has carried out a crime. In this case, the powers of the police constable are *restorative*: he wishes to play his part in rectifying a wrong which has already occurred, which may be defined as the purpose of bringing suspects to justice; and
- may be able to use powers of arrest in other specified circumstances, for example in regard to the prevention or investigation of terrorism. We shall simply refer to these as 'special' powers. Special powers may lead to the greatest controversy, in that they maximise the opportunity of the constable to use his discretion and may also render his actions unaccountable under the caveat of official secrecy.

It should be stressed that the powers of the police constable are original. He cannot be ordered to make an arrest by a senior officer. If his arrest should later prove to have been unlawful, he is responsible for his actions in court. His powers derive from and are not substantially greater than those of the ordinary citizen, the major difference being that the ordinary citizen may only make an arrest to deal with an immediate event and risks an action for civil damages (or even arrest himself) if he has made a mistake. A police officer may also arrest someone under a warrant of arrest issuesd by a court.

Once he does arrest someone, the police officer concerned must take them to a 'designated' police station, where the arrested person becomes the responsibility of the custody sergeant whose powers are regulated by the Police and Criminal Evidence Act of 1984 and its codes. PACE came into law so as to regularise police behaviour and prevent abuse, for example in regard to the treatment of vulnerable people such as juveniles or the mentally or physically challenged.[3] The Director of

---

2. In this context, please see the time-honoured offence of breach of the peace.

3. Some people are more susceptible to police interrogation than others, and more likely to confess to a crime that they did not in fact commit. The Criminal Justice System must and does protect the vulnerable, and the presumption of innocence and fundamental principle that guilt in a criminal trial must be established 'beyond reasonable doubt', are also to the advantage of the accused. Nevertheless, miscarriages of justice do occur and PACE itself was also a response to a number of high profile instances.

Public Prosecutions (DPP) has power to issue guidance for use by police custody officers.[4]

Bail

An arrested person can be granted bail by the police during an investigation, for re-appearance at a police station; or, after being charged with a criminal offence, to attend at a magistrates' court. Otherwise he will be kept in the cells until the court opens. The police can grant conditional bail and also what is known as street bail: quite literally 'on the street' when someone is arrested rather after they have been taken to the police station. All such events must be recorded. When police officers execute court warrants (above) these may be 'backed for bail' also.

PACE and the PACE Codes

What follows is not intended as a complete guide, simply a foretaste of police powers and their constraints. Other rules cover exceptional situations and generally speaking, in the current age of terrorism, police powers have increased.

On arrest

Where someone is arrested by a constable he or she must ordinarily be taken to a police station as soon as is reasonably practicable (except, of course, if already there or if he is given street bail (above)). The PACE procedures stand at the heart of this aspect of police work and are unavoidable if the situation is one where there is a need to hold an offender without charge in what is known as 'police detention'.

At the police station

If someone attends voluntarily at a police station or other place or accompanies a constable there without being arrested, he or she is entitled to leave at any time unless told that he is being arrested, the reasons for which must be explained to him. The arrested person will also be informed of certain rights, i.e:

- to consult the PACE Codes of Practice;
- to have someone informed of his or her arrest; and
- to consult a solicitor.

After 24 hours

No one may be kept in police detention for more than 24 hours without being charged. Usually, this may be extended up to 36 hours by a senior police officer.

---

4. See, e.g. the new section 37A to D of PACE as inserted by Schedule 2 to the 2003 Act.

Beyond 36 hours
Where continued detention *is* authorised by a senior officer, the detained person must still be released after 36 hours unless an application is made to a magistrates' court for what is known as a warrant of further detention; which can be issued for up to 36 hours at a time but not beyond 96 hours overall.

Review of police detention
Periodic reviews of the circumstances of police detention are carried out independently of custody officers and usually by a senior officer. PACE lays down a timetable. The detainee or his or her solicitor is entitled to make representations throughout.[5]

Documentation
Where a defendant is charged by the police related documentation including a bail notice will tell the accused person what happens next and when to appear at court (assuming that he or she is not kept in the cells and taken directly to court).

Review by the Crown prosecutor
The next stage is a statutory review of the case file by a Crown prosecutor. The police and CPS are often now located in joint Criminal Justice Units (CJUs) or Trial Units in relation to the Crown Court. The police always used to take the decision whether or not someone should be charged with an offence but this is now a matter for the CPS except in urgent or minor cases.

Diversion from prosecution
As an alternative to prosecution, there are well-established mechanisms for police cautions where people admit an offence. This extends to 'conditional cautions', whereby requirements can be added to such a warning. Diversion can involve a 'referral' elswhere, e.g. concerning a drugs problem or mental impairment. Decisions whether to issue a caution are now taken by the CPS, but administered by a senior police officer. There is a scheme for juveniles known as 'warnings and reprimands'.

Comprehensive regulation
Overall, police activities in regard to arresting, detaining and charging suspected offenders are highly regulated. Where terrorism is under investigation, it is fair to say

---

5. Special provisions apply generally to juveniles when the custody officer must, if practicable, ascertain the identity of the person who is responsible for his or her welfare and inform that person that the juvenile has been arrested, and the reason why he or she is detained. If the juvenile is known to be subject to a supervision order, reasonable steps must be taken to notify the supervisor. The custody officer must also, as soon as practicable, inform an 'appropriate adult' of the grounds for detention and the juvenile's whereabouts and ask the adult to come to the police station to see the juvenile. A custody officer who authorises an arrested juvenile to be kept in police custody must ensure that, after being charged, the arrested juvenile is moved to local authority accommodation.

that greater powers apply. It is also worth noting that police powers on arrest, detention and charge embody the principles in Article 5 of the European Convention On
Human Rights already noted—a convention which British lawyers helped to draft.

GENERAL PURPOSE POLICE WORK

Police work (outside CID, traffic duties and certain specialised functions) is carried
out by the following groups, operating either alone or as mixed teams. They are:

- police constables (PCs)
- police community support officers (PCSOs)
- special constables
- police staff (formerly known as support staff)

The modern police service is a mixed community, as is shown by the 2008 employment figures for the Devon and Cornwall Constabulary:

Police	3523
Police staff	2046
Special constables	549
Police community support officers	317
Other employees	47

We may also note that the police co-operate with other agencies and interested
parties, partly as a result of the Crime and Disorder Act 1998 which resulted in
the Crime and Disorder Reduction Partnerships (CDRPs) mentioned in *Chapter
3*. This means that what once may have been considered purely police work is now
a shared activity. This chapter explores the police role as carried out by the police
'family', whilst bearing in mind that many activities have some implication for other
units outside the police service.

Police constables
The office of constable is an ancient one and the police constable has a symbolic as
well as an actual significance. He is the bedrock of policing, and all other services
develop from him. Chief constables are also constables. If a police service were to
consist of only one person, that person would be a police constable.

Recruitment and training
Members of the public who wish to join the police service usually apply for a va-

cancy in a particular force, and join its waiting list. They must be of satisfactory physique, health and character, and pass an aptitude test for policing Anyone is entitled to apply to become a police officer, but not everyone is accepted; and standards for acceptability change over time. There used, for example, to be a height requirement, which has now been abolished. Is it an automatic disqualification if a potential recruit has relatives with criminal convictions, or indeed may himself have been convicted of a minor offence? Should the police service go out of its way to attempt to recruit more candidates from certain backgrounds who are traditionally under-represented in the police—bearing in mind that positive action is legal but that positive discrimination is illegal? These can be very challenging issues! A police service that strives to police by consent will do its best to represent the community as a whole in its ranks.

The approved candidate joins the police service as a probationary police constable, and undergoes a lengthy period of training that combines theory and practice, at least part of which is spent understudying the job on the street as a sort of working apprentice, and part of which is spent in the classroom. He is attested as a police officer early on in his probationary period, and is thus a sworn police officer almost from the start. He may be dismissed at any point in the probationary period if he is found to be unsuitable for police work. Most probationers, however, are successful in completing their training; and once they have done so are more difficult to dismiss.

Norms, values and standards

How is an ordinary person transformed into being a police officer? The process is a surprisingly straightforward one. He or she may have spent a long time in trying to join, and already have police acquaintances or connexions, so that the job is already half done. Secondly, the police service ensures that its mores, values and attitudes are absorbed both consciously and sub-consciously by new recruits from the start of their service. It insists that the uniform is worn from day one, including a police hat, and that probationers are neat, tidy and presentable. The officers chosen as directing staff are generally excellent role models, and full of practical advice. The work itself is presented as being interesting, challenging and learnable. And the greatest source of pressure, both to conform and succeed, is the peer group itself: the group of young probationers in which each individual is immersed, and which very rapidly establishes the appropriate norms.

Does the police service clone its young police officers? No; but it does exercise a remarkable pressure to conform, as does any other occupation which takes itself seriously. Later, police constables may have to be re-programmed, as it were, if they go on to join CID or another department. Until then, the initial process of acculturation—we should not call it indoctrination, for it is not so formalised—aims to develop authenticity.

The result is the police culture, which has sometimes been heavily criticised. Police officers have been accused of being insular, conservative-minded, authoritarian, and racist and sexist in their attitudes. If these attitudes were once absorbed in police training, that is no longer the case; and it is expecting rather too much, we feel, that probationers should not absorb the prevailing mores and attitudes of their profession, as they learn how to practise it.

Constables wear a uniform, are generally unarmed (although they may carry non-lethal batons, CS-gas sprays or Taser-guns), and perform their duties either on foot or by bicycle, or by car. They carry out reassurance patrolling, respond to 999 calls for police assistance, search for missing persons, guard crime scenes, and perform a wide variety of other tasks as what is effectively a general pool of police labour.[6] They may have a specific territorial responsibility, and they are, or were, the face of the police service for the public. They are highly trained, and nowadays reasonably well remunerated. It is possible and commonplace for a police officer to spend his entire service of 30 years as a police constable, and there is no pressure to seek promotion. CID, traffic, firearms units, special branch, and so on, are all recruited from the uniform branch, which is thus a reservoir of talent for specialist tasks, as well as a branch in its own right.

Promotion

Police constables seeking promotion to sergeant and beyond may apply from any branch. Originally, promotion to sergeant and inspector was a twofold process:

- the officer who wished to be promoted sat and passed a written examination, set to a national standard by the Police Training Centre at Harrogate in Yorkshire, which was largely a test of his knowledge of the law; and
- then joined a list of those eligible for promotion in force, and waited his chance. Officers could also apply for a vacancy at a higher level in another force, or seek acting status in a higher rank by fulfilling a specialised role, for example in national police training, and hope that their higher status would be confirmed in due course.

The sergeants' and inspectors' promotion examinations were added to under the practice-based system of police promotion known as OSPRE, (Objective Structured Performance Related Examination) whereby candidates' suitability for the role of sergeant or inspector is assessed by role play.

---

6. Paradoxically, the British bobby may be patrolling the streets one day as a symbol of policing by consent and back on those same streets on the following evening in full riot gear, as a demonstration goes sour and leads to violence. Some States have separate riot police. The UK does not; although in the larger forces it may be possible to specialise in 'public order' duties for a period during one's career.

The OSPRE assessment system has proved enduringly controversial, and may be reformed. A test of legal knowledge may not have been a good predictor of one's ability to perform the role of sergeant or inspector, but at least the testing process itself was relatively uncontroversial: the candidate either knew the law, or he did not. OSPRE is a very different kettle of fish, and presents many opportunities for grievance.

An alternative promotion system now in practice in some forces is to replace role play by assessment of the promoted officer's practical competence in the workplace during a probationary period.

Police community support officers

The creation of PCSOs as a result of the Police Reform Act 2002, has been a controversial measure, urged by some chief officers and opposed by others. It was not popular with the Police Federation, to which PCSOs do not belong, and which described it as 'policing on the cheap'; but it is, perhaps, an inevitable consequence of the better pay and conditions of service offered to the full police constable.

PCSOs receive less training than regular officers, and are paid less for carrying out more restricted duties. (There is a discernible trend for some PCSOs to apply to become and in some cases progress to becoming police officers but there are no formal arrangements to encourage this.) They do not have the same powers of arrest as regular police officers, and their performance in what they do has on occasion been criticised as the public has expected a normal police service. We suspect that they are here to stay, and will become a part of the normal policing landscape.

Special constables

Special constables are, from one perspective, an historical and professional anomaly, best reformed out of existence. From another, they are an essential part of good citizenship. Special constables are ordinary members of the public who volunteer to give up some of their time, unpaid, to assist the regular police. They wear much the same uniform as regular police officers, receive some training, are sworn police officers, and have the same powers of arrest as full police officers, i.e., more power than PCSOs. They are expected to work a minimum of four hours a week.

No politician is likely to condemn the institution of the special constable, which provides an opportunity for the ordinary citizen to make a practical contribution to the safety and security of the neighbourhood: and indeed, special constables can be a valuable asset in policing local events. They may be of especial help in responding to predictable seasonal fluctuations in the local demand for policing, for example in a coastal resort whose population quadruples in the summer months. There is an analogy with other public services such as the fire brigade, which also consists of both full-time professionals and part-time volunteers, and provides a similar opportunity for local people to serve their community. The involvement and uses of special constables might be taken further, and at present they remain a good idea whose potential has not been fully exploited.

Special constables are not unique to the UK, and have their equivalents overseas. We note that a Garda Reserve was established in Ireland under 2005 legislation, and that such reserves are now on patrol on a voluntary and unpaid basis to assist the regular police. They need not be Irish citizens, as both EU and EEC and Swiss nationals are eligible to apply to join, as are refugees whose status is accepted under the refugee act, as well as persons who have been resident in Ireland for a specified period.

In the United States, the National Guard has provided an opportunity for public-spirited citizens to serve the community, although as part of the armed services rather than as the American equivalent of special constables. In the aftermath of the attacks of 9/11 and the creation of 'homeland security', American citizens have many more opportunities to serve the community in a voluntary capacity.

Police staff

Police or support staff are an essential part of modern policing and in some cases represent the force to the public: scenes of crimes officers (SOCOs) and front counter staff, for example, may be support staff rather than police officers, and chief constables have the authority to 'civilianise' other posts if they deem it desirable.

Supposedly, the employment of such staff allows sworn police officers to concentrate on the activities for which their training and powers are necessary. In reality, as surveys by such organizations as HM Inspectorate of Constabulary (HMIC) and the Audit Commission have shown, there is usually a gap between intention and result. The core role of the police officer—what a sworn officer and no one else can do—has been subject to continual and sometimes inconsistent revision, but never conclusively defined; and there remain significant variations and anomalies in the employment and treatment of support staff.

Since 1996, support staff have been the responsibility of the chief constable and not the police authority. Their integration might have been taken further, and relationships have been known to break down, as in Devon and Cornwall in 2006, in a major dispute over support staff pay which was followed by the resignation of the chief constable. Many questions remain to be resolved, and the police service still needs to address this issue, as HMIC has recommended.

Comment

We have seen that what was once a task carried out by a single institution—the omnicompetent police constable—has become something shared by a number of respondents. Those employed within the police 'family', as it were, tend to be loyal to the police service, for reasons too obvious to mention. Nevertheless, there are a large number of anomalies that remain to be resolved before police services are fully integrated; and some strategic thinking is necessary.

We go on to reflect on some of the challenges facing everyone who works for the police service, and not just its sworn officers or official leaders; and are indebted to our colleague Dr Robert Adlam for the fivefold analysis that follows.

CONTEXTS FOR POLICING

A useful way to consider the role of the police is to look at various aspects of policing from different perspectives of which the following five areas can be taken as representative:

1. The constitutional context

Police work takes place in a constitutional context. It requires an understanding of the underlying features of a liberal democracy and the need to apply them in policing. This applies to all roles and at all levels, for example with:

- a constable exercising powers of arrest and stop and search;
- an information technology specialist needing to consider the rights that apply, such as privacy and freedom of information, in planning a new data storage system;
- a press and public relations officer preparing for a media briefing about a missing child;
- a community relations specialist considering how to build a proper relationship with a newly-arrived immigrant community; or
- a chief officer who is reviewing policy in a particular area in the light of a new political imperative.

2. The politico-legal context

All governments make politico-legal changes in the unceasing drive to reduce crime and increase public security. Police leadership needs to be able to cope with a changing politico-legal environment, in which change does not necessarily flow in an orderly and logical sequence. Those who make the law, as well as those who apply it, must be responsive to changing events and pressures, as 9/11 made clear: there is now a far greater pressure for both measures and policies that will promote public safety in the age of global terrorism, that could not have been predicted before Al Qaeda's attacks.

Events in London in July 2005 have reinforced this pressure, and in the balance between liberty and security which has dominated public debate since terrorism moved to centre-stage on the political agenda, the shift has been towards greater security and the erosion of civil liberties. The police follow rather than set public policy, but are in a position to influence it by offering a disinterested and professional opinion.

3. The public sector

The police are part of the public sector, but there are significant differences between policing and other public sector activities that have especial significance for the police, such as the complexity of police accountability and governance and the breadth of the role of police. High levels of accountability, transparency and public participation are key defining factors for the exercise of police leadership.

The public good

Police leadership must be based upon a proper understanding of the idea of the 'public good'. Whilst it may sometimes be helpful in preventing professional arrogance to think of those who use public services as customers who have a right to be served, consumerism is, by itself, no guarantee of the public interest. The tasks of the public domain include the balancing of interests and the search for collective values. Public sector leadership necessarily involves:

- appreciating diversity;
- building and testing for consensus;
- managing and resolving conflict; and
- applying a responsibility to focus scarce resources in achieving the valued ends shared by the collective.

In short, public sector leadership is especially concerned with realising the common good. In consequence, public sector leaders are obliged to forge partnerships with collectives, communities, organizations and agencies that contribute to the common or public good.

4. The nature of police work itself

Police work is in some ways different to other work. For example, the ambiguity of fundamental purpose, the adversarial nature of certain police encounters, and the 'management of restraint' are recurrent features of police practice. No single feature of police work is unique. However, the combination of unusual factors, linked to the absolute need for integrity in practice under the extraordinary pressures which police work can mount, present a particular challenge. The principles and methods which may be successfully applied in other contexts may not be transferable to policing, or may lead to unintended consequences. Hence and according to ACPO:

> There is uncertainty about the ultimate goal. What is it? To preserve the Queen's Peace? Uphold the Rule of Law? Improve community relations? Help to maintain the 'status quo'? All these are open to individual interpretation. In fact, police staff arguably have the vaguest of remits—to undertake a multitude of tasks but with unclear objectives; objectives which depend upon their personal interpretations of what the law, the local community or national policies appear to be looking for. (ACPO 1993)

5. The psychological and ethical context

On a day to day basis, police work is characterised by the:

- need for instant decisions;
- reliance upon individual skills, judgement and initiative;
- emotional demands of policing;
- physical dangers of policing; and
- influence of the police officer's image.

> Again, ACPO has noted that:
>
> In most occupations, frontline staff have only routine, relatively unemotional contacts with other people. In contrast, police officers frequently operate in an emotionally charged environment. This can be caused by dealing with a crisis (for example a road traffic accident, a sudden death, being the victim of a crime, etc.) or, alternatively, enforcing the criminal law or responding to other 'conflict' situations which are themselves stressful for every one present ... To add to this, the police have close relationships with only a quarter of the population, the most deprived. It can be difficult for officers to maintain professional detachment—still less to have any measure of sympathy ... The emotional stress of policing cannot be underestimated ... (ACPO 1993, pp. 24 and 25)

Significantly, the authors of the above extracts go on to underline how, in the absence of safeguards, including support systems, the 'canteen culture' of the police is given room to thrive; whilst police leaders are perceived as not understanding the circumstances and realities of 'frontline policing'.

Police work takes place in a psychological and ethical context. Its leadership requires a psychological understanding of the sustained impact of police work upon the mentality and personality of the staff concerned, both individually and collectively. Police work can be damaging, and its practitioners need support.

Having reflected on police work in general, let us now go on to consider some of its aspects in particular.

PUBLIC ORDER OR PUBLIC SAFETY?

It is a remarkable feature of police work that some of it appears to have little connexion with Peel's original purposes in founding the modern police service in 1829—although, in the first example that we are about to discuss, it must be admitted that the Football Association did not exist in 1829.

Football and crowd control
The development of organized, professional sport was a consequence of the same process of industrialisation and urbanisation that led to the emergence of modern policing, and it was inevitable that in the end the one should embrace the other (For a fascinating account of the origins of modern sport, see *The Edwardians*, by Roy Hattersley). It might be argued that the police have no place in policing a private football match. After all, the match is a private event, taking place on private land, and if it is between professional teams, its intention is to raise money. It is a voluntary activity, in which neither players nor spectators are required to play a part; and it has no necessary connexion with crime. Indeed, the perfect match, as far as the police were concerned, would be one at which their presence proved unnecessary. However, despite the current emphasis on charging for their services, the police do attend and police football matches, or at least the major ones, where there may be a threat to public order; and therein lies the key to our dilemma.

The police are concerned to protect public safety, and any very large gathering of people may pose a threat to public safety. A professional football club, or at least one of the large and more successful ones, should be ready and willing to police its own events, by the use of trained stewards, and indeed this does occur: but nevertheless, there is still a role for a professional police service in proving the trained leadership, command and control that such events require. In essence, the situation is very simple: where there is a potential threat to public order, there will the police be found; and so they should be.

Hence we may expect a police presence at a rally, a demonstration, a religious gathering, a sporting event, a festival, and even a flower show, if it be sufficiently large and attracts a sufficient crowd.

What is the role of the police on such an occasion? In essence, it is to preserve the Queen's Peace: and whilst it may be difficult to define what exactly this means, in the abstract, it is easy enough to recognise when the Queen's Peace has been broken. We would suggest that the reason why the police provide a service, at least on occasion, that seems to go beyond the formal limits and boundaries to their official duties, is threefold:

- it is in the tradition of British policing, and is therefore, at least to some people, in no further need of justification;
- no other organization is set up to provide the service needed, on a 24/7 basis, and the police may therefore take a legitimate pride in the service that they provide, and the opportunity afforded to exercise and test their skills for use in emergency; and
- providing a generally useful service is part of the structure of policing by consent. It is a source of positive relations between police and public which means that help, co-operation and information will be forthcoming when needed, from the public to the police.

Firearms and lethal force

We now move from one extreme to the other, or so it seems: from the role of the police as a social agency, concerned to facilitate the public's right to enjoy itself in a safe and secure environment, to its role as the guardians of life and death; for the police may claim a monopoly on the use of lethal force within the United Kingdom.

As already described earlier in this chapter, they are permitted to use such force under certain conditions, here, primarily only when it is absolutely necessary in order to protect life, and any occasion when the police do use lethal force is almost certain to lead to widespread publicity and possible condemnation. It may also lead to legal consequences for the officers concerned.

Suicide bombings have exacerbated the situation and heightened the tension associated with the lethal use of force. Should trained police officers shoot to kill, if confronted with a suicide bomber? The lethal shooting of Jean Charles de Menezes at Stockwell underground station on 22 July 2005 led to an international controversy, the consequences of which are still with us; and is part of a long line of such controversies which must arise when instant decisions on life or death or serious injury, are made on incomplete information. Please do not read this as a general apologia for policing. When the police get it wrong, and they do, they must face the consequences. What we are seeking to establish at this point is the inherent difficulty of some of the challenges that are faced by police officers. The unlawful killing of another human being constitutes either murder or manslaughter,[7] and murder

---

7. There are also some more specific or related categories of offence, such as causing death by dangerous driving,

is generally regarded as the most serious crime on the Statute Book. Police officers, however, will not be convicted of either murder or manslaughter if their action in killing someone can be shown to have been not unlawful.

The Stockwell shooting

In the de Menezes case the police shot and killed a Brazilian electrician resident in London because they believed him to be a suicide bomber who was about to detonate a bomb. There had been a number of failed bomb detonations on 21 July 2005, and the metropolis was in a state of heightened tension. The police belief about Jean Charles de Menezes's criminality and intentions was entirely false, based upon a surveillance operation that had gone wrong, and they rapidly apologised for their lethal error and offered compensation. The situation soon worsened to become an international incident, with widespread ramifications and repercussions. We shall restrain our comments to the lawfulness of the use of lethal force, whilst recognising that the real controversy is about the reasonableness of the police chain of actions that led to the shooting, perhaps more than the shooting itself.

The first question, as we see it, is this: would the police be entitled to use lethal force to prevent a suicide bombing? We explore the law below, and, subject to knowing the precise facts, the short answer is 'yes': the use of lethal force *can* be legally justified in some circumstances.

We would also suggest, in line with the findings of the European Court of Human Rights in assessing similar shootings, that a general judgement also needs to be made. The police service that:

- is known to take its duties seriously;
- selects and trains its officers with great care, particularly in the use of lethal force;
- trains for extreme cases regularly and realistically; and
- maintains proper command and control systems, so that its decision-making system is both dynamic and accountable

is more likely to receive a favourable assessment than its opposite. The police service that does none of those things falls at the first hurdle.

The Metropolitan Police Serrvice (MPS) is a highly trained and professional organization. Nevertheless, it got it wrong on 22 July 2005. We would suggest that the fatality was the result of a combination of circumstances rather than the result of one mistake alone. We do not dispute that the police would have been justified in using lethal force, if there were no alternative to preventing a suicide bombing. The controversy that arose as a result of the shooting suggests that some believed the

---

infanticide and arson with intent to endanger life.

shooting to be a tragic but understandable error, whereas others believed that it was an unreasonable decision and an unjustified act, the culmination of a chain of errors that should not have occurred.

It is not our purpose here to reach a definitive judgment on the reasonableness of the police action in this particular case. We may conclude, however, that the police use of lethal force in any circumstances is quite naturally and properly liable to lead to an investigation (it is, in fact, an Independent Police Complaints Commission (IPCC) set procedure), and that the police must think, plan, train and train again to make sure that their procedures withstand objective scrutiny. The relevant law is traceable to the following sources:

- the Common Law rights of self-defence and protection of other persons;
- section 3 Criminal Law Act 1967;
- section 117 Police and Criminal Evidence Act 1984 (PACE)—which empowers a constable to use reasonable force in exercising powers under PACE; and
- human rights legislation from the UK and international instruments (which we shall now explore).

The Right to Life

According to the Universal Declaration of Human Rights, Article 3, everyone has the right to life, liberty and security of person; and under the European Convention On Human Rights, Article 2:

1. Everyone's right to life shall be protected by law. No one shall be deprived of his life intentionally save in the execution of a sentence of a court following his conviction of a crime for which this penalty is provided by law.
2. Deprivation of life shall not be regarded as inflicted in contravention of this article when it results from the use of force which is no more than absolutely necessary:
   (a) in defence of any person from unlawful violence;
   (b) in order to effect a lawful arrest or to prevent the escape of a person lawfully detained;
   (c) in action lawfully taken for the purpose of quelling a riot or insurrection.

As indicated, in addition to human rights law, which is legally binding, police actions should be guided by international declarations and national codes.

The UN Code of Conduct for Law Enforcement Officials

Article 3 requires compliance with the principles of necessity and proportionality by police when they use force. The *Commentary* to the Article states that police may only use such force as is reasonably necessary for the prevention of crime or in effecting or in assisting in the lawful arrest of offenders or suspected offenders. It requires that firearms should not be used except when a suspected offender offers armed resistance or otherwise jeopardises the lives of others and less extreme measures are not sufficient to restrain or apprehend the suspected offender. Clearly, a suicide bomber jeopardises the lives of others as well as his own life.

Basic principles

The 'Basic Principals on the Use of Force and Firearms by Law Enforcement Officials' is a detailed and very practical instrument consisting of 26 Principles. It sets standards in respect of all aspects of the use of force and firearms by police, including the provision of equipment to allow for a differentiated use of force; selection and training of police; the responsibility of senior officials for the actions of their subordinates; and a requirement for proper reporting and review procedures when force or firearms are used by police. Under Basic Principle 9 firearms may only be used against persons in response to an imminent threat of death or serious injury.

Prevention and investigation

'The Principles on the Effective Prevention and Investigation of Extra-Legal, Arbitrary and Summary Executions' is a detailed instrument consisting of 20 principles designed to prevent unlawful killings by State officials and to secure proper investigation of any such killings when they occur. In particular Principle 2 requires governments to ensure strict control, including a clear chain of command, over all officials responsible for apprehension, arrest, detention, custody and imprisonment, as well as those officials authorised by law to use force and firearms.

Findings and decisions of treaty bodies

These include:

- the use of force must be no more than absolutely necessary for the achievement of one of the purposes set out in sub-paragraphs a, b or c of Article 2, paragraph 2 of the Convention;
- in establishing whether the use of force was 'strictly proportionate' regard must be had to the nature of the aim pursued, the dangers of life and limb inherent in the situation, and the degree of the risk that the force employed might result in loss of life;
- the European Court of Human Rights has stated that it must scrutinise not only whether the force used was strictly proportionate to the aim of protecting lives but whether the operation (for example, to arrest suspects) was planned and controlled so as to minimise, to the greatest extent possible, recourse to lethal force.

Comment

The ordinary police officer is not expected to know the decisions of the European Court of Human Rights in detail, but must have a clear understanding of the operating principles involved. In regard to Article 2, human rights training for British police officers is based on the following principles:

- Article 2, the right to life, is what is known as 'qualified right' as opposed to an 'absolute right'. There are occasions when it may be breached;

- actions taken in breach of a qualified right must be legal, necessary and proportionate, and the process must be accountable. In other words, the police officers involved must be able to present a reasoned account of their actions in breaching a qualified right;

- if there is an alternative to the use of lethal force that achieves the same effect, then it should be used. In practical terms, this means that police firearms units are now equipping and training themselves in the use of items such as stun-guns, designed to be effective under some circumstances in subduing a threat of lethal violence, but not lethal in themselves.

Legality

British Common Law defines what is illegal, not what is legal, and leaves the decision as to what is legal initially to the discretion of the police officer in question and ultimately to the courts if he gets this wrong. Human rights law operates from the other approach. Police officers must justify their conduct from what is declared to be permissible.

Necessity and proportionality

It might be thought, that these two words amount to the same thing. If something is necessary, then surely it must also be proportionate? Not so. It may be necessary to use force but there still remains the question of how much. So, for example, a firearm should not be used if a Taser-gun is available and can achieve the required objective of incapacitating a person safely, without the use of lethal force, and removing the threat.

European Court of Human Rights judges do not set themselves up as experts on police operations, and are open to technical argument and the wisdom of professional experience: nevertheless, the principle of proportionality is perhaps the most important concept in any interpretation of the application of human rights.

THE EMERGENCE OF A RISK AVERSE CULTURE

The non-police reader may be beginning to wonder why anyone might join the police service at all, wherein conduct of any kind may be subject to stressful scrutiny; and having joined, why he might seek to volunteer for firearms training as an additional source of difficulty and stress. The answer is, of course, that:

- it is not expected that the duties of a police officer should appeal to all citizens;
- any police officer, having joined, should receive the right training, equipment and leadership in order to enable him to be able to face and cope with the difficulties presented by his choice of career; and
- if he does face especial challenges, and has acted in good faith and by making an honest and reasonable decision under such knowledge and understanding of the circumstances as was available to him at the time, then his organization and managers should back and support him, rather than place him under the additional stress of official suspicion and a presumption of guilt.

However, not all police officers rise to the challenge, and Sir Ronnie Flanagan, the chief inspector of police, has articulated in forcible terms his detestation of the risk-averse culture which has arisen in the police service, partly because of the issue of the responsibility of the chief police officers for the health and safety of the officers under their command, and which is, in Sir Ronnie's opinion, capable of destroying both the reputation and effectiveness of modern policing. He presents his overview as follows (Flanagan, 2008).

A vision of successful 21st century policing

Policing in England and Wales finds itself 'at a crossroads'. The range and scale of the challenges which it faces means that very serious decisions must be taken, not simply by the police service itself but by everyone involved in policing, about how we can best succeed over the next decade and beyond. One option would be to match the growing complexity of modern policing by seeking to specify every outcome and control and bureaucratize every aspect and process, from the centre to the force and within the force from the chief constable to the constable, in an attempt to cover every risk and meet every demand. To me, however, such a response would fail to acknowledge that a fundamentally different, more dynamic model is essential.

Sir Ronnie Flanagan recommends that the police service adopts a new approach to assessing risk. Risk is something to be managed, rather than avoided altogether; and there must be occasions when the police service takes risks in order to carry out its primary duty of protecting the public. Moreover, risk assessment should not become a bureaucratic exercise in retrospective accountability, a substitute for real thought, as it were, but a dynamic activity of its own. Risk is normally assessed in terms of likelihood and potential for harm. In other words, an organization must take seriously even a low risk of something happening, if its potential consequences are catastrophic; hence emergency planning.

Risk aversion in practice

A case study can make the point rather more effectively than an abstract analysis, and we now quote from the executive summary of a report into a shooting at Highmoor Cross within the jurisdiction of the Thames Valley Police, which illustrates very clearly the downside of risk aversion. The facts were that two sisters, Vicky Horgan, 27, and Emma Walton, 25, were shot dead by Vicky's estranged husband, Stuart Horgan, in Highmoor Cross, Oxfordshire, in June 2004. The police reacted wrongly, and the report explains how.

Executive Summary

- On 9 June 2004 Chief Constable Peter Neyroud commissioned a review of the practices and procedures adopted by Thames Valley Police in connection with the fatal shootings at Highmoor Cross on Sunday 6 June 2004. The Independent Police Complaints Commission agreed to oversee this review in the interests of public confidence.

- The purpose of the review was to address public concern about the police response: that it took too long for the police to get to the scene and to get urgent medical help to the victims.

- The review concludes that the delay in attending the scene cannot be justified.

- The reasons for the delay are not due to the failings of the individuals involved in the response. The failings are embedded in Thames Valley Police policy and training in responding to firearms incidents.

- Essentially, current policy seeks to eliminate risk rather than manage it. The direct result of this was that the police priority in response to the emergency calls was to locate the offender rather than get to the victims, and an overly cautious approach to the deployment of armed officers.

- This report recommends that the policy in relation to spontaneous firearms incidents needs to be replaced. The new policy must provide clear direction and guidance on dynamic risk assessment, to respond to situations where people are believed to be hurt. It should include a presumption that unless there are good reasons for not doing so, the command function must take place near the scene. These policies need to be supported by new and better training.

- The review also identifies national issues for firearms policy and training. The IPCC will take these up with the Association of Chief Police Officers to seek to ensure that lessons can be learned at all levels as a result of this tragedy.

Comment

We do not include this summary and analysis as typical of police work in general, nor of the Thames Valley Police in particular; and we note that the ambulance service is also criticised. What is clear, however, is that the police service itself has recognised that a 'risk-aversion culture' is the wrong one; and there are many other examples that might have been chosen.

We do not believe that the great majority of police officers join the service in order to shirk their duty, let alone the common obligations that humanity places upon them, and that were shown by the other inhabitants of Highmoor Cross; and we are quite sure that an over-emphasis upon 'health and safety' is resented by the average police officer as much as his armchair critic, for it removes the officer's discretion in making the right decision as to what to do in the circumstances as he perceives them at the time, and in the light of his professional experience and judgment.

Protection against the misuse of lethal force

The police service has a duty to protect the public against the illegal use of force, whether lethal or otherwise, both under Common Law and human rights legislation; and this raises some interesting questions about how the police should interpret their duties and go about their work.

Let us take a very high-profile example: the case of Salman Rushdie. The writer (now Sir) Salman Rushdie was made the subject of a 'fatwa' in 1989. The police had a duty to protect his life, and Mr Rushdie received police protection, and in effect lived in hiding until the fatwa was considered less of a real and immediate threat.

What proportion of its resources, should the MPS have devoted to protecting him? Enough, we would suggest, to show that it was taking the threat seriously and taking reasonable precautions in an unreasonable situation.

No one's life can be protected against every possible eventuality, as countless political assassinations have shown, from John F Kennedy to Benazir Bhutto; and no human rights court would have criticised the police had the fatwa been carried out, if it could have been shown that the police had been taking reasonable precautions at the time. Threat cannot be eliminated: it can only be guarded against.

Suppose, *per imposibile,* that the MPS had devoted its entire resources to protecting Salman Rushdie. That would have been unnecessary, counter-productive, and in neglect of its other duties, since many other people would have died or been injured as a result of the loss of police protection. Police work is about judgement, and the Human Rights Act 1998 does not change that, although it has brought a new vocabulary into use. The police should take reasonable precautions against a known threat. But they cannot protect everyone, and they cannot protect anyone *in toto.*

The use of deception

Police work, as the distinguished Australian police scholar Seumas Miller has written (Miller, 2005, and elsewhere), is distinguished from other occupations by its need to violate ethical norms for the public good. Thus, as we have already seen, the police have a right to the use of lethal force. Secondly, as Miller puts it, 'a distinctive feature of policing is its unavoidable and routine use of harmful methods, e.g. coercion and deception, that are considered to be morally unacceptable in ordinary circumstances'.

Deception is an everyday part of policing, and test-purchasing is an everyday example of its use. A police officer learns that a shopkeeper is breaking the law in selling cigarettes to minors, and decides to find out whether or not this is true, by asking a minor or apparent minor to make a test purchase. The shopkeeper readily makes the sale, and the police officer makes an arrest. Was the shopkeeper deceived? Certainly: he did not know the reason for the exercise. The crucial issue is, was he coerced or misled into breaking the law? And the answer would appear to be 'no': he carried out a voluntary act when he might and should have acted otherwise. Therefore, a court would accept this deception, on the face of it, as a legitimate means to enforce the law and achieve the greater good.

Consider another example. The police learn that A wants to murder his wife B, and is looking for a private executioner or hit-man (C). A plain clothes police officer is persuaded to pretend to be C, and is given sufficient credibility to be able to play the role convincingly, which may involve ancillary deception. C makes contact with A, elicits the details that are needed, and arrests A for the intent to murder, or presents the information to his organization so that other officers are able to do so.

Did deception take place? Certainly: the police officer pretended to be a hit-man, which he was not. He may indeed have pretended, in order to obtain the confidence of the would-be murderer, that he, C, was in sympathy with A's aims, and believed that wives needed to be corrected from time-to-time, and if necessary murdered, which were not his true views. Thirdly, it is arguable that C was acting in breach of at least a verbal contract, in that he was agreeing to do something which he had no intention of doing: and that might make an interesting case in civil law.[8] But we are sure, as criminal case law shows, that the police service was justified in carrying out a major deception, in order to prevent murder and protect life.

The police service did not suggest to the would-be murderer, that he kill his wife. It did not entrap or entice him, into planning to do so. It did not act as an *agent provocateur,* creating crimes which would not otherwise have occurred in order to claim the credit for then solving them, like a fireman who first lights the fire and then puts it out. It became, more-or-less, a passive means whereby the would-be murderer A (who would be equally guilty in law of the crime, if in fact he did not pull the trigger himself but merely commissioned the event) was able to plan to facilitate the accomplishment of an already premeditated crime.

Legal proceedings as a result of deception

In the hypothetical case as just considered, the first aim of the police must be to prevent a murder from taking place; and the use of a bogus paid killer will achieve this. Could the information gathered by the undercover police officer or officers, be used against the would-be murderer in court, as evidence? That depends upon the circumstances. English law does not rule out improperly obtained evidence *per se,* as the fruit of the poisoned tree; but it does examine it very carefully.[9]

In the modern world, police work requires deception, which may go beyond suppressing the truth to suggesting what is false.[10] Should the police service take part in *sustained* deception? We believe that this question has already been answered. Any act of deception, in order to be successful, must contain within itself the capacity to be sustained if it is to be convincing; and we would argue that the reason for the deception is the primary moral issue, rather than its duration.

Some police services may see it as their duty to carry out sustained acts of deception, such as by infiltrating trained police officers, with the appropriate cover story, disguise and support mechanisms, into terrorist units or gangs of organized criminals (or even, for example, environmental protestors or political groupings, if their

---

8. Public policy would appear to be against the enforcement of any such 'contract', in the unlikely event that the law should accept that one exists. In the UK such situations are often approached with equivocation. A hit man might be both sentenced to life imprisonment and taxed on the proceeds – although the latter would nowadays probably be pursued by SOCA.

9. *R v Loosely* (2001), HL

10. *Suppresio veri and suggestio falsi.*

actions are seen as a sufficient threat).

We see such operations as potentially dangerous, and requiring a commitment to the sustained safety, and indeed the psychological and ethical wellbeing, of the infiltrator. The first question we should therefore ask is, is this act of infiltration really necessary? Is there another way, to gain the information required? Have all other channels been exploited, as far as it is possible to go? Having said all that, if the opportunity to infiltrate a terrorist unit presents itself, it would be an unusual police officer, we suspect, who turned down that opportunity out of hand.

THE ENDURING QUALITIES NEEDED IN POLICE WORK

Police work is not all dangerous, morally ambiguous or deeply challenging. Much of it is preventative, routine, and bureaucratic. It is often incomplete: the police officer is there to fulfil his task in what is part of a lengthier process, of which he may never know the final result. Moreover, police work often lacks the moral satisfaction of the wrong being rectified, or the good deed rewarded. A husband beats up his wife, yet again, and for one reason or another, the case does not arrive at court: the police officers concerned may be very frustrated, but there is nothing more that they can do.

Police work requires guile, subtlety and patience. It is right to believe that good will triumph; but the evidence does not always show that result. Good policing requires stoicism, and the ability to resist that corrosive cynicism which is the mark of the person who has lost his belief in human nature.

Passion and perspective

Another way of putting this is to say that the police officer needs to be able to achieve a balance between passion and perspective; and here we are much indebted to the work of the American political theorist William Ker Muir (1977), and the summaries of his work by my colleague Dr Robert Adlam, which have appeared in various sources. As Adlam puts it:

- What makes a good police officer?
- What type of organizational environment encourages good police work? (This is a fundamental question for leaders, managers and policy makers in police organizations).

One very sophisticated answer is given by Ker Muir (1977) in his book *Police: Street-corner Politicians*. There is no better way of beginning the serious study of police than by reading Ker Muir's study of the development of police officers. It may also explain some of the enduring and 'intractable' features of police culture.

Muir's general theory can be divided into three parts. The first is an analysis of the nature of coercive power and the special problems faced by people who assume responsibility for coercing others. Most of us have ways of avoiding the use of 'naked coercive power'. The police don't. So, Ker Muir examines the extraordinary situation facing police officers. In no time at all, he shows how police are caught up with the difficulties of dealing with people who are not amenable to the usual 'civilised' ways. The police face the 'bad', the 'mad', the 'sad', the 'dispossessed' and the 'detached'. In these circumstances very special skills are called upon if they are to 'return' these people to the ways and institutions of 'civilised' society. Ker Muir shows the kinds of choices facing police officers in these adversarial relationships; some of them lead to a crude, violent, insensitive, cruel style of policing; others reflect choices that lead to good relations with citizens and minimise the actual use of coercive force.

But why do some police adopt skilled, humane and effective styles whereas others remain ineffective, unskilled and/or cruel and insensitive? Here, in the second part of Muir's theory, there is an analysis of how coercive power affects personality and how personality affects the way different types of people respond to the challenges and responsibilities of using coercion. Muir, drawing closely from Weber's analysis of the tough business of politics, finds that, at the core of every police officer's life is a genuine moral dilemma—a dilemma in which every politician is also caught. To state it in its simplest terms, the dilemma is that every police officer (like every politician) must, on some occasion, use morally unpleasant, repugnant ('dirty') means in order to achieve morally good ends.

What makes both the police officer's and the politician's situation a genuine moral dilemma—a situation from which it is impossible to escape without committing a moral wrong—is that if either (police or politician) do employ 'dirty' means they become morally guilty for having done so but if they do not they become morally guilty for failing to achieve the good ends that can only be achieved by using 'dirty' means. (The type of 'dirty' means Weber and Ker Muir have in mind are: lies and threats, hurting or threatening to hurt people or to hurt the things they value dearly e.g. their liberty). The key point is that police cannot avoid some kind of profound moral challenge. Without being 'hard' in some way they may allow greater evils to prevail.

How do different police officers respond to all this? 'Only a minority cope well. 'If police are not careful they could hold on to their ideals but abandon respect for the 'civilised' means of achieving them. They can learn to lie, deceive, hurt, harm or injure others without suffering guilt or moral reservation. 'Or they could turn away from both the ideals to which policing aims as well as the imperative to use coercive means and, in effect, abandon 'being' a police officer. 'Or they can abandon their hopes for bringing about a better society and become obedient bureaucrats—enforcing law or regulations in a mechanical fashion.

Or they could become 'professionals'. But to become a professional they need to develop and cultivate two virtues. One is 'moral', the other 'intellectual'. The moral virtue is 'passion'. Passion is the strong conviction that the achievement of certain 'goods' are so important that it allows the police officer to reconcile him or herself to using morally dangerous, coercive or violent means to achieve them. The second virtue 'perspective' serves to counterbalance passion. Perspective is akin to having a sense of the 'big picture'. It enables the police officer to respect the suffering, sorrows, pain and sensitivities of others. Perspective teaches people not to have a cynical outlook on humankind but to recognise tragedy in the human condition. As Ker Muir puts it, those police who develop a 'tragic perspective' express three themes.

The first is that humankind is of one substance. Second, a complex causal pattern is at work in human affairs: accident, self-control and inevitable factors outside the control of an individual together have substantial influence over the destiny of any human being. Third, human solidarity is the foundation of a meaningful life.

Passion and perspective work together to discourage the destructive effects of having to exercise coercive power. Thus, a good police officer understands the psychological dynamics at work as a consequence of the obligation to use coercive force—and how to withstand its potentially corrupting or damaging effects. They come to develop 'passion' and 'perspective'.

And the type of 'organization' that encourages good police work? Well, it is one where the tough business of policing is addressed—through conversation (talk), through 'learning' about cities, communities, people; and through 'leadership'—the ethos, priorities and culture set by the leaders of the organization.

Crime Prevention and Crime Detection

CHAPTER SIX

Crime Prevention and Crime Detection

This chapter explores both the general role of the police as the leading crime prevention agency and the specific role of the Criminal Investigation Department (CID) in investigating and preventing crime. The police are not the only agency charged with preventing or investigating crime. Other agencies also do so, and indeed the list of organizations whose regulated activities include the investigation of crime has increased enormously in modern times and especially since the turn of the millenium. Under the Regulation of Investigatory Powers Act 2000 (RIPA) there were 792 organizations (as at July 2008) which were authorised to carry out surveillance operations, including 474 councils: a matter of current controversy, as some of their operations have been categorised as trivial pursuits. It could also be argued that every time a local council erects a new surveillance camera, it is a means towards the prevention of crime; and this is a fast growing activity in its own right (as well as a further source of controversy.) Nevertheless, the police remain the lead agency to deal with crime.

CIDs have a role in preventing crime as well as investigating it. As we shall see, the role of the CID has expanded and developed over the decades; and what is a naturally conservative organization, with a marked culture and *modus operandi* of its own, has had to become more adaptive and flexible in its response to the increasing pressures on the police imposed in the 21st Century.

We would conclude, however, that CIDs are still recognisably CIDs, and that if a detective from the past were somehow parachuted into a contemporary CID office he would not find the atmosphere entirely unfamiliar. There is an enduring culture to the CID. P A J Waddington wrote in 1999 on the so-called 'canteen culture' of the police both in the CID and more generally, that it has its good as well as its bad side.[1] Waddington argues that this culture does not deserve the wholesale criticism to which it has been subject, and that it is not proof in itself of institutional racism. Canteen humour should be recognisd as a form of catharsis, to be found in any professional sub-culture.

CRIME PREVENTION AS A POLICE ACTIVITY

If crime can be prevented, it need not be investigated. The New Police of 1829 were charged with the prevention of crime as a fundamental priority and the force

---

1. Waddington, P A J (1999), 'Police Canteen Sub-culture: An Appreciation', *British Journal of Criminology*, vol. 39, No. 2, pp 286-308.

was designed and supervised to achieve this objective. Police constables, who wore a distinctive uniform and could be seen from a long distance—hence the top hat, which later became the highly recognisable policeman's helmet—provided a visible deterrent to crime by patrolling the streets on fixed beats, such that the entire metropolitan area was regularly visited, and the ordinary citizen in need of assistance was easily able to find a police officer. For an urban and densely populated area in which progress was usually made on foot, this was a realistic and effective form of preventative policing, and a major deterrent to street crime, although its disadvantages may also be perceived.

Other forms of crime prevention were slower to emerge; and the modern police activities of offering advice to householders on crime prevention by means of improving security, and of attempting to 'design out crime' by giving advice on security to the planners of new housing estates, are products of a later era.

Twenty years ago, we should have been confident in writing that crime prevention (other than by visible patrolling, which also performs the function of reassuring the public) would remain the Cinderella of police work, and her Prince Charming was unlikely to arrive. Police culture did not 'rate' crime prevention, which was slow, methodical and painstaking work, distinctly lacking in the rush of adrenalin of the high speed car chase or the dangerous arrest; and this state of affairs, despite official rhetoric as to the value of preventing crime rather than investigating it once it has occurred, was unlikely to change.

Nowadays we must acknowledge a change of both attitude and approach. With the powerful driver of crime reduction targets, the attention of CID, at least in the metropolis, has increasingly been focussed on crime prevention. The Flying Squad (a term still in popular use despite more bureaucratic names) works closely with the cash-in-transit security industry, betting shops, banks and so on, in order to prevent armed or other robbery. Similarly, the Metropolitan Police Service (MPS) Homicide Command has been working with the concept of 'murder suppression'. This involves analysing murders and their causal factors and carrying out risk analysis and partnership working to prevent homicides in areas such as domestic violence and honour based violence. Operation Trident (shootings and murders affecting the black community) has an active crime reduction strand involving working with the community and other agencies. The MPS is also engaging in long-term violent crime reduction through working with organizations such as the Wave Trust, which we explore later.

What happens in London tends to find its way to other police forces; and we may conclude that whilst there has not been a sea-change in British policing, from the investigation of crime to its prevention in the first place, there is now a more active emphasis on crime prevention. Modern police officers recognise the benefits of problem-oriented policing, working on the causes and not just on the symptoms of crime; and whilst most may prefer the adrenalin rush of response or investigation, few think that this is efficacious on its own. How police work is assessed affects priorities, and short-term performance targets reinforce the natural preferences of police officers for immediacy and action.

Violent crime and its prevention

Is the propensity to commit crime predetermined? Are some people more inclined towards crime than others, by virtue of their genetic inheritance? The nature/nurture argument (Are criminals born or made?) has a new twist. According to the Wave Trust Report on Violence (2000), what counts most is experience in very early childhood. Some people are more disposed to commit crimes of violence against the person than others, since they cannot or do not wish to control their violent impulses; and those impulses develop very early on.

Failure to develop empathy

WAVE argues that the propensity to violence develops primarily from wrong treatment before the age of three. Empathy is the single greatest inhibitor of the development of propensity to violence. Empathy fails to develop when parents or prime carers fail to attune with their infants. Absence of such parental attunement combined with harsh discipline is a recipe for violent, anti-social offspring. The single most effective way to stop producing people with the propensity to violence is to ensure that infants are reared in an environment that fosters their development of empathy. The surest way to achieve this is by supporting parents in developing attunement with their infants.

WAVE's search for global best practice in the prevention of violence identified many effective early interventions. These include programmes which develop attunement and empathy in:

- tomorrow's parents while they are still in school;
- current parents; and
- parents-to-be.'

The implications of this report are considerable, for if its carefully-researched conclusions are accurate then society is putting the wrong emphasis, at least in part, on how it deals with violent crime.

Other methods of preventing crime

Crime prevention, or at least reduction, may be achieved by high-profile patrolling, giving advice on security, and helping to design areas to live, exercise, shop and work in which the thief, rapist, vandal or terrorist will find his intentions harder to pursue. Closed circuit television (CCTV) may provide an extra means of security and aid in both the prevention and investigation of crime, including by recording material evidence or countering an alibi. Products liable to be stolen may be modi-fied. Mobile telephones and other gadgets can, at least in theory, be programmed so that only the legal owner can use them. Cars can be made harder to steal, or seize up once in the wrong hands; and their position can be recorded on a security grid.

Every advance in technology presents new opportunities both to the criminal and to the police service which seeks to apprehend him, and we shall deal with the major topic of IT-related crime in the section on *Cybercrime* below, returning also to the subject of CCTV. For the moment, however, we believe that we are safe in concluding that crime can never be prevented altogether, and that some means of investigating it after the fact will always be necessary.

THE INVESTIGATION OF CRIME

When the first commissioners of the Metropolitan Police laid down its purposes, they included the investigation of crime as a major objective; and it has remained so ever since. Theoretically, that does not pre-suppose the need for a separate and specialised CID, and indeed there was no such department in the early MPS. In practice, it would be difficult to imagine a modern police force without one. Special-isation produces results, or should do; and the CID is the first, the largest—usually about 15 per cent of the size of the average police force—and the most heavily-attacked (and defended) specialist unit within the police service.

The purpose of the CID
The main purpose of the CID is to investigate and resolve serious crime, such as murder, rape, arson and armed robbery. Petty crime may require CID attention if it has become of major public concern, and if the techniques of the CID are amenable to its resolution. In theory, any crime merits investigation. At some point, however, a senior police officer who devoted disproportionate resources to the investigation of minor offences which were not of great concern to the public would rightly find himself the object of censure.

Detection of suspects
The Metropolitan Police Service as set up in 1829 was entirely uniformed, and no detective department was created until 1842. It became embroiled in a horse-race betting scandal in 1877, resulting in the 'Trial of the Detectives', as a result of which a number of senior police officers were imprisoned or dismissed. Sadly, this was not the last time that plainclothes police officers were to be brought to court to answer charges of corruption. CID was created to replace the previous system of unsuper-

vised work, in 1878. CID has expanded enormously since then, not only to other forces but in its internal sub-divisions. Police forces tend to form new units or sub-units as a new problem becomes apparent, or an old problem shifts up the political agenda, and many units have been added to CID over the years, some going on to become departments or sections in their own right.

Special Branch was first set up in 1886 as the Special Irish Branch of the MPS, to deal with Irish terrorism. Should Special Branch be classified as a section of CID, or as an independent unit? As its role has expanded, we see it as a separate unit. In the MPS, Special Branch has been absorbed into counter-terrorism; but this pattern has not yet been repeated in a national basis. Drugs squads began as a branch of CID. As this book goes to press knife crime is the top priority of the MPS, and a new unit has been set up to deal with it. That unit will undoubtedly consist of a mixture of uniformed and plainclothes police officers, the former drawn from the CID.

THREAT ASSESSMENT AND THE EVOLVING RESPONSE

Organized criminal groups are adaptive and frequently operate in more than one area of criminal activity. Drugs traffickers may also be importers of firearms. They may engage in illegal immigration or people-trafficking, be involved in money laundering and have other 'interests' such as robbery or fraud. The contemporary CID looks at the nature of their criminal adversaries, how they are structured and financed, what their distribution networks are like, how they recruit and deal with competitors, and other factors. Increasingly, the approach is not to focus on the type of crime being committed, but on the criminal network itself, and to prioritise it according to the harm it is adjudged to be causing to society.

The best use of police resources

Some crimes are described as victimless, since there is no obvious single victim: insurance fraud attacks a company, not an individual, and unemployment benefit fraud attacks the State. The police should investigate these cases, on many occasions in collaboration with other agencies, for in reality there is a victim: the company in question has shareholders, and everyone suffers when insurance rates go up, or certain items become uninsurable. Benefit fraud is a drain on the State's resources, and a cause of social aggravation; and we may conclude that in reality there is no such thing as a victimless crime. However, the resources that the police devote to investigating so-called 'victimless' crime must be a matter of professional judgement; and they are also entitled to take part in the national debate as to the best use of limited resources.

In regard to fraud, for example, which is the better approach? Law enforcement and prosecution, or an approach that favours prevention and regulation? For financial and commercial organizations, fraud may be a cost that is tolerated within a certain parameter. It could be reduced below this figure by greater investment in security and prevention, but the companies in question choose not to do so. Given this is a commercial decision, should the taxpayer (via the police) invest a great amount in dealing with crimes that are preventable?

Provisional assessment

CID was set up to investigate crimes that the uniformed police did not have the time, resources, or opportunity to investigate properly. Some of these crimes were invisible to patrolling officers, but were nevertheless a major problem for society.

The creation of a specialist unit gives opportunities for the cost-effective investigation of crime on a larger scale. Burglaries in a certain area, for example, may be discovered to be the work of an organized criminal gang; but the local uniformed police would have been unlikely to make this discovery, other things being equal, or indeed to have targeted that gang and put it out of action, even if they had gained some knowledge of its existence; for the role of the uniformed police is essentially reactive. The following generalisations are uttered with caution:

- the CID will continue, as a separate and specialised aspect of police work, since all large organizations undergo some speciality of function. However, to join CID may be less attractive to the uniformed police officer than it has been in the past;
- the CID will give birth to new sub-units and sub-divisions, as the changing pattern of crime follows political, economic, social and technological changes in society at large. In the larger British cities, the all-purpose detective who is required to investigate any crime may become a thing of the past;
- combatting international and organized crime will become increasingly important, and so will the need of the police service to take a more flexible approach towards it.
- IT-related crime will be of increasing concern, and we explore this topic later.

Rather than continue to look at the investigation of crime in the abstract, let us review a seminal investigation and its consequences, and then look at a more recent case which sets the investigation of crime in an international context.

Case study No 1: The Yorkshire Ripper

Peter Sutcliffe was convicted of the murder of 13 women at the end of a long campaign of terror which lasted from 1975 (he may have carried out previous crimes which did not arouse the same public concern) to 1980, and is now an inmate of Broadmoor Special Hospital. His campaign created immense fear amongst women, mainly in Yorkshire but also wider afield, and generated enormous publicity, much of it highly critical of the police, whose investigation appeared for a very long time to be going nowhere. A huge number of possible suspects were interviewed, and floors were reinforced because of the paperwork accumulated. Offender profiles, of an informal kind, were created. Geographical mapping was applied. What purported to be confessional tapes were apparently accepted at face value, and used to guide the investigation. Dogged senior detectives were interviewed by the media and said that it was only a matter of time. Psychologists, psychiatrists, and other criminal experts offered their advice. But the Yorkshire Ripper remained obstinately at large.

In the end, he was caught by good, practical police work, and not as the result of any sustained detective investigation into him as a prime suspect—although he should have been, as he had been interviewed on nine previous occasions before his final arrest, and a friend had denounced him to the police as the ripper. Sutcliffe was arrested in a red-light area, with a prostitute in his car, when the police discovered the car to have false number plates. An astute police officer went back to check the area where the arrest had been made, and found the weapons that Sutcliffe had used, hidden nearby. Sutcliffe resisted interrogation for some time, but finally confessed, claiming to have been guided by God.

This case taught the police many lessons, one of which was that they were simply unable to cope with the amount of paperwork that the case had generated: and as a result the ensuing Byford Report into the events led to the establishment of Holmes, a computer system developed by the Home Office which records the investigation, whilst in progress, of a crime and enables the collation and analysis of collected data such as the one which the West Yorkshire Police had found impossible to manage. The case reinforced the importance of maintaining objectivity during the course of a prolonged and high profile investigation; and it pointed to the importance of cultivating good relations with the media.

The media, which includes such specialist programmes as BBC TV's 'Crime-watch', can help enormously in the solution of crime: and a good media policy, in any case, presents the police in a better light and will encourage the public generally to support their efforts. On the other hand if the media becomes critical it can do great damage.

The need for reassurance

The police have a duty not only to prevent crime and to investigate it if it should have occurred, but to provide support to the victims of crime and their relatives and other interested parties, including those who fear that crime may be visited upon themselves or their nearest and dearest. In the case of the Yorkshire Ripper, when parents felt that their own daughter might be the next person to be attacked, this need for public reassurance was especially needful; but it applies to all crime.

Victim support

The police need, both for moral and practical reasons, to build a relationship with the victims of crime. Hence the appointment of family liaison officers, the tendency of senior investigating officers to refer to the social impact of the crime at press conferences, and so on. To express sympathy for the victims of a crime is not to lose objectivity, nor to be unable to continue the investigation with the right attitude. The grieving husband who appeals for witnesses to come forward and help the investigation of the murder of his wife, may be himself later arrested for the same crime; but that does not necessarily mean that the earlier actions of the police in promoting a public appeal for information were disingenuous.

The essence of successful policing is to react instantly and flexibly to changing circumstances, and to adopt new priorities accordingly. It is also, to be able to perform more than one task at the same time. The family liaison officer *is* appointed to help the family; *and* may also be a source of useful information to the senior investigating officer (SIO). In the morally complex world of applied policing, these two roles are not incompatible.

The importance of good police work

Finally, the case of the Yorkshire Ripper emphasises the importance of standard police work—with a little bit of imagination. Sutcliffe was caught, and ultimately convicted, because a non-specialist police officer did his job properly, showing enough initiative and discretion to ensure that it was not just a routine to him. Non-specific crime investigation works, and Sutcliffe was likely to be caught eventually. With the advantages of modern information technology, it is to be hoped that similar serial offenders are identified by the system, before routine police work may in any case lead to their capture.

In this context, we note that Steven Wright was arrested for the murder of five women in the Ipswich area in December 2006, and later convicted, as a result of a major inquiry by the Suffolk Constabulary, with national assistance, which rapidly produced results—although we are not entitled to claim that the investigation was so quickly successful, *because* of the reforms that followed the case of the Yorkshire ripper. Police work rarely lends itself to such simple cause and effect analysis.

Wright, who pleaded not guilty, was on the national database for a previous offence, and there was additional forensic evidence linking him to the scenes of crime. He claimed a series of coincidences had put him in the dock, and that the case against him was only circumstantial. The jury at his trial did not agree.

Information, intelligence and evidence

It would seem appropriate at this point to reflect on the difference between information and evidence. All police forces collect *information:* background knowledge about local, national and indeed international criminals, terrorists, drug-smugglers, and so on. Indeed, the ideal of community policing is based on the assumption that every police officer is a primary source of local information. *Intelligence* is information that has been assessed for reliability and accuracy; it has been converted into a form that can be actioned by law enforcement officers. It relates to the present and future, rather than the past.

Intelligence is not *evidence,* which may be used in court; but may be used to lead towards it. The supposition, from an informer, perhaps, that so-and-so is worthy of further attention, is not enough to put that person before a magistrate; but it may be a basis, together with other information, for specific attention to be paid to that person. The resources available to a modern police service are considerable, and their adroit use may lead to the emergence of evidence and the conviction of the offender which is the ultimate goal of crime investigation. (It is not the ultimate goal of the Criminal Justice System, which among other things is to rehabilitate the offender and hope to make him a good citizen; but that is a wider topic, and an area in which the police do not play a leading role, although they may contribute to the process).

Two developments have taken place since the Yorkshire Ripper case, which, although not directly arising as a result of it, have led to the improvement of the investigation of crime in general.

Firstly, there is now a National Intelligence Model (NIM), which provides a format for the systematic exploitation of intelligence. NIM is effectively the business management model for operational policing, and thus includes the investigation of crime under its broader remit. NIM was developed by the ACPO crime committee, the Home Office, and other interested parties such as HM Inspectorate of Constabulary (HMIC), acting in co-operation—an example of how the British police service changes and adapts by a process of liaison. Secondly, it is noticeable that many forces have appointed a senior officer as director of force intelligence, to reflect the importance accorded to this role. Good police work is pro-active as well as re-active, and seeks to systematise, collate and exploit the data that it gathers as a natural part of its general role, in order to investigate crime.

Offender profiling

It is at least arguable that the case of the Yorkshire Ripper might have been resolved more rapidly, if the police had made use (or better use) of the technique of 'offender profiling'. What is offender profiling, and how does it work? Suppose the existence of a serial offender at work. The first difficulty is for the police to recognise that offences A, B, C and D, in locations W, X, Y and Z, were in fact committed, or appear to have been committed, by the same person. Their second task is to identify what characteristics these crimes have in common, which may enable them to identify and arrest the perpetrator. The characteristics will not just include the *modus operandi* of the criminal (which will, in any case, already have helped to suggest that this is a serial offender at work). They will include something about his location, background, education, family circumstances, possible criminal record, mental propensities, and so on, all of which may help the police to identify the most likely suspect, from those people they have already interviewed; *and* to use the offender profile as generated as a basis for further investigation.

Offender profiling is, we would suggest, a mixture of art or craft and science, and an offender profile itself is not evidence. Does offender profiling work? The Yorkshire Ripper, when finally caught, did correspond to some extent to his offender profile: but the profile played no part in his capture. That gives us no conclusion on the usefulness and validity of offender profiling, which remains in the box of options open to SIO in seeking either how to locate the possible offender or how to interview him once arrested.

SIOs need experts in psychology to help them, as well as experts in other subjects; and it is the responsibility of the SIO to make best use of the expert in offender profiling, as with any other specialist adviser.

THE HOME OFFICE AND SCIENTIFIC SUPPORT

The Home Office maintains a strong interest in scientific discoveries and technological breakthroughs of police interest, and commissions work of its own. The responsible unit is the Home Office Scientific Development Branch.

Holmes (the Home Office Large Major Enquiry System) is an example of computer software developed by Home Office scientists, computer experts and police officers working together, and is designed to facilitate the collation and analysis of large amounts of data in relation to a crime or series of crimes. As we have seen, its development was prompted by necessity. Since detectives investigate crimes, it is detectives who must decide when to use Holmes, and learn how to use it.

The creation of the Police National Computer (PNC) was co-ordinated by the Home Office, and it is hard to imagine another development which has had a greater impact upon the police's ability to manage information and prevent and detect crime. We might also note that the Home Office promotes better technical communications. A former Police Information Technology Organisation (PITO) has been absorbed into the National Policing Improvement Agency (NPIA) which has an extraordinarily wide range of responsibilities.

Forensic Science Laboratories

These laboratories, which enable trained scientists from a variety of disciplines to assist the CID in examining the evidence found at the scene of the crime, and much else besides, were set up by the Home Office outside London and have now acquired quasi-commercial (similar to agency) status. Forensic Sciences Services Ltd is a government-owned company which has absorbed the previously separate system maintained by the MPS. (We may note that its competitor is LGC Forensics, and that the privatisation of forensic science has created issues for the police. Previously, advice could be sought without the complication of a commercial motivation influencing what was offered. Now the police must be alert to the possible mismatch in objectives, since the police will wish to minimise the forensic spend and the private provider is in business to make a profit. This problem is not unique to the provision of forensic services to the police, and has been addressed by various means in the public service).

The application of science to crime has yielded immense results, from 19th century techniques such as microscopic analysis, through the early-20th century development of fingerprinting, right up to the present-day development of DNA analysis.

Fingerprinting and other developments

The development and application of fingerprinting (the principle of which can be applied to other parts of the body, such as feet and ears) is an interesting example of an imperial power learning from its possessions overseas. Fingerprinting was in use as a means of identification in Bengal, India in the late 19th century, where the inspector general of police, a colonial civil servant named Sir Edward Henry, made sure that its use was extended to police work. He went on, not by coincidence, to be appointed Assistant Commissioner (Crime) at New Scotland Yard in 1901, and served as Commissioner of the Police of the Metropolis from 1903 to 1918. From its first uses in Bengal, fingerprinting became an integral part of police work first in London and thence throughout the UK and world; a development in which the Home Office played its part.

Other important technological developments have also been assisted by the Home Office Scientific Development Branch, such as technical surveillance or eavesdropping, electronic tracking, and the interception of communications.

In the past, individual chief constables have varied in their attitudes towards technology and technical developments. Hence, forces varied considerably in their approach towards the application of science and technology to the investigation of crime.

Although the UK has still not achieved a national police service, there are a sufficient number of co-ordinating mechanisms in place to ensure that technical advance is relatively uniform across the country, and that no police service remains untouched. Policing, by and large is a 'can do' culture, and police forces want to get results. Very naturally, they have a professional pride, and do not wish to be seen as backward either by the public at large or, perhaps more importantly, by their professional colleagues. They will, therefore, strive to keep abreast of new developments which are of proven benefit to the investigation of crime, and hope to achieve economies of scale in rationalising the use of resources.

DNA and the national DNA-database

DNA profiling was developed by the geneticist Sir Alec Jeffreys of Leicester University from 1984 onwards and has become of worldwide significance. The UK now has the largest DNA database in the world and this development has been of immeasurable significance in the resolution of crime, leading not only to the statistically indisputable identification of the authors of current crimes brought to police attention, but to the solution of previous crimes which had long been thought unsolvable, usually described by the Home Office and the media as 'cold crimes'. DNA identification can also be used for other crime-related purposes, such as identifying whether or not a claimed biological relationship is a true one. It has aroused controversy in its wake. Should everyone be included on the national DNA database?

The creation of the National DNA Database (NDNAD) is an example of a development which is intended to be benign, but which is also a potential source of conflict in the surveillance society of which we are already a part... The existence of NDNAD leads to a clash of principles in reality, which would otherwise remain academic.

An extreme view

Those who want law and order at almost any price will see the NDNAD as a marvellous means to solve crime, and one which should be wholly unfettered. Their ideal position would be to record the DNA of every person resident in or visiting the United Kingdom, who might possibly be suspected of having carried out a crime or who might be involved in doing so in the future; or who may never fall under suspicion, but needs to be included on the database in order to be identified and eliminated as a suspect in any inquiry where unidentified DNA has been discovered.

It will immediately be perceived that no-one can be excluded from such a database, and indeed it has been argued that only a total database would be entirely fair, as we should all be potential suspects, rather than only some of us as chosen on questionable grounds. The existence of such a database must be linked to its speculative searching for the perpetrator of any crime, if it is to justify its purpose and cost...

The current position

At present, the police are able to take DNA from anyone arrested for a criminal offence, and to put that DNA on the national database, whether or not the person is ever charged with a criminal offence. The DNA database is then searched automatically as new crimes are investigated or old crimes re-investigated.

The future

A truly national database would remove the stigma of being recorded on it. We have a right to privacy, and a right to a fair trial on a criminal charge, if the State should find evidence against us; but does that mean that we have a right to commit crimes undetected? The status quo is likely to change until our present qualms about the extension of the data available to the state, to be used both for present purposes and for purposes yet to be discovered, will seem as quaint as the early legislation that required a man to walk in front of a motor car with a red flag. Those changes need to take place as a result of informed public debate and not administrative convenience.

(Villiers, *Police Review*, May 2008)

Case study No 2: The disappearance of Madeleine McCann

This case, which remains unresolved, presents the inescapable characteristics of a *cause celebre;* and illustrates that the task of the police is not just to investigate and resolve crime, but to respond to the pressures of public opinion under the spotlight of the media.

Madeleine McCann disappeared on the evening of Thursday, 3 May 2007 in the resort of Praia da Luz in the Algarve, Portugal, a few days before her fourth birthday. Madeleine was on holiday with her parents, Kate and Gerry McCann, and siblings when she disappeared from an apartment in the central area of the resort. Madeleine's parents have said that they left her unsupervised in a ground floor bedroom with her two-year-old twin siblings while they ate at a restaurant about 120 metres away.

The initial investigation by the Polícia Judiciária (Portuguese criminal investigation police) concluded that she had been abducted. After further investigation, they subsequently stated that she might have died in her room (this hypothesis was believed to be based on forensic evidence). During the investigation there were a number of unconfirmed claimed sightings of Madeleine in Portugal and elsewhere and additional scientific evidence was obtained, although so far it has proved inconclusive.

The investigation involved the cooperation of the British and Portuguese police and demonstrated the differing methodologies employed by each, with regard to such aspects as the amount of information released to the public and the legal status of those involved in the case. The disappearance and its aftermath are notable for the breadth and longevity of the media coverage. This was initially due to the active involvement of the parents in publicising the case and to several awareness-raising campaigns by international celebrities. Interest was heightened when the parents were named as suspects, a status that was soon revised, and appears to have been based on a misinterpretation of technical evidence.

Comment

It is significant that the disappearance of Madeleine McCann, a British subject,took place on foreign territory, thereby enabling the popular British press to wave the Union Jack, and to assert to their own satisfaction that the Portuguese police were unable or unwilling to investigate this case properly, and should have called in the help of Scotland Yard from the start.

The media campaign associated with this case has been truly global. Nevertheless, official international police means of communication, such as Interpol missing persons notices, have still played their part. Many of the basic facts remain in dispute, and it is still not at all clear what happened on 3 May 2007. One is tempted to state, that almost whatever the police do in a media-drenched case such as this, they are bound to be criticised. Whatever in practice may have occurred, an ideal police investigation should have begun as soon as the disappearance was reported and the initial facts had been verified. The police should then have:

- put out an immediate alert to all police and customs units, especially at border posts, informing them of what had occurred and what to look for;
- made an immediate forensic investigation of the scene of the disappearance, sealing it until further notice;
- identified, located and interviewed anyone in the area at the time (the size of the relevant area for enquiries, to be a matter for the judgement of the SIO);
- made door-to-door enquiries in the area, or wider afield, to see what they might discover;
- appealed for further information by every means possible, including making best use of the media;
- appealed for information from relevant informants, through CID conduits;
- looked into the movements of possible suspects at the time of the crime, and investigated the likelihood that they might have been involved (in this case, suspects might have included the known members of any international paedophile organization who were known to abduct children, people with a relevant history of mental illness who were known to be in the area, people known to have a grudge against the McCanns and so on); and
- prepared itself for a lengthy and painstaking campaign, and made the necessary logistical and IT arrangements.

None of these measures would have guaranteed a successful investigation. They might, however, have reduced public criticism. Police work may be a craft, rather than a science; but there are some rules that apply to any investigation.

THE REALITY OF POLICE WORK: DETECTIVE SKILLS

The reality of police work is that the senior detective in a major investigation is at the centre of a bewildering kaleidoscope of shifting facts, rumours and interpretations. He cannot follow one lead or theory whilst at the same time ignoring others; and he must have a 'feel' for what is going on.

Like any good scientist, he is entitled and indeed required to formulate and test working hypotheses, as the enquiry continues and further information comes to light. Was this, perhaps, the work of so-and-so? No, he was in prison at the time. But no, in fact he wasn't: he had been given leave to attend his mother's funeral. Did he go to the funeral? Was he accompanied? Can it be shown that he has, in fact, an infallible alibi? A major police investigation requires the systematic and painstaking examination of an increasing mass of information, any part of which may prove to be of vital signficance.

Inductive and deductive reasoning

If we are able to make a decision by deductive reasoning, a true and valid conclusion may be infallibly derived from true and valid premises. What does that mean? Let us explore further, by means of an example.

- all left-handed, red-haired men are serial killers;
- Tom is a left-handed, red-haired man;
- therefore, Tom must be a serial killer.

The above is an example of a valid but untrue syllogism. The conclusion follows from the premises, but the major premise (that all left-handed, red-haired men are serial killers) is untrue. In fact, we are able to make very few statements about the social world which are universally true, unless they be true by definition. Sir Arthur Conan Doyle, the creator of the world's most famous fictional detective, frequently commits a logical fallacy in his portrayal of the great sleuth. Contrary to what he claims, Sherlock Holmes does not use *deduction:* he uses *induction,*

Inductive reasoning is in essence about probability, and no deduction follows infallibly from its premises. Most police work rests upon induction, and it is especially useful for SIOs. An inductive chain of reasoning might run something as follows (going back to our WAVE information for our example):

- the propensity to violence in young people develops primarily from wrong treatment before the age of three;
- empathy is the single greatest inhibitor of the development of propensity to violence;
- empathy fails to develop when parents or prime carers fail to attune with their infants;
- absence of such parental attunement combined with harsh discipline is a recipe for violent, antisocial offspring;
- John Smith (the example is hypothetical) is a young man whose background indicates that he was less likely to develop the capacity for empathy, than other more fortunate children.

Therefore, there is a certain possibility that John Smith will be both violent and antisocial (and likely to come to police notice); and there is an argument for saying that the police service should pay more attention to people of John Smith's background than others, both in attempting to investigate crime and to prevent its occurrence at the outset. We may note that all this lacks the comforting security of deductive reasoning, and cannot even reach the status of circumstantial evidence. We do not know how John Smith will turn out: we can only make assumptions and test them against the evidence.

Detectives can and must use inductive reasoning if they are to investigate and solve crime—provided that they preserve their professional integrity, maintain the importance of an open mind, and if possible, seek for evidence that falsifies rather than verifies their working assumptions. To seek for evidence that verifies an assumption, rather than to search for evidence that goes against it, may be something very much akin to prejudice; and as human beings, we are easily capable of giving undue credit to the evidence that supports the beliefs we already hold, and undervaluing, belittling or ignoring the evidence that goes against them.

The importance of judgement

Senior detective work is *judgement,* in which the calculations are unique to the case in question, but the experience that lies behind them has been gained from many other cases. The 'Murder Investigation Manual' and other publications may be full of helpful hints, tips and reminders, and any training course must be of advantage; but in the end, the SIO must rely on his own assessment of the situation, the facts as known, and his interpretation of the personalities concerned. More senior police officers know this, having been in that position themselves; their task is to support the SIO, but at the same time to make sure that he is keeping an open mind and running an open, legal, fair and professionally informed investigation, in which objectivity is maintained.

SIO and other detective training

The Police College created as a result of the recommendations of the Police Post-War Reform Committee in 1948 did not offer professional CID training on its curriculum, although it did stress the importance of ethics. Detectives learned their skills on the job, or on the occasional course at a regional detective training centre; and as the largest force, the MPS trained the most detectives. National Police Training was created in 1993, and as a result the National Crime Faculty (NCF) was set up at Bramshill, to include training as one of its responsibilities. This was a bold move with great potential, which, we believe it is fair to say, has not yet been consolidated.

The NCF became part of the National Centre for Policing Excellence, but both were short-lived. SIO and other specialised courses are still on offer, and specialised police training is now an area of somewhat bewildering complexity, in which a variety of agencies carry out a variety of tasks, of which we offer one example. The task of national co-ordination is yet another responsibility of the National Policing Improvement Agency (NPIA).

The National Centre for Applied Learning Technologies (NCALT) was set up as a partnership between the Metropolitan Police Service and Centrex (now NPIA). NCALT claims to be a national leader in Critical Incident simulation training, for which it invented the Hydra and Minerva systems.

Hydra is a syndicate-based command simulation system used to train police officers in the tactical and strategic management of both large-scale critical incidents and major crime investigations such as rape and murder. It allows command officers, who would typically be responsible for managing large teams at such incidents, to work together in syndicates on a common problem within a safe training environment where they can share best practice and exercise their command skills. Hydra has been developed to simulate more protracted incidents and investigations, which may take days or even weeks to resolve.

Minerva has been designed as a real-time command simulation system allowing a simulated incident, emergency or public order-style incident to unfold uninterrupted and in fast-time, from the point of first approach to the point at which effective incident management has been established, typically about two hours. In addition, Minerva is a team-based simulation system allowing for interaction and problem-solving between members of a command team.

Comment

The police service no longer possesses a national crime faculty, nor indeed a combined crime and operations faculty. We believe that its ideal remains to train every senior officer to a set standard, so that he or she cannot undertake a particular task—to act as an SIO, be in charge of public order and safety at a major football match, and so on—unless he can show that he has completed the appropriate course and passed its test. That state of affairs, which would mark the police service as a proper profession, has yet to be reached.

MYTHS AND REALITIES OF CID

We have touched on the realities of the investigation of crime, and it is worth pursuing this theme further. Everyday police work does not address *causes celebre*, and is not crisis driven. Nor is it, very often, what is portrayed in popular fiction. We are all familiar, and indeed over-familiar, with the work of CID from novels, plays, film and television. Inspector Morse of Thames Valley CID is a well-known example of an engrossing personality, whose work is dramatically convincing but in many ways lacks verisimilitude (which it does not require). Real CID work, however, tends to be rather different to what is shown on television. We have already explored in part the vital role played by scientific support, in considering the role of the Home Office. Let us move on to some other factors.

Time and cost

Most major crimes are solved, if they are going to be solved at all, within a matter of weeks. Obtaining evidence from a seized computer may take a little while, as does analysing telephone traffic and getting the information from service providers. However, once all this has been exploited, and if the trail has gone cold, it is unlikely that the crime will be solved.

Naturally, hope is not given up; and dedicated investigation over a lengthy period has paid off. There are unsolved crimes which are later re-investigated and solved, especially if technology advances to the point where old evidence can be re-evaluated, as with DNA (see above).

Moreover, some criminal offenders do feel both guilt and shame, and will confess to a crime years after it was committed—although in such cases there may have been no police input. There are cases which remain in the public eye, for one reason or another, long after interest might have been expected to fade: the murder of Stephen Lawrence (22 April 1993) and the disappearance of Madeleine McCann

(3 May 2007) (noted above) are conspicuous examples, although we must also ac-knowledge neither of these two cases has been resolved. Nevertheless, crimes can and do become more difficult to solve as time goes by, and the most likely sources of success are exhausted. Investigating crime should be approached in a businesslike way and the cost of a continued investigation must be weighed against its likelihood of success, unless there are other factors to be taken into account, such as political considerations—a loosely defined phrase. Is it right that the murder of a well-known public figure such as the television presenter Jill Dando (shot dead on 26 April 1999) should receive greater attention, and thereby resources, than the murder of someone who was not a celebrity? The issue is debatable on moral grounds; but it is certainly the case that where a murder has given rise to major public concern, the police are obliged to take that concern seriously; and the life of a celebrity may also offer greater avenues for inquiry.

The allocation of police resources is not an exact science, and never will be. Nev-ertheless, it is not an irrational or arbitrary process, and requires the same judgement as police work itself.

Teamwork

Good detective work rests on teamwork. Detectives usually operate in pairs, and often in teams; and it is dedicated teamwork, and following set procedures, rather than individual brilliance which tends, more often than not, to solve a crime. The role of the SIO is to co-ordinate the activity of the team, rather than to solve the crime single-handed.

Scientific support

Solving crimes also rests very much on the detailed and systematic use of forensic evidence, rather than the methods so popular in fiction. Sherlock Holmes, admit-tedly, was a pioneer of forensic examination, and Conan Doyle even gives him credit for a monograph on the characteristics of different types of cigar-ash; but the facili-ties available to the modern forensic science laboratory are of a different order to what can be discovered by a sleuth armed merely with a magnifying glass and an active curiosity.

The role of the crime scene examiner/scenes of crimes officer (SOCO) is critical. Far more serious crimes are solved by forensic evidence than anything else. With the pervasive presence of solicitors in interviews, the importance of interviewing has decreased; and it might be argued that it is the forensic practitioner, rather than the leading detective, who is the key figure in modern crime investigation. Nevertheless, the process of investigation needs to be co-ordinated, and prepared for use in court; and it is the responsibility of the SIO, working in conjunction with the Crown Prosecution Service, to ensure due process.

To search for the truth?

Many police officers have argued that the purpose of a criminal investigation is to search for the truth. Criminal barristers, on the other hand, tend to argue that the purpose of a criminal trial is to find out whether or not there is sufficient evidence to convict Suspect A of Crime B, beyond reasonable doubt, under the adversarial system of justice. These two objectives are not the same, and are part of the cause of the antipathy between the police service and the law which is evident on some occasions. It is the police who deal with the victims of crime, and are therefore, perhaps, more highly motivated than the barrister, to ensure that the guilty do not go unpunished: whereas the barrister may argue that it is just under such circumstances that the integrity of the investigation must be preserved.

In contrast, for example under the French system of investigation, the senior detective is officially directed by a judicial officer in any major criminal investigation and the discretion of the police is therefore officially circumscribed. The British system allows more latitude to the police. However, the police no longer conduct their own prosecutions, as they used to do. Since the creation of the Crown Prosecution Service in 1985, they present their best case to the CPS, whose task it also is, since 2003, to decide whether or not to bring a prosecution. CPS policy is to make this decision by applying certain criteria but, ultimately, on the basis of the likelihood of conviction. The CPS is spending public money in bringing a prosecution, and cannot mount a hopeless case for the moral satisfaction to which this may give rise.

The police investigation, therefore, must be as thorough and accountable as possible, both to persuade the CPS to proceed and to withstand technical objections by the defence, who will legitimately seek any legal means to ensure the failure of the case against any client who pleads not guilty. Disclosure, whereby the police may be required to produce any documentation acquired in the process of the investigation (and which could be used by the defence to counteract the prosecution) can be a contentious issue, and certainly adds to the clerical duties of the police service; this is not an issue that is likely to be raised in a television drama, but is of vital importance to successful police work.

The role of the police in carrying out an investigation is therefore part discretionary and part circumscribed; and we should mention that they are not obliged to mount an investigation of every allegation brought to their attention. Through case law, it is clear that the police are not obliged to investigate an allegation of crime if they judge that this would not be productive and would be a waste of scarce resources—for example, if the allegation has already been investigated elsewhere, such as by the Parliamentary Commissioner for Standards, on MPs' expenditure.

The presumption of innocence

It is a tradition of the Common Law that an accused person is innocent unless and until proved guilty; a presumption which is not expressly stated in the European

Convention On Human Rights, but which underlies Article 6 of the Convention, which confers the right to a fair trial. What this means, in practice, is that the accused does not have to prove his innocence: the prosecution has to prove his guilt, beyond reasonable doubt. The so-called right to silence is an interesting issue arising from this tradition. The accused need not answer allegations which are made against him, and failure to answer cannot generally be used as proof of his guilt—although the right to silence is not absolute and, since, 2003 adverse inferences can be drawn from silence before or at a trial, something that a suspect or accused person is warned about at appropriate stages, including by way of what is known as a police caution as to his rights at the time of arrest. Adverse inferences can be drawn from silence, by a jury or magistrates in certain circumstances. The Serious Fraud Office (SFO) has special powers and it can be an offence to fail to answer questions in certain circumstances.

We may note that although television detectives do not necessarily ignore this presumption, their methods of interrogation are on the whole far more rough-and-ready than would ever be officially accepted as part of a real criminal investigation. Fair enough: real investigations, like real trials, can be very dull. The purpose of a television drama is to entertain. The purpose of a criminal investigation is rather different.

The police interview

The formal interview is an important means for the police to investigate crime, if perhaps not as important as it used to be. Interviewing should be prepared for beforehand, and follow a recognised format which leads to a clear result; not something that always occurred in the past, when some police interviews led to false confessions or other improprieties, and thence to unsafe convictions; and many police interviews were poorly planned in a general sense, resulting in unclear results. There is now a national training programme.

It is clearly disadvantageous if the proof of an accused person's guilt rests purely on his confession, and other evidence should be sought. Some jurisdictions require other evidence. In Scotland for example, a criminal conviction cannot rest upon a confession alone.[2]

Police interviews are now tape-recorded, and if possible video-taped. This assists both sides in promoting a professional investigation.

The use of informers

Informers are highly important in the solution of crime, and likely to become more so under the influence of the doctrine of 'intelligence-led policing' (ILP). The ar-

---

2. Corroboration is required as a matter of law or practice in a small number of situations: as to which the reader should consult works on criminal law and the law of evidence.

gument of ILP is, in essence, that the police should concentrate their resources on resolving significant crime by the most effective means, rather than paying undue attention to relatively minor offences that the public finds irritating. The doctrine is strongly associated with the former Chief Constable of Kent Police (1993 to 2003) and President of the Association of Chief Police Officers (2001 to 2003), Sir David Phillips. Under it, the use of informers should be maximized as a cost-effective way to resolve series and serious crime.

Consequences of the Human Rights Act 1998

The 1998 Act, which came into force in 2000, prompted much discussion as to the rights and obligations of the State in regard to criminal investigations. It articulated a right to privacy, which even suspected criminals had a right to enjoy. But the right is a qualified one, and the State (and therefore, its medium, the police or any other designated investigative agency) has a right and indeed a duty to violate privacy in order to investigate crime, provided that its actions are legal, necessary and proportionate.

In order to regulate the invasion of privacy and to render the process lawful, the government passed the Regulation of Investigatory Powers Act 2000 (RIPA), under which officers of the rank of superintendent formally authorise surveillance operations and which created the acronym CHIS (dee the *Glossary*). RIPA has regulated and formalised what was once informal practice.

Selecting and training the detectives

What sort of person makes a good detective?:

> There are certain specialist posts, particularly in the detective branch, the requisite qualities for which differ in some respects from the qualities needed in an ordinary police officer; in some quarters of our large cities, for example, an intimate knowledge of the district and its inhabitants might be of more value to a detective than a high degree of general knowledge and police ability. Moreover, some detectives owe their success to a 'flair' which it is difficult to define but is not necessarily accompanied by any particular aptitude for the normal kind of police studies. Again, a detective officer, even of fairly high rank, is not called upon to exercise the same quality of leadership as the officer whose main duty is to organize and command a large body of men. (Police Post-War Committee (1946))

The CID has traditionally been regarded as a craft, and crafts tend to be self-selecting, and to create an aura of mystery around themselves. There is still a distinct sub-culture to CID, which is regarded as an elite in policing, at least by many of those who have joined it. Detectives, by tradition, never wear uniform, unless on a command course at Bramshill; and this specialism generates a somewhat false air of glamour, quite unlike normal policing.

Indeed, the work of a detective is different to the work of the ordinary constable, and does emphasise the importance of initiative and discretion, in many cases. However, the majority of detectives spend most of their time in the office, preparing and reviewing cases, and not meeting informers or taking part in high-speed car chases or making high profile arrests.

Moreover, the comparative attractiveness of CID work has lessened with the advent of Special Priority Payments (frequently paid to uniform officers on shifts) and flexible shift systems (ten-hour shifts, more days off) for uniform response officers.

Sir John (now Lord) Stevens, the high profile MPS commissioner from 2000 to 20005, wrote in his autobiography that there is definitely an instinct or 'nose' to being a good detective, and that his 'nose' had led him to make many successful arrests when patrolling the streets of London as a young detective. If there is such a thing as a detective's 'nose', its acquisition is certainly not taught on CID courses; and we should prefer to highlight Sir John's remark, that his instinct in pursuing any high level investigation was to find out the facts, and see where they led him. That would seem an admirable policy for any detective.

Direct entry for specialists

The French, amongst other continental police forces, recruit people directly into their equivalent of CID (which is of an *officially* higher status than normal policing), on the basis of their aptitude for the work; but the UK has resisted that policy, and all British recruits to CID must have served in uniform first. The advantages of the British system are claimed to be as follows:

- the detective (or detective aide, when he is first appointed and on probation) knows what the uniformed constable does, and has had a general police training;
- senior CID officers have a chance to weigh up new uniformed constables generally, and to decide who may be suited to work in CID; and
- interchange of manpower between CID and uniformed officers at various levels helps to break down the psychological barriers between the two organizations and to remind them that they share the same overall aim. It is of particular benefit to potential senior officers to have had practical experience of work both inside and outside of the CID.

The major disadvantage of the British system, especially when linked to limited tenure of office, is that it wastes the advantages of specialisation. Much of detective work is extremely specialised. Work in computer crime, or fraud, may require a particularly high level of acquired skill in its practitioners. Typically, a fraud case may be highly complicated, demand a detailed knowledge of company law, and take years to bring to court. Those who specialise in such work will need specialised training and lengthy experience to prove their worth, which would be wasted were they then posted to other duties. If, however, they remain with their specialisation, then their chances of promotion are significantly diminished.

Under the French system, the computer or fraud specialist is recruited direct into CID, and practises his chosen skill immediately. he is a specialist already, and does not need further training; and the system recognizes and rewards him for his speciality. It is a significant advantage.

National Crime Squad and National Criminal Intelligence Service
Regional crime squads were first set up in the 1970s, and were an important development. Criminals did not (and do not) necessarily confine themselves to working in one police force's area, and there was a considerable advantage to be derived from setting up regional crime squads, consisting of specially chosen and highly experienced detectives, who could pursue their enquiries into patterns of major crime, without being unduly troubled by divisional or police force boundaries.

These detectives did not have the normal case-load to carry, and could therefore be flooded into an area where there was a significant hope of solving a significant crime. Their remit included drugs.

The National Criminal Intelligence Service (NCIS) was set up in 1992 to co-ordinate and assist the investigation of both national and international crime and criminals in so far as they affected the United Kingdom. The NCIS investigated drugs offences as well as other types of crime, and contained customs officers as well as police officers.

In 1997, the National Crime Squad (NCS) was created. In 2006, both units were united in a new Serious and Organized Crime Agency (SOCA), to be joined by specialist investigators from HM Customs & Excise and UK Immigration.[3]

THE SERIOUS ORGANIZED CRIME AGENCY (SOCA)

SOCA was an attempt by government to tackle serious and organized crime believed to be beyond the reach and resources of previously existing law-enforcement agencies. Although it has been described as the British Federal Bureau of Investigation (FBI), it is significantly different: the real, USA FBI has greater powers, a higher status, and is an integral part of a federal system of government. Nevertheless,

---

3. Which later became part of HM Revenue & Customs and the Border Agency respectively,

SOCA is a highly interesting development. SOCA's priorities are drug trafficking and organized immigration crime.

The assessment of the effectiveness of any new national organization such as SOCA is always bound to generate interest, and probably controversy. The Asset Recovery Agency, established under the Proceeds of Crime Act 2002 to co-ordinate activity across the UK in recovering criminally obtained assets was found to be costing more money than it recovered, and in April 2008 was disbanded as a separate entity and its mission of tracking-down and recovering the proceeds of crime absorbed into SOCA.

The Serious Fraud Office, which has been in existence for rather longer, was criticized in 2008 for its declining effectiveness, and has a similar problem in proving value for money; although it is not yet clear what may be the long-term consequences of this for the SFO itself.

Assessment

It is to be hoped that SOCA will prove its enduring worth. The problem it faces is not in knowing that drugs-trafficking and organized immigration crime are major problems for British society, and that to combat them effectively is a worthwhile aim. The major problem is that both these activities are essentially international in scope and therefore any successful campaign against them must be the result of well co-ordinated international co-operation. To this end, many of SOCA's personnel are stationed abroad; and only a sustained long-term investment is likely to produce results. Co-operation is the name of the game, and all government agencies, including the secret services MI5, MI6 and GCHQ, have needed to find a way to co-operate and to share information, which they may have previously found difficult or indeed impossible. International liaison, for example with Interpol and Europol, creates further challenges.

CYBERCRIME

We are living in a period of profound technological change. Developments in IT, including the internet, have created both new opportunities for criminals to commit crime and for the police to detect crimes and bring offenders to justice. Let us follow the example of the National Hi-Tech Crime Unit (now also absorbed into SOCA (above)), and classify crime as falling into one of two types:

A. Crimes which predate computers, but which the new era has made it easier for criminals to commit, or has enabled them to carry out in new ways.

Old crimes, new ways ('old wine in new bottles')
Examples would include fraud, theft, money laundering, sexual harassment, hate crime and pornography.

B. Crimes which are only possible because of new IT and in particular the internet.

New crimes, new ways
Examples would include hacking, viral attacks and website defacement; and we may separate B from A by means of the so-called transformation test. Could this crime still occur, if the relevant IT were not available?)

Crimes under B take place in cyberspace and have naturally been labelled 'cybercrime".[4] This raises various issues for the police, such as:

- who polices cyberspace, which is outside any normal territorial jurisdiction?
- where is the trial to take place for cybercrime, if anywhere?;
- what if something is a crime in country A, but not in country B?;
- what is to count as evidence, to be used in framing what charges?; and
- who pays for policing cyberspace, and what proportion of its resources should a police service allocate to this sort of crime?

Here are some of the relevant considerations for the UK:

- of the 140,000 police officers in the UK, it is estimated that less than 500 have the specialist skills and knowledge to combat computer-based crime;
- the 2008 ACPO National Strategic Assessment states that 90% of e-crime is not reported;
- the estimated value of on-line fraud is £52 billion worldwide - believed now to be greater than that generated by illegal drug sales; and
- evidence is beginning to emerge that people are becoming more worried about criminals attacking them through their computers than burglars breaking into their home. This is probably a reflection that burglary is a crime that has gone down substantially whilst e-crime has gone up and is a rational assessment of the risks of being a victim of crime.

---

4. Or sometimes e-crime.

Imagine ...

Imagine that you are sitting at home, reading your e-mails, and receive what seems to be a very interesting offer from what appears to be an official and indeed a highly prestigious West African source. All you need to do is to supply a few mundane but very necessary details, and you will be the lucky—no, the deserved *recipient of untold riches ...*

A robust argument would be that the victim of such a scam has only himself to blame if he is deceived, and it is not the purpose of the (criminal) law to prevent people from being victims of their own folly. This may be a high technology crime; but fraud has been with us for a very long time (as has identity theft, by one means or another) and there is nothing essentially new here.

Why take IT-related crime more seriously?

- IT-related crime, and indeed financial crime more generally, creates major problems for the economy and needs to be addressed as a strategic priority. Banking, industry and commerce need to rest upon secure foundations, and it is necessary to police them. Commercial organizations that encourage their customers to believe in the reliability of security systems which are not in fact secure must accept some measure of blame, and responsibility for, the consequences—which they may have tried to evade. Nevertheless, the police still need to be involved.
- the police must adjust to the real needs of the 21st century, and cease to make the most loudly articulated local views their top priority for action. Policing should be both intelligence-led and locally accountable (admittedly, a difficult combination). It must address fraud, so-called 'white-collar' crime, and IT crime as well as the other claims on its priorities.
- cybercrime itself creates new ways to make victims' lives miserable, for example by electronic stalking. This crime has nothing to do with high-level financial affairs and everything to do with low-level human misery and the police can and should do something about it. To do so, they need technical awareness.

We have referred previously to the importance of preventing crime before it occurs, rather than attempting to investigate it after the event. Cybercrime emerges from the interaction between new technology and human imagination, perverted by wickedness. Just as new technology presents opportunities for crime, so it also presents opportunities for the resolution of that crime (and for the resolution of crime in general). The police need to be in on the ground floor, as it were: taking an interest in new developments before their criminal possibilities are seen and exploited by the criminal element. That interest is a strategic investment which will pay increasing dividends.

In his thoughtful analysis of cybercrime, Majid Yar (*Cybercrime and Society,* Sage Publications, 2006) presents a fourfold possible classification system for such crimes, and refers to crimes against:

- the person;
- property
- morality; and
- the State.

Yar's inclusive classification is a useful one. Cybercrime can affect every aspect of police work.

RIGHT VERSUS RIGHT

The clash between the right to privacy and the right to freedom of expression is a matter of ongoing debate. In investigating the private lives of prominent individuals, newspapers may claim that it is in the public interest that some aspects of their private lives be exposed.[5] The celebrities in question may claim that they have the same right to privacy as any other citizen. The public may be interested in something; but that does not mean that to satisfy their perhaps prurient curiosity is in the public interest.

Changing mores

Consider the private life of a Government Minister. Is it in the public interest that he be exposed as a homosexual, something which is true but which he had sought to keep private? When adult male homosexuality was illegal, it could have been argued that the matter should be raised for several reasons, including that:

- the Minister was, presumably, breaking the law; and
- in doing so, or indeed in leading a secret life whether or not he was breaking the law, he was exposing himself to blackmail and his government to potential embarrassment.

Adult male homosexuality in private was decriminalised in 1967 and the arguments for exposure are now less persuasive, even if they might still be raised.

---

5. In July 2008 Max Mosley was awarded £60,000 and costs against the *News of the World* in a privacy case involving a Nazi-style orgy and later started out on a campaign to establish a general right to privacy.

Confidentiality

As a result of their legitimate professional activities, police officers tend to discover information about members of the public that those members of the public would prefer to remain private; and the police are expected to use their discretion in respecting confidentiality.

Suppose, for example, that A's alibi in regard to crime B is, that at the time of the crime, he was engaged in an adulterous affair with C. The police check the story out with C, perhaps against her will. Should the police then broadcast to D, C's husband, that C has been having an affair with A? Surely not. Adultery is not a crime and the police had no reason to investigate C's affairs, other than to check A's alibi. The need to respect confidentiality is usually cited in ethical codes; and the abuse of police access to privileged information is a disciplinary offence.[6]

The limits to freedom of expression

The right to freedom of expression is not absolute. Police powers to restrict that right must depend on the perceived circumstances. Consider the following contrast.

> A respected academic, in examining the foundations of a set of religious beliefs, discovers, or claims to have discovered, that some of the statements made by its founder are fraudulent. He publishes his views in a learned journal of limited circulation (it may also be accessed via the internet, by those who wish to pay). No police action follows.

> The same academic, having, as it happens, had rather too much to drink, finds himself in a neighbourhood where there is a concentration of adherents of the religion in question. He becomes involved in an argument with some of those locals, and puts forward the views he has already articulated in print. Hostility is expressed and a confrontation develops. Others join the group and threaten violence. The academic redoubles his arguments.

> A passing policeman arrests him for a breach of the peace, and removes him from the scene.

---

6. Principle 7 of the current ethical code refers to confidentiality, and states that police officers (should) treat information with respect and access or disclose it only for a legitimate police purpose.

Comment

We would assume that the reasonable person would agree with the police re-action on both occasions (although there may be others who might also have been arrested on the second occasion, depending upon circumstances). The views that the academic is expressing may be substantially the same, but the circumstances are very different. He has a right to freedom of expression: but that does not extend to the right to shout 'Fire!' if there is not one in a crowded auditorium.

CONCLUSION

Times change, and the CID changes with them. The CID began as the first special-ised sub-unit within policing, and has given birth to other sub-units as new needs have emerged and old ones have been re-addressed. Crimes which make little public impact, or which are intrinsically difficult to solve, or require specialised investment, will remain, we suspect, comparatively under-resourced; and the crime that catches the public's eye will always attract major police attention. It is therefore right and proper that environmental crime should rise up the agenda, and that police forces (or other law enforcement agencies charged with specialist tasks) should now be devoting resources to this vital area of public concern.

Some crimes may appear to be of a different order to what has gone on before—suicide bombings in London, for example, as the result of the radicalisation of Is-lamic youth (and converts to radical Islam). But we would suggest that although the motives of the bomber may be new to British society, the means to combat this sort of crime, which requires not only excellent intelligence work but an equal commit-ment to the value of community policing, are not new.

New technology presents new opportunities to criminals. For example, internet connexions and websites provide a means whereby paedophiles (if necessary, oper-ating under an assumed identity) can 'groom' potential victims, whom they could not otherwise have contacted. Indeed, the internet itself provides opportunities for identity theft which would not otherwise have existed. But the advance of technol-ogy provides opportunities to the police as well as to the criminal—the intelligence to be derived, for one simple and telling example, from the adroit exploitation of mobile phone records—and we are not convinced that the advantages are all to the criminal, for advances in IT offer formidable opportunities to a progressive police service such as those provided by Global Satellite Positioning (GSP). (The UK now has its first directly internet-related specialist internet-based policing agency, the Child Exploitation and Online Protection Agency (CEOP).

The British police service, like others, must remain alert to changes in technology as in other areas, and their implications for policing. They show every sign of being so aware; and whilst there remains a case for a national police service with a national detective branch and national crime faculty, so that standards may be set and maintained as with any other national enterprise, we suspect that such reforms will remain in the indefinite future.

Terrorism

Terrorism

Terrorism is clearly one of the major problems facing any police service, in that it is a cause of huge public fear and uncertainty. Moreover, if the police exceed or abuse their powers in combating terrorism, they will be roundly criticised for doing so. On the other hand, the British public appears to accept that terrorism:

- is a challenge to the public safety as a whole, and the police need to address it with vigour;
- requires special counter-measures, which will restrict civil liberties; and
- is a genuine challenge to good policing, and the police will make mistakes in dealing with it,

MODERN TERRORISM LEGISLATION

The practice of terrorism has expanded from the actions of the IRA to the activities of Islamist terrorists, taking in other groups en route. To explore how terrorism may be defined (and thereby countered), we begin with this century's legislation, which shows the current response to the contemporary threat of terrorism .

The Terrorism Act 2000

Terrorism is defined under the 2000 Act so as to encompass the 'the use or threat of action' where 'the use or threat is made for the purpose of advancing a political, religious or ideological cause'. Such action must also fall within section 1(2) of the Act, i.e. must:

a. involve serious violence against a person,
b. involve serious damage to property,
c. endanger a person's life, other than that of the person committing the action,
d. create a serious risk to the health or safety of the public or a section of the public, or
e. be designed seriously to interfere with or seriously to disrupt an electronic system.

We may also note that under section 1(3) of the 2000 Act the use or threat of action falling within (a)-(d) above which involves the use of firearms or explosives amounts to terrorism whether or not the use or threat is designed to influence the government or to intimidate the public or a section of the public. The relevant events may take place abroad as well as on home soil: it is still terrorism.

Further legislation followed the 2000 Act, which we summarise below based on Home Office explanatory materials. The Home Office has also noted that the legislation goes beyond countering terrorism and also serves other purposes.

Anti-Terrorism, Crime and Security Act 2001 (ATCSA)

The ATCSA was introduced in order to provide stronger powers to the police to investigate and prevent terrorist activity and other serious crime.

According to the Home Office, the measures were intended to:

- cut off terrorist funding;
- ensure that government departments and agencies could collect and share information required for countering the terrorist threat;
- streamline relevant immigration procedures;
- ensure the security of the nuclear and aviation industries;
- improve security of dangerous substances that might be targeted/used by terrorists;
- extend police powers available to relevant forces; and
- ensure that we could meet our European obligations in the area of police and judicial co-operation and our international obligations to counter bribery and corruption.

The Prevention of Terrorism Act 2005

This Act introduced control orders (see *Glossary*): a form of restriction of liberty which does not amount to imprisonment (and which under a totalitarian regime would be called house arrest). That Act allows for them to be made against any suspected terrorist, whether a UK national or a non-UK national, or whether the terrorist activity is international or domestic. The Home Secretary is required to report to Parliament as soon as reasonably possible after the end of the relevant three-month period on how control order powers have been exercised during that time.

The Terrorism Act 2006

The 2006 Act specifically aims to make it more difficult for extremists to abuse 'the freedoms we cherish' (original Home Office wording), in order encourage others to commit terrorist acts. It creates a number of new offences. It makes it a criminal offence to commit:

- acts preparatory to terrorism
  This aims to capture those planning serious acts of terrorism.

- encouragement to terrorism

  This makes it a criminal offence to directly or indirectly incite or encourage others to commit acts of terrorism. This will include the glorification of terrorism, where this may be understood as encouraging the emulation of terrorism.

- dissemination of terrorist publications

  This will cover the sale, loan, or other dissemination of terrorist publications. This will include those publications that encourage terrorism, and those that provide assistance to terrorists.

- terrorist training offences

  This makes sure that anyone who gives or receives training in terrorist techniques can be prosecuted. The Act also criminalises attendance at a place of terrorist training.

The 2006 Act also made amendments to existing legislation, including:

- introducing warrants to enable the police to search any property owned or controlled by a terrorist suspect;
- extending terrorism stop and search powers to cover bays and estuaries;
- extending police powers to detain suspects after arrest for up to 28 days (though periods of more than two days must be approved by a judicial authority);
- improved search powers at ports; and
- increased flexibility of the proscription regime, including the power to proscribe groups that glorify terrorism.

Comment

Much of this legislation, in all four acts, is a response to Islamist terrorism, which we now explore.

Islamist Terrorism

Islamist terrorism differs from what has been experienced before, for example in terrorist actions by the IRA, in at least as follows:

- it marks the advent of suicide bombing as a laudable and indeed glorified choice, rather than a risk to be avoided if possible;
- it is marked by the absence of warning and the intention to commit unpreventable

mass destruction;
- there is an absence of terrorist demands, except in so far as their actions have some link to a globalised conflict;
- the background of the terrorists does not include a link to criminality, so far as we are aware; and
- it is associated with the idea of 'radicalisation'.

There is no doubt that Islamist terrorism presents a major threat to British and other societies. Indeed, it has been declared *the* major threat by all relevant agencies, and therefore their priority. Does that mean that any measures can be justified to counter Islamist terrorism? May the police act as they see fit, against what has been described as an unprecedented threat? Clearly not.

Counter-terrorism

To prevent terrorism's success requires several things:

- the right political, social and economic policies;
- a well-organised and professional police service, which includes an effective intelligence department;
- good fortune—as the detailed study of any counter-terrorist operation will reveal; and
- a clear idea of what it is that needs to be protected, and what measures cannot be used to do so—such as torturing suspects.

Terrorism nothing new

Terrorism is nothing new—the Special Irish Branch of the MPS was founded in 1886—and there is little new about the principles of counter-terrorism. Some citizens, whether politicians or police officers, will always seek more powers, in order to combat a threat which is no longer hypothetical but real. Others will place an abiding emphasis upon the liberties that are being defended, and oppose the need of the state to increase its powers to the point where we no longer live in a free society.

Is there a solution to the threat of terrorism? Clearly, not an easy one: but we believe that it places an even greater emphasis on the need for policing by consent. Here as elsewhere, the supposed alternative between community and intelligence-led policing is a false one. No-one becomes an active, practising terrorist overnight; and a police service that is trusted by the community has a better chance of identifying the terrorist and neutralizing the threat that he represents, than a police service that is simply relying on the latest technology to do so—no matter how tempting the possibilities that modern technology (noted in *Chapter 6*) may seem to offer.

A Bill before Parliament at the time of writing proposes powers re the plotting of emails and internet use and enhancements to surveillance and interception of communications powers to enable the foiling of terrorist plots via intelligence and material that may justify an arrest, raid or detention but may not be capable of being used in court. Such matters stress the sensitive nature of policing in this area and the pace of change.

Regulating Police Behaviour:
Ethics, Discipline and Human Rights

Regulating Police Behaviour:
Ethics, Discipline and Human Rights

Ethics implies a fundamental choice. We face a conflict between right and wrong, or between two rights; and we do not know what to do. Police work presents many such challenges; but we should not, perhaps, exaggerate the ethical dilemmas of policing. Most police officers and support staff in a State that respects fundamental human rights, upholds the Rule of Law, and practises some form of democratic government, should be able to form a clear view as to what it is possible to do in most circumstances, without undue stress either in terms of decision-making powers or matters of conscience. Police work is sometimes difficult and sometimes unpredictable; but it is not always so.

Annex A to this chapter contains a number of hypotheticals for the reader to ponder, which may indicate some of the situations where it is not so clear as to what should be done. We are indebted to *Police Review* for their kind permission to reproduce some of this material, which appeared in one form or another in that journal. We would recommend to readers that they consider these cases at their leisure, before reading on.

ETHICAL ANALYSIS

What do the cases in *Annex A* have in common? The first two cases are historical, and it is always difficult to know what people would have felt, who were brought up under very different circumstances to our own. Nevertheless, if we are to believe that there is something universal about ethics, time, place and culture may differ, but the essential principles remain the same.

Do they? Our first comment is to question that assumption. Not all our readers, we suspect, will find all the hypotheticals ethically challenging; and not all our readers will perceive the same challenge.

Secondly, ethical challenges may be a challenge to character, rather than being an ethical dilemma as such. We know what we should be like, as police officers, for it is indicated in the statement of common purpose and values that is quoted later in this chapter, or the police code of ethics. The difficulty lies, in living up to that challenge. We want to clear the high-jump, but the bar may be too high.

Thirdly, ethical challenges may present a genuine ethical dilemma. What do we mean by that? A choice of courses of action, either of which could be justified on ethical criteria, is an ethical dilemma; and perhaps we can most easily illustrate this with an argument from government expenditure. Let us suppose, that a government has to decide how to spend a windfall tax, and has clarified three main options. Many schools are in disrepair, and in urgent need of attention. Many National Health Service (NHS) hospitals are dirty, and more money could usefully be spent on medical hygiene. Thirdly, the nation is over-committed abroad and needs to increase its defence expenditure if fewer lives are to be lost. Each of these options is valid, and each could do with a detailed investigation as to how the money could most wisely be spent in order to achieve maximum benefit. What is not in doubt, however, is that each is a worthy objective, and that to choose between them must in the end be just that: a choice.

No 'ready reckoner' on ethics: The analogy from medical practice

The medical profession recognises, through the work of the professional ethics committee of the General Medical Council (GMC), that there is no 'ready reckoner' on ethics. Ethical problems and dilemmas need to be addressed as they arise, by the group of dedicated and professional people who are immediately concerned with their resolution. They may disagree. They may view ethical problems in different ways, and from different standpoints. They may reach a solution about patient *y*, which does not appear entirely consistent with the way in which they previously resolved the case of patient *x*; for circumstances alter cases and their solutions. And they must, of course, take into account the views of the patient: for we have moved away, by and large, from the era of benevolent paternalism into the more challenging arena of informed consent.

A group of conscientious and dedicated practitioners who are determined to reach an ethically justifiable solution by means of an open and honest discussion that takes into account the particular features of a case, and who may have different personal values, will not be afraid of disagreement: but they will in the end reach an individual solution to an individual case which is compatible with the general principles of their profession.

The essence of professional decision-making is to be able to reach a robust and defensible solution, based on the application of clear and consistent principles to the facts as known at the time, supported by the moral courage to do what may be legitimately criticised from another perspective.

Professional solutions to everyday problems

Police officers are not trained to achieve technically-based solutions to technical problems, as might engineers or surgeons; and they are not responsible for deciding the priorities of government expenditure. The problems that the police service faces are the problems of the public writ large, such as the vandalism, petty crime and persistent burglary that have destroyed the quality of life on a housing estate. In such a situation, the police can only operate with public consent; and one of the most challenging aspects of police work in such circumstances is to find out what the public wants and will approve, especially in a diverse community.

DECIDING SUCCESS

Let us consider the area of the prevention and investigation of crime on a housing estate, and how to define and recognise a successful policy. Successful crime prevention is, at least in theory, easy to measure: there is no crime.

However, there are at least four major snags here. Firstly, real and reported crime may not coincide. Secondly, crime may be displaced or diverted rather than prevented by crime prevention measures such as deterrent patrolling. Thirdly, a negative effect cannot be conclusively established since we cannot prove a causal link. If burglaries decline in a certain area, and if we have increased foot patrols in that area, then we may be tempted to argue that increased foot patrols caused the decline in burglaries. However, there may have been other reasons; or the decline may have been a random (i.e. uncaused) event. Fourthly, crime prevention cannot be achieved by the police acting alone. They must act in co-operation with other agencies in order to address the causes as well as the manifestation of crime and disorderly behaviour.

We must therefore find a number of ways to measure (or perhaps a better word would be to estimate) the effectiveness of crime prevention; and a qualitative survey of the effectiveness of police work in reducing crime and fear of crime, may be as or more important than a quantitative survey. Crime investigation also gives rise to problems in the definition and assessment of success. What is successful crime investigation? Here are two possibilities, and we would suggest that a successful crime investigation policy works towards resolving the two, but never abandons integrity.

1. Results
The crime is detected:

- and the criminal charged, prosecuted and sentenced;
- and the criminal charged and prosecuted: the prosecution fails, for reasons which are not to the discredit of the Police Service;
- but no charges are brought, for reasons which are not to the discredit of the Police Service; or
- as above, with the addition that police resources have been used as efficiently as possible in detecting the crime.

2. Process

- Officially prescribed procedures are followed in full.
- Victims and others involved in the criminal justice process (such as the accused) are fully satisfied with the process followed.
- Human rights are fully respected.
- The process accords with the highest moral standards.
- There are no complaints; or, any complaints are fully resolved.

ETHICAL FRAMEWORKS AND FOUNDATIONS

The oath of office
All police officers are sworn in as constables by taking an oath of attestation (or making an affirmation) as follows:

> I do solemnly and sincerely declare and affirm that I will well and truly serve the Queen in the office of constable, with fairness, integrity, diligence and impartiality, upholding fundamental human rights and according equal respect to all people; and that I will, to the best of my power, cause the peace to be kept and preserved and prevent all offences against people and property; and that while I continue to hold the said office I will, to the best of my skill and knowledge, discharge all the duties thereof faithfully according to law.

There is as yet no equivalent declaration for police community support officers (PCSOs) and support staff as part of the wider police family. The distinction between 'sworn' and 'unsworn' police staff is important in legal terms, as sworn police officers have greater statutory and inherent powers. However, all members of the police family need to feel that they are working to a common purpose under shared values, and one of the ways of creating a sense of unity would be by a common declaration.

Codes of discipline and ethics
The discipline code is an essential part of maintaining the ethical fabric of a police service. Staff must know what they can and cannot do, and the penalties that apply for misbehaviour, as well as the processes by which its occurrence will be investigated; and so must the public to whom the Police Service is ultimately accountable under the doctrine of policing by consent. The Police Service is a disciplined service.

There has been a long debate about the relationship between discipline and ethics in the Police Service. If the service has a disciplinary code, does it also need a code of ethics? Alternatively, if it has a code of ethics, does it need a disciplinary code? This debate, like that over the difference between leadership and management, is capable of prolongation into infinity, and we shall express our own view succinctly. The Police Service needs both a disciplinary code and a code of ethics, the latter being aspirational.

The British Police Service is committed to developing a national code of police ethics under Article 63 of the European Code of Police Ethics (2001) and the Northern Ireland Police Service has already done so. A national code of police ethics, once developed and applied, will be of practical help in further developing the quality of British police leadership.

The European Convention on Human Rights (ECHR)

As the Council of Europe has recognised, the ECHR does not provide a substitute for a national code of police ethics, although there is a positive relationship between the two. Put simply, human rights are part of professional ethics, and not *vice versa*. Knowledge of human rights and willingness to uphold and apply them is necessary but not sufficient for ethical police leadership.

The Statement of Common Purpose and Values (SOCPV)

The SOCPV has already been noted in *Chapter 2*. We find the statement reproduced in that chapter extremely useful. It is short, clear and pungent, and has national acceptance. It offers part of the function of a code of ethics but is not a substitute.

Police force mission statements

All or most police forces have mission statements, which may or may not be variations on the SOCPV, and they may be used by local leadership on a local basis.

European Code of Police Ethics (2001)

The police in democracies help to sustain the values of democracy, and are themselves imbued with the self-same values. In general, the public consent to and, indeed, welcome the exercise of legitimate authority by the police so long as the police are seen to carry out their tasks in an ethically acceptable manner. In turn, the police have every right to expect that the public will support and co-operate with them in their policing activities when doing so. These ideas about democratic policing are at the heart of the Council of Europe.

The Rule of Law

The police objective of upholding the Rule of Law encompasses two distinct but inter-related duties, i.e. that of:

- upholding the properly enacted and constituted law of the State, including securing a general condition of public tranquillity, and of
- keeping strictly within prescribed powers, abstaining from arbitrary action and respecting the individual rights and freedoms of members of the public.

The Rule of Law is focused not only on *what* is done but on *how* it is done. In carrying out their duties, police need to respect citizens' individual rights, including human rights and freedoms, and avoid arbitrary or unlawful action. This is fundamental to the meaning of the Rule of Law and therefore to the whole meaning and purpose of police duty in a democracy.

AN ETHICAL CULTURE THAT WORKS

A culture of ethical policing requires a 'visible and personal commitment to the values and principles of ethical policing' (Neyroud and Beckley, 2001). This applies to all police officers. There is an additional responsibility placed upon those who have achieved higher rank. In order to be able to practise ethical and effective police leadership, police leaders need:

- technical and professional knowledge;
- physical and emotional resilience;
- a strong personal ethical framework and orientation; and
- the ability to relate and apply core values to the task in hand.

Warren Bennis (1989) describes the essential journey of becoming an effective leader as 'the process of becoming an integrated human being'. The development of a strong ethical framework on which to build leadership forms the keystone of success. The integration that is required includes the ability to meld one's personal value system with that of the Police Service and thereby achieve a personal congruence that enables police leaders to act with confidence and integrity.

Once that framework has been developed and tested on the anvil of personal experience, how is it to be applied more widely? This requires unceasing vigilance, tailored to the character of police work and the proper functioning of its chain of command.

Discretion and its management

All police officers are required to use their judgement and exercise discretion in enforcing the law at all levels of police work. More difficult decisions are not automatically referred up the scale of command for the judgement of more senior officers, since time and circumstances may not allow for this, and it would in any case run counter to police tradition and practice. Police constables have to exercise discretion just as much or indeed more than their seniors.

> *Is this a breach of the peace or not? Do I make an arrest, or is there a better way to preserve or restore the Queen's Peace?*

Only the police officer at the scene can decide, for only he or she can appreciate the full facts of the situation as it evolves and evaluate the probable *immediate* consequences of the various options available to the officer on the spot. On the other hand, there will be occasions when the judgement of the more senior officer is either required or at least desirable:

- where time and circumstances allow, senior consideration may add value to the quality of the decision made;
- there may be far-reaching consequences to a simple executive act that take it from beyond the tactical to the strategic arena;
- force or national policy may be affected;
- other agencies (or working partners) may be involved;
- the actions of a number of police officers may need to be co-ordinated in order to obtain a proper response to an incident;
- in the case of an intelligence operation, only the senior officer may know 'the full picture'.

In these and other circumstances, where the decision as to what to do need not be made at the point of impact, senior consideration may have merit. These considerations, however, do not remove the need for discretion (and accountability) on the part of the officer making the decision. Law enforcement is a matter of judgement, in which knowledge of the law is not enough to be a complete police officer. Discretion requires judgement, and judgement requires ethics.

The reasons for an arrest

We have already mentioned in *Chapter 5* the powers that a police officer has to make an arrest. But an individual decision based on an exercise of personal discretion still falls to be made by the officer concerned under his 'original authority'. Let us suppose that Police Constable John Smith fails to make an arrest, where you as his senior officer might have supposed that an arrest was desirable. If the police officer states that he failed to make an arrest because:

- he was about to go off duty; or
- he was put off by the amount of paperwork that would be involved; or
- the person who should have been arrested was so aggressive in his demeanour that

the officer in question was scared to take action; or
- he had already achieved his arrest quota for that period

then, on the face of it, these are not commendable examples of an exercising of discretion. Discretion does not allow the police officer to shirk his duty under unpleasant, disturbing or threatening circumstances.

If, on the other hand, the officer were able to show that:

- an arrest at that time and place would have lead to a more serious breach of the peace, or
- there were other and better ways available to deal with the problem at the time, or
- there were other sources of evidence available so that an arrest could be made at greater convenience at a later date

then on the face of it these are better reasons for the exercise of discretion. What is in place, in fact, is a double exercise of discretion: firstly, by the executive officer and secondly by his or her senior officer. In summary:

- the use of discretion is inescapable in police work;
- its indispensability prevents the use of simple management systems and techniques such as algorithms to dictate appropriate behaviour; and
- a knowledge of the law is not enough for proper police work, for which a sense of moral awareness is indispensable.

The need for a learning organization

Police leaders need to make sure that the organization of which they are in charge and for whose actions they are accountable has a climate that is conducive to learning and develops a body of corporate knowledge in order to sustain the craft-based decisions of its practitioners. A climate of fear does not promote learning, and nor does an over-emphasis upon individual decision-making and accountability.

Police officers, like other professionals such as surgeons whose work has come under scrutiny, need to be able to make morally sustainable decisions that will stand up to scrutiny both by their superiors and in a court of law. They cannot avoid moral dilemmas in what they do and they must expect some of their cases to fail. They remain in the arena, saving life and preventing crime, whilst applying the fundamental virtue of integrity.

WORKING THROUGH ETHICAL DILEMMAS

What is the difference between an ethical or moral problem and an ethical dilemma?

Let us make another contrast. Police corruption is a moral problem that needs to be addressed where it exists. It is not, however, a moral dilemma: for there is no *moral* argument in favour of corruption (defined as the misuse or abuse of one's official position for personal gain). Its investigation, given the moral consensus that exists that corruption is indefensible, is largely a matter of applying well-known detective techniques by those who have *not* been corrupted—who may be outsiders to the organization in question.

Compare, on the other hand, a conflict of ideals. Suppose that you, as a conscientious and dedicated police leader, wish to make use of the background and skills of a member of your staff in order to infiltrate and sabotage the work of a criminal gang engaged in people-smuggling. The police officer in question, detective constable Chan, is willing; he has the skills needed for the task, as far as you can judge; his background and personal circumstances are suited to the work in hand; and he will receive special training and support. The work is of great potential value and there appears to be no realistic alternative to the use of a police undercover officer if the gang is to be put out of action.

However, when you wake up and think about this case in the middle of the night (as you sometimes do, although you would deny it to casual acquaintances at work), you have your doubts.

Is Chan really up to it, despite his enthusiasm?

Does he fully understand the risks and possible long term implications of deep-cover work, for himself? Do you?

Are you justified in making use of his willingness to volunteer for what must remain, despite all the risk assessments you may apply, an uncharted voyage to an unknown destination?

We are not suggesting that this project should not be undertaken. Nor are we asserting that it is immoral *per se*. We are indicating that one desirable outcome, the investigation of crime, may clash with another: your duty of care for DC Chan. Where two virtuous possibilities clash, we have a moral dilemma.

Resolving moral dilemmas

Moral dilemmas are more easily identified than solved. Moreover, police officers tend to be practical folk, not over-patient with the meanderings of moral discourse.

Chan volunteered, didn't he? So what's the problem?

The first issue that has to be addressed, therefore, is recognising that a moral problem or dilemma exists. In other words, the person, unit or organization needs to be aware of a problem that cannot simply be resolved by recourse to law, human rights doctrine, precedent or authority—although all of these factors will probably be relevant to its resolution.

Milan Pagon (Villiers and Adlam, 2004) states that 'a lot of time and effort needs to be put into education and training in police ethics, before police officers, when faced with a moral problem, will:

- automatically consider all the alternatives available to them;
- not make decisions based on prejudice or impulse;
- submit their decisions to reason and change them, if such a change seems reasonable; and
- give equal consideration to the rights, interests and choices of all parties to the situation in question.'

Taking these points into account, our model is as follows.

Ethical problem-solving

- recognise that the problem exists;
- find out as much as you can about the background to the problem, in an open and non-prejudicial atmosphere. As part of this process:
  — consider the facts, finding out what is known and what is assumed;
  — challenge received opinion and conventional wisdom in a disinterested search for the truth;
- expose and explore core values. Is this a moral challenge or a moral dilemma? If a dilemma, what are the virtues in conflict?;
- encourage an open-minded and positive resolution to the issue, based on a consensus of moral values where possible. The solution achieved should be fair, consistent with generally recognised moral principles, capable of defence in the public arena and able to withstand the test of time.

CONCLUSION

In this chapter we have argued that ethical policing encompasses an active respect for human rights and its core virtue is integrity. We have defined successful policing as related to both process and outcome, for example in regard to the investigation of crime. The ideal outcome is one in which due process leads to lawful conviction. It must be borne in mind, however, that many highly desirable police activities, such as preventing crime or building better community relations, are difficult if not impossible to measure in terms of quantifiable results. They should still be undertaken, and other means found to assess their impact.

We have provided guidance on how to deal with the moral dilemmas that are an inescapable part of police work and presented a model for investigating and resolving them. We have reviewed the ethical frameworks that have guided policing in the past and will do so in the future. Among other things we have:

- pointed to the symbolic importance of the oath of office and recommended its wider application;
- re-affirmed the usefulness of the SOCPV; and
- emphasised the importance of the development of a national code of police ethics.

Police work is a test of character as much as the capacity for abstract ethical reasoning; and character, as Aristotle said, emerges from practice.

ANNEX A

Hypotheticals

Slavery

A police official is on duty in a State that does not practise slavery in the United States of America, some years before the Civil War (1861-65). He becomes aware that a slave fugitive from a southern, slave-owning state is seeking refuge in his area. The law (the Fugitive Slave Law of 1850) says that the slave should be arrested and returned whence he came, to his owner. What should the police official do?

Discussion

What are the options open to the police officer?

- *To obey the law as it stands, without further ado. Duty must outweigh conscience, if conscience is disturbed.*

It is not the role of the police officer to disobey or subvert the law; and he cannot change it. Others will do so soon enough, if the law is fundamentally wrong. Moreover, in enforcing the law 'without fear or favour' he will be demonstrating its iniquities to those who have eyes to see, and it will be changed the faster. Finally, if he chooses to disobey one law because his conscience tells him it is wrong, he may then disobey or subvert other laws. As a police officer, his duty is to uphold the Rule of Law, which means the laws themselves: not to pick and choose those that he personally approves, and ignore the rest.

- *To ignore what is before his eyes, as inconspicuously as he can, and let the slave find his destiny without State interference.*

This may be a tempting option from the humanitarian point of view, but it could easily be argued that it is profoundly wrong. It does not necessarily resolve the plight of the fleeing slave, for he may be arrested by another. It does not change the law; and it is a breach of duty, whether the reason be good or bad, and setves a dangerous precedent.

- *To take direct action to assist the slave.*

This is the action of a good person, rather than a good police officer.

Comment

It is to be hoped that in a liberal democracy, the police officer should not be troubled by his conscience in enforcing the law. However, police officers operate at the margin, where principles can be questioned; and even a modern liberal democracy can be harsh on some. For example, the illegal immigrant may be seen as the modern equivalent of the fleeing slave.

Goods trains

A decent-minded railway police officer in Nazi Germany, who does not belong to the Nazi party himself and did not vote Hitler into power, has been told to pass through certain trains and not to concern himself with what those trains are carrying. The trains arrive, and there are signs that he cannot ignore that something very odd is going on, involving human suffering. Should he ignore those signs, and obey his orders? Or should he investigate further, on his own initiative?

Comment

Some of the same issues arise as in the runaway slave, and this is, again, a fundamental conflict of duty and conscience. A railway official in Nazi Germany faces potentially disastrous consequences if he defies the State, both for himself and his family. Moreover, as an official employed by a fundamentally immoral regime, it could be argued that he has already compromised himself, even if he does not take action in this case. The argument that as an official he must obey his orders, and that that obligation absolves him from any personal responsibility for their consequences, was dismissed at the War Crimes Trial at Nuremberg.

The party

Two constables attend a noisy party complaint[1]. A large number of aggressive-looking men, clad in motor-cycle gear, emerge from the house and challenge them. The

---

1. This evocative dilemma was first brought to our attention by Roger Watson as part of his Master's Thesis for the Curtin University of Technology in Western Australia in 1998. We are grateful for permission to publish it.

group separates the two constables.

Constable A gets back into the police vehicle and the group surrounds his partner, B. A immediately radios for urgent support. Meanwhile, B is being pushed, verbally threatened and ridiculed.

A notes that B is not actually being battered. He decides to lock himself in the van, take detailed notes of the incident as it transpires and wait until support arrives.

Support arrives in a few minutes and ten men are arrested. A's notes prove to be instrumental in formulating charges. Moreover, B is not actually hurt. However, B tells his sergeant, C, that he will not, under any circumstances, ever again work with A.

C calls A into his office, where he tells him that he is a coward, that he cannot be trusted, and that unless he dramatically changes his ways his future in the police service is limited. He then transfers him to a non-operational position.

Comment

This scenario raises issues of professional standards and loyalty, and is perhaps best reviewed in discussion with others, where fundamental differences of view may emerge. In regard to the second issue, the reaction of the sergeant to the apparent cowardice, as he perceives it, of the police officer who locked himself in the van, agreement may be easier to reach. In regard to the behaviour of the apparently cowardly officer, much will depend on his credibility in offering an alternative explanation for his conduct to that assumed by the sergeant; and his credibility will result, at least in part, from the evidence of his previous behaviour. Resolving ethical dilemmas does not simply require an understanding of theory: one also needs to be able to find out the facts.

Policing protest

A county police force polices a scientific establishment where vivisection is practised under State licence. A major demonstration is to take place at the site, with whose aims some officers are entirely in sympathy. Because of their antipathy to vivisection, some of them do not wish to police the demonstration. One officer has asked not to carry out policing duties in this setting, and has offered to work elsewhere. Should he be allowed to do so? What are the wider issues arising, and what are the arguments for and against allowing him to express his conscience?

Comment

This scenario contrasts duty and conscience once again, and raises the issue of consistency of approach. Readers will be able to think of similar situations for themselves, in which some police officers will not wish to carry out some duties. How is the police service to cope with this, ethically and effectively? Should all police officers be expected to carry out all lawful duties, or is there some room for discretion here?

False testimony?

A police officer, A, is under pressure to support his colleague, B and collude in corroborating an item of evidence that A cannot in fact verify from his own observation, in order to convict a notorious criminal, C.

Comment

Strictly speaking, this problem does not present an ethical dilemma so much as a challenge to resolution. As a police officer, A is dedicated to policing under due process in order to uphold the Rule of Law. Therefore, he cannot tell a lie (or omit to tell the truth) in order to support B's testimony, no matter how desirable the outcome (the conviction of the notorious criminal, C.) However, dilemmas of this sort are frequent in policing, and present a major and recurring temptation. On utilitarian grounds, it is relatively easy to find reasons why the conviction of C may do more for the greatest happiness of the greatest number—*in the short term*—than the actions of the police officer who refuses to collude in a deception and practise 'noble cause' corruption. Moreover, there may be an issue here about loyalty versus integrity. We suggest that an open discussion of the temptations that police officers face, and an exchange of their own accounts as to how they have grappled with such dilemmas, may do more to improve practical police ethics than any textbook.

ANNEX B

The Virtue of Integrity

The Police Leadership Qualities Framework (PLQF) rests upon the indispensable virtue of integrity. Police officers and staff must display integrity in whatever they do. Milan Pagon (Villiers and Adlam, 2004) offers a useful synthesis of views as to the meaning of integrity, quoting from Delattre and Becker amongst others.

Delattre (1996) defines integrity as:

'the settled disposition, the resolve and determination, the established habit of doing right where there is no one to make you do it but yourself' (p. 325).

Becker (1998) states that:

'integrity is the principle of being principled, practising what one preaches regardless of emotional or social pressure, and not allowing any irrational consideration to overwhelm one's rational convictions' (p. 158).

Integrity in policing, then, means that police officers genuinely accept the values and moral standards of policing. They possess the virtues of their profession, and they consistently act, out of their own will, in accordance with those values, standards and virtues, even in the face of external pressures.

Policing and the Future

Policing and the Future

Modern policing arose from the industrial revolution of 1760 to 1830. It was a consequence of widespread industrialisation and urbanisation, which irrevocably altered previous patterns of social and political control. These social trends have continued and have been multiplied by globalisation, so that it might be argued that there is a strategic priority for policing to adapt to the new circumstances of a post-modern and indeed post-industrial society, in which an expanding population reflects a high level of immigration from areas in which there is little or no tradition of policing by consent. (In a so-called 'failed state' such as Somalia, there may be little or no recent tradition of policing at all).

The percentage of the British population from a non-white ethnic minority background is now eight per cent (*Social Trends Overview, 2005: 35 Years of Social Change*);[1] and whilst this is not in itself an indication that policing will be more difficult, it is surely an indication that it must change.

The British tradition of policing, which arose as much as anything as a means to police the population without an unnecessary and counter-productive reliance on coercion, is of policing by consent. However, as we wrote in *Chapter One*, policing by consent is not a static concept, but a dynamic one. Is there a need for a new articulation of policing by consent, based on a more active interpretation of the existing model? Has British society changed to such an extent, that a fundamental change in policing is necessary? Can a multi-ethnic and multi-racial society be policed under a tradition that had developed under very different conditions?

FROM NEIGHBOURHOOD TO NATIONAL POLICING

The government's Green Paper (2008), 'Policing Our Communities Together', does not develop such a model, although it suggests a series of practical reforms, many of

---

1. The same report stated that 29 per cent of the population in London was from minority ethnic groups, and that the percentage increased to 41 per cent of those under 15. It also stated that the UK as a whole has an ageing population; that more people live alone, especially men; that there are more one-parent families, usually headed by women; that fewer people marry; that more children are illegitimate (but more to co-habiting couples than single mothers); and that more women are remaining childless, or having fewer children. Around one in five women in England and Wales currently reaching the end of their fertile life are childless, compared with one in ten women born in the mid-1940s. Women are becoming more important in the workplace, although many work part-time. These underlying social trends may be less dramatic than immigration issues, but are an equal if not a greater source of change for the police, both in how it polices and how it recruits its own workforce.

which build on what has already been discussed in this work;[2] and we have already considered in outline its suggested reforms in regard to the composition of police authorities. We would note that the Green Paper recognises that the police are to a large extent judged by their effectiveness in addressing local concerns.

The Green Paper acknowledges the importance of these in referring to the Louise Casey Review, 'Engaging Communities in Fighting Crime' (2008). The top ten policing approaches that the review found the public want to see are:

- **a service that takes action** – responsive, approachable, coming out quickly when called to incidents, acting on, following up and feeding back on progress to members of the public when they report crime and anti-social behaviour.
- **a visible, uniformed police presence**, with police freed up from unnecessary red tape and health and safety restrictions, fewer constables and PCSOs taken off patrols to perform 'administrative' tasks, and there when needed, not just a nine-to-five service.
- **PCSOs who are clearly distinguishable as part of the police service**, with uniforms, equipment and powers that match their role in patrolling communities, supporting local police and tackling anti-social behaviour.
- **named contacts** and clear information about who is responsible for what locally, and how to contact them in both emergency and non-emergency situations.
- **face-to-face access** at a police station, a surgery or a street meeting.
- **continuity in the local policing team**, with officers and PCSOs serving a minimum of two years in the neighbourhood so that they get to know areas and communities well and gain communities' respect and trust.
- **a better service for victims** of crime, especially repeat victims, returning regularly to check they are alright and to help minimise further victimisation.
- **sensitivity over reporting** crime and giving evidence, protecting anonymity.
- **good engagement with the community** to identify their priorities for action and to give feedback on action and outcomes on cases of greatest community concern.
- **clear leadership from the police** on crime – with the backing of other organizations like the local council, prosecutors, the courts and probation services.

These ten issues, we would suggest, are suitable check-points for the current working of policing by consent, and have much to recommend them. We note that Professor PAJ Waddington wrote in *Police Review* (August 2008) that the Green Paper refers to *consumers* of police services, and states:

---

2. And some of which seek to recreate what was previously in existence under another name, such as a National College for Police Leadership in place of the former Police Staff College at Bramshill, on the same site.

This is a profound constitutional change. For the past couple of centuries the people of this country have been regarded as 'citizens'. Citizenship is quite different to consumerism, for it is based on indivisible rights. Every citizen, no matter how humble their status, has the right to be treated on the same terms as every other. Thus the police were seen as servants, not of the majority wishes, but of the highest civic virtue—justice, about which the Green Paper says little or nothing.

Dr Robert Adlam and I wrote in 2004 that 'in our view there are seven requisites for a safe, just and tolerant society'. Although interdependent and not wholly distinct from each other, they can usefully be described separately.

A safe just and tolerant society is made possible if the following seven conditions are met:

1. It is an open society.
2. It practises pluralist democracy.
3. It is governed by the Rule of Law.
4. It upholds human rights and fundamental freedoms.
5. It expresses an active and shared concept of citizenship. Its members cannot be so selfish, egotistic, or simply self-absorbed as to be indifferent either towards the welfare of others or the common good. They have duties, responsibilities and obligations as well as rights, and go beyond tolerance to show care and compassion for others.
6. In recognition of human fallibility and the continuing need to strive for virtue, it places an emphasis on education in the fullest sense... including education in the rights and responsibilities of citizenship. Education develops the capacity for informed and rational decision-making, and thereby reduces ignorance, prejudice and fear. The educated person is able to resist indoctrination and see through propaganda.
7. Finally, a safe, just and tolerant society needs to recognise the necessary limits to toleration and to have a fair, impartial and effective means to control intolerable behaviour' (i.e. a good police service.)

(Villiers and Adlam, Policing a Safe, Just and Tolernt Society, 2004)

We believe that these comments still apply.

POLICE REFORM: MODERNISATION AND DISCONTENT

Police reform is a continuing activity which will never be complete. At the same time, any government which wishes to reform policing in any radical sense faces a dilemma. To improve efficiency requires the increasing centralisation of account-ability and control, or so it would appear. But improving efficiency may not be the first priority; and in any case, 'Statist' solutions are not necessarily the answer.

Local concerns

By tradition, policing in the UK is a local concern. [3] It reflects local concerns and lo-cal issues, which may be seen as quite different to national priorities. Local commu-nities are much more concerned with local crime, vandalism, anti-social behaviour and nuisance than with national and international issues; and the national policing budget does not appear to be of relevance to them.

Local police stations

By and large, they would prefer a police service that is responsive to local demands than one which satisfies national or indeed regional criteria for efficiency. Hence the consistent demand by the public that local police stations be kept open and manned, even if the police force itself believes that it can present a more cost-effective service by reducing its points of contact and centralising its services. [4]

Government policy

The government has set out to:

- standardize police policies, procedures and practices on a national basis, so that one police force is comparable to another, whatever its local traditions and apparent differences;
- link comparative performance against set targets to significant rewards and punish-ments which ensure police participation;
- create national units for identified national needs, such as the Serious Organized Crime Agency (SOCA) or National Policing Improvement Agency (NPIA); and at the same time
- it has found ways and means to increase its power in the so-called tripartite relation-ship, which is now balanced in its favour.

A national police service is no longer under discussion (as it was, for example, in

---

3. With the partial exception of the MPS, which confounds most generalisations about British policing, and which in practice needs to concern itself with national and international policing issues as well as the polic-ing of the capital itself.

4. The same argument applies to the retention of local railway stations, bus services, post offices, cottage hospi-tals, and the like, and the arguments cross a range of criteria. It is a mistake to see the debate as being simply about saving money. It is, in part, about the need to preserve a rural infrastructure; and the nature of govern-ment itself, which rests upon a social contract which must reflect some expression of the general will.

1962), since its advantages, as far as central government is concerned, have been achieved by other means—with the additional benefit that the continued existence of a number of forces encourages competition on grounds of efficiency, and enables the government to identify and individually address those forces, units and activities that are not achieving what they should.

Abiding concerns

We referred in *Chapter 1* to the policing of Jersey and Pitcairn. Both are settled communities, with their attendant problems. *Unsettled* minority groups, such as gypsies, who are by definition travelling people, create very different problems for the police, and the long history of police relationships with the gypsies is an equally long history of prejudice and misunderstanding, in which the police have been placed under pressure by settled communities to deal with the intruders in their midst. Gypsies and travellers, like prostitutes and other hitherto unheard groups, have found a voice and are now participating in the public debate.

The community in general, whatever its racial, religious, ethnic and other differences, has certain expectations in regard to the type of service it expects from the police. Those expectations transcend boundaries of race, national origin, religious affiliation, and so on. Whatever their origin, people want the police to deal effectively with the crime, vandalism and anti-social behaviour which reduces or ruins their quality of life. They may also wish them to deal with sections of their own community, who present a particular problem.

Some sections of the population may see the police as being prejudiced against them. This view, whether based on fact, rumour, ideology, or a combination of those and other factors, is highly dangerous to the police, since it means that they cannot police by consent. In an atmosphere of constant criticism and distrust their morale must be affected, and their relationship with the community in general must suffer. They must go the extra mile to address the problem.

Notwithstanding the above, the police cannot afford to treat part of the community as above the law. All laws apply to all citizens. This is the Rule of Law mentioned in earlier chapters, and every citizen has a duty to uphold the law and assist the police.

Community policing, in its broadest sense, should not be an afterthought to real police work, but an integral part of police strategy. To this end, we are not entirely convinced that the creation and use of police community support officers (PCSOs) is an unalloyed benefit. *All* police officers are PCSOs.

AUTONOMY AND CONTROL

In this book we have attempted to present a model of policing by consent which has evolved organically as a practical and accepted means to keep the Queen's Peace, with a fundamental emphasis on:

- the original powers of the office of constable;
- the importance of discretion for all police officers; and
- the chief officer's need for operational independence.

The British police service has attempted to maintain a distance between itself and direct political control, whether that control be local, regional or national; and we would argue that a degree of autonomy is needed for the police to be able to uphold the confidence of the citizenry in its elected representatives, and truly to police 'without fear or favour'.[5]

We would further suggest that a police service is judged by its effectiveness in achieving socially desirable aims, rather than by its efficiency in addressing imposed objectives. Who counts the cost of finding a missing child?

Police virtues

There are four main ways in which a police officer may damage a member of the public, in the course of his duties.

- the police officer may take away his life or health;
- he may take away his liberty;
- he may take away his possessions; or
- he may take away his reputation, either with his nearest associates, including his family, or with the public as a whole.

There are circumstances under which any of these actions may be justified; and although all of them are protected under human rights legislation, those rights are qualified (the only unqualified right is the right not to be tortured, which can never be justified under any circumstances). The police thus possess formidable powers; and when we remember that those powers are often exercised by the most junior officers, without supervision, under emergency circumstances where an immediate decision is needed, and with incomplete information, it will be understood that

---

5. The British Prime Minister, Tony Blair, was questioned (as a witness) in 2006 in connexion with the cash for honours scandal—whereas the President of France, M. Jacques Chirac, could not be questioned about alleged corruption whilst still president.

policing is of its very nature a difficult and challenging occupation which requires persons of the highest quality to accept its responsibilities.

Increasing powers?

The powers of the police are increasing as the century unfolds, not only in regard to addressing terrorism by a variety of means, such as in the imposition of control orders, but in controlling the population at large. This can lead to what seem on the face of it to be abuses of police powers, for example when old age pensioners are sprayed with pepper spray by police officers who are too quick to resort to the use of force; or anti-social behaviour orders are sought and imposed when an informal measure would have been more appropriate. ASBOs raise a number of concerns, which are briefly reviewed in the *Glossary*.

Some police officers are concerned that modern technology is reducing the appropriate use of discretion and forcing them to act simply as the implementers of State policy. Speed cameras, for example, do not take into account any of the conditions prevailing at the time of the offence: speeding is speeding, and a fixed penalty ticket is issued. Police officers thus lose the opportunity to exercise judgement, serve the interests of justice, and build a better relationship with the public.

Adlam and Villiers wrote in 2003:

> [Thus] the cardinal [police] virtue becomes the proper cultivation and use of judgement. This in its turn requires professional knowledge, independence of mind and confidence in oneself, practice in the exercise of discretion, and the capacity for sympathetic imagination into the minds and motives of others.... It also requires that the State should regard the achievement of proper policing as a long-term investment, requiring the cultivation of disinterested virtue. In practical terms, this means that the police officer must not be under the immediate direction of the State and its functionaries, but have a certain degree of independence...

> ... Edwin Delattre argued that the police service necessarily imposes exceptional demands upon those who choose to accept its discipline. He referred to:

> The tradition that calls upon all who bear positions of public trust to live up to higher intellectual and moral standards than are required of other citizens and residents... In giving authority and powers that the rest of us do not have to public servants, we gain a reciprocal right to hold them accountable to fulfil their duties wisely, competently, and honourably...'

> In practice, the most effective forms of policing… are matters of leading, not merely following or reacting; and they succeed when police earn and come to possess, by their exemplary conduct and by the consistency of their words, policies, and deeds with the Rule of Law and the ideals of integrity, service, and concern for public safety, the trust and cooperation of a significant portion of the public.
>
> (Adlam and Villiers, *Police Leadership in the 21st Century*, 2003)

A conservative view?

So far, our position might bend described as a conservative one, in which we might be said to have concentrated on identifying the advantages of the *status quo* from the police's perspective—which may not be quite as grounded in historical fact (for example in regard to the tradition of operational independence) as it would like to believe.

To that criticism, whether abstract or applied, we would offer two counter-arguments. Firstly, we agree that the police service needs to provide value for money, and an effective substitute for the pressures of market competition needs to be found. To create a partial monopoly, as the government has done in awarding certain duties entirely or mainly to the police service, is to create the possibility of waste or corruption. The negative possibilities of a monopoly should not be exploited by any public service, whether intentionally or unintentionally.

The government has attempted to find a substitute for the pressures of market forces in performance management. This policy has been heavily criticised throughout the public sector, whether in health, education or policing; and we would suggest that it is a policy that has failed. We would further suggest that the quality of police leadership is the key factor; and that good leadership requires nurturing and trust. Good leaders are self-motivated and set themselves much harder targets to achieve than any government requirement. Those targets include the reputation of the police service, its acceptability to the community as a whole, and the ways in which it best helps the most vulnerable elements of society.

Social divisions have always existed, and those divisions have an additional significance if multiplied by race, religion and ethnicity. A multi-racial and multi-religious society may require sensitive policing—for example, in regard to the question of how to question a female witness to an event, when the witness's husband is convinced that it is he who should answer the questions on her behalf (leaving aside the question of the language employed). But it does not change the fundamental role of the police, which is to find out what the witness saw, in order to assist the investigation of a crime.

Laws and rules

In one sense, policing is a simple task. Police officers put themselves at the point of conflict, real or potential, and endeavour to keep or restore the peace. In order to be able to do so, they need not so much a strong arm (although that may be necessary on occasion), or an intimate knowledge of the law, as a ready tongue and a large measure of common sense.

Police officers may enforce the law on occasion; but it could be argued that their true purpose is, far more often, to explain the rules. As Peter Winch pointed out in *The Idea of a Social Science* (first published fifty years ago in 1958) rules and laws are not the same. The law is something external to us. We have a constitutional and in many cases a moral obligation to obey it, and if we do not do so, and we are discovered, then we shall face a punishment: but it is not the same as a rule. We may attempt to live our life without laws: but we cannot do so without rules. Laws tell us what we should not do. Rules allow us to develop life as a communal activity. Laws are applied, whereas rules are negotiated. Laws need to be accepted. Rules need to be understood.

SOME CLOSING THOUGHTS

Any introduction to policing must be an exercise in judgment for its author, and his long-suffering editor—a series of decisions as to what to leave out, as well as what to include, and a confirmation of the vital purpose of the book.

This is not a book about police powers in any technical sense, and does not offer its readers detailed instructions on how to be a practising police officer. It will, we hope, reach a wider audience than that, for everyone has an interest in policing, and is concerned with the practice of policing in a vibrant democracy—and some of the best questions are asked by the police themselves, who confront daily and in practice the major dilemmas of their demanding profession.

We have concentrated upon the analysis of British policing, and our book is in essence about the theory and practice of policing by consent. What is that essence? We shall summarise it as follows.

The fundamental task of the police is to keep the peace and uphold fundamental human rights and freedoms. All other duties follow from there, and all other tasks, including the enforcement of the law, are secondary. The police service is not, primarily, a law enforcement agency, and indeed there are other agencies that are in some ways better suited to that specific task, for they may concentrate upon particular aspects of the law and refine its enforcement. The police officer has a wider role. The police officer:

- has original authority;
- has operational independence;
- upholds the Rule of Law, and is subject to that same rule of law himself in everything that he does;
- must follow due process;
- is accountable for everything that he does, in a variety of ways and by a variety of means, not only by formal mechanisms but by his own participation in the democratic life of the nation. Accountability is both contemporary and retrospective. Fear of being criticised or censured after the event must never deter a police officer from acting to the best of his ability in carrying out his fundamental duties; and
- represents the whole of the public whom he polices, and not just a part of it.

Police work is both challenging and rewarding. It is an honourable profession, and its goals cannot be achieved without the active co-operation of the public. The most valuable weapons of the police officer are judgement and good sense.

Glossary of Words, Phrases, Acronyms and Abbreviations

Glossary of Words, Phrases, Acronyms and Abbreviations

AA (1) appropriate adult, who should, e.g. be present when a juvenile is arrested, questioned etc. under *PACE* below; (2) Alcoholics Anonymous.

ABC acceptable behaviour contract, e.g. with the probation service or a youth justice team, etc. as part of crime prevention and changing poor behaviour.

ABH actual bodily harm

ACC assistant chief constable

accused person someone charged with an offence but whose case is yet to come to trial and who is entitled to the presumption of innocence. Contrast *suspect*.

ACPO Association of Chief Police Officers. Hence also ACPO(S), where 'S' = Scotland.

ACR automatic crime recording

ACU Area Crime Unit

advice (1) informal words of warning or caution from a police officer; (2) legal, professional or other expert advice, including from the *CPS* to the police

AFR automatic fingerprint recognition

AG (or A-G) Attorney General

Altaris One of the modern police command and control computer system; an 'IT management solution'.

AMP Association of Muslim Police

ANPR automatic [vehicle] number plate recognition, in conjunction with *CCTV*, speed cameras, etc.

APA Association of Police Authorities

APS accelerated promotion scheme.

ALR alarm receiving centre; usually operated by private sector contractors, e.g. to monitor burglar alarms

arrest exerting physical control over the person (or 'body') of a *suspect* or someone who is unlawfully at large. Note especially the chain of events involving arrest on suspicion of an offence and the process of police detention under *PACE* described in *Chapter 5*. Note also the relationship to *bail* (below) and/or custody and the role of the custody sergeant described in that chapter. Arrest may also occur under a court warrant (aka a 'bench warrant').

ART/V armed response team/vehicle

ASB/ASBO anti-social behaviour/anti-social behaviour order. ASB has been increasingly targeted by government since 1998 including via its Respect Agenda. Compare *CRASBO*.

BA The UK Border Agency (sometimes called 'Border Force'): see bia.homeoffice.gov.uk

bail a *suspect* or *accused person* can be released on police bail to attend at a police station or court; or be kept in the cells until the court opens, or in police detention if matters remain under investigation (hence the popular expression 'helping the police with their inquiries'). Note especially the interaction between *PACE* and the Bail Act 1976. See generally the outline in *Chapter 5*.

BCS British Crime Survey: a Home Office survey measuring public perceptions of crime and 'fear of crime'

BCU (1) Basic Command Unit; (2) Borough Command Unit.

Black Maria colloquial term for a 'police van' dating from the time when all such vehicles were black

BME black and minority ethnic (e.g. people, issues)

Bramshill Short for Bramshill House, a Jacobean mansion in Hampshire, which was purchased by the Home Office in 1956 for use as a national Police College (*Chapter 2*). It was renamed Police Staff College (1979), later CENTREX. It is now part of the *NPIA* (below).

brief a solicitor or, more usually, a barrister who 'works to a brief' (papers setting out the facts, evidence and issues)

briefing a session at which police officers are 'put in the picture' re matters of the day, the progress of an investigation, etc., or e.g. a senior officer is updated. See also *NBM* and *NEB* below.

BTP British Transport Police

camera See *CCTV*, *speed camera*, *in camera*

caution (or police caution). A warning: (1) to an accused on being arrested concerning his or her rights; (2) as an alternative to prosecution and sentence (see *Chapter 5*); or (3) one given in court when an accused is asked to decide whether he or she wants to be tried in the magistrates' court or Crown Court re an *either way offence*.

CBO (1) community beat officer; (2) civil behaviour order (such as a football banning order; or a restraining order to prevent harassment)

CC chief constable

C&C command and control

CCTV closed circuit television

CCU (1) Complex Crimes Unit; (2) Computer Crime Unit.

CCRC Criminal Cases Review Commission which refers alleged or suspected miscarriages of justice to the Court of Appeal

CDO civilian detention officer (who may be encountered, e.g. in a police custody suite)

CDRP Crime and Disorder Reduction Partnership (see *Chapter 5*)

CDS Criminal Defence Service (dealing with State funded legal aid)

CEO court enforcement officer

CEOP Child Exploitation and Online Protection Centre: see *Chapter 6*

charge a formal allegation of an offence which tuns a suspect into an accused person: *Chapter 5*

child someone under 14 years of age. Ten is the age of criminal responsibility in England and Wales, so that in this context child means someone aged 10-14. Child can have other legal meanings.

CHIS covert human intelligence source. Broadly speaking, an informer

Ch/Spr chief superintendent

CI crime incident

CICB/C/S Criminal Injuries Compensation Board/ Commission/Scheme

CID (1) normally Criminal Investigations Department; but note also the use of (2) Criminal Intelligence Department.

C/Insp Chief Inspector

CIU Crash Investigation Unit

CJA Criminal Justice Act, e.g. CJA 1991, 2003

CJS Criminal Justice System. Note also cjsonline.org

CJU Criminal Justice Unit: usually a joint police/CPS unit re prosecutions before magistrates

CMS case(file) management system

CO custody officer: usually meaning someone who works in the police custody suite. Custody officers can be civilian employees rather than police officers. Hence also *CDO* above.

'cold case' One where the case file was closed at an earlier time, that is reopened and reviewed (hence also the term 'cold case review').

community policing policing with the involvement and support of the community, in which citizens may play an active part re, e.g. crimeprevention/

crime reduction. But note variations in the use of this term according to local circumstances

cordon a barrier placed around a crime scene or an accident: 'police tape' or a physical police presence to seal off the location

CPA (1) crime pattern analysis; (2) Child Protection Agency.

CPIA Criminal Procedure and Investigations Act 1996

CPO crime prevention officer

CPS Crown Prosecution Service

CPU Child Protection Unit

CRASBO criminal anti-social behaviour order which can be made to run alongside any sentence given by a criminal court (similar to an *ASBO*)

CRB (1) Criminal Records Bureau. (2) Crime Reporting Bureau.

CRO (1) Criminal Records Office: hence references to 'an offender's CRO', i.e. his or her criminal record; (2) crime reduction officer.

CRU central referral unit

CS (1) crime scene; (2) CS spray used to incapacitate violent or disorderly people.

CSM crime scene manager

CSR confidential source register (in conjunction with *CHIS*)

CSO short form of PCSO: see later

CSU court support unit

C/Supt chief superintendent

CTC counter-terrorist check

CTL custody time limit, i.e. for bringing a case to trial when someone is denied bail

CTS counter terrorist search

custody sergeant a police officer of this rank nominated to take key responsibilities under PACE re arrest, detention, bail and charge: *Chapter 5*

Crimestoppers leading crime prevention charity: see crimestoppers-uk.org

CJU Criminal Justice Unit: a *CPS* or CPS/police unit, often re Crown Court cases

Cybercrime crime atributable to the internet and cyberspace as defined in *Chapter 6*.

CYPA (or C&YPA) Children and Young Persons Act, e.g. 1933, 1969

DAT drug action team: a multi-agency team to deal with drug misusers

DC (1) detective constable; (2) detention centre, now usually an immigration detention centre (aka holding centre). Similar to a low security prison.

DCC deputy chief constable

DCI detective chief inspector

designated police station one designated by the chief constable for *PACE* purposes as per *Chapter 5*

detention without trial Once someone is charged, then as a matter of general principle the case must be pursued expeditiously. In the UK there is no prolonged detention without trial, only detention without charge within the limits set by *PACE* and special rules re terrorism: see *Chapter 5*. The control order mentioned in *Chapter 7* came about because the higher courts ruled that attempts by the Home Office to hold terrorist suspects longer than usual without charge or trial were unlawful.

DI detective inspector

DIC (1) drunk in charge; (2) Driver Improvement Course (as an alternative to prosecution or disqualification by a court).

DIO (1) drugs intelligence officer; (2) divisional intelligence officer. For the difference between 'information' and 'intelligence', see *Chapter 6*.

DIU divisional intelligence unit

disclosure showing information or evidence to the 'other side', ahead of a criminal charge or trial. Accused people must now divulge more than in the past: see specialist works.

DNA deoxyribonucleic acid. DNA evidence is now critical in many cases. Note also, 'enhanced DNA', where a microscopic sample is 'grown' until strong enough to be produce a match (or 'hit'); and familial DNA, that of a blood relative. See generally *Chapter 6*.

DPG Diplomatic Protection Group (a unit of the Metropolitan Police)

DPP Director of Public Prosecutions (the head of the CPS)

DS (1) short for D/Sgt/Supt, i.e. detective sergeant/superintendent; (2) duty solicitor: one 'on call' or 'stand-by' from the CDS in case someone is arrested/detained and requires legal aid.

DSU (1) Divisional Support Unit; (2) Dog Support Unit.

DTTO Drugs Testing and Treatment Order (made by a court)

Due process fundamental principle which obliges all CJS personal to deal with cases in compliance with law, procedure and practice

DV (1) domestic violence; (2) developed vetting. Hence DVC domestic violence/vetting/coordinator and DVLO domestic violence/vetting liaison officer.

DVLA/C Driving Vehicle Licensing Authority/Centre (aka 'Swansea')

ECHR European Convention On Human Rights (note also European Court of Human Rights: but this is usually signified by Eur. Ct. HR)

EGT/U Evidence Gathering Team/Unit

either way offence One triable in the Crown Court or magistrates' court depending on a court procedure known as 'allocation and sending'

ELO explosives liaison officer

EPIC Emergency Procedures Information Centre

ETA expected/earliest time of arrival, i.e. by police at a crime scene, incident, etc.

emergency citizens have long been able to call the police emergency number 999; and in modern times a non-emergency number 101. Non-urgent matters can now be reported via the internet.

EP emergency preparedness

ESP employer support policing, e.g. re initiatives such as Bus Beat, Campus Beat, Hospital Watch and Shop Watch.

Europol See *Chapter 3*

exclusion zone one designated: (1) re an emergency, crime scene, etc; or (2) generally to prevent disorder, particularly re juveniles

FBI Federal Bureau of Investigation (USA). Hence terms such as 'FBI-style'.

FBO football banning order

FCC Force Communications Centre

FEC Force Enquiry Centre

FEO firearms enquiry officer

FIR force information room

FIU (1) Force Intelligence Unit; (2) Football Intelligence Unit.

FLC family liaison co-ordinator

FLO (1) football liaison officer; (2) family liaison officer

FO firearms/force officer (or sometimes AFO = authorised firearms/force officer)

FPN/D fixed penalty notice/for disorder

FPT (1) fingerprint maybe written Fpt); (2) fixed penalty ticket

FSO Force Standing Order

FSS/L Forensic Science Service/Laboratory: see Chapter 6.

FSU (1) Force Support Unit; (2) Firearms Support Unit.

FTA fail to appear (e.g. in response to bail or at a police station, etc. to give a sample)

FTD [physically and mentally] fit to detain

FWTO force weapons training officer

GA Gamblers Anonymous

GBH grievous bodily harm

GCHQ General Communications Headquarters: the government 'listening station' in Cheltenham

GLO gypsy liaison officer

golden hour The first hour after a crime has occuredwhen the evidence is fresh, said by experienced investigators to be when most crimes are solved

H2H house to house inquiries

hate crime generic term for crimes targeted against particular groups on the basis of their religious beliefs, sexuality or disabilities, etc.

HDC home detention curfew (enforced by electronic tagging whilst someone is on leave from prison)

HET house entry team, i.e. for a police raid

High tech crime (or hi-tech crime): see IT-related crime and *Cybercrime* in *Chapter 6*.

house-to-house i.e. inquiries by knocking on doors

as part of an investigation, usually re a serious crime such as murder

HM Her Majesty's (as in HMIC = HM Inspectorate of Constabulary; HMP = HM Prison; HMPS = HM Prison Service; HMR&C = HM Revenue & Customs; HMSO = Her Majesty's Stationery Office)

HO Home Office. Hence HOC/G = Home Office Circular/Guidance; *Holmes* below; HORT/1 = Home Office Road Traffic Form 1 (as issued to people stopped for certain traffic offences).

Holmes Home Office Major Enquiry System (now Holmes 2): see *Chapter 6*

'hot pursuit pursuing fleeing offenders, usually in a police car. A controversial aspect of police work

HR/HRA human rights/Human Rights Act 1998

HS Home Secretary

HSC Health and Safety Commission

HSE Health and Safety Executive

ICP incident control point

ICPO International Criminal Police Organisation

ICRP International Commission on Radiological Protection

ICV independent custody visitor: an ordinary member of the local community appointed to make sure that the welfare of people detained at a police station is maintained. They call unannounced, write short reports and play a key role in maintaining public confidence re this aspect of police work. ICVA = Independent Custody Visitors Association: see further icva.org.uk

ID Identification. Hence ID card, etc.

IED improvised explosive device (a home made bomb)

IEU Incident Enquiry Unit

IIMARCH Information, Intention, Method, Administration, Risk assessment, Communication and Human rights

IIO initial investigating officer

ILET International Liaison and Enquiry Team

IMB Independent Monitoring Board (at the local prison and comparable to *ICVs*)

in camera 'in private' in rare circumstances when a court closes its doors to the public, as where national security or threat to life and limb is involved

indictable offence One triable in the Crown Court by a judge and jury. Some offences are 'indictable only' (e.g. arson, murder, rape), others *either way offences* (above)

Insp inspector

Intelligence-led policing Policing on the basis of verified and/or analysed data, information, etc. For the distinction between 'information' and 'intelligence', see *Chapter 6*.

intercept See *IOC*

Interpol International Police Organization: for the origins, status and present role, see *Chapter 3*.

IO investigating officer

IOC interception of communications. Hence IOCA (A for 'Act')

IPA International Police Association

IPCC Independent Police Complaints Authority

IPTF International Police Task Force

IPU International Police Unit

ISO information security officer

IWF Internet Watch Foundation

john doe (and in politically correct times jane doe). Names, American in origin, given to unidentified corpses. In the UK, descriptions such as A (or, e.g. Adam), B, C, etc. seem to be preferred; or indicative names, such as 'Mr Seagull' after a body was found washed up on a Dorset beach in 2002.

JIC joint intelligence coordinator

JP justice of the peace (a synonym for 'magistrate')

JTAC Joint Threat Assessment Committee (national)

LAGLO lesbian and gay liaison officer

LALO local government liaison officer

LEC local emergency centre

licence 'on licence' means that a prisoner is now on parole or some other form of prison release licence and may be subject to recall to prison, e.g. for misbehaviour. Hence, also, 'life licence' re a life sentence prisoners. Such people may be subject to police monitoring, especially high risk offenders and through *MAPPA*.

Liberty The National Council for Civil Liberties

LIO local intelligence officer

LO liaison officer (hence, e.g. FLA = family LO; LAGLO = Lesbians and Gays LO; VLO = victims LO)

Macpherson Report That into matters arising from the investigation into the murder of Stephen Lawrence (see main index)

MAPPA Multi-Agency Public Protection Arrangements (with the police as a key player)

MCIT Major Crime Investigation Team

MCT Major Crime Team

MDP Ministry of Defence Police

MFH missing from home

MHA Mental Health Act

MID motor insurers database

MIR major incident room

misper short for 'a missing person'

MIST major incident support team

mitigation A claim that an offence is less serious than is claimed by the police/prosecutor (usually put forward in court as a 'plea in mitigation')

MO modus operandi (way of operating; usually with reference to a *suspect*)

MOD Ministry of Defence

Moriarty See *Police Law* below

MP (1) military police; (2) member of parliament

MPA Metropolitan Police Authority: the police authority for Greater London (excluding the City of London)

MPB Missing Persons Bureau (national)

MPF Metropolitan Police Federation

MPR missing person report

MPS Metropolitan Police Service

MRT mountain rescue team

MSU Mobile Support Unit

NA Narcotics Anonymous

Nacro Formerly called the National Association for the Care and Resettlement of Offenders but now just Nacro: see nacro.otg.uk

NAFIS National Automated Fingerprint Identification System

NAI non-accidental injury: a euphemistic term for unexplained suspicious injury, often to a child or partner

NAIR National Arrangements for Incidents Involving Radioactivity

NARPO National Association of Retired Police Officers

NBM National Briefing Model (see *briefing* above)

NCCL National Council for Civil Liberties (aka Liberty)

NCF (1) National Crime Faculty; (2) National Competency Framework.

NCIS National Criminal Intelligence Service (former: see *Chapter 6*)

NCRS National Crime Recording Standard

NCS National Crime Squad (former: see *Chapter 6*)

Neighbourhood Watch a voluntary sector scheme in which neighbours act to keep watch/be vigilant re each others property. Hence also, e.g. Boat Watch, Business Watch, Factory Watch, Farm Watch, Pub Watch, School Watch and Shop Watch.

NFA (1) no further action, i.e. with an investigation or prosecution; (2) no fixed abode.

NFIU National Football Intelligence Unit

NIS National Identification Service (or Scheme)

no case to answer term used in court where there is insufficent evidence to call for a defence from the accused; and hence by the *CPS*/police in analogous circumstances duuring an investigation

'no crime' a formula of words used to record an event or behaviour that does not amount to a conviction, such as a fixed penalty notice for disorder (*FPN/D*)

NOMS National Offender Management Service: the umbrella organization for HM Prison Service (HMPS) and the National Probation Service (NPS).

NPIA National Policing Improvement Agency

NPP National Policing Plan

NPS (1) National Policing Strategy; (2) National Probation Service.

NPT (1) National Police Training (now superseded); (2) Neighbourhood Policing Team.

NS (1) national security; (2) national standards (re various public services).

NSPCC National Society for the Prevention of Cruelty to Children

NSY New Scotland Yard

NVC non verbal communication (such as winks, nods and body language)

NW Neighbourhood Watch: see, also, that entry above

OAP (1) Offences Against the Person Act 1861 (which covers many assaults and other attacks on the phisical integrity of a person); (2) old age pensioner (note also the term 'grey crime' for that committed by older people, which is a growing phenomenon).

OCU Operational Command Unit (compare BCU)

offender Someone who has been convicted by a court. An alternative word to 'criminal' (which some people see as sterotyping and possibly unfair, especially when speaking of minor offenders).

OIC (1) officer in charge; (2) officer in the case.

OIOC officer in overall command (aka 'commander')

on-the-spot fine A 'ticket' issued by a police officer (or authorised person). See *FPN/D*; *summary justice*.

operation police operations are usually identified by giving them a name. e.g. Kratos for post-September 11 UK policing of terrorist threats such as suicide bombings; Operation Ore re internet-based paedophile offences; Operation Trident to re gun crime and Operation Compass to target missing persons.

organized crime Crime carried out as if by way of a business venture or other legitimate operation and usually meaning on an appreciable scale. Hence, e.g. the *SOCA* below and the existence of an Organized Crime, Drugs and International Group.

OSC (1) Office of the Surveillance Commissioners; (2) Off-site Support Centre.

OSCT Office for Security and Counter Terrorism

OSU Operational Support Unit

OTD other than dwelling, usually 'burglary OTD'

PACE Police and Criminal Evidence Act 1984. Hence also the 'PACE codes' made under the 1984 Act.

PC (1) Police Constable (hence, also, WPC below); (2) previous conviction (below); (3) Privy Council; (4) probation centre; (5) politically correct.

PCA (1) Police Complaints Authority (former: now the *IPCC*); (2) Proceeds of Crime Act 2002.

PCSO (1) police community support officer; or sometimes (2) police community safety officer

PDO potentially dangerous offender

PDU [police] Probationer Development Unit

PER prisoner escort record

PF See *Police Federation*

PFX police radio

PHU prisoner handling unit

PIC personal injury collision

PII public interest immunity, i.e. from prosecution: consult specialist works

PIM post-incident manager

PIO (1) principle investigating officer; (2) Public Information Office.

PITO Police Information Technology Organisation (former): see *Chapter 6*

PM post mortem

PMS (1) Police Management System; (2) prisoner management system (sometimes reffered to as 'PMS2')

PNB (1) pocket notebook; (2) Police Negotiating Board.

PNC Police National Computer

PN/D penalty notice for disorder; but usually *FPN/D*

POA Public Order Act

Police Federation (PF) The Police Federation of England and Wales is a staff association for all police constables, sergeants and inspectors (including chief inspectors). It was created by the Police Act 1919, passed a year after a crippling strike by the unrecognised National Union of Police and Prison Officers (NUPPO). See polfed.org

Police Law leading work on this topic that replaced 'Moriarty', known to generations of officers as the 'police bible': Police Law (10th edn. 2007), English J and Card R, Blackstone Press.

police officer's notebook (or 'pocket book'): a small book for noting down daily occurrences, facts, details, etc. that may later be used to refresh memory before making a witness statement or in court. Nowadays increasingly an electronic pocketbook.

policing by consent the idea that policing takes place with the consent of citizens, which it is important to maintain if, e.g. people are to support and trust the police and have confidence in them. This does not mean that consent is needed for day to day items, rather those of a broad and general nature: see *Chapter 9.*

police rules a reference to those contained in manuals, standards, force standing orders, and e.g. the *PACE* codes

POLSA police search adviser

POT (1) public order training; (2) prevention of terrorism.

POTF Persistent Offender Task Force (either the national forum or local arrangements)

POU Public Order Unit

PPE personal protective equipment

previous/previous convictions An offender's existing criminal record or 'form'.

PPU (1) Police Protection Unit; (2) Prisoner Processing Unit.

PRA Police Reform Act 2002

PRIME problem solving in multi-agency environments

PSA Police Superintendent's Association. see police suprs.com

PSDB Police Scientific Development Branch

PSNI Police Service of Northern Ireland. Founded in 2000 to replace the *RUC* (below)

PSSO Police Standards and Skills Organization

(former)

PSU Police Support Unit

PTC Police Training Centre

QC Queen's Counsel (a senior barrister aka a 'silk', usually seen in the Crown Court)

QGM Queen's Gallantry Medal

QPM Queen's Police Medal (or 'Queen's policeman').

OSPRE Objective Structured Performance Related Examination

R Regina (or Rex): all prosecutions are brought in the name of the Crown.

raid An unannounced visit by the police (or other law enforcement agents) with a view to arrest, search and/or seizure of unlawful/contraband items and/or for evidence. In many instances, police need a court warrant re a search and/or advance authorisation by a senior officer, but not if already lawfully on the premises or the offence demands emergency entry.

remand A court order obliging someone to reappear at a later court hearing, 'on bail' or 'in custody'.

restraining order A court order aimed at harassment or preventing other specific activities.

RIC remand in custody (see generally *remand* above)

RIPA Regulation of Investigatory Powers Act 2000

RJ restorative justice

ROSH risk of serious harm

ROSPA Royal Society for the Prevention of Accidents

ROTI record of taped-recorded interview

ROVI record of video-recorded interview

RPET Road Policing Enquiry Team

RSI (1) roadside interview; (2) in popular speech, repetitive strain injury

RSO (1) road safety officer; (2) registered sex offender.

RSPB Royal Society for the Protection of Birds

RSPCA Royal Society for the Prevention of Cruelty to Animals

RTA/I road traffic accident/incident

RTRA Road Traffic Regulations Act

RUC Royal Ulster Constabulary. Now replaced by the *PSNI* (above)

Rule of Law Everyone is subject to the law equally and no-one is above the law, police, citizens, judges politicians. One aim of policing is to support and maintain the Rule of Law as opposed to a tendency to anarchy and disorder. There are anomolies, such as soverign immunity, duplomatic immunity and public interest immunity: consult specialist works.

RVP rendezvous point

SA specialist advisor

Safer Neighbourhoods an initiative to this end

SAR suspicious activity report. SARs target proceeds of crime and money laundering via, e.g. banks, lawyers, accountants and businesses who may, e.g. encounter offences when dealings with clients or customers and must report their supicions.

SARA Scanning Analysis Response Centre

SB Special Branch

SC (1) security check; (2) Special Course: *Chapter 4*

SCC Senior Command Course: *Chapter 4*

SCD Specialist Crime Directorate (of the MPS)

sectioned ('being sectioned') A medical practitioner can order someone who is mentally-impaired into hospital which will often trigger a need for police support and liaison.

SEG special escort group (usually of the *MODP*)

SEO [police] station enquiry officer

SFO Serious Fraud Office: see sfo.gov.uk

SI Statutory Instrument: see also *statutory* below

SIO senior investigating officer

SLP self-loading pistol

SMART Specific, Measurable, Achievable, Relevant, Time-framed

SO Standing Order

SOCA Serious Organized Crime Agency: *Chapter 6*

SOCO scenes of crime officer

source a police *intelligence* source (see also *CHIS*)

SOCPV Statement of Common Purposes and Values

Special Branch Special Branch of the *MPS*. Now known by other names according to its exact function, e.g. Counter Terrorism Command (CTC)

SSU scientific support unit

statutory laid down by Parliament in legislation, i.e. in a statute (aka an Act) or other statutory measures under an Act, often called 'delegated legislation' or 'statutory instruments'. The two forms are also known as primary and secondary legislation.

sting example of a word (one of many) with connotations on either side of the police/offender divide, i.e. to signify (1) a scam or con in which the victim has been lead into a trap; and (2) a raid in which offenders are taken by surprise.

stinger device which uses metal spikes to puncture car tyres and that can be rolled out by police across a road to stop a fleeing vehicle

Stockholm syndrome (aka Stockholm bank syndrome). The idea (not unchallenged) that victims, especially hostages, may warm to their captors or perpetrators of abuse over time, as against the police or authorities who are trying to rescue them; a theory now associated with various scenarios including terrorism/terrorists, controlling behaviour and domestic violence. Based on events at a five day siege at Kreditbanken, Norrmalmstorg, Stockholm, Sweden (1973). A psychological (but not medically recognised) condition credited to Nils Bejerot, the psychaitrist who assisted police at the time.

stop and search stopping and searching people in the streets, usually meaning under *sus* laws, below.

summary justice (1) instant justice by handing out a ticket, *FPN/D* or 'one the spot fine'; (2) that in a magistrates' court (which is aka a court of summary jurisdiction).

summary offence one triable only in the magistrates' court (in normal circumstances)

Supt superintendent

sus short for suspicion, especially in the context of a search of an invidual for, e.g. drugs, knives, firearms underwhat are known as the 'sus laws'

suspect Someone who is under suspicion but who has not been charged with an offence (when he or she becomes 'an accused person'). Hence also, e.g. 'prime suspect'.

SVS Stolen Vehicle Squad

TA tactical advisor

tagging electronic monitoring (under a court order or on *HDC* above)

tampering, i.e. with (1) a motor vehicle; (2) evidence; (3) a jury (all criminal offences).

target i.e. (1) of a raid, operation or blitz; (2) set by a police force or government; (3) a suspect; or (4) of an offence, e.g. the victim or property concerned.

Taser-gun (or just Taser which is a brand name) A type of stun gun used by police officers (who are not in the Great Britain routinely armed with guns) to incapacitate people deemed to be dangerous; as rolled out nationwide to UK Police forces from 2004 onwards; with 8,000 further Tasers and training re their use announced in 2008. The 'M26 Taser' originates in the USA; and is a form of 'less lethal force'. It fires twin needle-tipped darts (aka barbs) using compressed nitrogen, for up to six metres. These deliver a rapid series of 50,000 volt pulses (static electric shocks) via wires connected to the Taser; at a power of just 26 watts. The same effect can be achieved by pressing the gun against the body of the target. Either causes temporary muscle cramps; without further affecting someone in normal health. It can penetrate clothing for five millimetres. Whenever a Taser is drawn this is reported to the *IPCC*.

TFT/U Tactical Firearms Team/Unit

TI trace and interview

ticket Colloquial term for: (1) a fixed penalty notice; (2) a parole or other licence re release from prison, etc. (aka a ticket of leave, especially with regard to the temporary release of a prisoner).

TIA tactical interview advisor

TIC After someone is convicted of a criminal offence he or she can ask the court to take into consideration other offences which he or she admits but re which he or she has not been charged, i.e. in deciding upon the appropriate level of sentence for the offence of which he or she stands convicted. Hence a list of TICs produced by the prosecutor and agreed by the offender. Once an offence has been properly TIC'd it cannot be the subject of a later prosecution. There has been some controversy in the past re the 'trading' of TICs as between offenders (especially prisoners) and the alacrity with which the police were prepared to write off offences in this way in order to enhance clear up rates; now subject to closer scrutiny.

TP test-purchase

TPU Team Policing Unit

traffic short for road traffic, see *RT* above

TSU Technological Support Unit

Tulliallan The Scottish Police Training College located at Tulliallan north of Edinburgh, responsible for all Scottish police training

TU Trial Unit (usually meaning re the Crown Court)

TWC (aka 'twocking') taking [a motor vehicle] without consent

UDT unarmed defence tactic

UKAEAC UK Atomic Energy Authority Constabulary. see generally www.ukaea.org.uk

UK Borders full name of the *BA*

UKIS United Kingdom Immigration Service

UWSU Underwater Search Unit

VASCAR visual average speed camera (or calculator) and recorder

VEL Vehicle Excise Licence

VIB Vehicle Investigation Branch

VIP very important person

VIPER Video Identification Parade Electronic Recording

VODS vehicle online descriptive search

VP vulnerable person who is, e.g. old, a child, mentally impaired, a sex offender or ex-police officer in prison

VPS victim personal statement

VRS Vehicle Rectification Scheme (sometimes VDRS: D for 'defect')

VS Victim Support: see victimsupport.org.uk

YCO youth case officer

WFD warrant of further detention: see *Chapter 5*

YIP Youth Inclusion Programme

YJB Youth Justice Board

YJS Youth Justice System

YOI young offender institution

YOT youth offending team

YRP youth referral panel

YSP Youth Support Panel

YP (1) young person (14-17 years); (2) young prisoner (18-21).

ZT zero-tolerance. A publicised policing strategy of virtually automatic arrest, prosecution, etc. even for minor offences, so that people know what to expect.

Timeline

1285	Statute of Winchester regulates law and order and formalises the hue and cry
1652–1658	An experiment with national policing under the Lord Protector, Oliver Cromwell
1829	Sir Robert Peel creates the Metropolitan Police Service (MPS) (as 'the New Police')
1842	Creation of the detective branch of the MPS, later known as the CID (1878): *Chapter 6*
1856	County and Borough Police Act which leads among other things to the formation and work of Her Majesty's Inspectorate of Constabulary (HMIC): *Chapters 2* and *3*
1861	Offences Against the Person Act 1861
1886	Creation of the Special Branch of the MPS, first known as the 'Special Irish Branch' (to deal with Fenian outrages). The first intelligence gathering agency of the MPS, it goes on to deal with all forms of 'political' crime, and precedes the formation of MI5 (the security service, founded 1905).
Early-1900s	First use of fingerprinting: *Chapter 6*
1910	Siege of Sydney Street. An active Home Secretary, Winston Churchill, directs troops against anarchists in London. Tonypandy disturbances when the same Home Secretary sends troops and MPS officers to deal with serious industrial unrest in South Wales.

1914	First meeting of a group of police officers and others in Monaco, which eventually became Interpol: *Chapter 3*
1919	Police strikes in London and Liverpool
1919-1921	Irish War of Independence, leading to the formation of the Irish Free State (later the Republic of Ireland) and the separate province of Northern Ireland which remains part of the UK. The Royal Irish Constabulary (RIC) and Dublin Metropolitan Police are abolished. Northern Ireland forms its own police force, the Royal Ulster Constabulary (RUC). Although RUC officers carry arms and live in barracks, it is not a gendarmerie in the full sense.
1920	Formation of Royal Canadian Mounted Police (RCMP) First Firearms Control Act: *Chapter 2*
1923	Interpol 'revived': *Chapter 3*
1934	Trenchard Scheme of police training initiated: *Chapter 2*
1936	Public Order Act follows on from unrest and disorder
1946	Police Post-War reform Committee: *Chapter 6*
1948	Creation of the national Police College (later renamed the Police Staff College). It moves from Warwickshire to Bramshill, Hampshire in 1956 and remains known by that name nationally and internationally. *Chapters 3* and *4*.
1960	Royal Commission on the Police
1964	Police Act: stemming from the Royal Commission above.
1967	Shotguns to be licensed for the first time: *Chapter 2*

1969	As a result of a prolonged civil rights campaign in Northern Ireland, and a renewal of IRA activity, that province is plunged into crisis, and the British army called onto the streets; where it remains for over three decades. (The RUC faces unprecedented difficulties and suffers huge losses: an illustration of the difficulties of policing without consent.) Capital punishment abolished after its suspension in 1965
1970s	Regional Crime Squads and later the National Criminal Intelligence Service (NCIS) (1992) and National Crime Squad (NCS) (1997): *Chapter 6* and see the note at 2005 below.
1976	Bail Act endorses a supect's 'general right to bail': see generally arrest, detention, etc. within *Chapter 5*
1984	The Police and Criminal Evidence Act (PACE) and PACE codes affect all aspects of investigations, etc: *Chapter 5*. Brixton Riots and the Scarman Inquiry Miners' strike DNA profiling developed and becomes progressively key to a whole range of investigations: *Chapter 6*
1985	Formation of the Crown Prosecution Service (CPS). The police now no longer prosecute their own cases as they did from the earliest days. 'Blue Book' issued by the MPS: *Chapter 1*
1985 and 1990	Schengen Agreement, a move towards abolishing internal border controls within the EU, comes into force in two parts. The UK and Ireland do not accept the agreement and retain their own border controls. Security arrangements follow to increase EU security in the absence of internal border controls, including the eventual creation of Europol (below).

1990	Statement of Common Purposes and Values: *Chapter 1*
1993	National police traning and the creation of a National Crime Faculty (NCF): *Chapter 6*
1999	The Stephen Lawrence murder and inquiry. The MPS is dubbed 'institutionally racist' (as later are other CJS agencies), leading to legislation and changes across the system
	Europol created: *Chapter 3*
1998	Human Rights Act (HRA) passed by Parliament
	Crime and Disorder Act provides a legal basis and framework for police services and local authorities and other agencies to co-operate in reducing crime (known as 'partnership' and hence also Crime Reduction Partnerships (CDPs). It also introduces the anti-social behaviour order.
2000	The HRA comes into force. A massive police training programme follows. The impact is less dramatic than anticipated but accountability acquires a new language: police actions now need to be justified as lawful, necessary and proportionate, rather than simply in terms of reasonableness.
	Metropolitan Police Authority (MPA) created: MPS no longer directly accountable to Home Secretary: *Chapter 3*
	Terrorism Act (plus others in the wake of 9/11): *Chapter 7*
2001	RUC becomes the Police Service of Northern Ireland
2002	Police Reform Act (including the creation of PCSOs: *Chapter 5*)

2005	Serious Organized Crime Agency created, encompassing the former duties of the NCIS, NCS above and certain other nation-wide police responsibilities.
	National Policing Improvement Agency (NPIA)
	Stockwell shooting: *Chapter 5*
2007	Slimmed down version of the Home Office created to concentrate on internal and external security, public safety and border controls (the latter via a new UK Border Agency).
2008	'Casey Review' (and associated developments) and the Green Paper 'Policing Our Communities Together': *Chapters 2, 9*

References

Adlam, Robert, and Villiers, Peter (2003), *Police Leadership in the 21st Century: Philosophy, doctrine and developments*, Hampshire: Waterside Press.

ACPO (1990), *Statement of Common Purpose and Values,* London: Assocation of Chief Police Officers.

ACPO (1993), *Getting Things Right*, London: Assocation of Chief Police Officers.

Argyle, Michael (1969), *Social Interaction*, London: Tavistock Publications.

Becker, T E (1998), 'Integrity in Organisations: Beyond Honesty and Conscientiousness', *Academy of Management Review*, 23(1), 154-161.

Bennis, Warren (1989), *On Becoming a Leader*, New York: Perseus Publishing.

Burns, James MacGregor (1978), *Leadership*, New York: Harper Row.

Canter, David (2003), *Mapping Murder*, London: Virgin Books.

Critchley, T. A. (1966), *A History of the Police in England and Wales*, London: Constable.

Delattre, Edwin (1996), *Character and Cops*, Washington, DC: the AEI Press.

Emsley, Clive (1991), *The English Police: a political and social history,* London: Longmans and New York: St Martin's Press.

Flanagan, Sir Ronnie (2008), *The Independent Review of Policing*, London: HMIC.

Gibson, Bryan (2008), *The New Home Office*, Hampshire: Waterside Press.

Heidensohn, Frances (1992), *Women in Control: The Role of Women in Law Enforcement*, Oxford: Clarendon.

Ker Muir, William (1977), *Police: Street-corner politicians,* Chicago: Chicago University Press.

Kleinig, John (1996), *The Ethics of Policing*, Cambridge: Cambridge University Press.

Macpherson, Sir William of Cluny (1999), *The Stephen Lawrence Inquiry*, Cm.4262, London: Stationery Office.

Miller, Seumas and Blackler, John (2005), *Ethical Issues in Policing*, Hampshire: Ashgate.

NPIA (2006), *The Police Leadership Qualities Framework*, Hampshire: National Policing Improvement Agency.

Neyroud, Peter and Beckley, Alan (2001), *Policing, Ethics and Human Rights*, Willan: Cullompton.

Newman, Sir Kenneth, and Laugharne, Albert (1985), *The Principles of Policing and Guidance for Professional Behaviour*, London: Metropolitan Police.

Reiner, Robert (1991), *Chief Constables: Bobbies, Bosses or Bureaucrats?*, London: Oxford University Press.

Silvestri, Marisa (2007), "Doing" Police Leadership: Enter the "New Street Macho", *Policing and Society* Vol. 17, No. I, March, pp. 38-58.

Stevens, John (Lord Stevens of Kirkwhelpington) (2005), *Not for the Faint-Hearted*, London: Orion.

Villiers, Peter and Adlam, Robert (2004), *Policing a safe, just and tolerant society*, Hampshire: Waterside Press.

Waddington, PAJ (1999), Police (Canteen) Culture: An Appreciation, *British Journal of Criminology*, 39, 287-309.

Winch, Peter (1958), '*The Idea of a Social Science and its Relation to Philosophy*, London: Routledge.

Index